DATE DUE

Oct. 4, 2013

Demco No. 62-0549

431 CANAL STREET
NEW YORK, NY 10013

Making New York Dominican

THE CITY IN THE TWENTY-FIRST CENTURY

Eugenie L. Birch and Susan M. Wachter, Series Editors

A complete list of books in the series
is available from the publisher.

Making New York Dominican

Small Business, Politics, and Everyday Life

Christian Krohn-Hansen

PENN

UNIVERSITY OF PENNSYLVANIA PRESS

PHILADELPHIA

Copyright © 2013 University of Pennsylvania Press

All rights reserved. Except for brief quotations used for purposes of review or scholarly citation, none of this book may be reproduced in any form by any means without written permission from the publisher.

Published by
University of Pennsylvania Press
Philadelphia, Pennsylvania 19104-4112
www.upenn.edu/pennpress

Printed in the United States of America
on acid-free paper

2 4 6 8 10 9 7 5 3 1

Library of Congress Cataloging-in-Publication Data

Krohn-Hansen, Christian, 1957–
   Making New York Dominican : small business, politics, and everyday life / Christian Krohn-Hansen.—1st ed.
     p. cm.—(The city in the twenty-first century)
   Includes bibliogaphical references and index.
   ISBN 978-0-8122-4461-8 (hardcover : alk. paper)
   Dominican Americans—New York (State)—New York—Economic conditions—21st century. 2. Dominican Americans—New York (State)—New York—Politics and government—21st century. 3. Dominican Americans—New York (State)—New York—Social life and customs—21st century. 4. Small business—New York (State)—New York—History—21st century. 5. New York (N.Y.)—Ethnic relations—History—21st century. I. Title. II. Series: City in the twenty-first century
F128.9.D6K76   2013
305.8968'72930730747—dc23   2012018056

CONTENTS

Introduction	1
PART I	29
1. From Quisqueya to New York City	31
2. Origin Stories	47
PART II	91
3. From Bodegas to Supermarkets	93
4. From Livery Cabs to Black Cars	134
PART III	171
5. Dominicans and Hispanics	173
6. Up Against the Big Money	201
7. In Search of Dignity	230
Conclusion	264

Notes	269
References	285
Index	299
Acknowledgments	310

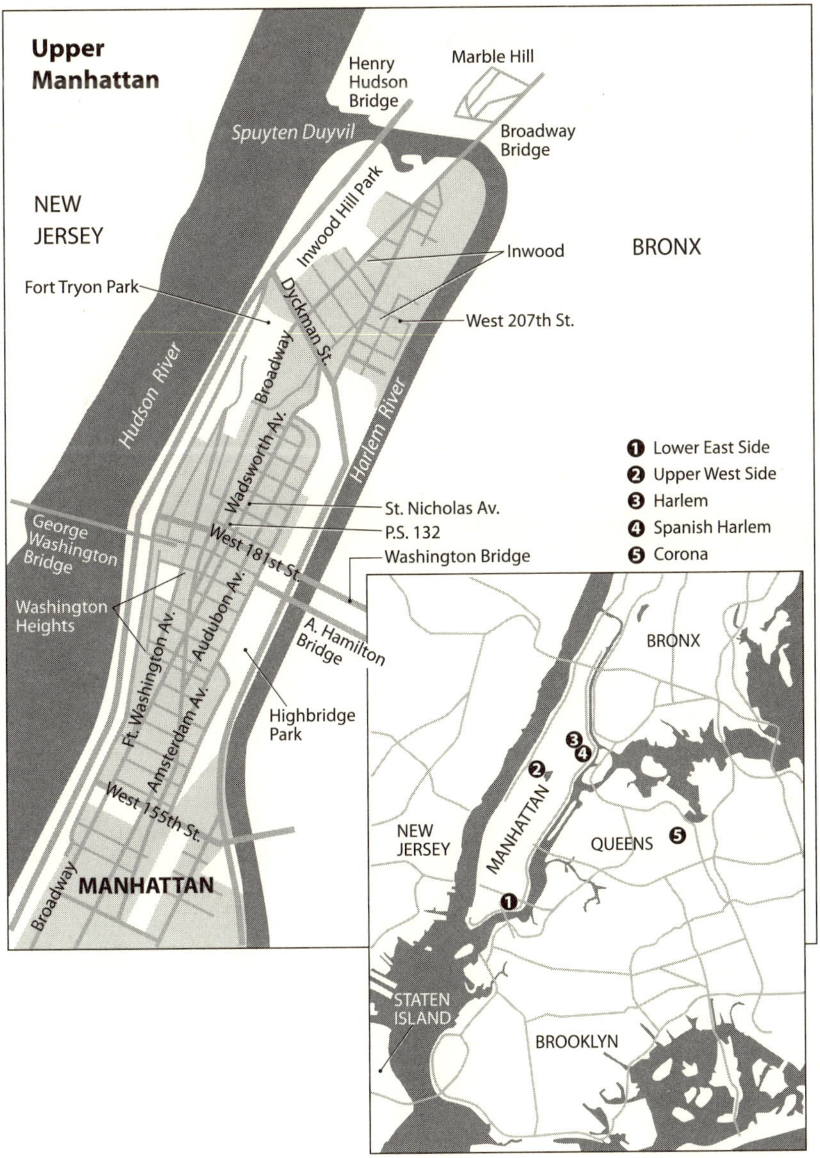

Figure 1. Upper Manhattan.

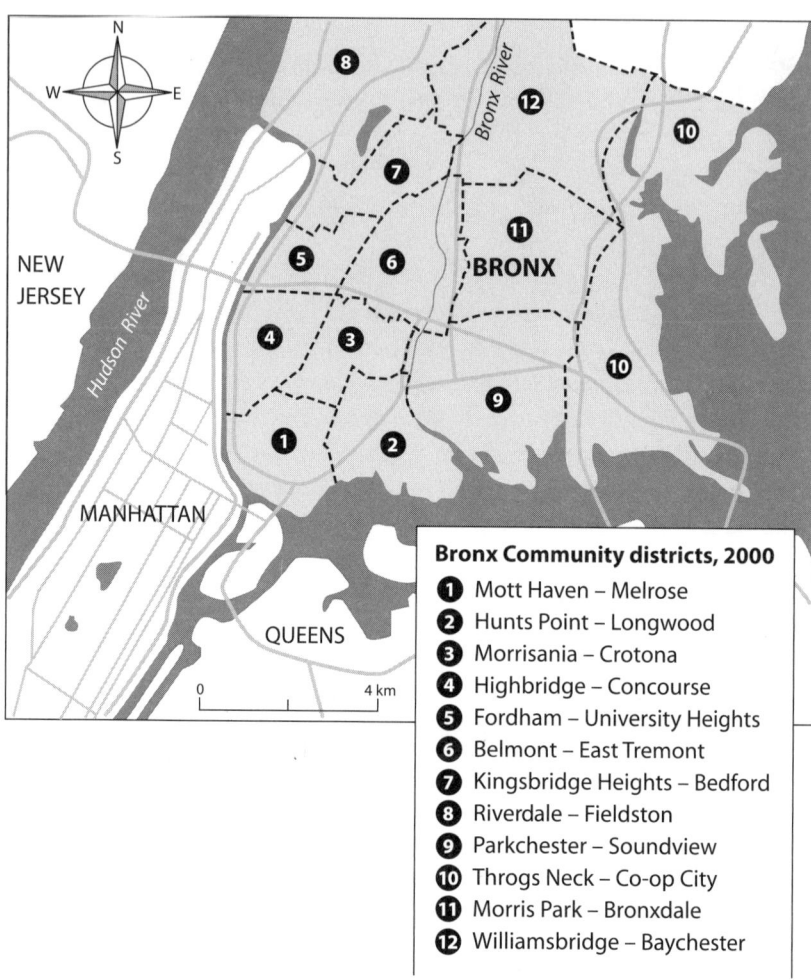

Figure 2. Bronx Community districts, 2000.

Introduction

It was a hot Tuesday afternoon in late August 2002, and I was in La Nueva España, a small restaurant on 207th Street in Inwood, at the northernmost point of Manhattan. The restaurant, owned and run by a Dominican, served mainly Dominican food, and most of the guests were first- and second-generation Dominican immigrants. The man sitting with me at the table was the reason I had come. These days La Nueva España functioned as his regular café. He was a friend of the owner and lived with a sister in a tenement around the corner. José Delio Marte was a Dominican immigrant who had arrived in New York City in 1965, at eighteen.[1] While his first jobs in New York had been factory jobs in midtown, he had spent most of the last thirty-seven years as an owner and operator of small businesses, mostly *bodegas*, small, Spanish-speaking Dominican neighborhood or street-corner grocery stores, in Upper Manhattan. During these years, he had seen the city and northern Manhattan change conspicuously: he had seen the Dominican community emerge.

I had met with him for the first time a couple of weeks previously. Then as now, I had asked him to tell me about the Dominican immigration to the city and about the creation and the construction of New York's Dominican community. I had asked him to tell me why, and how, he and so many other Dominican immigrants had ended up in small businesses—taxicab operations, neighborhood grocery stores, restaurants, travel agencies, beauty parlors, car-repair shops, small and medium-sized supermarkets, and other enterprises.

One of Inwood's busiest commercial streets is 207th Street. This short stretch on the northern tip of Manhattan has two subway stations, one for the 1 train on Tenth Avenue, and one for the A train on Broadway. Next to La Nueva España was a McDonalds. A few of the businesses on 207th Street were owned by Americans of Arab ancestry, and a couple were Mexican, but the great majority were run by Dominicans. The language on the sidewalks and in the stores was Spanish, and most of the livery cabs that cruised the neighborhood were owned and driven by Dominicans. Inwood was dominated by Dominicans. The area was multiethnic, but most of the population were first- and second-generation Dominican immigrants. Close to the restaurant where I was sitting with José, State Assembly member Adriano Espaillat had his office. In 1996, Espaillat had become the first Dominican to serve in the State Assembly, after unseating John Brian Murtaugh, an Irish-descended incumbent who had represented Manhattan's 72nd District for sixteen years.[2]

José saw as key that a growing number of Dominican immigrants had bought or created their own small economic ventures. If one wanted to understand the emergence of today's New York City Dominican community, he emphasized, one had to attempt to understand this history, of how the city had ended up with a considerable number of Dominican-owned small businesses. So much else in New York's Dominican community's history, he went on, had been tied to this development. Most decisive, he claimed, had been the appearance of the Dominican bodega. (In Cuba and Puerto Rico, a small neighborhood grocery store is referred to as a *bodega*, and New York's Latinos similarly call the city's small groceries *bodegas*.) As he put it, "Yes, I've always said that the basis of the emergence of today's strong Dominican community in New York was the bodega. The bodegas produced the large homes that [a few] Dominicans now own in New Jersey. The bodegas created the large [Dominican-owned] supermarkets."

José was bearer of history and memory. At the same time, he was a practical man, businesslike. Little in him appeared static. He seemed to take for granted that most things in life are historical, changeable. Over the years he had bought, run, and sold a series of stores; many of the businesses had been sold, often to another Dominican immigrant, after a year or two. He had operated in a large area. Most of the stores he had owned had been located in Upper Manhattan between 168th and 225th Streets, but he had also operated in the Bronx.

José had also been, for more than two decades, one of Dominican Upper Manhattan's neighborhood activists and grass-roots politicians. He had often functioned as an advocate of the Washington Heights and Inwood area's Dominican and other small-business owners and had been quoted in the city's newspapers. He had decried and fought against abusive landlords, rising rents, galloping energy costs, and unfair fines. When I met with him, he was president of a Dominican small-business association in Washington Heights and Inwood, called the Federation of Dominican and Hispanic Merchants and Businessmen. In spite of the impressive name, the organization was small; it was only a loosely organized network of friends and acquaintances. José's "association" belonged to an umbrella organization, the New York State Federation of Hispanic Chambers of Commerce, consisting of more than thirty large and small Hispanic or Latino organizations and associations in the New York area. The organization was headed by Alfredo Placeres, a lawyer and political activist of Cuban descent.

José and I spoke Spanish. He referred to himself as *"dominicano"* or "Dominican." But he used this term interchangeably with *"hispano"* or "Hispanic" and *"latino"* or "Latino." In short, he spoke of New York's Dominicans as *dominicanos* but also as *hispanos* and *latinos*.

* * *

Considerable emigration from the Dominican Republic to the United States began in the early 1960s after the assassination of General Rafael Leónidas Trujillo, who ruled the country dictatorially from 1930 to 1961. Most of these Dominicans settled in New York City. According to the 1990 U.S. Census, 93 percent of all persons of Dominican ancestry in the country resided in four states: 70 percent in New York, 11 percent in New Jersey, 7 percent in Florida, and 5 percent in Massachusetts (Hernández et al. 1995: 6). An overwhelming majority of those in New York lived in New York City. The growth of the Dominican population in the city has been staggering. The Dominican Republic, in absolute numbers, sent the most immigrants to New York City during the 1970s and 1980s and maintained that position in the early 1990s. In 1995, the former Soviet Union became the number one source of immigrants to New York City (Ricourt 2002: 35). But since 1995, this relatively small, Spanish-speaking Caribbean nation has sent great numbers of immigrants to New York. According to the City of New York Department of City Planning (1993), the Dominican population grew from 125,380 in 1980 to 332,713 in 1990, 4.5 percent of the entire city's population. Ten years later, in 2000, the city's Dominicans had grown to 547,379; in 2009, the figure was 588,865 (Bergad 2011: 5).[3]

Washington Heights and Inwood, or Manhattan north of Harlem, remains a decisive part, not to say the heart, of the Dominican community in New York City. In the early 1990s, Upper Manhattan housed about one-third of all Dominicans in the city (Pessar 1995: 24). The rest reside in the Bronx, Queens, and Brooklyn.

The Dominican migrants' massive arrival in New York took place when the United States was undergoing socioeconomic changes that would have a considerable impact on the need for labor. Over the last fifty years, New York has seen a spectacular economic restructuring; the service sector has replaced an economy once based on industrial production. More than 520,000 manufacturing jobs in New York disappeared between 1967 and 1987 alone (Hernández et al. 1995: 41). This became important for the city's Dominicans. In the 1960s and 1970s, a significant number of Dominicans in New York were factory workers, employed in light manufacturing, particularly in the garment industry (Grasmuck and Pessar 1991). But during the 1980s, Dominican immigrants in the manufacturing industry declined. In 1979, 49 percent of all Dominican workers, but only 18 percent of New York City's total labor force, were engaged in manufacturing. In 1989, only ten years later, the percentage of Dominican immigrants in manufacturing had declined to 26 (Hernández et al. 1995: 42–45). After that the figure continued to drop. But more and more Dominican New Yorkers were found in other parts of the economy. An increasing number found jobs in the service sector, and more became self-employed. In 1991, sociologists Alejandro Portes and Luis Guarnizo estimated that 20,000 businesses in New York City were owned and operated by Dominican immigrants. They claimed that Dominicans particularly owned cab operations, bodegas, small and medium-sized independent supermarkets, restaurants, travel agencies, beauty parlors, and sweat shops (Portes and Guarnizo 1991: 61; see also Guarnizo 1992: 110–14).

The Dominicans were the first group among the people migrating to the United States after 1965 who secured electoral representation in both the New York City Council and the New York State Assembly.[4] The great majority of Dominican New Yorkers continue to have fairly low incomes, but despite their immigrant status and limited economic resources, the Dominicans have become an ethnic political force in today's New York.

In this book, I examine everyday life among Dominican New Yorkers. I analyze Dominican immigrants' economic and political practices and constructions of identity, of belonging. I seek to understand how forms of globalization and migration are transforming contemporary urban landscapes in the United States. As Nancy Foner put it in 2001, "At the dawn of a new millennium, New York is again an immigrant city.... In 1970, 18 percent of New York City's residents were foreign-born, the lowest percentage of the century. By 1998, immigrants constituted over a third of the city's population, fast approaching levels at the turn of the twentieth century" (Foner 2001: 1).

How have the Dominicans influenced New York City? And, conversely, how has the move to New York affected their lives? How may we usefully understand "the Dominicanization" of New York City, the emergence and construction of a Dominican community? I examine Dominicanization in New York City as a historically constituted power process of social differentiation and cultural production. I seek to answer the following questions. How did Dominican immigrants obtain money? How did they get their own small businesses, and how did they run them? What characterized their daily rhythms and routines, their everyday practices? What distinguished the Dominican community's forms of political activism and political culture? What part did the Dominicans play in New York's political life, in the city's constant struggles over property, power, influence and meaning? How did Dominican New Yorkers identify racially and ethnically?

This study is based on intermittent fieldwork undertaken in New York City from 2002 to September 2008, but also on a longer research interest in, or contact with, Dominicans. I carried out thirteen months of "classic" anthropological fieldwork in and around the community of La Descubierta in the southwestern part of the Dominican Republic in 1991–92. In 1997, I spent three months in the Dominican capital and various regions of the country; I worked in libraries, traveled, and talked with people. I have published on features of the Dominican Republic's political, social, and cultural history since the mid-1990s (for some works, see Krohn-Hansen 1995, 1996, 1997, 2001, 2005, 2009).

I lived in the heart of the Dominican community in Washington Heights for six months in the second half of 2002. My landlady, Magdalena Flores, a first-generation Dominican immigrant in her early seventies, rented an apartment in a five-story tenement a few blocks north of 181st Street, between Audubon and Amsterdam. I rented one of her bedrooms. The apartment was not large: a small living room, kitchen, bathroom, and two bedrooms. Although she mostly lived alone in the apartment, she had four daughters and a son and nine grandchildren in New York City. Two of the daughters and five of the grandchildren lived nearby.

How did I end up staying with Magdalena? The first time I met her was a Sunday in late June 2002. For about two weeks, I had tried to find housing in the Dominican areas of Washington Heights. This Sunday morning I had had an appointment with a Dominican real estate broker in northern Manhattan. But his fee, which he charged compatriots and others who used him, proved to be huge. Depressed, I sat down to have a coffee and read *El Diario/La Prensa*, one of the city's dailies in Spanish. I decided to do what I had already attempted a few times, to ask people in bodegas and on tenement stoops if they knew about a room for rent. Outside the tenement where Magdalena lived, I asked a man in Spanish if he knew about a room. He summoned Magdalena. While the man lived on the third floor, Magdalena's apartment was on the first. Magdalena said that the price was $100 a week. She showed me the room and the rest of the apartment. I said it looked fine and that I wanted to take it and move in two days later.

Later, I sat on the bed in my new room, and one of Magdalena's daughters, Rosanna, arrived with her two children and one of her nieces, a college student. Rosanna asked me many questions about who I was and what I did, saw my papers, and got phone numbers of people at Queens College where I was affiliated. She explained that I looked all right, but that it was necessary to be careful—this was less than a year after 9/11. (A year later, Rosanna and her sisters laughed at this first meeting; Rosanna said to me with a grin, "Christian, you weren't a part of the Taliban!") I had already said to Magdalena that I would probably need a small desk and a small refrigerator in my room. Having heard this, Rosanna and her niece immediately decided to drive me to a store in the Bronx. Rosanna did not own a car, but the niece drove her mother's car. We returned with a desk and a refrigerator, and two days later I moved in.

Magdalena's bathroom had a tub with a shower. But when I lived there, the bathroom was in bad shape. The absentee landlord, a Jewish American who lived in Brooklyn and had bought Magdalena's tenement with three others in the same block, spent six months on small repair work; one of the walls had been left unfinished. Meanwhile one could not shower without causing more damage. The tenement had ten apartments, two on each floor. Five apartments had three bedrooms, five had two. All the tenants but one were Dominican immigrants; one was a Puerto Rican woman. Magdalena knew all the others. By 2002, she had lived in this building for over sixteen years, and most of the tenants had also lived there for years. The other tenements in the vicinity were also populated by Dominican immigrants.

After 2002, I lived mostly in Oslo but returned for shorter visits: three times in 2003, twice in 2004, once in 2007, and once in 2008. Each visit lasted between one and five weeks, most about two or three. The fieldwork consisted mainly of participant observation and informal conversations and interviews in Upper Manhattan. The bulk of my data were produced in Washington Heights and Inwood. But I worked in many other areas of the city. Some of my data were gathered among Dominicans in various neighborhoods in the South Bronx. In addition, I collected data—through participant observation and conversations and interviews—in parts of Harlem, in midtown and downtown Manhattan, and in parts of Queens.

Most of my informants were Dominicans. Some were or had been factory workers. The majority had worked, or were still working, in industrial jobs in New Jersey. Some had jobs in the city's service sector. A few had got work in big corporations, such as Verizon or IBM. A number were seniors, and others were children or young people who attended school. But the majority of my informants belonged to the small-business economy. Many were self-employed, each person running a small venture or a series of businesses. Others were wage workers in the small-business sector. Quite a few among my informants took part in politics also. They struggled for Dominicans' and others' rights. Many belonged to associations or organizations. Some were well-known community activists and grass-roots politicians. A few, less than a handful, were among New York's elected officials.

Making New York Dominican conveys considerably more about the worlds of Dominican immigrant men than about those of Dominican immigrant women. Why? The two parts of the city's Dominican small-business economy that I particularly examine in this book—the Dominican-controlled parts of New York's grocery store industry and cab industry—are worlds dominated by men. The Dominican small-business economy also contains many women; Dominican immigrant women seek paid work outside the household (in factories, in small businesses, etc.), and New York's Dominican businesses are owned by both women and men; a few Dominican immigrant women own and operate supermarkets, and some work as taxi drivers. I discuss women's socioeconomic strategies also—but I have substantially more to say about the activities and strategies of men.

One last comment about gender bias: the building of a Dominican community in New York has been rooted in a form of daily life in which the principal parts have been played by women. The Dominican immigrant population in New York has for a long time been characterized by high rates of marital instability and of women being heads of households (Gurak and Kritz 1982: 20; Grasmuck and Pessar 1991: 159). In *The Mobility of Workers Under Advanced Capitalism* (2002: 100), Ramona Hernández notes, "In 1990 the average Dominican household [in the New York metropolitan area] contained 4.7 persons. Almost one out of every two of these households was headed by a single woman, and over 50 percent of them fell below the official level of poverty." Hernández uses public statistical data—that is, data that probably hide a certain underreporting of (more or less peripheral) husbands and sources of income (see, for example, Duany 1994: 25–27). But the proportion of single female household heads is high. Most of these female heads are the main economic providers of their households. Migration from the island to the United States often contributes to a certain restructuring of gender relationships and families. As the men's typical sources of authority are eroded, the women's forms of autonomy increase correspondingly (Pessar 1987, 1994; Grasmuck and Pessar 1991; Levitt 2001; Ricourt and Danta 2003).

Dominican immigrant women in New York draw massively on their networks of female kin and acquaintances. They obtain housing and work through relatives, neighbors, and friends; it is the same with childcare and forms of schooling and education. In Washington Heights, the most important reciprocity networks among Dominican women were based on kinship. Much daily interaction and informal mutual exchange occurred between women who were relatives—mother and daughter, sisters, grandmothers and granddaughters, aunts and nieces. Women helped each other with everything—from cooking and errands to paper work and money. Rearing children and young people, or primary socialization, in the Dominican immigrant community in New York is almost completely dependent on these informal female networks.

Living in Magdalena's small apartment, I was gradually incorporated into one version of these networks. Magdalena's four daughters and son resided in the city: Ramona, Carmen, Rosanna, Amelia, and Domingo. Ramona, her eldest, was in her late forties, an unemployed widow with four grown children. She lived with her youngest daughter, Evelyn, who was twenty-two and a single mother with a three-and-a-half-year-old daughter, now the household's breadwinner and head. She worked in a small Dominican-owned supermarket in Washington Heights, and the three lived in a tenement on Jerome Avenue in the Bronx, a twenty-five-minute bus ride from Magdalena's apartment.

Carmen, who worked for America West airline at John F. Kennedy Airport, lived in a different part of the Bronx. She was about forty and lived with her three youngest children, who were in their teens and went to school. Carmen's eldest daughter was twenty-one and went to college in upstate New York. Carmen had recently divorced after over twenty years of marriage. Later, she had bought a co-op in the western Bronx; before this, she had lived in the same tenement as her mother.

Magdalena's two other daughters, Rosanna and Amelia, lived in Washington Heights. Both were single mothers. Rosanna, who was thirty-eight and worked in a hotel, had a ten-year-old daughter and a seven-year-old son.

The three lived only four blocks from Rosanna's mother's apartment. The two children had the same father, who lived in the Dominican Republic. Amelia, who was in her mid-thirties and worked part-time as a hairdresser, had three children, a son and two daughters, with three different fathers (who lived in the Dominican Republic and the United States). The children lived with their mother and went to high school. Amelia's apartment was five minutes' walk from Magdalena's.

Magdalena's son, Domingo, lived in a tenement in the western Bronx and worked as a driver. His partner was a first-generation immigrant woman from Ecuador. The couple did not have children, but Domingo had a daughter with another woman.

This family, or this network, embodied an immigration history. Magdalena had grown up in the countryside outside San Pedro de Macorís (in the Dominican southeast) and had raised her children alone. Her husband, who died in the early 1970s, had had another family elsewhere in the country—eight children with another woman. At first Magdalena and her children lived in the countryside, growing coffee, vegetables, and fruit and raising animals. Later the family moved to San Pedro de Macorís where Magdalena had relatives, so that the children could attend high school. The first of Magdalena's children to migrate to the United States was Carmen. Carmen's husband had already moved to Washington Heights and worked in a factory in New Jersey; in 1980, Carmen joined him. At the time, she was seventeen or eighteen. Six years later, Magdalena followed her daughter under the United States' family reunion rules. For the first two years Magdalena lived in the apartment of Carmen and her husband, before she obtained her own apartment, the one she still had in 2002, and a job in a factory in New Jersey. Some six years after Magdalena's arrival in the U.S., in 1992, she was followed by the rest of her children with their children—again under the family reunion rules.

The flow of information and reciprocity in this network, especially among the women, was striking. Magdalena and her daughters phoned one another frequently, sometimes several times a day. The daughters used their mother's apartment as a meeting place—when I came home, I often met one or two of the daughters and some grandchildren in the apartment. They would cook together and share a meal. And they helped each other with a range of other activities, from shopping to child care to visits to a public office or a doctor. Magdalena, Rosanna, and Amelia had a common deposit account. Carmen had her own savings. The contact between Domingo and the others was less frequent, but he too helped his family with both favors and money—for example, when Magdalena's washing machine had stopped working and needed repair or when his mother became ill and was taken to a hospital.

Another man who belonged to Magdalena's network was Francisco Paredes, a forty-one-year-old Dominican immigrant who worked in a factory in New Jersey. He was from the same part of the Dominican Republic, and Magdalena and her children had known him since he was a boy. In 2002, Francisco lived with his wife and a child in the same tenement as Rosanna. He and Rosanna, and he and Amelia were *compadres* or ritual coparents. Francisco often visited Magdalena, especially on Sundays, and he often phoned her. Magdalena said, "He isn't a relative by blood, but he is a part of the family."

The core of this network (which included many others besides) had its own rituals. On most Sundays, a couple of the daughters spent a good deal of the day in their mother's apartment. Many grandchildren entered and left—some sat down on Magdalena's bed, while others watched TV or played on the pavement outside the building. Sometimes Francisco came, or Domingo—or both. They sat down in the living room and had a chat and shared a meal. At noon or in the early afternoon, Magdalena and her daughter(s) had prepared a large *almuerzo* or lunch—a Dominican meal, perhaps chicken with rice and beans and a salad. Everyone ate. On a couple of occasions, they did not cook their meal themselves but ordered Chinese takeaway from a place around the corner. On a hot Sunday in August, the daughters and their children went together to Coney Island to spend some hours on the beach—on that Sunday the apartment remained almost empty. But this was an exception; on most Sundays the family gathered in Magdalena's apartment. Becoming a part of this (female-dominated) network helped me tremendously in my work. The close contact with these women's everyday life made me better understand many processes in the city's Dominican immigrant community.[5]

This is not a book about a "Dominican enclave" or an "immigrant ghetto." The trope of the ethnic enclave and its equivalents, the "immigrant ghetto" and the "immigrant inner city" (understood as a world apart, as a society by itself, a form of nation in the nation), has often been employed in descriptions and studies of international migrants residing and working in U.S. cities. I seek to write against this form of representation, for three reasons.

First, the image of the ethnic enclave helps to give shape to and reproduce a veiling and mystifying dichotomy. It helps to produce a false distinction between two entities, two societies—the enclave or the ghetto (viewed as an isolated community) and the (typically ill-specified and little analyzed) American "mainstream." What is perhaps most unsatisfactory about the concept of the ethnic enclave is the extent to which it has served, and continues to serve, to block attempts to understand not absence of integration but the opposite: namely, specific forms of incorporation into a more comprehensive configuration of power and meaning. The lives and activities of New York's Dominican immigrants must be viewed as an integral part of an order that remains organized around clear asymmetries in political power and economic resources stretching beyond the imagined frontiers of the inner city—or the city's Dominican enclave. This book is not about a kind of parallel sociocultural universe. It is instead about connections—between Dominican New Yorkers' economic and political practices and ways of thinking and the much larger historical, political, economic, and cultural field within which they operate and upon whose existence their practices and ways of thinking are premised.

Second, the use of the enclave model in immigration studies seems to reproduce old, ill-founded ideas about rootedness and stability. It helps to create fictions of stable, migrant life where (temporary or relative) stability only corresponds to a part of the story. The enclave focus often makes researchers pay insufficient attention to immigrants' movements between "the enclave" and other places in the city and to their forms of displacement in the receiver country. Dominican immigrants are usually pretty much on the move. For example, Ramona and her daughter Evelyn lived, as noted, in the Bronx; the family had previously resided in Washington Heights but had had to move when Ramona no longer could pay the rent. But when I lived in Washington Heights, Ramona's and Evelyn's goal was to move back into this neighborhood. Another informant, a woman of Dominican origins in her forties, ran a small travel agency in Washington Heights and lived with her family in a tenement a couple of blocks away but had previously lived both in the South Bronx and in New Jersey.

Stories like these seem fairly representative. Some may have had to move because they needed a cheaper apartment or had gotten a new job in a new neighborhood. Others had sold their business and moved because they had not succeeded. Still others had sold a business and moved because they had wanted to expand. The imagery of immigrant enclaves is not adequate if we wish to map and represent the sociospatial landscapes of Dominican New Yorkers. Ideas about enclaves assume that people treat a given place—that of "the enclave"—as the principal environment to which they adapt themselves, so that the researcher pays too little attention both to movements farther afield and to displacements or to processes that challenge the usefulness of the enclave focus from the outset.

Third, using the enclave framework easily makes us overlook the mutual effect that immigrant groups may have on each other—and more generally, the significance of interactions across racial or ethnic boundaries. The central distinguishing mark of the enclave perspective is, as I have already underscored, that it presumes the separability of groups. It assumes that a given immigrant population can be understood if it is treated as if it were a discrete, bounded entity. But by dealing with immigrants in today's United States as if they form nations within the nation, we neglect and silence significant components of the process of immigrants' adjustment to American society.

Since the 1960s, large numbers of Dominican immigrants have secured a new home in the many tenements of New York City. First-generation Dominican immigrants "accepted" not being granted what Renato Rosaldo (1994: 402) has called "first-class" (political, social, and cultural) citizenship. Instead, they came to share neighborhoods with representatives of other minorities—with African Americans, Puerto Ricans, and members of the various new immigrant groups (Sanjek 1998; Ricourt and Danta 2003; Hoffnung-Garskof 2008). In 1993, Jorge Duany sampled 125 apartments and 352 persons residing within four towering buildings in the center of Dominican Washington Heights. The block was chosen by Duany precisely "because of its high concentration of Dominican residents." But one-fifth of the residents in the tenements were of non-Dominican origin—Ecuadorans, Puerto Ricans, Cubans, Mexicans, other Hispanics, non-Hispanic blacks, and non-Hispanic whites (Duany 1994: 13–15).

We ought to situate the migrants in concrete space. New York's residence patterns express striking segregation (Massey and Denton 1993). But the historical processes that shaped segregation also produced a situation in which many Dominican immigrants daily interacted across ethnic and racial boundaries—in tenements, neighborhood stores, neighborhood laundries, neighborhood parks, neighborhood child-care centers, neighborhood school yards, neighborhood churches, neighborhood hospitals, neighborhood senior centers, and buses and subways (Domínguez 1973, 1978; Georges 1984; Ricourt and Danta 2003: 24–56; Hoffnung-Garskof 2008: 97–162). The same applies to the job market—or the workplaces. Small businesses have been bought, sold, and run not in isolation from the city's ethnic and racial diversity but as part of it. Dominican small-business owners and employees have had to interact with representatives of the city's police and other authorities, with representatives of large and small companies, and with landlords and moneylenders; and these have often not been Dominicans. Likewise with the textile industry and other industries, factories have been multiethnic and multiracial (Waldinger 1986; Grasmuck and Pessar 1991: 162–98).

The stories of ethnic enclaves help shore up and render natural a specific political form—the nation-state model. Nationalists understand themselves as anchored in a particular piece of land. The classic ethnographic project, too, had an agrarian orientation (Gupta and Ferguson 1997: 8), and like the nation-state project, anthropology used to link the society or community to nature, to bind together the two "natural" parts of the society or community—the people and the place (Hart 2003: 2). Using the enclave image does the same thing. Narratives of ethnic enclaves in a city like New York help segregate populations and identities spatially, each in its fixed, urban territory. The enclave model in immigration studies reproduces infertile ideas of territorially rooted communities and stable, localized cultures and silences an interconnected world.

Understanding International Migration

Since the mid-twentieth century, millions of people from the global periphery have sought a better life in the cities of Western Europe and North America (Sassen-Koob 1982; Sassen [1991] 2001; Sanjek 1998; Trouillot 2003). The Dominicanization in New York City should be viewed as a component of these vast movements and interactions of people.

In this book, I argue that it is crucial to seek to analyze four sets of processes—or, if one wishes, four dimensions of the immigrants' lives: (1) the immigrants' forms of work, that is, their production of money and capital; (2) their everyday lives; (3) their forms of participation in political life; and (4) their negotiation and building of identities. This division is analytical. In reality, or empirically, the four sets of processes overlap. Let us consider each in turn.

Money

The most penetrating anthropological works on the new immigration, or on effects of the new immigration, that have appeared during the last couple of decades have, as I see it, a basic feature in common (in spite of their many significant differences, theoretically and methodically): these works all build on detailed examinations of the migrants' economic practices and strategies (for a few examples, see Grasmuck and Pessar 1991; Lamphere et al. 1994; Sanjek 1998; MacGaffey and Bazenguissa-Ganga 2000; and Stoller 2002). This should not surprise us. Labor migrants often have long working days; many work extremely hard to make and save money. If we want to be able to understand the lives of the immigrants, we have to seek to understand their economic conditions and their economic projects.

As Roger Sanjek (1998: 119–40) conceptualizes it, contemporary New York City has three economies, each increasingly divergent from the others. The first is the "speculative electronic economy," formerly called "Wall Street," based on global trading in currency and security values, producing great wealth for those at its command posts but employing ever fewer city residents and "dispersing nationally and worldwide." Then, there is the city's "real economy" of goods and services, providing the basics of daily life: food, clothing, machinery, housing, transportation, health care, repairs: "Its decline as a source of employment for neighborhood New Yorkers between 1980 and 1996 was due in part to job dispersal to the suburbs and other regions of the United States, and in part to new productive technologies and downsizing policies that required fewer workers. Damage to the real economy occurred as the speculative-electronic economy siphoned off productive capital to pursue paper gain. This resulted in job loss, wage stagnation and decline, erosion of health insurance, and pension insecurity." And finally there is the "underground economy" that has grown massively with the decline of the "real economy": sophisticated tax avoidance especially, but also such off-the-books pursuits as flea markets, street peddling, scavenging, illegal rooming houses, sweatshops, gambling, car theft, drug dealing, and prostitution (Sanjek 1998: 119).

Most New York City Dominicans are found in the real economy where they work in low-wage jobs and also use informal, off-the-books business-and-labor opportunities to make money. Some belong primarily to the underground economy. As previously said, from the late 1970s onward, the proportion of Dominican immigrants engaged in New York's service sector increased steadily, and more and more became self-employed. In this book, I examine in particular the Dominican immigrant community's small-business economy, though I do discuss also a part of the activities and everyday life of Dominicans working in other parts of the economy such as industry. I examine especially Dominican immigrants' integration into two sectors: the city's cab industry and grocery industry. But I look also at the Dominican immigrant community's ways of exploiting other niches—such as the restaurant industry, the travel-agency business, the beauty-shop business, and the repair-shop industry.

This study of Dominican immigrants' income-producing strategies seeks to avoid a model of "the economy" (or of "capitalism," or for that matter, of "neoliberalism") that sees the economy (or capitalism or neoliberalism) as an economic order governed by universal laws. Instead I set out from a premise that all forms of economic action are shaped by, and articulate, historically specific notions and values—that is, culture. In other words, we always need a cultural analysis of economic activities. This general anthropological position has been powerfully asserted by Sylvia Yanagisako in her *Producing Culture and Capital* (2002)—and in this study I am inspired by her thinking. A key is to seek to think of *both* "the cultural" *and* "the economic" as processes—that is, in dynamic, processual terms. Or in the words of Yanagisako, "Treating capitalism as a culturally enabled process through which people continually rethink and reformulate goals, meanings, and practices allows us to better comprehend the creative, unfolding dynamic of capitalist action" (2002: 6).

Two important questions arise: How did Dominican immigrants find work? And how did they organize their enterprises? Not surprisingly, I found that they relied massively on personal relations based on kinship, ethnicity, nationality, and friendship from workplace and/or locality. Such relations were mobilized for most purposes. They were used, for example, to obtain information and assistance, to assemble capital, to get credit, to find premises, to recruit employees, and to secure customers. In fact, in this study I examine Dominican New Yorkers' income-generating activities as networks. What do I mean by a "network"? In my view, the economic-cultural networks of the city's Dominican immigrants include three components. We should examine (1) *the people involved*, that is, the ties between them and their forms of exchange, help, collaboration, and conflict; (2) *the arenas or premises in which goods and services are sold*; and (3) *the goods and services that circulate in the networks*. Networks are not only about relations between people; they are also about particular places and particular things or objects—specific goods and services. This approach draws on the work of Janet MacGaffey and Rémy Bazenguissa-Ganga and their impressive study *Congo-Paris* (2000, esp. 12-14).[6]

First-generation immigrants, including first-generation Dominican New Yorkers, are economically and socially dissimilar. While most first-generation Dominican immigrants in New York certainly remain poor or relatively poor, there are exceptions. A small minority, have, as we shall see in this book, managed to make a good deal of money; a few have become "success stories"; some have even begun to play golf. The point is simple but important. Immigrants, like others, are not "all the same." They, like others, should be understood with reference to class.

Everyday Life

Social and cultural anthropologists have for nearly a century based much of their work on the following key idea: if one wishes to understand a society, one needs first to comprehend this society's everyday life. This has unique, but often unrecognized, significance; a society's economic, cultural, and political institutions are typically rooted in the organization of everyday life, in the small scale and prosaic—indeed, in the forms, practices, and activities of society's most basic entity, the household. Anthropology has known this at least since the early 1920s. Bronisław Malinowski once wrote (in the second appendix to the first volume of *Coral Gardens and Their Magic*, called "Confessions of Ignorance and Failure: Gaps and Side-Steps"): "A general source of inadequacies in all my material, whether photographic or linguistic or descriptive, consists in the fact that, like every ethnographer, I was lured by the dramatic, exceptional and sensational. . . . I have also neglected much of the everyday, inconspicuous, drab and small-scale in my study of Trobriand life. The only comfort which I may derive is that . . . my mistakes may be of use to others" (1935: 462). In spite of these confessions, Malinowski gave us an exceptional contribution, a set of insights and a corpus that helped create a new standard for a science. There were at least two reasons for this. Malinowski had the opportunity to live in the same field site for a long time. Second, he managed, no matter what he maintains in the quotation above, to observe and document an enormous amount of ordinary everyday life—what his Trobriand informants usually did, not only what they typically told him they did.

In studies of international migrants, it has often proved to be difficult, too difficult, to live up to anthropology's expectations. Often time in the field has been strongly limited by restricted funding or other practical circumstances. Or the researcher found that doing anthropology in the city (that is, in a large-scale, completely urban, fragmented field) demanded and justified a new way of working ethnographically, an altered form of knowledge production. But often this meant in practice, as I see it, that the researcher quite simply relied too much on the interview as a source of data collection.

What particular insight lies, then, in the "everyday, inconspicuous, drab and small-scale" when the goal is to understand the life and strategies of a group of labor migrants? As I have already insisted, it is a sine qua non to attempt to understand the migrants' culture—their orientations, ideas, and values. But culture does not exist in isolation from social action. One thing that cultural theorists, including anthropologists, have recognized after the last decades' turn away from forms of structuralism may be summed up in the following manner: social actors' cultural worlds are produced through everyday practices that are themselves culturally formed (Williams 1977; Ortner 1999); hence a migrant group's cultural ideas and values are shaped through these everyday practices, including what are conventionally classified as "economic" practices, "kinship" practices, "political" practices, "ritual" practices, and so on. (In other words, let us not assume that social actors shape and sustain their ideas and practices according to the analytic classifications [domains and institutions] of researchers.)

The use of interviews is necessary; a significant part of the data that I employ in this book has been produced through interviews—a series of informal, semistructured conversations between an informant and me. But it is important to combine the use of interviews with other forms of production of data. I emphasize two other forms.

First, the researcher should spend sufficient time in the immigrants' neighborhoods—on their sidewalks and streets. He or she needs to be able to observe ordinary everyday life in tenements, restaurants, associations, and businesses. This is necessary if one wishes to understand the key process that I mentioned above, the dialectic interplay between ordinary everyday practice and production and reproduction of culture, between action and meaning. Clifford Geertz once wrote that "the normal activities of ordinary men in everyday life" are typically guided by "half-formed, taken-for-granted, indifferently systematized notions" (1973: 362). I agree—and to be able to examine and comprehend such notions we need to do more than just converse with people. We should immerse ourselves in their everyday life.

Second, it is important to spend sufficient time at the level of the household. The household is not only a uniquely significant arena as society's building block; it also functions in practice as a mediation process, on a small scale. Through the daily activities of the household's members, a series of social domains—like economic processes, kinship, neighborliness, socialization, friendship, schooling and education, ethnic and racial identity production, and political participation—get continuously linked up, united. The organization of this everyday complexity (or the organization of this constant mediation or traffic across domains in the household, on a small scale) is crucial to study. In my opinion, immigration researchers need to live for a time in one of the immigrants' homes, in one of their apartments, to live for some time together with some of their informants.

Politics

The Dominican small-business sector is not just an economic (and cultural) force; it has also yielded forms of political activity. Dominican New Yorkers who own small economic ventures, or who work in the city's taxi industry, have joined forces and created collectivities or industrial bodies—small-business associations and trade unions. These organizations are political actors. Many fight against increasing rents and higher taxes and sponsor social and cultural events and (Dominican and Latino) political leaders running for office. Some form part of broad multiracial and multiethnic alliances and coalitions struggling against new giant stores or megastores. All have as their primary task to promote and defend the members' economic interests.

In my view, it is imperative for migration research to study this type of political activity. Today—after the last decades' brutal neoliberal restructuring—many migrants across the world seem forced to seek to support themselves and their families through forms of entrepreneurship and/or wage work in the informal economy. As Sian Lazar (2008) has noted about Bolivia, with economic restructuring, "Organized labor has not been entirely broken but is beginning to reconstitute itself as a political subject. As Hardt and Negri (2005) argue, this political subject is not the working class as we traditionally understand it, but the urban poor" (Lazar 2008: 178). In other words, if we wish to comprehend how representatives of the popular classes in today's world make money, organize their everyday life, and construct identities, we need to understand their political activities. We must examine in what ways they seek to defend and promote their material, symbolic, and other interests; and for that reason it should be obligatory to study the political practices of small-business associations and trade unions.[7]

Dominican immigrants have also acted politically in other ways, through other channels. Many of the city's Dominicans belong to one or more Dominican recreational or social *clubes* or clubs. Many of the *clubes* are politically active; they express and support moral and political claims, take political initiatives, and form part of political grass-roots alliances. Others have created nonprofits that sponsor everything from local economic development to enhanced rights for immigrants to improved local housing. Dominican parents residing in Washington Heights and Inwood—and in other parts of the city—have for decades fought for more and better public schools for their children (see, for example, Hoffnung-Garskof 2008: 132–62; Georges 1984). Most Dominican New Yorkers have been, and still are, Democrats, not Republicans (Hispanic Federation 2002: 5).

It has often been said that international migrants are more preoccupied with the political processes in their original homeland than with taking part in the political life in the receiver country. This contains a kernel of truth. But many migrants act and struggle politically in their new homeland. Quite a few immigrants are politically active simultaneously in both places—both in their original homeland and in their new homeland. Sometimes things change as time goes by, after the migrants have spent more years in the receiver country. As we shall see later in this study, such things are not static. In this book, I look primarily at political activity in the United States, in the New York area. I examine especially forms of political culture and activism in two important parts of the Dominican immigrant community—or among two key groups, Dominicans working in (1) the city's grocery industry and (2) New York's taxi industry.

Investigations along these lines require, and I stress this, a broader view of politics than is most often applied—whether we are speaking of migration studies or other forms of social research. We need thoroughly anthropological thinking about the study of politics. Here, this means two things. First, studies of politics should be anchored in examination of people's everyday life. Political struggles are not confined to a narrow set of arenas. Researchers thus need to shift from a focus on studies of "politics" (in its narrow meaning) to a focus on investigations of power, meaning, and history: we should aim to understand what constitutes "the political" about the processes we study but recognize that the political, or politics, must not be treated as a separate domain or field but must be examined as articulations between power relations, cultural processes, and historical trajectories.

The second important point relates to the way we assess the necessity of studying cultural meaning when our goal is to be able to grasp politics. Just like economic life, political life cannot be understood in isolation from culture. As I see it, too much analysis of contemporary politics continues to be reductionist; it ignores the tremendous significance of symbolic forms, or meanings and values, in the making and remaking of configurations of power in today's world. In clear contrast to this, I set out from the premise that we need to investigate how leaders and masses involved in the construction of contemporary forms of politics shape and reshape categories and meanings and understand their worlds. Structures of inequality and domination are constituted with the aid of categories and meanings. We should, therefore, see political life as continuous negotiation of meaning and fighting over it. Politics is a realm both of tactical behavior and struggle and of activity taking place through complex symbolic processes.

Belonging

Over the past decades, the literature on international migration has increasingly expressed a new important interest, in the so-called transnational migrant circuit (see, for example, Rouse [1991] 2002; Glick Schiller et al. 1992; Appadurai 1996; Guarnizo 1997; Ong 1998; Levitt 2001; Duany 2002; Smith 2006; Olwig 2007). Analysts have maintained that groups of migrants have created a new sort of social space or community or sociospatial relations that force social theory to question the received ways of understanding international migration—that is, that migrants have not abandoned one nation-state for another but have generated communities stretching across national boundaries; they belong simultaneously to more than one nation-state and, thus, to no one nation-state in particular: they are transnational. As Roger Rouse formulated it in an already classic essay, the Mexican labor migrants among whom he conducted research moved to the U.S. community of Redwood City, on the northern edge of California's Silicon Valley, but were still far from severing their links to their native community, the rural town of Aguililla in the state of Michoacán, the telephone being particularly significant in weaving together a "transnational circuit" (Rouse [1991] 2002: 162).

Certainly it is necessary to examine the transnational circuit—or more generally, those activities and relations that bind together the sender and receiver countries. This is definitely also the case with the Dominican New Yorkers, as will become apparent in this study. Most if not all of those I met with were part of a transnational circuit. There is now a constant circulation of people, capital, and information between most areas of the Dominican Republic and New York (Hendricks 1974; Georges 1990; Duany 1994; Pessar 1997; Levitt 2001; Ricourt 2002; Hoffnung-Garskof 2008). Increasing access to the telephone and more recently to the Internet has been important. Many called relatives in the Dominican Republic daily or weekly from their Washington Heights homes. I frequently found my landlady walking around in the apartment while talking on the phone with a relative in the southeastern Dominican Republic. Altered forms of communication have made it possible to take part in everyday forms of decision making on the island, even from Manhattan, the Bronx, Queens, and Brooklyn.

That said, I think the last three decades' interest in the transnational, or in effects of transnational flows, has in some ways been exaggerated. Certainly, we must study the circuit, but I disagree with some others about the implications of the existence of circuits and forms of cultural bifocality. People have written as if increased trade and migration really are making national borders increasingly irrelevant. But this does not square with what we know of history. As David Graeber has put it, "while world trade has increased, overall migration rates are nothing like what they were 100 (let alone 200 or 300) years ago, and the only element that is entirely new here is the presence of the borders themselves. The modern 'interstate system' that carves up the earth through thousands of highly patrolled and regulated borders was only fully completed quite recently" (Graeber 2002: 1225).[8] This is not the first time in history that migrants belong to more than one cultural world or construct diasporic attachments (Sanjek 2003: 321–28; Mintz 1998: 123–26).

My point is that we should not exaggerate the degree of change world society has seen over the past few decades. First, the end of Western empire is not behind us. World society may be said to be fragmented and in some ways increasingly decentered, but it has nevertheless an extremely recognizable structure. A striking share of capital investments today continues to take place in highly limited parts of the world (Trouillot 2003: 47–78). People from the Caribbean, Latin America, the Middle East, Asia, Africa, and Eastern Europe travel to the global center, in particular its cities, to sell their labor at a better price than it obtains in their home country. Second, there are clear signs that the nation-state (as model and reality) remains powerful. That is, it is important not to overlook or minimize either the continued, perhaps growing, strength of the nation form globally (Verdery 1999; Duany 2002; Lomnitz 2005) or the fact that many forms of nation-state building in the global center, far from being eaten away by today's transnational migrant circuits, are entirely premised on them (Stolcke 1995; Hansen and Stepputat 2005).

Given this, we clearly need to ask how migrants from the global periphery have influenced the large cities of North America and Western Europe. And, conversely, how has the move to the core of the Western empire affected their lives—that is, in which ways have the migrants become a part of the receiver countries? These are the general questions that have driven me in this book. This is primarily a study of immigration processes.

In such studies, we seem forced to treat constructions of belonging. We have to study the migrants' production—or negotiation and building—of forms of belonging, or identity, in the receiver country (in terms of race, [pan]ethnicity, religion, nationality, and so on). In the subsequent chapters, I focus particularly on how Dominican New Yorkers viewed themselves in terms of race, ethnicity, and panethnicity. How did they identify themselves racially and ethnically? To what extent did they continue to define themselves as "Dominicans"? To what extent did they see themselves as "(U.S.) Hispanics" or "(U.S.) Latinos"?

The production of collective and individual identities in a society is a power process, involving a range of political, economic, social, cultural, material, and aesthetic practices and networks. By "identities," I refer to a series of domains or fields that are crucial for people's experience of community and belonging—kinship, family, race, ethnicity, nationality, religion, the arts, and cultural production. An identity is best understood as a form of production—as historically specific ideas and practices. The production of identities is inextricably linked to the three other fields that I have mentioned above—that is, the practice of politics, the organization and management of the everyday life, and the participation in the economy.

Racial and ethnic identities are not only a product but also the condition of politics. In Steven Gregory's instructive words, "the social construction of identity or the 'fixing' of racialized, gendered, and other subject positions within a given social order is not only political, it is also the precondition of politics. From this perspective, the identity of black people in the United States has everything to do with politics" (1998: 13). It is the same with economic participation and everyday life. Dominican New Yorkers' economic roles and everyday rhythms and routines provide them with belonging—with experiences of identity as Dominicans and Hispanics. At the same time, their experiences of who and what they are racially and ethnically help to give form to their economic practices and decisions and to the way in which they organize and live their everyday lives (for example, in the household).

Dominicans, Latinos, and New York City Since the 1970s

Most of the data I discuss in this book are derived from processes and events from the late 1960s and early 1970s to the present; the book covers especially the period from the late 1970s and early 1980s until around 2005. Two processes that have helped transform American cities since the 1960s have been what authors have described as the increasing U.S. Latinization and the nation's (and most of the rest of the world's) emphatic turn toward neoliberalism in political-economic practices and thinking since the 1970s (see, e.g., Bergad and Klein 2010; Gutiérrez 2006; Harvey 2005). Both processes have been and remain vividly at play in New York, and one of my most basic goals may therefore be summarized as to demonstrate, and in this way help call attention to, important parts of the Dominican migrants' contribution to the remaking of U.S. cities in general and New York City in particular, in this context.

Much has already been written about both processes, so my goal is relatively modest. Through this study, I seek primarily to help render visible the Dominican New Yorkers, with their practices and forms of thinking, as a component of the last decades' changes in the Empire City. But to be able to do this, it is first necessary to say a little bit more about New York's recent history. Below I sketch the contours of the history of the city's Latinization, before I roughly outline the history of how New York became a neoliberal city.

New York City crossed the "majority-minority" threshold in the early 1990s. The city's white population fell from 85.3 percent in 1960 to 76.6 percent in 1970, 60.7 percent in 1980, 52.3 percent in 1990, and 44.7 percent in 2000.[9] New York City's Latino population increased from 23.7 percent of all New Yorkers in 1990 to 27 percent in 2000. By 2000 the city's black population stood at 26.6 percent, down from 28.7 percent in 1990, and the Asian population at 9.9 percent, up from 7 percent. In other words, Latinos are the city's biggest minority group.

The history of the Caribbeanization and Latinization of New York takes us back at least to the first part of the nineteenth century. In the words of Nancy Raquel Mirabal,

> With its long history of Puerto Rican and Cuban migration and settlement, along with it being the site where José Martí based his political operation and subsequently organized the Partido Revolucionario Cubano (PRC), New York was one of the few places where Puerto

Ricans and Cubans lived and worked for a significant amount of time. By the 1830s Puerto Ricans and Cubans had fashioned an anticolonial movement. Political organizations, exile newspapers, cultural clubs, and revolutionary groups were already present in New York. As a thriving political community, the city was transformed into one of the most important and necessary sites for Puerto Ricans and Cubans to reimagine a distinct Antillean nation and identity while still remaining loyal to their own notions of what constituted an individual Puerto Rican and Cuban nation. (Mirabal 2001: 58–59)

Puerto Rico has a curious status in the contemporary Western world. As one of Spain's last two colonies in Latin America and the Caribbean (along with Cuba), Puerto Rico experienced the longest period of Hispanic influence in the region. In 1898, however, the United States occupied the island during the Spanish-Cuban-American-Filipino War. Nineteen years later, the U.S. Congress granted citizenship to all persons born in Puerto Rico but did not incorporate the island as a territory. Until now, the island has remained a colonial dependency, even though it gained a limited sort of self-government as a Commonwealth in 1952. The penetration of U.S. capital into the Puerto Rican economy after the Spanish-Cuban-American-Filipino War nearly destroyed the traditional pattern of individual land ownership and consolidated the dominance of a group of U.S. corporations. This caused thousands of Puerto Ricans to migrate, first to the island's urban centers and then across the ocean (Sánchez Korrol 1994: 25, 27). The 1930 Census registered a growth of more than 100 percent (to 110,223 individuals) in what was then called the Hispanic population of New York City, with a substantial increase of Puerto Ricans to 44,908 (40.7 percent) (Laó-Montes 2001: 19–20). Between 1940 and 1960, the number of Puerto Ricans residing in the continental United States increased from 70,000 to 893,000, and the preferred destination was New York City (Ricourt and Danta 2003: 3). The growth in the Puerto Rican population was tremendous, to the point that by 1965 Puerto Ricans were by far the largest Latino group in the city and for a while (say, up to around 1960) their presence in New York became practically coextensive with the Latino presence (Sánchez Korrol 1994).

The period from the late 1950s to the mid-1970s also saw two other major migrations from the Spanish-speaking Caribbean to the city—the first after the Cuban Revolution of 1959 and the second with the Dominican political and social changes beginning in 1961 (with the assassination of Trujillo):

After the 1959 Cuban revolution, the New York Cuban population grew from 42,694 in 1960 to a peak of 84,179 in 1970. The significantly white upper- and middle-class composition of the first post-1959 Cuban migration[10] and the substantial financial and political aids provided by the U.S. government to them as part of Cold War anticommunist policies (such as the Cuban Refugee Program of 1961 and the Cuban Adjustment Act of 1966) facilitated the ability of the new immigrants to obtain an unparalleled degree of economic success and cultural recognition.... The very possibilities for success led many Cubans to relocate (the censuses of 1980 and 1990 indicated a decrease of Cubans in New York from 63,189 to 56,041, respectively) to places where they could predominate (especially Miami and West New Jersey) and where they accumulated not only economic and symbolic capital but also demographic leadership and political power. (Laó-Montes 2001: 21)

Considerable numbers of Ecuadorans, Colombians, and other South Americans, as well as Central Americans of diverse nationalities (Guatemalans, Hondurans, Panamanians, and Salvadorans), entered New York in the 1960s, 1970s, and later. In the 1980s, the migration of Mexicans to New York City also took off, and Mexicans have for some years been by far the fastest growing of the city's Latino nationalities (Limonic 2008: 3–4; Smith 2006: 19–23). According to U.S. Census data, in 2000 the city's 808,400 Puerto Ricans accounted for 37.6 percent of the total Latino population (down from 49.5 percent in 1990), 530,787 Dominicans, 24.7 percent (up from 19.1 percent), 185,885 Mexicans, 8.6 percent (up from 3.2 percent), 139,015 Ecuadorans, 6.5 percent (up from 4.5 percent), 104,232 Colombians, 4.8 percent (down from 4.9 percent), 46,225, Cubans, 2.1 percent (down from 3.3 percent), and 336,421 other Latin Americans/Latinos, 15.6 percent (up from 15.4 percent). By 2007, the city's Mexicans had increased to 289,755, 12.4 percent of the total Latino population (Limonic 2008: 3).

As an outcome of these migration streams, by 1980 many parts of the city had a substantial Latino population. The historically Puerto Rican areas in Manhattan (particularly "El Barrio," East Harlem), the south Bronx, and parts of Brooklyn remained fairly strongly Puerto Rican, but the area north of Harlem in Manhattan became a heavily Dominican neighborhood. In Queens, however, there was no majority group among the borough's diverse Spanish-speaking Caribbean and Latin American residents. Neighborhoods in Queens were above all multi-Latino (Ricourt and Danta 2003; Sanjek 1998).

Unlike past European and contemporary Asian immigrants to the United States, Latinos from different countries share a language. Most Latino New Yorkers do speak (at least a bit of) English, but for first-generation immigrants, and also for long-established bilingual or English-dominant residents, Spanish retains a special position, enabling Latinos from different countries easily to communicate and interact with each other. But there are also profound differences among New York and United States Latinos. First, Latinos from different countries are products of different political and social histories, have dissimilar national identities, and embody different class positions and racial identities (Arreola 2004; Suárez-Orozco and Páez 2002). Second, although lumped together under the monolithic label of "Latino" (or "Hispanic") ethnicity, distinct Latino groups are divided by clear citizenship inequalities (Oboler 2006; Smith 2005; De Genova and Ramos-Zayas 2003). Puerto Ricans are by definition U.S. citizens. Cubans have often been treated by the U.S. authorities as political refugees. The rest—Dominicans, Colombians, Ecuadorans, Mexicans, Peruvians, and so on—have for the most part been illegal or legal labor immigrants.

Neoliberalism—the political and economic theory that values market exchange as an ethic in itself and maintains that the social good will be maximized by maximizing the extent and frequency of market transactions— became gradually hegemonic in thought and practice in a large part of the world from the early 1970s onward. Its strengthened position depended on a transformation of the role of the state so that deregulation, privatization, finance, and withdrawal of the authorities from many areas of social provision were given priority; public interventions in the economy were reduced, while the obligations of the state to help secure the welfare of its citizens were weakened (for examples, see Sassen [1991] 2001; Comaroff and Comaroff 2001; Ong 2006; Gregory 2007). In his *A Brief History of Neoliberalism* (2005), David Harvey has offered an analysis of how neoliberalization conquered the world. Harvey sees New York City's fiscal crisis in the mid-1970s as a key event. In Harvey's words, "The management of the New York fiscal crisis pioneered the way for neoliberal practices both domestically under Reagan and internationally through the IMF in the 1980s. It established the principle that in the event of a conflict between the integrity of financial institutions and bondholders' returns, on the one hand, and the well-being of the citizens on the other, the former was to be privileged" (2005: 48).

Harvey, summing up the situation in New York in the mid-1970s, notes that, after the impoverishment of central New York due to "capitalist restructuring and deindustrialization" and "rapid suburbanization," there followed "explosive social unrest" in the 1960s; expansion of public employment and public provision—facilitated in part by generous federal funding—was seen as the solution to this, but "faced with fiscal difficulties, President Nixon simply declared the urban crisis over in the early 1970s" and funding declined. After this, the city's debt mounted, and "in 1975 a powerful cabal of investment bankers . . . pushed the city into technical bankruptcy." The bailout that followed entailed the construction of new institutions that took over the management of the city budget; the effect of their management was "to curb the aspirations of the city's powerful municipal unions, to implement wage freezes and cutbacks in public employment and social provision (education, public health, transport services), and to impose user fees. . . . The final indignity was the requirement that municipal unions should invest their pension funds in city bonds." This, says Harvey, "amounted to a coup by the financial institutions against the democratically elected government of New York City, and it was every bit as effective as the military coup that had earlier occurred in Chile" (2005: 45).[11]

All this created a tough, not to say brutal world, and it was in this social climate that new waves of migrants continued to enter the city. This was a universe with a "good business climate," but also with a striking and growing gap between rich and poor and disheartening levels of violence. The aftereffects of the 1975 fiscal crisis—diminished social infrastructure, crowded schools, a deteriorated subway system (due to lack of investment or even basic maintenance), reduced building inspections, weakened public safety, and other consequences of fiscal austerity—defined the condition in the city for over two decades. Overall, the city's budget shrank 22 percent between 1975 and 1983, and service cuts affected every aspect of the masses' everyday life (Sanjek 1998: 93). To quote Harvey again, "Working-class and ethnic-immigrant New York was thrust back into the shadows" (2005: 47).

As stated, my goal is to direct attention to the Dominican immigrants—given the above outlined landscape. I wish to analyze how they managed and in which ways they contributed to the restructuring of the city.

* * *

Chapter 1 offers a brief history of the Dominican Republic and of the Dominican exodus to the United States and outlines some main features of Dominican history in New York.

Chapter 2 presents a (mostly oral—or "street") history of Dominican immigrants and small business in New York City. The chapter examines accounts by Dominican New Yorkers of how they and others had contributed to the creation and the construction of a set of important economic-social niches (the city's Dominican-run grocery store, the city's Dominican-owned taxi operation, and so on).

Chapters 3 and 4 shift the focus to the time of the field research. In these two chapters, I ask how the Dominican immigrants' businesses are organized. Or, how do they come into being, and how are they run? While Chapter 3 examines Dominican enterprises in a range of different industries (from the grocery business to the restaurant industry to the beauty-shop business), Chapter 4 is entirely devoted to an analysis of the Dominican car services.

Chapters 5, 6, and 7 examine the history of the Dominicanization in New York in part as a history of political action (including collective struggle) and in part as a story of forms of negotiation of identity—of belonging. In Chapter 5, I outline some answers to the following questions. How did the Dominican New Yorkers I met define themselves racially and ethnically? In which ways did they produce and sustain their identity as Dominicans? In which ways did Dominican New Yorkers contribute to the city's and the United States' construction of Hispanic or Latino panethnicity? In Chapters 6 and 7, I analyze forms of political activity and political struggle among Dominican New Yorkers who operated small businesses. I do this through investigation of two histories: in Chapter 6, the history of the emergence of the National Supermarkets Association; in Chapter 7, that of the creation of the New York State Federation of Taxi Drivers. These two bodies were no doubt the two strongest of the Dominican-controlled interest organizations in the city at the time of the fieldwork—and both were completely dominated by New York-based Dominicans.

PART I

CHAPTER 1

From Quisqueya to New York City

"Quisqueya" is the indigenous name for the Caribbean island of Hispaniola (or, in Spanish, Española), which lies between Cuba and Puerto Rico. Hispaniola is divided into two nations—the Dominican Republic (which occupies the eastern two-thirds of the island) and Haiti (which occupies the remaining western third of the island). Nowadays, Manhattan north of Harlem is often referred to as "Quisqueya on the Hudson" or "Quisqueya Heights"—Washington Heights being New York City's name for Manhattan north of Harlem (see, for example, Duany's title from 1994).[1]

The history of emigration from the Dominican Republic differs markedly from the pattern characteristic of the Anglophone Caribbean, where seasonal or temporary migration in search of work within the Caribbean and more recently to Europe and North America has been important since the nineteenth century (Olwig 1993; Maurer 1997). Mass emigration from the Dominican Republic is a new phenomenon, dating only from the early 1960s. Indeed, for over 130 years, or since the late 1870s, the Dominican Republic has been an importer of labor, primarily from the English-speaking West Indies and Haiti (Bryan 1985; Martínez 1995, 1999).

Why has the Dominican Republic become a significant supplier of migrants? While most by far of those who have emigrated have been driven by a desire for economic progress—an improved income—the earliest large-scale migration from the Dominican Republic to the United States generally, and New York more especially, was politically motivated. To explain this, I must first say a bit more about the Dominican Republic's political and social history. This chapter is meant as an introduction—it sketches a background and a set of contexts for the analyses that follow in the rest of the book.[2]

The Making of a Migration Movement

A watershed in the history of the Dominican Republic, independent since 1844, was the U.S. occupation from 1916 to 1924.[3] The U.S. occupation regime created an effective national military institution in a country that had previously had none. Among the first class of native officers who graduated from the new military academy in 1921 was Rafael Trujillo, who rose to command the modernized military the United States had helped establish and then overthrew the elected government and ruled the Dominican Republic from 1930 until his assassination in 1961.

Trujillo's rule was marked by grotesque violence and abuse, and he used state power to amass a spectacular fortune. The regime's greatest crime was the 1937 massacre of thousands of Haitian peasants and workers in the Dominican-Haitian borderlands, a still greater number being expelled from the country (Fiehrer 1990; Turits 2003: 144–80).[4] Hundreds of Dominicans were also killed by his agents, although Trujillo generally employed means of domination and repression short of actual liquidation (Galíndez 1958: 129; Vega 1986).

The dictator's Dominican Republic was basically a peasant society, and even Trujillo's rule (often viewed by scholars, novelists, and foreign observers as totally despotic, a regime with little or no backing in society) had, in fact, a substantial social basis and significant spheres of acceptance (see, for example, Walker 1970; Turits 2003; Derby 2009; Krohn-Hansen 2009). The thirty-one-year regime mediated important socioeconomic changes, especially through agrarian policies that benefited the country's large independent peasant population. In the mid-1930s, 82 percent of the population was rural; in 1960, 70 percent remained rural, still one of the highest proportions in Latin America and the Caribbean (Turits 2003: 265). In his *Foundations of Despotism* (2003), Turits has shown how reforms by the Trujillo state changed the nascent processes of restructuring in the countryside that had threatened Dominican peasants when Trujillo seized power—changes energized by new production of sugar for the world market, by increased commercialization of land, and by new property laws. By implementing policies that in practice sustained the peasants' free access to land during a phase of national economic growth, the dictator secured rural backing. In Turits's terms, Trujillo promoted a peasant-based modernity (2003: 81–82).

Massive emigration from the Dominican Republic to the United States began in 1962 after the death of Trujillo, who had severely restricted movement out of the country to conserve the domestic agricultural and industrial labor supply (Georges 1990: 29).⁵ In 1962, there were perhaps as many as 15,000 Dominicans in New York, including many who had arrived in the year since the dictatorship's end. But just four decades later, moderate estimates put the Dominican population in the United States at around 1.12 million—and by far most of these lived in New York City (Hoffnung-Garskof 2008: 4).

After Trujillo was assassinated, relatively free elections followed in 1962, the first of their kind since 1924. Those elections resulted in an overwhelming victory for Juan Bosch, leader of the Partido Revolucionario Dominicano (PRD), which he had founded in Cuba in 1939. Although Bosch's political ideas were far more "reformist" than "revolutionary," he was soon labeled communist (by members of the armed forces, businessmen, and industrialists), and after only seven months, his government was overthrown by a military coup. The triumvirate regime that followed stayed in power with the support of the Trujilloist generals in the army and the United States. In April 1965, civil war broke out in the capital between pro-Bosch and anti-Bosch forces. Peace, or a second Pax Americana, was then imposed, when President Lyndon Johnson on April 28, 1965, ordered 42,000 U.S. marines to Santo Domingo to stop Bosch and prevent the establishment of "a second Cuba in America."

During this politically turbulent period, Dominican emigration to the United States jumped to about 10,000 legal migrants per year, while there were also 20,000–30,000 tourists per year, many of whom overstayed to work (Hoffnung-Garskof 2008: 69). Most of this earliest mass emigration was politically driven, or rather strongly shaped by Dominican and U.S. foreign policy and security concerns (68–96).⁶ At first the emigrants were mostly middle-class people, worried about the progressive rule by President Bosch. Soon their unease shifted to the civil unrest after Bosch's defeat. But U.S. visas were not at all reserved for conservative or indeed reactionary (white or light-skinned) middle-class Dominicans. The U.S. ambassador to the Dominican Republic during the early 1960s worked actively, with the president's backing, to issue more visas to Dominicans. Thus it became possible for quite a few progressive supporters of Bosch in the 1965 crisis to obtain visas, including leaders and activists of left-wing and social-democratic parties, trade union organizers, barrio militants, and radical students from the nation's oldest and largest university, the Autonomous University of Santo Domingo (UASD) (Georges 1984; Hoffnung-Garskof 2008: 68–80). Many of these individuals chose to leave for New York after the U.S. military intervention in 1965.

Others were in reality forced to leave the country; they were deported under the terms of an agreement between the two governments (Martin 1966; Hoffnung-Garskof 2008: 77–79).

Fairly soon, however, the Dominican exodus was primarily a response to (1) the manner in which the Dominican state-building project was managed and (2) the living conditions of vast segments of the population. After Trujillo's death, Dominican ruling elites gradually shifted from a more self-sufficient agriculture-based economy to a new economic model, "an increasingly neoliberal version of modernity" (Turits 2003: 263). But the bulk of the population drew relatively little benefit from what occurred. The changed political and economic system made the old rich richer, created some new categories of rich, and (at least up to the late 1970s) expanded the middle class slightly; but it only improved to a modest extent the basic conditions of the masses. Hence increasing numbers of Dominicans chose to seek their fortunes in New York—or more generally, abroad.

The three decades from 1966 to 1996 were dominated by Joaquín Balaguer. He ruled the nation first from 1966 to 1978 and then from 1986 to 1996. Earlier, Trujillo had ruled for some time without holding the title of president, through puppet presidents of whom the last was Joaquín Balaguer. A lawyer and shrewd politician, Balaguer was also a prolific author who published many books. He occupied a set of important positions under Trujillo and was one of the regime's leading ideologues.

After a brief exile in New York following the dictator's death, Balaguer founded the Partido Reformista (PR) in 1964 and gained the support of army officers. His first twelve years in power (1966–78) were violently repressive and have been described as "Trujillismo without Trujillo" (Black 1986: 42). The elections in 1966 were organized in an atmosphere of extended civil war. With U.S. troops in the country and while terrorist campaigns against Bosch's PRD killed hundreds of the party's activists and Bosch himself feared for his life, Balaguer won with 57 percent of the vote to Bosch's 39 percent. The nation suffered for some eight years under Balaguer's state-sponsored terror. Paramilitary groups killed more than 4,000 Dominicans between 1966 and 1974 (Moya Pons 1990: 528).

Balaguer gave up power in 1978 after the elections that year had triggered loud allegations of fraud.[7] Eight years later, he regained the Dominican presidency and then was reelected once more in 1990. When he stepped down from office for the last time in 1996, he had once again been forced to resign, having lost credibility in a spectacular way. The opposition and foreign observers had condemned the presidential elections of 1994, which Balaguer (now ninety years old) was declared to have won, as scandalously rigged (Hartlyn 1998: 251–54).

But Balaguer also enjoyed ample support in important sectors of society. He used the nation's large public sector for patronage politics. Across the country, public sector jobs were given almost exclusively to members of the president's own party. After 1966, the number of public sector employees increased steadily, boosted by massive U.S. aid plus a favorable U.S. sugar quota (Moya Pons 1990: 531; Betances 1995: 120, 123), conspicuous economic growth with more foreign investment and tourism (Kryzanek and Wiarda 1988: 49–50, 137–38), and a public sector wage freeze from 1966 to 1978 (Kearney 1986: 151). In the 1960s and 1970s, there was also a marked increase in the national rates of enrollment of students pursuing higher education. Postsecondary enrollment grew from 3,400 in 1960 to 23,500 in 1970 and then rose sharply to 139,300 in 1982 (Grasmuck and Pessar 1991: 36). But in spite of the national economic growth, a large number of Dominicans, including graduates, actually saw their meager incomes fall during the 1970s: "A look at the changes in the distribution of income in Dominican society during the 1970s would show that the poor became poorer, but the other social strata largely benefited" (Torres-Saillant and Hernández 1998: 54–55).

An almost complete turnaround in the national economy came in the late 1970s and early 1980s. In 1977, petroleum costs absorbed 60 percent of sugar export earnings, but the figure had increased to 133 percent in 1982 (Kryzanek and Wiarda 1988: 138–39). By the 1978 election, clear signs of an end to the economic boom were already present. In addition, leaders of the opposition had finally managed to put aside their differences and shape a viable coalition. Their presidential candidate was Antonio Guzmán, whose main promise was to get rid of the repression and establish democracy. Guzmán's party, the PRD, thereafter remained in power for eight years. Another PRD leader, Salvador Jorge Blanco, was elected president for the period 1982–86.[8]

By 1981 "it was already evident that the entire public sector was on the edge of bankruptcy" (Moya Pons 1990: 537). Negotiations on the Dominican debt problem with the International Monetary Fund (IMF) and bilateral creditors followed. And predictably enough, the 1980s and the early 1990s saw a general pauperization of the population and a reduction of the middle class. Indeed, by the early 1990s, the purchasing power of the nation's minimum wage was half its value in the 1970s—and salary readjustments in the country's large, most modern companies had brought these companies' wages down to around 60 percent of the value they had had in the 1970s (Torres-Saillant and Hernández 1998: 59). At the same time, the distance in wages between the island and New York (based on the annual average exchange rate and the two countries' minimum monthly salaries) continued to increase. In 1975, the minimum monthly wage for full-time work in the United States was four times that in the Dominican Republic; a decade later, it was between six and seven times, by 1991, thirteen times Santo Domingo's minimum salary (Grasmuck and Pessar 1991: 46–47; Guarnizo 1992: 63).

The natural outcome was, as we know, a continued tremendous Dominican migration to the United States. As noted, the Dominican Republic was the country sending the most immigrants to New York City in the 1970s and 1980s, and kept that position in the early 1990s. In 1995 the former Soviet Union became the primary source of immigrants to the city (Ricourt 2002: 35). But since 1995, the Dominican Republic has supplied enormous numbers of immigrants to New York.[9] Statistical data for 2009 indicated that the city's official Dominicans had grown by some 41,000 from 2000 to 2009 (from 547,379 to 588,865) (Bergad 2011: 5). Not only has the volume of the exodus grown but so has the geographical and socioeconomic variation this migration stream contains. Dominican migrants to New York have already for a long time come from most areas of the country. In the 1960s and 1970s, relatively many came from the middle sectors of society; but after the country was hit by growing economic crisis from the late 1970s onward, the migration stream broadened considerably to include a colossal number of ordinary (or fairly poor) Dominicans from both urban and rural areas, as well as a wide range of highly educated professionals.

Most Dominicans who travel to New York arrive in the city with some form of visa to the United States (Georges 1990: 81–92; Hoffnung-Garskof 2008: 74–80, 90–93); hence the social composition of the Dominican migration stream to New York has been shaped not only by processes on the island but also by U.S. immigration policies.[10] U.S. visas are essentially of two types: immigrant (sometimes described as residence) and nonimmigrant (tourist and student) visas. An immigrant visa allows wage employment, is usually valid without time limitation, and gives the right to apply ultimately for citizenship. The majority of the United States' legal immigrants are granted visas under a family unification stipulation; they have been spouses, children, parents, or siblings of an adult U.S. citizen or spouses or unmarried children of a permanent resident. A minority are granted visas because they are regarded as persons (professionals or workers) with needed skills. The tourist and student visas usually prohibit wage employment and are valid for only a limited period. But many arriving on such visas, often using forged documentation,[11] have overstayed the granted time period. The great majority of those who begin their sojourn in New York in this manner manage subsequently—say, after three to six years—to regularize their status, that is, become legal residents (although most often at considerable expense) (see, for example, Georges 1990: 90–92; and Grasmuck and Pessar 1991: 171–74). Many Dominicans with whom I became acquainted in the field, in Washington Heights and elsewhere in New York, belonged to this category.

After becoming legal residents, Dominican immigrants typically start applying for additional visas for family members still on the island; they become the pioneers or anchors to which sets of future migrants tie themselves. Thus, the practice and sustenance of kinship—or the production and sustenance of what Dominicans describe as *la familia*, or the extended family—have functioned, and continue to function, as a key mechanism in the history of the Dominicanization of New York. When Dominicans (on the island and in New York) discuss migration to the United States, they frequently speak about the *cadena*—the chain of migrant kin binding the sending community in the Dominican Republic to the immigrant community in the Empire City.

In sum, after 1966, Balaguer and Dominican leaders more generally came to rely on a migration-dependent political-economic project (or a migration-dependent form of state building and economic development). But the roots of the last two hundred years of political, economic, and social development on Hispaniola lie in colonialism and imperialism (Hansen and Stepputat 2005). What is today the Dominican Republic's territory belonged for about three hundred years to the Spanish Empire. From the late nineteenth century, the Dominican Republic's history has, to a striking extent, been shaped by U.S. military, political, and economic concerns. The United States occupied the country militarily in 1916–24 and again in 1965. Both Trujillo and Balaguer were in practice helped to power through U.S. activities on the island.

Settling in New York

As two prominent U.S. migration sociologists have put it, "Migration is a network-driven process, and the operation of kin and friendship ties is nowhere more effective than in guiding new arrivals toward preestablished ethnic communities" (Portes and Rumbaut 1996: 32). Dominican newcomers to the U.S. are typically helped in decisive ways by already established relatives or friends. The new arrival is temporarily lodged in the apartment of a relative or friend. Close kin and acquaintances in the city attempt also to find employment for the newcomer.

According to the U.S. Census Bureau, in 2007 38.9 percent of New York City's Dominicans resided in the Bronx, 28.8 percent in Manhattan, 16 percent in Queens, 15.8 percent in Brooklyn, and only 0.4 percent in Staten Island.[12] If we examine borough residential data for the same year a bit more closely, we see that in 2007 Puerto Ricans remained the largest group among all Latinos in the Bronx; Puerto Ricans (44.3 percent) and Dominicans (32.8 percent) accounted for 77.1 percent of the Bronx's Latino population. But Dominicans remained the largest group in Manhattan. In 2007, Dominicans made up 41.9 percent of all Manhattan Latinos, while Puerto Ricans were 27.5 percent; together these two groups accounted for 69.4 percent of all Latinos in the borough. In Brooklyn, 39 percent of all Latinos were Puerto Ricans, 18.5 percent Dominicans, and 17.2 percent Mexicans. Queens continued to have the most equitable distribution of Latino groups, and no one nationality was predominant in 2007. Ecuadorans at 18.5 percent were the largest nationality, but only by a small margin over Puerto Ricans at 17.2 percent; Dominicans were 15.5 percent, Colombians 13.4 percent, and Mexicans 12.5 percent of the Latino population of Queens.

As the above figures show, in 2007 more than two-thirds of the city's Dominicans lived in the Bronx (38.9 percent) and Manhattan (28.8 percent). Most Dominicans residing in the Bronx are found in the borough's southern and western parts, in areas relatively near northern Manhattan (where we find Inwood, Washington Heights, Harlem, and East Harlem). Most Dominicans residing in Manhattan live north of the Harlem area, or in Washington Heights and Inwood. But a good many also live in the Harlem area (including East Harlem). City bus routes connect the Washington Heights area and the Bronx neighborhoods Dominicans have settled in.

Among Dominicans, there has been a gradual shift away from the previous matrix of Dominican settlement in Washington Heights and Inwood toward the southern and western Bronx. In 1980, the census showed that Manhattan alone accounted for 50 percent of the total Dominican population in the city; in 1990 the figure had fallen to 41.1 percent, in 2000 to 34.3 percent, and in 2007 to 28.8 percent. At the same time, whereas 14.1 percent of the city's Dominicans resided in the Bronx in 1980, a decade later the figure had reached 26.2 percent; in 2000 33.5 percent; and in 2007 38.9 percent (Torres-Saillant and Hernández 1998: 63; Limonic 2008: 4, 7–8).

Despite this change, northern Manhattan remains an area of special significance for a majority of the city's Dominicans. The area continues to be *the* Dominican area of the city—and it continues to be dominated demographically by Dominicans.

In the late 1960s and early 1970s when anthropologist Glenn Hendricks conducted his pioneering study of the Dominican migration to New York, he found that the city's Dominicans at that time were concentrated in three areas—the Lower East Side of Manhattan in the heart of what had once been a mostly Italian area; the Corona-Jackson Heights section of Queens; and the Upper West Side of Manhattan from about 70th Street to the George Washington Bridge on 179th Street. But Hendricks added that more and more Dominicans in those days were moving to Brooklyn and the Bronx—and he acknowledged that, although the city's Dominicans were concentrated in three main areas, it was not reasonable to maintain that they resided "only in these places" (Hendricks 1974: 80). According to Hendricks, there was a rough ranking of living areas among the city's immigrants. In the Lower East Side in those days, he notes, although people complained about the environment, "the neighborhood's low rents and proximity to work [for example, in the clothing manufacturing industry where many were employed], and subway lines by which one can visit those living in other parts of the city, provide sufficient reason to remain" (1974: 80–81).

During the 1960s and 1970s, the more economically secure Dominicans left the Lower East Side and began to settle elsewhere—in neighborhoods of higher standing in Queens (in Corona or Jackson Heights, for example), on Long Island (for example, in Rockville Center), and in New Jersey (for example, in Paterson, Perth Amboy, or Union City). In the mid- and late 1960s, more and more Dominicans were moving to the Corona area of Queens:

> This transitional area next to Flushing Meadows had earlier been populated by Germans, Irish, and later Italians; after World War II blacks bought property in the area, and this group, composed largely of civil servants, in turn became part of the rush to the mushrooming suburbs on Long Island. They gladly sold or rented their aging two-story houses to Dominicans and other Latin Americans. The prices paid were often highly inflated—according to a local real estate agent, rents and sale prices could be doubled by such transactions, even though

some of the long-time residents, especially the Italians, resisted the influx of this new group of "foreigners." (Hendricks 1974: 81)[13]

By the early 1970s Corona housed two small garment factories and a series of small economic enterprises (grocery stores, restaurants, barber shops, etc.) owned by Dominican immigrants. Next to the Corona area in Queens are Jackson Heights and Elmhurst, both areas of better housing. By the early 1970s both areas had become the residential centers for lower-middle-class Latinos, including upwardly mobile Puerto Ricans, and a few relatively successful Dominican immigrants (Hendricks 1974: 82).

Another housing variation is found on the Upper West Side, in the whole Washington Heights-Inwood area, and in most of the southern and western Bronx. Here one mainly finds five- and six-story tenements; some apartments are large, while others consist of two or three rooms. The renters are essentially households made up of close kin. But one also finds dormitory-type arrangements, with provisions either for boarding or for shared cooking facilities.

How can one briefly summarize the social history of Washington Heights and Inwood? How did it happen that precisely this area emerged as the heart of the Dominican community in the city? What characterized the living conditions in the Dominicanized parts of Washington Heights and Inwood at the time of the fieldwork? Below I attempt to outline some answers to these questions.

Dominican Upper Manhattan

The Dominicanization of Washington Heights and Inwood was shaped by the New York region's power relations and systems of classification. The political economy and a set of social and cultural logics structure settlement processes and hence the production of place in the city (Gregory 1998). New migrant waves to the city cannot evade this condition.

The opening decades of the twentieth century saw a considerable northward migration of African Americans from the U.S. South. Between 1890 and 1910, the black population of Manhattan more than doubled. In turn, New York and other northern cities saw a general trend toward a hardening of the "color line" (Osofsky [1966] 1996). In this period, black settlement in Manhattan was shifting "uptown" to Harlem, and Harlem became the specific center of this movement. Subject to discrimination, blacks in Harlem and elsewhere not only occupied the worst housing but also paid the highest rents (Gregory 1998: 25). Black migration from the South intensified during and after World War II. In already congested black areas such as Harlem, this produced a dramatic housing shortage, aggravated by an enormous increase in the migration of Puerto Ricans to the city and state-sponsored "slum" clearance projects. Robert Caro (1975: 966) has written about the late 1940s and 1950s:

> Crowd as they would into slums, there would not be enough room in the slums for them. So they would move into areas adjacent to the slums, into areas in which landlords, without incentives to keep up their property anyway because of the slums' proximity, would see an opportunity for financial profit and take it by breaking up large apartments into small and by cutting down on maintenance and repair. The slums would spill over their boundaries.

The southern and eastern part of today's Dominican Washington Heights north of Harlem was one of these areas adjacent to "the slums" where racially and ethnically structured public- and private-sector practices interacted with local conditions to change the neighborhood.

The area north of Harlem was the last part of Manhattan to be urbanized. Indeed, it remained fairly rustic right up to the end of the nineteenth century. In historian Steven Lowenstein's words,

> In many ways the story of the development of Washington Heights [including the Inwood area] from a semirural to a densely urban district parallels similar stories about other middle-class New York neighborhoods. At first the neighborhood was considered far from downtown, but the development of subway and bus links to the city's center led to rapid development. Eventually all of Washington Heights was covered with apartment buildings, mostly of the red brick five- and six-story variety. The number of private homes was tiny.
>
> The date of development differed in various parts of the Washington Heights area. In general the southern and eastern apartments date from the pre-World War I era, while most of the houses in the north (Inwood, the area north of Dyckman Street) and west (west of Broadway, north of 181st Street) were built in the 1920s and 1930s. (Lowenstein 1989: 39)

In those days, Lowenstein continues, the Washington Heights area was considered a middle-class neighborhood:

> Its population was mixed between native-born and immigrant inhabitants. For many, perhaps most, of the immigrant residents, Washington Heights was an area of second settlement to which they had moved as their social standing had improved. The chief ethnic groups in Washington Heights at the time were an older and declining Protestant group made up of persons of English and German extraction, and newer residents including Irish, Jews, and Greeks. The Jews in 1930 made up about three-eights of the population. The Irish were smaller in number, and the Greeks still smaller. The Jews tended to be more heavily concentrated in the western sections and the Irish in the eastern area around Amsterdam Avenue. (1989: 42)

In the years before World War II, Washington Heights became the home of thousands of Jewish refugees from Nazi Germany. Although the German Jews never became a majority of the neighborhood's population, they gave it much of its distinctive tone up to the 1960s and the 1970s—to the extent that Washington Heights and Inwood were regarded for a long period as a solidly Jewish area (Lowenstein 1989: 212–38).

The changes that eventually resulted in a massive Dominicanization began in some sections of Washington Heights long before others. The German Jews inhabiting the southern part of Manhattan north of Harlem were already beginning to move away in the late 1950s. In contrast, Jews farther north, even ten years later, felt themselves to be still in a phase of expansion. Those who moved into Washington Heights were African Americans, Puerto Ricans, Cubans, and Dominicans. At first, whites of the area referred to the three groups of Latinos indiscriminately as "Puerto Ricans," but Puerto Ricans were outnumbered as early as 1965 by Cubans and Dominicans in northern Manhattan. While the Cuban Manhattan community soon began to decline, scores of immigrant Dominicans moved into the Washington Heights-Inwood area's tenement buildings. By the late 1970s, most main commercial streets of northern Manhattan had a distinctively Latino or Dominican flavor with many Spanish language signs. The other side was an equally dramatic exodus of whites. Between 1960 and 1980, the size of the German Jewish community in Washington Heights fell by over 50 percent (Lowenstein 1989: 212), reflecting a citywide wave of selling in neighborhoods where

African Americans, Puerto Ricans, and new immigrant groups—like the Dominicans—were settling and a more general postwar exodus of whites from the city to the suburbs (Brodkin 1998; Gregory 1998).

The exact boundaries of the Washington Heights area have been relatively fluid. In the minds of many in the city, Washington Heights is quite simply that area to the north and west of Harlem. But the neighborhood's southern boundary has moved and continues to move. In the words of Lowenstein (1989: 40), as the black population of Harlem in the mid-twentieth century "expanded geographically, the newly black areas were no longer thought of as Washington Heights but as a new part of Harlem, and the southern boundary was 'moved' to the north." Today, Washington Heights's core area may be said to be the area from 155th Street (in the south) to Dyckman Street (in the north). The area north of Dyckman Street is Inwood. This part of northern Manhattan is sometimes considered as a separate neighborhood and sometimes as a part of Washington Heights.

Within the central part of Washington Heights (between 155th Street and Dyckman), there is a marked internal socioeconomic differentiation. Simplifying, the further north and west one goes, the more reputable the area; the further east and south, the less reputable. The clearest socioeconomic distance exists between the area in the northwest, just south of Fort Tryon Park, which is the most prestigious area, and the far poorer neighborhood east of Broadway between 165th and 181st Streets. This difference was already great over seventy years ago (Lowenstein 1989: 44) and remained highly striking even when I lived in Washington Heights, that is, even after most by far of this part of the city had undergone a noticeable social decline.

Latinos made up 67 percent of the population of Washington Heights and Inwood in 1990. Fifteen years later the figure had grown to 73 percent. The corresponding figures for non-Hispanic whites were 18 percent in 1990 and 14 percent in 2005; for non-Hispanic blacks 12 percent in 1990 and 7 percent in 2005; for Asians 2 percent in 1990 and 3 percent in 2005; and for others 1 percent in 1990 and 3 percent in 2005 (Bergad 2008: 4).[14]

In 1990, Dominicans accounted for 43 percent of the area's total population (of 206,592 individuals) and 65 percent of all Latinos in the district. In 2005, the figures had grown to 53 percent of the total population (of 211,884) and 73 percent of all Latinos (Bergad 2008: 5).[15]

The annual median household income of all Washington Heights and Inwood residents increased considerably from 1990 to 2005. In 1990 it was $25,271, in 2000 $34,800, and in 2005 $39,422. But when median household income data are examined by racial/ethnic group great differences appear. Non-Hispanic whites and Asians had the highest annual median household incomes: $56,312 and $60,611 in 2005. In comparison, the annual median household income among the area's Dominicans increased from $21,036 in 1990 to $32,000 in 2000 and then rose marginally to $32,801 in 2005. The percentage of Dominican households in Washington Heights and Inwood earning under $20,000 yearly fell clearly between 1990 and 2000, from 47 percent to 31 percent, and then grew to 37 percent in 2005. At the other end of the income hierarchy, about 12 percent of Dominican households made over $50,000 yearly in 1990; this rose to 28 percent ten years later and remained stable in 2005 at 28 percent (Bergad 2008: 7–8, 10–11).

In 1990, only 6 percent of Washington Heights and Inwood Dominicans twenty-five and over had achieved a B.A. or higher degree. Ten years later the figure had grown to 8 percent, and in 2005 to 12 percent (Bergad 2008: 17).[16] An increasing percentage of foreign-born Dominicans living in Washington Heights and Inwood became U.S. citizens between 1990 and 2005; only 21 percent were naturalized citizens in 1990, but fifteen years later, this figure was 45 percent. Yet if we look at all citizens among the area's Dominicans, naturalized and domestic-born, it is clear that a greater percentage of Washington Heights and Inwood Dominicans were citizens between 1990 and 2005. This mirrored the clear growth in the number of U.S.-born Dominicans as well as increasing rates of naturalization. In 1990, 45 percent of all Dominicans living in Washington Heights and Inwood were U.S. citizens. In 2005, this figure had risen conspicuously, to 68 percent (Bergad 2008: 18–19).

Dominican Bronx

Historian Evelyn Gonzalez opens her absorbing narrative of the Bronx by describing how "The home of the Yankees, the Bronx Zoo, and the Cross-Bronx Expressway" became "a national symbol of urban deterioration. Neighborhoods that had held generations of Bronx families disappeared under waves of arson, crime, and housing abandonment, with solid blocks of brick apartment buildings turning into rubble-filled empty acres," while white people moved out: "South Bronx, in particular, went from being two-thirds white in 1950 to two-thirds African American and Hispanic by 1960. Forty years later, by 2000, the entire borough was almost all of black and Spanish-speaking ancestry" (Gonzalez 2004: 1).

Since its devastation in the 1960s and 1970s, this part of the city has undergone revitalization and renewal. But there is much more to the Bronx than just its crisis and resurgence. The area has a long history of social and demographic changes.

The borough is separated from Manhattan by the Harlem River and divided by the Bronx River. In 2000, the section west of the Bronx River (closest to Manhattan) housed 60 percent of the borough's total population of 1,332,650; the figures were 58 percent and 1,168,972 two decades earlier, and 70 percent and 1,424,815 in 1960 (Gonzalez 2004: 4).

The southern section of the Bronx was a landed property called Morrisania. In the 1840s, Morrisania was still the agricultural hinterland for the still small city of New York only a bit further to the south. Some decades later, or in the years from 1880 to 1930, the Bronx "was one of the fastest growing urban areas in the world . . . [and the borough] became famous for its stable ethnic neighborhoods and housing units that on average were better than those of Brooklyn and Manhattan" (Gonzalez 2004: 5). As noted, this had changed by 1960. Demographic and racial-ethnic changes, housing depreciation, and residents' search for better homes were aggravated by housing shortage, creation and construction of new suburbs, economic transformations, and a set of other circumstances.

About three decades later, the South Bronx was rebuilt and renewed. "The critical year was 1987 and the catalyst was Mayor Ed Koch's $5.1 billion capital housing program. In April 1986, Mayor Koch announced the city would rehabilitate its entire stock of city-owned buildings, both abandoned and occupied, and build new housing on its vacant city-owned land." After just three years, the authorities' measures had already produced more than 15,000 apartments in the South Bronx (Gonzalez 2004: 137–38).

Who resided in the Bronx in 2000? Whites had continued to move out, but from 1980 on new groups of blacks and Latinos had settled in the borough. African Americans had been joined by blacks from the Caribbean and West Africa, while Puerto Ricans had been joined by other Latinos—Dominicans, Cubans, Colombians, Mexicans, and so on:

> By 2000, this new Hispanic community extended beyond the South Bronx to Fordham, Kingsbridge, and Norwood and across the Bronx River to Clasons Point, Soundview, and Castle Hill. The black population, meanwhile, spread across the South Bronx from Sedgwick Avenue to Crotona Park and across the Bronx River into Williamsbridge,

Wakefield, and Eastchester. Each of these groups predominated in certain spots, but both lived alongside each other throughout the borough. Whites lived in Riverdale and in the farthest parts of the eastern Bronx. (Gonzalez 2004: 145)

While a number of Dominican immigrants lived in the Bronx during the late 1960s and 1970s, the Dominican presence in the borough and particularly in the West Bronx is a fairly recent phenomenon. In 1990, 71.3 percent of the borough's total Dominican population (of 87,261) resided in three community districts in the southwestern Bronx: Highbridge-Concourse, Fordham-University Heights, and Kingsbridge Heights-Bedford (Ricourt 2002: 48, 50). Although these parts of the borough are still the areas of greatest concentration of Dominicans, the years after 1990 have seen a considerable spreading of Dominicans into other parts of the Bronx.

There is no question that some, perhaps many Dominican households have left Upper Manhattan for lower-rent neighborhoods in the Bronx or elsewhere during the last couple of decades and particularly from 2000 onward. Hard data show that "overall there has been absolutely no systematic movement of people" out of Washington Heights and Inwood since 1990 (Bergad 2008: 22), but among Dominicans there definitely has been, particularly after 2000, a slowdown in migration from the Dominican Republic to northern Manhattan. This is revealed if we look at the proportions of the Dominican population in Washington Heights and Inwood that were respectively foreign- and U.S.-born. The percentage of foreign-born Dominicans in Washington Heights and Inwood remained stable between 1990 and 2000 and then fell considerably by 2005 (Bergad 2008: 10). More and more Dominicans now move directly from the Dominican Republic to other parts of the city than northern Manhattan, especially to the Bronx.

In this chapter, I have sought to outline two histories: first, the history of how the Dominican Republic became a major supplier of immigrants to New York City, and second, the history of where in the city the Dominican migrants have settled. In the next chapter, I continue to inquire into the past, asking about the history of the Dominican-owned small businesses in New York. Or put differently, how did it happen that the city during a few decades got a large number of Dominican-owned enterprises?

CHAPTER 2

Origin Stories

In 1991, Dominican immigrants owned around 80 percent of the approximately 9,000 bodegas and independent groceries controlled by Latinos in New York City (Martinez Alequin 1991; Silverman 1991). By the late 1980s, one researcher counted an average of twelve Dominican businesses per block between 157th and 191st Streets in Washington Heights (Mahler 1989); 90 percent of the cabs in Upper Manhattan in the early 1990s were owned by Dominican immigrants (Portes and Guarnizo 1991: 61). Until the early 1980s the number of economic enterprises in the city owned by Dominicans was still not very large (Guarnizo 1992: 110). Most have therefore been bought or opened during the past three decades.

But there is no doubt that Dominican New Yorkers have been solidly creating small economic ventures for quite a long time. In the 1960s and 1970s, Dominicans ran small enterprises in Queens, particularly in Corona, and Dominican-owned businesses were found in Manhattan's Lower East Side and Upper West Side and in parts of the Bronx and Brooklyn (Guarnizo 1992: 113–14). In a 1976 *New York Daily News* article about Upper Manhattan, "Washington Heights and Changing Times," journalist John Lewis claimed, "Evidence of the changes can be seen everywhere. Irish grocery stores are now Spanish [*sic*] bodegas. Along the central shopping district on W. 181st St. several older, well-known stores have closed because the merchants said that they could not compete with Hispanic merchants who cater to the needs of the growing Hispanic population" (Lewis 1976).

Although we already have a sizable scholarly literature on Dominicans in New York, we have little oral history of the emergence of a broad field of Dominican-owned small businesses in the city. The literature contains little ethnographically shaped narration of this part of the history of how immigrants from the Dominican Republic entered, and were incorporated into,

New York. This chapter takes a first step to alter this. In much of the chapter, informants remember and narrate how they and others took part in the creation of a set of economic and social fields—like the Dominican-owned bodega, the Dominican-controlled cab operation, and the Dominican restaurant. Some of this takes us back to the mid- and late 1960s, but the bulk focuses on the 1970s and 1980s.

We should view this oral history as origin stories, narratives of creation and emergence, which are important because they help to frame, make sense of, and orient the present. The history conveyed by my informants does indeed reflect the actual history, or the truth, but its most important aspect is linked to the basic perspective it conveyed. Its greatest value lies in the access it offers to a historically, socially, and culturally constituted mentality, a set of views on the past and the present that express a perspective on the world. My concern in this chapter is less to present a seamless, let alone exhaustive, account of Dominican immigrants' businesses in various parts of the city than to draw attention to and focus on specific processes. Again, the account with its foci has been shaped by the stories, or the purposeful acts of memory, of Dominican New Yorkers with whom I worked.

There are four reasons I regard the following history as key. First, time and again during the fieldwork, I was struck by the degree to which Dominican immigrants I met incorporated a historical consciousness. Their memories were not only of early years in the Dominican Republic but also of how they had witnessed and taken part in central transformations in New York. What I could see in the field was that people continually recollected and reworked components of their own, or the Dominican immigrants', history in the city to provide context and meaning, as well as authority, to interpretations of contemporary social conditions and relationships. In daily life, public events, and political meetings, Dominican New Yorkers used a rich knowledge of economic and social relations and of power struggles reaching at least four decades back into their community's history and that of the larger United States society. This chapter shows a part of the knowledge people drew on. Later chapters demonstrate in more detail ways in which such knowledge was used.

Second, when New York City Dominicans told about how they and other Dominican immigrants had been able to develop networks of small businesses in the city, they often focused on important transformations in the city three or four decades earlier. They confirmed that the demographic, economic, and social processes that changed the Big Apple's neighborhoods rapidly and dramatically in the 1960s, 1970s, and 1980s were of vital significance to the creation of new forms of entrepreneurship and of Dominican immigrants' small businesses. People anchored their stories of the emergence of Dominican-owned businesses in a broader history of the sweeping structural changes in the New York landscape in the 1970s and 1980s. As they viewed it, these changes made both necessary and possible new economic and social forms and practices, which Dominican immigrants and others engaged in small businesses had developed.

Third, a majority of the Dominican immigrants engaged in the small-business economy in New York City in the 1970s and 1980s had immigrated with little money, a relatively limited education, and little ability to understand English. Many had started as undocumented migrants—for example, they had entered the United States legally as tourists but overstayed the terms of their visas. How could someone arriving with such disadvantages buy and run a business in New York? This chapter provides some answers.

Dominicans who set themselves up in the city's small-business economy did so with the aid of particular cultural forms and practices, which were imported from the Dominican Republic and then adapted and modified. The history in this chapter documents this, the fourth reason I regard it as important. The part played by cultural processes in the emergence of a New York City Dominican small-business economy can hardly be overrated. Here, I am content quite simply to demonstrate the role of culture. Subsequent chapters analyze more thoroughly the relationship between the making and remaking of businesses and the production of cultural forms and practices.

What follows is divided into six main parts. The first three examine the history of the Dominican-owned grocery stores and supermarkets and the fourth that of the Dominican cab operations. The last two look briefly at some features of the histories of two other niches: the Dominican restaurant and the Dominican beauty parlor.[1]

Two Success Stories

Early in the fieldwork, I met José Delio Marte. He had immigrated as a young man in 1965 and was a veteran in northern Manhattan's Dominican American community. Having bought and sold a string of small businesses, mostly bodegas, he had also played a role as an activist and leader at the grass-roots level among New York City Dominican small-business owners and in the

Dominican community in northern Manhattan. In the Dominican parts of Washington Heights and Inwood, José had a name. When I contacted Alfredo Placeres and Hugo Díaz, a Cuban American and an Argentine American, respectively president and vice-president of the New York State Federation of Hispanic Chambers of Commerce, José was recommended because, as they put it, he had been among the pioneers and knew much early history.

When I met José, he lived partly in northern Manhattan and partly in his house in Santo Domingo. In his late fifties, his plan was to soon retire to the Dominican capital for good. But he still owned businesses in northern Manhattan. When he was in New York, he lived in his sister's apartment in a tenement in Inwood. His "office" was a table in a Dominican popular restaurant owned by one of his friends, on 207th Street. A dapper figure in a nice suit and a tie, José was of rural stock. He was born in the Dominican countryside, in Duarte province in the northern part of the country, and after more than thirty-seven years in New York, he still spoke English with such a heavy accent that it was almost impossible to understand. We always spoke Spanish—most often over a cup of coffee in his regular café.

In New York in 1965, José had found work in the city's garment industry, in the Jewish-owned sweatshops and factories situated in midtown Manhattan. Besides working in the garment industry, he had even harder jobs in an egg business and a butcher's enterprise. Those who entered the country from the Dominican Republic in 1965 all started to work in factories, José reiterated. But some, like him, looked for a way to buy their own business. A big obstacle, of course, was the lack of money. How did people raise capital?

José said he and others tried to save money. They did not use banks but kept their savings at home. They did not have papers. As undocumented migrants, they could not open bank accounts. One of the things many did to increase their savings, José went on, was to participate in *sanes* or *sociedades*, rotating credit associations informally organized by small groups of Dominican immigrants and other Hispanics. A *san* or *sociedad* typically included ten individual members, men and women. Each contributed a fixed amount of money, usually weekly or monthly, and each in turn received the pooled contributions.[2] People viewed participating in a *san* or *sociedad* as a good way to raise slightly larger sums than they could save on their own.

The *san* or *sociedad* institution, as José proudly underscored, was imported from the Dominican Republic. *Sanes* or *sociedades* were, and still are, organized and used on the island, and they continue to play a role in today's New York. In the Dominican Republic, it is common to call the rotating credit association a "*san*," but in New York, Dominicans use both words, although many seem to use the term *sociedad* more frequently than *san*. In Puerto Rico, the common term has been *sociedad*, not *san*. A Dominican immigrant said to me that Dominicans in New York often used *san* if all the members of the savings group were Dominicans but *sociedad* when the group included other categories of Latinos, for example, Puerto Ricans. In the Dominican Republic, it has been common for the person who organizes the *san* to receive compensation from the rest of the group. But in New York, this has not been the norm; among Dominicans there, all have received exactly the same.[3] In New York, Dominican immigrants have used their informal savings groups to accumulate funds for various purposes—for travel costs, rents, TVs, cars, homes, and small businesses (Sassen-Koob 1987: 265–66; Ricourt and Danta 2003: 35). According to Saskia Sassen-Koob, Dominican New Yorkers in the 1960s and 1970s employed these *sanes* to save money for a broad range of activities, "a fact," she writes, "which may explain at least in part the rising number of small shop owners in the community" (1987: 266).

The first *san* on Manhattan in which José participated was organized by a Dominican woman he did not know before. He had heard from a friend that she wanted to organize a *san* with a weekly contribution of 50 dollars. When he called her, she had already found six of the ten members she needed. José recruited himself, a sister, a brother, and a friend. Thereafter, he and his sister had continued to save, keeping what they had managed to put aside at home.

But the capital needed to buy a small store on Manhattan was considerable, even in the late 1960s. Again, how did they do it? According to José, what really had an effect was Dominicans' ability to mobilize and draw on *la familia* or the extended family. As he would explain over and over again, "We joined kinsmen. We united family groups and pooled the family's savings and those of friends." With the capital you had been able to raise in this way you went to see a professional moneylender. If you had, for example, $4,000 or $5,000 or $10,000, you could borrow the rest of what you needed:

> Here, in those days, if you had for example 4,000 or 5,000 dollars, you went to the moneylenders and you could get 10,000 or 20,000, you see? It wasn't legal, of course, to borrow money in this way, it was illegal. But there was no alternative, for you couldn't get a loan from a bank or from other institutions, and we didn't have the various sorts of institutions we have today.... Those who lent money were Jews and Italians. So, what they did was ... let me give you an example:

If I wanted to buy a business for 15,000 dollars and had 5,000, they lent me 10,000. But all remained in their name, the business belonged to them, and only when I had paid off the loan did they transfer the business to me and I became owner. If I borrowed 10,000 dollars, they charged me 20,000 dollars, but there was no other way out. There was no other way to obtain your own business. In this way the [Dominican] bodega industry came into being.

In our conversations, José listed many of the bodegas and other business enterprises he had had a stake in over the years he had lived on northern Manhattan. He had early on become owner of a bodega, La Marquetita, situated on Amsterdam Avenue and 169th Street. After that, I counted at least nine more stores, but I am pretty sure that he could have remembered a few more. Many of the stores were bodegas that he had bought or created and later sold. In Inwood, he had owned bodegas on Dyckman Street, on 193rd Street, at an address close to 207th Street, and on 225th Street. Beyond bodegas and small supermarkets, he had held stakes in an unsuccessful business that had sought to distribute meat to Hispanics and in a store in Inwood selling fur coats.

To own a bodega was, in practice, often to own two different businesses simultaneously, José explained. You had a grocery store, and you had a place for illegal sale of lottery tickets:

> The issue of the lottery tickets is important. Today they say that the bodegas have become places for illicit practices, run by criminals. No . . . the illegal tickets which are now sold in the bodegas, and by Dominicans, they were sold also by the Italians. We learnt from them and from the Irish [people who owned and operated grocery stores earlier]. For when you buy a bodega [nowadays], sometimes—often— it costs $50,000. So I said, "Well, the bodega costs 50,000 and the spot for sale of lottery tickets 15,000. You have to pay me 65,000 dollars." One bought two businesses, a bodega and a place for sale of lottery tickets.

Why bodegas? I asked José. Why did Dominican immigrants choose the grocery store, not some other economic niche in the city?

> The bodega . . . people arrived from the Dominican Republic, and they worked in a bodega. Each product [sold in a bodega] has a picture or

mark on the product. For example, [demonstrating] this bag is sugar; on the bag there is a picture of someone cutting cane. A man doesn't have to speak English to sell sugar. People said [in English], "I need one pound of sugar." He looked at the bag. But he didn't know English. Well, he understood, had a feeling. But in the beginning, of course, one always hired a Puerto Rican or an African American [one who knew English], one hired a Puerto Rican or an African American to work in the store. To be able to run your bodega, you had to be able to deal with the authorities; you went to the police, and the bodega was visited by inspectors. It was necessary to be able to communicate.

According to José, hiring someone who was more familiar with the country's culture and spoke English was far more common previously, when the development of Dominican-owned grocery stores in New York City still was in an early phase.

The Dominicans who pioneered the bodega business opened a space that could be filled by others. José remembered a couple of men who had been among the first to import Dominican products. One had started to import plantain and yucca from his native town, Mocca, for sale in New York City. The other had been among the first Dominican traders to distribute Dominican products at the Bronx Terminal Market.[4]

But as José saw it, nothing could be compared to the bodega. Nothing else had played the part the Dominican-owned bodega had played:

> The large and luxurious houses in New Jersey today have their roots in the bodega. The supermarkets, the big supermarkets, have their roots in the bodega. Various sorts of tourist projects on the island have their roots in the bodega. The development of housing projects in Santo Domingo—the sale of newly erected apartments and houses—is anchored in the bodega. Because . . . from the bodegas, one went on to the supermarkets, and one diversified and did new things. That's the way it was; that's how this changed.

José exaggerated. But as we shall see later, his claim was not so far from the truth. Many Dominicans who became owners of supermarkets in New York started with some kind of small grocery store, a neighborhood bodega. The Dominican bodega was, as we have seen, based on two forms of resources: credit and extended mutual help between family members. In addition, it was based on self-exploitation—and exploitation of family labor and other forms of labor. Dominican *bodegueros* maintained a grueling work schedule, working long hours; I shall return to this.

José saw the emergence of Dominican-owned businesses in New York in the light of transformations in the city. Time and again, he drew pictures of a New York City that had changed dramatically over the past decades. His story was about the city's economic and demographic restructuring since the 1960s—and he told about forms of racism and about the politics of place. In the 1970s, he said,

> factories were closed and businesses [in the neighborhoods in the inner city] were shut down and abandoned. They started to set the Bronx on fire, burning down all those buildings and homes, you saw arson everywhere. They saw our presence, the presence of the Latinos, as a threat. I am referring to the *anglos* [whites]. They started to sell their properties. They started to burn down their properties so they could get their insurance money. And they left for the suburbs because they didn't want to live together with us, an inferior race.

In José's view, Dominican immigrants and others—other Hispanics and blacks—breathed new life into, and developed, buildings, businesses and neighborhoods the white middle class had fled. Now, he said, whites are once again eager to do business and live in these neighborhoods, which they had left in fear in the 1960s and the 1970s and which thereafter became predominantly black and Hispanic:

> Why is the *anglo* [again] in all these areas [of the city]? He didn't want to live along with us, but God has punished him and they're returning again. But they have come back after first having left. All this became populated by Latinos and blacks. Now it is OK to be in the company of Latinos, because the Latino has now demonstrated that he came to work, that he came to produce and develop. He has shown that he was able to change the face of these neighborhoods, these parts of the city which were replete with poverty, filled with garbage and scum. Where properties had been left burned down there are now new buildings, and in those buildings you find apartments, they're productive, right? Today everybody wants to understand this phenomenon [the conspicuous commercial and political growth of the

New York City Dominican community that helped transform parts of the inner city].

Against the backdrop of this story of continuous change, José explained how Dominican grocery store owners had replaced earlier groups of grocery store owners. El Barrio or East Harlem was dominated by Puerto Ricans; they owned bodegas in other parts of the city also. But, as José would emphasize, New York's grocery stores were never owned mainly by Puerto Ricans. On the contrary, in many neighborhoods, they were owned by Irish, Italians, Jews, Greeks, Germans, or Poles (see also Ricourt and Danta 2003: 47–48). However, José acknowledged that often a Dominican immigrant who bought a bodega in parts of Manhattan or in the Bronx in the 1960s and 1970s bought it from a Puerto Rican. The Puerto Ricans, he said, sold their bodegas to Dominicans because they had reached a certain age and wanted to retire. As a U.S. citizen, the Puerto Rican *bodeguero* had a right to a certain old-age insurance. His children had often gone to college; at any rate, they did not want to take over their father's store.

Dominican bodega owners were facing a set of challenges. One of these was the increasing levels of crime and violence in the neighborhoods in which the stores were situated. In the 1970s, the 1980s and the first part of the 1990s, alarming numbers of bodega owners and employees were killed by robbers in holdups; forty-seven in 1992 alone in New York City (Bragg 1994). As José put it (again, exaggerating), "in the mid- and late 1970s, when you left home, you had to carry your rosary and say a lot of prayers because not so many *bodegueros* returned home." Another difficulty Dominican *bodegueros* had to deal with was discrimination. José vividly remembered how his relations with corporate America, or big companies, had been difficult and had used to anger him. Big companies like Coca Cola and Pepsi Cola used to treat the *bodeguero* badly, he said. "They supplied our stores, but abused their power." Other companies had refused supplies, saying that the bodega's turnover was too small. This was for a long time the case, for example, with the Sara Lee Corporation, a company that manufactured popular bakery products, like cakes, muffins, and biscuits. Another big company that used to deny supplies was the wholesale baking company supplying one of the country's most popular bread products, Wonder Bread. José explained how he had had to obtain the Wonder Bread products he needed for his bodega through a deal with the owner of a nearby supermarket. This changed gradually, however, and all companies began to sell also to the Dominican immigrants' bodegas. José also deplored the conduct of the city's authorities. According to him, health inspectors and other inspectors, and representatives of the police and the justice system, had too often treated the *bodeguero* with lack of respect and justice.

Another challenge for Dominican *bodegueros* was rising rents in the 1980s and the 1990s. As José and other Dominican small-business owners saw it, most landlords were exploiters who would raise the rent, however unfairly, whenever it was possible. As José drily put it, "The landlords started to increase the rent as we did better and prospered." But, he immediately added, the Dominican store owners had had a powerful countermeasure—an incredible capacity to work long hours, to engage in self-exploitation and exploitation of others, often family members, who helped maintain the bodega's viability, to keep it open and going: "They doubled the rent; but we [the *bodegueros*] tripled the working hours. Many businesses are open twenty-four hours, you see?" (When I lived in northern Manhattan in 2002, most if not all Dominican-owned bodegas were open seven days a week, from around seven in the morning until around midnight or later.) José went on, "If you start a business and your goal is to make a certain amount of money in five years, a Dominican can do it in two-and-a-half years, and he doesn't have to sell drugs, nor sell illegal lottery tickets or steal or kill. No, the reason he can do it is that he triples the working hours."

José stressed the hardships the Dominican immigrant community in the city had experienced. His story was about the abuse of power, about discrimination and violence, and about hard labor, but it was also a history of heroism. Against all odds, people like himself, a group of Dominicans of peasant stock in the Big Apple or undocumented and penniless immigrants, had been able to make it. On its way, the city's Dominican community had helped change, and breathe new life into, once-infamous neighborhoods. Dominicans' hard work and businesses had transformed the inner city, neighborhoods that were about to dissolve under waves of white flight, arson, crime, and housing abandonment. To a man like José, the image of Dominican immigrants who breathed life into "dead" neighborhoods was more than a metaphor:

> Here [in Washington Heights and Inwood in the 1960s], the bodegas and other stores didn't open on Sundays. Here, people [the *anglos*] worked only eight hours. You had a bodega, but closed at 7 or 8 in the evening. It was the same with the supermarkets, the pharmacies, the travel agencies, etcetera etcetera. But after we the Dominicans came, this changed.

In the late 1980s, a small group of Dominican immigrants who had become owners of a set of independent small and medium-sized *supermercados* or supermarkets in different parts of New York City held an informal meeting in a restaurant in Washington Heights. Thereafter, they founded a small-business association for supermarket owners, the National Supermarkets Association. This association quickly evolved into the strongest of the Dominican New Yorkers' business associations. In spite of its name, most if not all members were first-generation Dominican immigrants who operated businesses in the New York region, most in the inner city. While I conducted my research, its executive director was Luis A. Salcedo, a man in his late forties and himself a first-generation Dominican immigrant who had become a supermarket owner. Below I sketch how Luis, during our conversations in his office in 2002 and 2003, explained the way Dominicans had gradually become owners of a large proportion of the independent, small and medium-sized supermarkets in New York City. As we shall see, there is a considerable overlap between Luis's story and the history that José told. Echoing José, Luis exclaimed one day during our conversations, "We [Dominicans] revolutionized the [supermarket] industry [in the city's once-infamous neighborhoods]!"

Luis was not only a formal spokesman for the community of New York City Dominican owners of independent supermarkets but also a representative of this community in a deeper sense. The vast majority of those Dominicans who now controlled supermarkets were between 40 and 55 and had arrived with little money. Some were women, but most were men. Many had started their career as employees and had later invested in a small bodega or restaurant. They had all drawn heavily on mutual help, cooperation, and support among close kinsmen and friends.

Luis migrated to New York City in 1974. The oldest of eleven children, he had been the first to migrate. By 1986, both his parents and all his siblings had also moved to New York. After working for about ten years as a waiter in restaurants and saving money, Luis had bought his first business, together with a cousin, in 1984, a small coffee shop in Brooklyn. Six years later, he and the same cousin had together invested in a large bodega in the Bronx. A few years later, he became owner of his first supermarket, a store in Harlem. When I met him in 2002, he had sold the supermarket in Harlem but was owner of two independent supermarkets, one in the Bronx and one in Brooklyn; and he continued to own what had been his first business, the coffee shop in Brooklyn.

Both José and Luis, certainly, spoke from the position of an immigrant who had experienced upward mobility. They *were* success stories. Individual and collective acts of memory are shaped by, and express, not only constructions of (trans)nationality, race, and (pan)ethnicity but also constructions of class and gender. The vast majority of Dominican New Yorkers had not experienced the economic success these two had achieved. On the contrary, very many continued to be poor (Hernández et al. 1995; Torres-Saillant and Hernández 1998: 67–70). Many saw themselves as immigrants who were better off than they would probably have been back home but none the less poor. Most Dominicans who owned, or were employed in, a small business worked hard and made relatively little or very little money. Many Dominican-owned enterprises had failed—the business had gone bankrupt, and people had lost their savings. In spite of this, we should view the stories of José and Luis as important and representative. They articulated ideas and perspectives that carried weight in New York's Dominican community and mobilized people, propelled them to act, and they told about representative processes—a set of processes that had helped and were still helping give shape to the economic, social, and political life in the wider Dominican community in the city.

In 2002, the National Supermarkets Association's headquarters were situated in Queens, on the third floor of a modern office building close to the Whitestone Expressway. The headquarters contained the offices of Luis and his secretary, a small kitchen, and a large meeting room. The secretary answered the phone in Spanish and English; of Dominican origin, she was fluent in both languages. Luis's mother tongue was Spanish, but he spoke English well. He too spoke on the phone sometimes in Spanish and sometimes in English. Our conversations were a mixture of the two languages; sometimes I would start in English, and he replied in Spanish; or I started in Spanish, and he switched to English.

To be a member of the National Supermarkets Association, a person needed to have a stake in a supermarket. To be owner of a bodega was not sufficient. When the association was founded in 1989, a supermarket was informally defined as a store covering 6,000 square feet or more, "a store that will probably have a turnover—I don't know—it was 60,000 dollars a week and up," Luis said. Most bodegas are much smaller, between 1,000 and 2,000 square feet.

In 2002, the Dominican supermarket association had about 125 members, who owned around 300 stores. Most of these stores were small and medium-sized independent supermarkets situated in areas of the city with large proportions of African Americans, Latinos, and members of other minorities (like the "new" immigrants from Asia, West Africa, and the former Soviet Union). That these supermarkets were classified as "independent" is important. Today in the United States, a large supermarket typically forms part of a chain, which is owned by a corporation. The independent supermarket, on the other hand, is not part of a chain but individually owned. It is also much smaller than the chains' typical megastores. In the 1960s and 1970s, many of the neighborhoods in New York City where we now find Dominican-owned small and medium-sized independent supermarkets had supermarkets belonging to chains, as well as individually owned supermarkets. But with the economic and demographic transformations in the city, the chains moved out of many neighborhoods in the inner city. Similarly, the individually owned supermarkets came to be abandoned and sold by their owners. Luis recalled that, before the mid-1970s, "we had chains, which in fact were not the size of [today's] Pathmarks and Waldbaums, but we had—I remember Bohack's, we had Fedco, we had Red Apple, we had A&P, we had Shopwell, we had Key-Food." But then "they actually ran away. They left. They left. Then we [Dominican entrepreneurs] saw those opportunities, and we came into it"; this happened from the 1970s on, which was a period of change.

Luis then started to explain how two big competing grocery wholesalers in the New York City metropolitan area, Krasdale Foods and White Rose Food, and a third company, Associated Wholesalers, had helped restructure the retailing of foods in the city from the mid-1970s. Krasdale Foods has been supplying groceries in the New York area for about a century. As a wholesale food distributor, the company serves independent clients, ranging from small bodegas to larger supermarkets. It is owned by the founding Krasdale family. In 1972, Krasdale Foods opened a brand new distribution center at Hunt's Point, in the Bronx, and thereafter went to market seeking local chain and other business. But as noted, in the 1970s, the chains were withdrawing from many neighborhoods.

In 1975, Krasdale Foods created C-Town. C-Town supermarkets are independently owned stores that operate under a common name, C-Town. In addition to the common store banner, they have a unified advertising program produced by Krasdale. Although C-Town is not a chain store, each C-Town owner pays a sum to Krasdale Foods for the common advertising, which is done daily through New York City's newspapers and other channels. In addition, each C-Town owner, in practice, buys a large proportion of his or her supplies from Krasdale, and Krasdale has often, especially in earlier days, helped the owner obtain and renovate the store by lending money and by delivering the first supplies on credit. In the 1970s, the 1980s, and much of the 1990s, individual store owners typically borrowed from Krasdale, not from banks; they were charged considerable interest. Later, Krasdale created two more store names—Bravo and Aim. An owner of a Bravo or Aim had the same type of relationship to Krasdale Foods as the owner of a C-Town. Krasdale created the new names to avoid a situation with two or more C-Towns destructively competing with each other. Luis recalled that Krasdale had originally used the name K-Town but, when sued by the Kmart chain, had to change it to C-Town, while the Bravo name was started in 1990 to allow for competitors in the same area as a C-Town.

A main competitor of Krasdale Foods was White Rose Food. Today a division of Di Giorgio Corporation, White Rose has existed for over a century and is a large grocery distributor in New York City. When I conducted my research, White Rose had created two store names, Met and Pioneer. Owners of Mets and Pioneers were financed and supplied by White Rose Foods. In the beginning, however, White Rose had not wanted to lend money to and supply individuals who sought to buy and develop their own independent supermarkets, and this had opened a niche for a third company, New York-based Associated Wholesalers, which from the mid- and late 1970s had established itself in a role as a broker. Associated Wholesalers offered store owners credit at interest and saw that they obtained supplies, but it has never itself been a distributor of groceries, instead buying supplies for the stores from White Rose. In this way, White Rose reduced its risk. It did business with Associated, not with the individual store owner. For its part, Associated charged a profit in its transactions with the store owners.

To be able to organize and develop its transactions, Associated created its own independent supermarket name, Associated. When I lived in New York, a large proportion of the Dominican immigrants who owned supermarkets had stores called C-Town, Bravo, Aim, Met, Pioneer, or Associated. Others owned and operated independent stores with other names—Fine Fare, Foodtown, Key Food, Compare, Corona, or Price Choice. The latter three names—Compare, Corona, and Price Choice—represented Dominican American inventions; these three names had been created not by big companies like Krasdale and White Rose but by a few of the most successful Dominican immigrants who owned supermarkets.

Before Dominicans started to buy supermarkets, Luis claimed, many of the independently owned supermarkets in the city had been owned by Jews coming from Europe. Particularly in the 1970s and early 1980s, he went on, it was fairly easy to buy a run-down supermarket. Since many of the stores were old, they had to be renovated and remodeled. Stores were provided with new piping, new floors, new cold-storage chambers, and so on. In the late 1970s and in the 1980s, a number of Dominican immigrants had already accumulated considerable experience; they had managed bodegas, restaurants, and other kinds of small businesses. A few now started to enter the city's supermarket industry. They received help from Krasdale and Associated, two competing companies that needed and sought partners. The capital needed to obtain a supermarket was assembled in nearly the same way that had been used previously. Dominicans who bought supermarkets drew heavily on mutual help among close kinsmen and friends, pooling family resources. In addition, they used moneylenders or received a loan from Krasdale or Associated. Not until the late 1990s did many Dominican supermarket owners begin switching to the banks. According to Luis, running an independent supermarket was not so different from running a bodega: "First, when you open [the supermarket], you don't have working hours, you don't have time off"—as in a *bodega*; "When you start a business, you have to work very hard until the business allows you to do anything, without a vacation during two, three, four, five years."

Dominican supermarket owners' dominant story of the appearance of Dominican-owned businesses was almost identical to that told by José or by so many of the city's Dominican small-business owners. As Luis proudly summed it up, the Dominican small and medium-sized inner-city supermarket had "revolutionized" the industry. Dominican immigrants had played an important part, he claimed, as the city's neighborhoods had changed economically and demographically:

> In the mid-1970s, the neighborhoods which now have Dominican stores were neighborhoods that had been deserted, completely abandoned. The big stores or supermarkets which these areas had were the stores that had traditionally existed—supermarkets that were adapted to the traditional American. I don't want to go much into the issue of race and color, but the fact is that this traditional supermarket was a supermarket for a white American. Then the Latinos started to arrive in great numbers. They [the *anglos*] began to become afraid, and they didn't understand how one dealt with these people [the Latinos]. They didn't understand what kind of products our compatriots [Latinos] wanted. So what happens? If you have a supermarket here, for

example an A&P, that never sold plantain, that never sold yucca—all those things [which Latinos demand]. So what happens? The whites left and the Latinos arrived. But the supermarket lost clients. Business began to be bad. And finally they [the *anglos*] left, closing their stores. And the neighborhoods started to deteriorate. They backed out, left, and shut down. Then the Dominicans started. And in this case, especially the Dominicans—for they saw an opportunity. Dominicans who had bought a bodega said, "Oh! They shut down the supermarket! And I have a bodega. Perhaps I could open a bigger store, perhaps I could open a supermarket."

The next two sections sketch features of the life histories of two men. Both arrived as immigrants with little money, and both worked for some years as New York City *bodegueros*. One became wealthy; when I met him, he owned a series of supermarkets. For his part, his compatriot never made it as a *bodeguero*; when his career as a *bodeguero* ended, he lost his savings, and he started to drive a cab. There are two reasons I want to sketch these biographies. First, they document more concretely some of the historical and social processes we already have looked at in the chapter. The second reason is that the social field of Dominican immigrants' small businesses is highly heterogeneous, containing considerable social differences, and also functioning itself as a contributor to the production of social inequality, that is, to the broader production of class in society. The histories below underscore this.

Another Success Story

Eligio Peña has been a pioneer and a leader among the Dominican New Yorkers who control supermarkets. In 2002, he and his brothers were owners of eighteen supermarkets, mostly on Long Island and in Connecticut. The following story is essentially based on a six-hour conversation I had with him on a Saturday in November 2002, mostly at a diner located across the George Washington Bridge from Washington Heights. Eligio told me about his life—about his early years in New York and the development of his businesses. In 1989, Eligio was the key figure when the National Supermarkets Association came to be created.

Born in 1951, Eligio lived his first nineteen years on the island. Arriving in New York in 1970, he first lived in an uncle's apartment in Brooklyn and found work in a factory. In addition, he took an evening course in English. (When I met him in 2002, we spoke Spanish; his English was still not good, but he managed.) Another uncle owned a bodega on Longwood Avenue in the Bronx. He now offered Eligio a job in his store. A few months later, Eligio got a new job in another bodega that paid better. In this job, he lasted about six months. His uncle in Brooklyn, in whose apartment he had stayed on his arrival in the city, owned a bodega together with a friend. The two were what New York Dominicans call *socios* or business partners; each owned half the business. Such a partnership is called a *sociedad*. In the New York City Dominican community, to start a business with the aid of a form of *sociedad* or partnership is common. Eligio's uncle in Brooklyn and his *socio* had decided to end their partnership, and the uncle needed a new partner to run the bodega. He asked Eligio to become his *socio*, with each owning half of the store. The basis for the partnership was that Eligio, who had already learned a good deal about how to run a bodega and knew some English, would work in the store, while his uncle knew little about the day-to-day running of a bodega. In this way, Eligio in fact became a *socio* without having to raise any money. The only one who invested capital was his uncle, who had already bought the store. The bodega did well. But Eligio did not like the way his uncle bossed him about. After half a year, they ended their partnership, the uncle paying Eligio 50 percent of the store's value. Eligio then bought a new bodega alone—in northeastern Brooklyn, on Dumont Avenue—in 1971. According to Eligio, the bodegas in those days were cheap; to buy his first, he spent only $10,000.

A few years later, Eligio had sold his bodega and invested most of his money in a yellow taxi medallion. After a while, he bought two more medallions, to be able to go to school and study in the evening. He got an equivalent of a high-school diploma. Thereafter, he took some classes in business administration and other subjects at Baruch College—but without graduating. Working as a taxi driver, he got to know most of the city, and one day in 1978, he spotted what seemed to him to be a great bodega—what he described as *un bodegón*. Larger than a normal bodega, it was situated in Woodside in Queens. As he said when I met him many years later, this was a neighborhood that, in those days—the late 1970s—was changing a lot from *blanco* to *hispano*, from white to Hispanic. He saw that the bodega was in need of some renovation but that its location was good. This time, though, Eligio could not afford to buy alone; the store was too big. However, he had his brothers. After he had married and managed to become a legal resident in the early 1970s, he had helped others in the family to move to New York, and he now had his father and three brothers in the city. In 1978, he and his brothers pooled their resources, founded a family company, and bought the store: "At that time my capital was about 35,000 dollars—that was what I had. My brothers had to invest some 2,000 dollars, 3,000 dollars. So what we did was to create a company with shares. Each bought shares in the company [or the bodega]. Those who worked in the company were paid a salary by it; the others just made money from their shares. . . . Yes, this bodega is actually what created what the family is today."

In 1980, Eligio married again, and he and his wife soon had children. In the same year, in 1980, he said to his brothers that they ought to sell the bodega and instead buy a supermarket. But his brothers said "no," arguing that a supermarket was a too difficult task. For his part, Eligio told his brothers, "The whites own supermarkets and the Hispanics bodegas. There is more money in supermarkets than in bodegas." In those days, he explained to me in 2002, the supermarkets were cheap. A&P and the other chains were leaving; they were withdrawing from the inner city. A supermarket that today may cost $2 million, he continued, could at that time be bought for $50,000. In 1980, Eligio sold his share in the bodega to three of his brothers. Then he bought a rundown supermarket on Bowen Street in downtown Brooklyn. How did he pick it? I asked. He had often passed the store. It used to be a chain store, an A&P. In 1979, A&P sold it to people of Middle Eastern origin (*arabes*). But these new owners, Eligio said, were not able to run it with a profit. Having bought it, Eligio and his wife remodeled it and sought to fill it with the groceries they believed people in the neighborhood wanted.

Eligio's first supermarket was an Associated. This meant three things: the supermarket had been bought with a loan from the company Associated Wholesalers, it was supplied with the aid of Associated Wholesalers, and the supermarket's name was Associated. In the following years, Eligio continued to cooperate with Associated. In the 1980s, he and his brothers bought more rundown supermarkets—always with a loan and credit from Associated. He explained this by saying that in the 1980s no bank was willing to lend them money, but Associated for its part could borrow what the company needed from Chase Manhattan. Thereafter, Associated charged Eligio and the rest of the independent supermarket owners a high interest on their loans. White Rose Foods supplied the groceries. The bills for this, however, were not sent to the individual store, but, instead, directly to Associated. Again, Associated charged Eligio and the other store owners for the service.

The great majority of Dominicans who became owners of supermarkets began their careers in the city more or less like Eligio. According to Eligio, there was a clear pattern:

> Of the hundreds of Dominican-owned supermarkets I know of only two or three that are owned by people over 60. The majority are around 50. They are people who arrived [from the Dominican Republic] at the age of 18, 19, 20, 21.
>
> C: And many started in bodegas?
>
> E: Of course, in bodegas. You know, my history is the history of nearly all the supermarkets.
>
> C: Yes?
>
> E: Everybody the same story. They came here, they looked for work, a job in a bodega... [The pattern is] bodegas, bodega partners, bodega owners, supermarket partners, supermarket owners, owner of one, owner of two, owner of three... it's the same story [*bodegas, socios de bodegas, dueños de bodegas, socios de supermercado, dueños de supermercado, dueño de uno, dueño de dos, dueño de tres... es la misma historia*].

However, Eligio's success had by far exceeded the usual or typical. In the 1990s, he continued to grow his businesses. When I met him in 2002, he was far wealthier than most of the other Dominicans in the supermarket industry. Not only did he and his brothers own an impressive number of supermarkets, but he had also developed his own line or "chain" of supermarkets, the Compare supermarkets. In 2002, there were 32 independent Compare supermarkets—in New York's inner city, on Long Island, and in Connecticut and North Carolina. Of these 18 were owned by Eligio and his brothers, as he said, by *la familia*. The Compare name had been invented by Eligio and the name itself was his private property. The owners of the 14 Compare supermarkets not owned by the family had paid Eligio for the right to use the name.

Why and how did Eligio create the name "Compare"? In the mid-1980s, he said, he had gradually become convinced that the name "Associated" was not very good. As he put it, "People liked what we had in the store, but they didn't understand the name Associated, the Hispanics. You know, in New York, there are many nationalities. I began to think that we should have a supermarket name that was more suited to the [Spanish-speaking, recently arrived] immigrants." He decided on "Compare" because it is easy to remember and means the same in Spanish and English: "The name Compare invites you to 'compare' my supermarket to other supermarkets." In addition, he explained, over the past couple of decades, scores of rural Mexicans have arrived in New York. "These people are from the countryside and have just arrived. So when we decided on 'Compare' we thought also of the recently arrived Mexicans. These people wouldn't even go to their Compare; no, they would go to their 'Compadre' ['Co-parent'], who for them is a very important figure, the *compadre*—very important."[5]

In 1986, Eligio asked permission from Associated Wholesalers to replace "Associated" with "Compare." The company, controlled by Jewish Americans, turned the proposition down. Three years later, however, in 1989, Eligio managed to impose his will. It started when Associated made him a business proposition. An independent supermarket on Long Island had gone bankrupt, and Associated owned the building. Associated now proposed that Eligio should take over the store and restructure it. Eligio said "yes," but on two conditions: first, that Associated gave the family the option to buy the building that housed the store, which meant the family would control the property and not pay rent; second, that Associated gave him the right to call the store "Compare."

A Story of Survival

I met Benito Paulino in November 2002. Having read an interview with him in *El Taxista*, a journal in Spanish that is circulated and read in the New York City Dominican community of taxi drivers, I went to see him. He had just been elected head of a Dominican-controlled livery-cab operation in the Bronx. I went to ask him about the history of the livery-cab operation he now headed and what he wanted to do as the enterprise's head.

Benito was from the Dominican southeast, from San Pedro de Macorís. Now in his mid-forties, he had immigrated in 1984. When I met him in 2002, he lived in an apartment in the Bronx with his wife and son. In San Pedro de Macorís, he had built himself a house. Before he became a livery-cab driver, he had tried his luck as a New York City *bodeguero*. He bought his first bodega in 1989 and sold it two years later. Then he bought a new bodega. His life as a *bodeguero* ended in 1993, and since then he had been a livery-cab driver.

In San Pedro de Macorís, one of Benito's uncles had run a grocery store, and having been more or less brought up in that store, Benito already knew a good deal about running a small business when he migrated. From 1985 to 1989, he worked as a manager of a bodega in the Bronx. Soon, however, his goal was to get his own business. The store he bought in 1989 was located in Williamsbridge in the Bronx, and he bought it together with a *socio*, the father of his sister and his own stepfather. In all, he and his stepfather had had $11,000. They had borrowed the rest of what they needed—$45,000—from Cuban moneylenders; for the next two years, they had repaid the moneylenders weekly. They paid back more than $74,000 for the $45,000, but they made it—after the two years, the loan was repaid. In addition to Benito and his stepfather, Benito's mother worked daily in the store. The business was entirely based on the family's labor. It was open seven days a week, from seven in the morning until midnight.

The store was sold in 1991. The sale left Benito with $20,000 and his stepfather with $28,000. According to Benito, they sold because they were tired and because they wanted to dispose of what they had gained. In addition, Benito wanted to have a business alone. So he bought a new bodega soon afterward, this time on his own. The new store was situated on Creston Avenue in the Bronx. Commercially, it had a better location than his previous store, and it was also slightly larger. The price was $135,000. Benito's own capital at the time was $38,000 (the $20,000 he had obtained when he sold his previous bodega plus his savings). From the same moneylenders he had used previously, he borrowed $60,000. The remaining amount, or $37,000, he owed to the man who sold him the store. The agreement was that Benito would pay him what he owed him when he had paid off his debt to the moneylenders. The first year, Benito paid what he owed on time. But after the first year, things started to go badly. Shortly afterward, he lost his store because he could not pay what he owed. After the loss of the store, he still owed $25,000. As he said laconically in 2002, "And in that way began my life as a taxi driver, to be able to pay what I owed."

Asked to explain why things had gone well with the first bodega and badly with the next, Benito emphasized two circumstances. The first of these had to do with recruiting and paying labor. As he said, in the first bodega, his mother had helped a lot. In his store on Creston Avenue, on the other hand, he had had to pay wages of two employees. During the time he owned the bodega, he had hired three people, one Dominican, one Puerto Rican, and one Mexican. In addition, his mother had helped him from time to time, but not like before.

The second circumstance Benito mentioned was tied to his own behavior.

At the time, he said, he was still unmarried. While he had owned the first store, his self-discipline had been strong. But after a while on Creston Avenue, this time not surrounded by his family, he had started to act more carelessly as an owner, keeping his business under less close observation and spending more money on women.

In 2002, he was clear on one point: if he could have chosen again, he would have chosen being a livery driver over being a *bodeguero*. Why? "Because, with the taxi, I have my time free from work. In the bodega, there is no time free from work. In the bodega, I had to work from seven in the morning until midnight. A bodega may give you more money, but the price is very high, the price is work all the time."

Over the past three decades, the economic conditions for Dominican owners of *bodegas* and other small stores have worsened. Today in New York City, it is difficult for ordinary Dominican small-business owners to pull through, and many of the Dominican-owned stores represent nothing but survival strategies. This is due to at least three circumstances. First, as noted, bodegas and other stores were less expensive in the 1970s and early 1980s. People had to invest considerably less money to obtain their own business; Eligio, for example, bought a bodega in Brooklyn in 1971. Second, since the early 1980s, the rents paid by most of the city's small-business owners have increased significantly. In the mid-1980s, Mayor Edward Koch opposed commercial rent regulation. But under election-year pressure, Roger Sanjek writes, he appointed a commission to study the issue: "When Koch's commission, composed mainly of Manhattan bankers and developers, reported in 1986, it acknowledged that a quarter of small-business owners considered rent increases their most serious problem but nevertheless recommended against rent regulation" (Sanjek 1998: 345). Subsequently, rents continued to rise. When I conducted my field research, most Dominicans engaged in small business in northern Manhattan described rent increases as one of their biggest difficulties.

Third, as manufacturing in New York continued to decline while new waves of Dominicans and other groups of immigrants continued to enter the city, more people became self-employed. One result is that neighborhoods have become crowded with small bodegas and other kinds of mom-and-pop stores, and competition between small businesses situated on the same block or street has intensified. Today in parts of Washington Heights and Inwood, for example, a Dominican *bodeguero* who looks out the window from his store may quite often see the store entrance or the store signs of a couple of other Dominican-owned bodegas. The fact that so many want, or are forced, to try to develop their own small economic ventures explains in part (the possibility of) the high rents and the fact that bodegas and other small businesses are now bought at high prices.

In such an economic context, many fail. Like Benito, they do well enough for a period, but subsequently go bankrupt and have to find another source of income. Others are able to keep their business floating, but their income remains limited. Only a few have been very successful, such as those who control supermarkets. But as we have seen, a significant number of those Dominican immigrants who owned supermarkets when I carried out the fieldwork had immigrated earlier, in the 1970s and 1980s or during a period when it still had been possible to obtain a small business at a limited price.

A Story of Struggle

The city's taxicabs are operated by private companies and licensed by the New York City Taxi and Limousine Commission. There are three categories of taxis: "medallion taxis," which are the familiar yellow taxis, "livery cabs," and "black cars." Black-car services are primarily used by corporate clients; a ride is paid for by a voucher, not in cash. Yellow cabs patrol a large part of Manhattan and may be hailed with a raised hand. Livery cabs offer most of the taxi services outside Manhattan's central and lower areas—in northern Manhattan, the Bronx, Queens, and Brooklyn. Legally, livery-cab drivers are not allowed to pick up passengers who hail them on the street but can only respond to telephone calls to a licensed dispatch service or livery-car service. Yet, in practice, they cruise for street hails. Drivers of both yellow cabs and livery cabs are paid in cash, but only yellow cabs use a meter.

Of the roughly 41,000 livery cabs that operated in New York City at the time of my fieldwork, a very large proportion were owned and driven by Dominicans. The head of the strongest of the associations representing the city's livery-cab drivers, the New York State Federation of Taxi Drivers, was Fernando Mateo, one of the most prominent New York City Dominican leaders. In northern Manhattan and in large parts of the Bronx, Dominican immigrants completely dominate the industry: a vast majority of the drivers are Dominican, and Dominicans own and run the livery-car companies or dispatch services. Dominicans also run livery-car services in Queens and Brooklyn. While a few of these Dominican-controlled livery-car services are individually owned, the great majority are cooperatives. Each has been founded, and is owned and run, by a group of Dominican drivers together. Owners and drivers call their company "*la base*" or "the base." The group of owners is called *los socios*, or owners or partners. The number of *socios* varies; in some bases it may be forty to sixty; in others only ten or twelve. The vast majority of *socios* work themselves as livery-cab drivers. In addition to the *socios*, each car service or base has a number of drivers who belong to the company without being *socios* or owners. Large Dominican-owned livery-car services in northern Manhattan included between 300 and 400 *socios* and drivers. These people earned their bread and butter as livery-cab drivers; few had other jobs besides taxi-driving.

Most drivers stop by their base daily. Usually the base is situated in a small, rented space on the first floor in a tenement building in, or near, an important shopping area or a large public institution like a hospital, a school, or an old people's home. Here are the radio dispatch service, the office of the base's elected president, and the offices or desks of one or two secretaries. Sometimes the base also includes a meeting room. Small businesses situated next to the base are used by the drivers: not only the drivers' households but also bodegas, small restaurants, barber shops, car-repair shops, and insurance brokers depend on the livery-car services. These other businesses are generally not owned and run by the base, but by others. They may be located on the first floor in the same building as the base or in nearby buildings around the base.

The history of the emergence of New York City's livery-cab industry takes us back at least to the 1960s and 1970s. In the 1960s, New York's medallion or yellow cabs, the majority of the city's legal taxis at the time, hardly drove outside the "nice" parts of Manhattan. African Americans, Puerto Ricans, and immigrants started to drive legal and illegal cabs where the yellows would not venture, in the city's lower-income neighborhoods. Eventually, there were so many unlicensed or "gypsy" cabs that the city enacted new ordinances in the 1980s to bring the unregulated cars under its control. In 1987, when the livery-car services were required to register with the New York City Taxi and Limousine Commission, there were almost 40,000 livery and gypsy cabs (compared with 11,700 yellow taxis) (Schaller Consulting 2004: 30; Sanjek 1998: 187).

In part to address livery-cab issues, City Council in 1971 created the New York City Taxi and Limousine Commission, although this agency did not finally gain jurisdiction over livery cabs until sixteen years later. Today, the

Taxi and Limousine Commission is the city agency responsible for licensing the city's yellow cabs, livery cabs, black cars, commuter vans, and a number of other vehicles. This agency is also responsible for licensing the several hundred car services or base stations from which the livery cabs operate. The Taxi and Limousine Commission, however, does a good deal more than just issue licenses. It also enacts regulations, inspects vehicles used as cabs, and enforces local laws and regulations. As a city agency regulating a private industry, the Taxi and Limousine Commission investigates passenger complaints, adjudicates summonses for rule violations, and imposes fines, suspensions and revocations where it finds them appropriate. It has over 400 employees to carry out these tasks. Street enforcement of taxicab laws and rules, however, is assigned to the New York City Police Department's Taxi Unit. The Taxi and Limousine Commission Board consists of nine members, eight of them unsalaried commissioners. The salaried chair/commissioner presides over regularly scheduled public Commission meetings and is the full-time executive head of the agency. Five commissioners are appointed at the recommendation of City Council and represent the boroughs of the city, thus maintaining a role for the City Council and more generally the city's politicians in taxi regulation. The other four are appointed by the mayor, who also designates the chairperson.

My account of how veterans in northern Manhattan's Dominican livery bases described the industry's history relies heavily on the narratives of a couple of key informants, but their story is representative. The main features of this history are not contested among Upper Manhattan's Dominican base owners and drivers. On the contrary, they are often taken for granted. Key components of this history provide context and meaning to base owners' and drivers' interpretations of contemporary economic and social realities.

In New York City, liveries were a source of contention from their birth. While a number of elected officials defended them as community businesses providing needed transportation, the yellow-taxi industry attacked them as illegal, unsafe, and encroaching on yellow taxis' rights. Despite controversy, the livery industry, as we have seen, not only survived but also grew rapidly. Meanwhile, the Taxi and Limousine Commission remained dominated by groups with stakes in the yellow-taxi industry. Such was the general picture during the three decades from 1971, the year the Commission was established, until 2002, the year I started my research. This has had an important effect. More than other groups with whom I worked, the community of Dominican base owners and drivers embodied a history of struggle and resistance. From the beginning, livery drivers were "on the outside." They were not only involved in a day-to-day battle to make money, but many also took part in a larger struggle. Base owners and drivers were forced to endure, and face, what they viewed as an unfair and hostile environment: representatives of the police, the Taxi and Limousine Commission, the yellow-taxi industry, and the cab-insurance industry. These forces, in the livery industry's eyes, sought to prevent base owners and drivers from exercising a basic right: to survive and provide food, clothes, and a home for one's family. During my fieldwork, Dominican base owners and drivers reminded me of this again and again.

In Washington Heights, many Dominicans explained that people chose to become taxi drivers because they did not want to work in a factory. Working in a factory left people with too little space for independence and flexibility. A man who drove a livery cab was basically his own boss. He could work when he wanted to, and he could travel back to the island or somewhere else, stay for two or three or more months if he wanted or needed to, and thereafter return to his work in New York. Some of the livery drivers I met were people who had migrated after first completing university training in the Dominican Republic. While they spoke little English and had no chance of obtaining a job as professionals, they had not been willing to reduce themselves to slaving in a factory. Others were people who combined working with going to school or college. They drove a livery in the night and studied in the day; or they drove in the day and took classes in the evening.

One of the many in Washington Heights's livery bases who celebrated the independence of the livery driver compared to the oppression—or lack of autonomy and respect—suffered by the factory worker was Nelson Camacho. The first time I met Camacho was early in my fieldwork. I met him on the street in front of his base, located on Amsterdam Avenue between 166th and 167th Streets. That time we just met; I had not called before I showed up, and Camacho was in a hurry. Subsequently, we met many times. Often dressed in a blue baseball cap, white shirt, colorful tie, and khaki pants, Camacho was friendly and extroverted. Then in his mid-fifties, he had come from Santo Domingo in 1980 and been part of the livery industry ever since. His base had been the base where I first found him; his home was in a tenement on East 181st Street. Camacho became one of my most important sources of information in Washington Heights.

Before I went to his base the first time, I had asked José Delio Marte whom I could contact in the Washington Heights livery industry. He had given me one name: Nelson Camacho. Camacho not only knew a lot about the history of the livery industry (he even kept a rudimentary private archive—a small pile of copies of letters and newspaper articles—in his home that documented important events in the industry's history, to which he gave me access), but he had also been active in community building and politics. When I met him, he was head of La Hermandad Quisqueyana Community Center, one of many social clubs organized by Dominican immigrants. He had worked for one of the three large Dominican political parties, the Partido Revolucionario Dominicano. In New York City, he had worked during many years for the Democrats. Beyond this he had run his own small business. A couple of blocks beyond his base station on Amsterdam Avenue, he owned a small business that acted as an intermediary in the sale of motor insurance. The last time I saw Camacho, in early 2004, he had just sold his business, using the proceeds to buy two apartments in the Dominican capital. He and his wife had decided to move back to Santo Domingo because his health was no longer as strong as it used to be. Their son, a man of around thirty, would stay in Washington Heights; he had no wish to return. Several of Camacho's brothers and sisters also lived in the United States; his other brothers and sisters, as well as his mother, lived in the Dominican capital. In the following years, Camacho and his wife expected to spend time in both countries.

I asked Camacho how the Washington Heights livery industry was created. His story began in the 1970s and was focused on two interrelated processes. The first had to do with interethnic interaction and ethnic succession. As Camacho recalled it, the founders and pioneers of the livery industry had been Puerto Rican. In the late 1970s and early 1980s, Dominican drivers entered a group of Puerto Rican-owned bases. For a few years, Puerto Ricans and Dominicans built the industry together. Subsequently, it came to be entirely dominated by Dominicans, while the number of bases, most of them cooperatives, skyrocketed.[6] The other process to which Camacho drew attention revolved around collective action and organized resistance. To defend their interests, a number of base owners and drivers created a common political organization, the Committee for the Defense of the Nonmedallion Cab Drivers, or El Comité pro Defensa de los Taxistas sin Medallón. And they organized demonstrations and protests. In the 1960s and 1970s, Camacho said,

> The yellow taxis only operated in the lower areas, in downtown and midtown Manhattan. The other areas of the city, the poor barrios, didn't have transportation. Then the Puerto Ricans, who are the

pioneers in this struggle, begin to offer service, with the so-called gypsies [*gitanos*]. Gypsies were cabs that weren't regulated by the city. No, they just took any car they had and offered service. That way this industry started, it began with the gypsies. Later, around 1980, there was already an industry, and a handful of bases had been established. The city said it had to regulate the industry, since there were too many gypsies. But [the industry had people who defended it; in the early 1980s] we had a Puerto Rican who had been part of this industry, José Rivera ["*Entonces, había un puertorriqueño que había nacido en esta industria*"]. [On other occasions Camacho called José Rivera "*el padre de nuestra industria de taxi libre*," "the father of our livery-cab industry." When Camacho and I spoke, in 2002, José Rivera was an Assemblyman and one of the New York City Puerto Rican community's top leaders.] And we had the Reverend Ruben Díaz, and Fernando Ferrer [two others of today's top New York City Puerto Rican leaders], and a man called Freddy Pérez was a Puerto Rican community activist. And then the first groups of Dominicans appear, around 1980.

I asked, "May one say that the first Dominican livery drivers began to work in Puerto Rican bases?" Camacho replied, "Yes, I think so. It's obvious, because [bases like] America, Highbridge, San Juan, which were some of the first Dominican livery bases, were Puerto Rican bases." But later Dominicans began to take over bases. "And then we came up with the idea of forming a union for livery-cab drivers. For the city had already started to put pressure on us and to make a series of demands." So, to save the industry, they established an organization to say to the city that, while regulation was needed, it must be "in a way that allows us to develop and continue to live."

In the early 1980s, the authorities tried increasingly to bring the city's taxi industry under their regulation and control. Of the around 35,000 nonmedallion cabs that operated in the city at the time, only some 2,000 were registered with the New York City Taxi and Limousine Commission as was required. This led New York State Governor Mario Cuomo to sign a bill that considerably strengthened the authorities' regulatory power over the livery industry. The law gave the Taxi and Limousine Commission the right to hear cases involving violations of its regulations by nonmedallion, or livery-cab, drivers and owners—not only by those of yellow taxis as before. The power to hear cases involving violations by gypsy and livery drivers rested with the Criminal Court, which was overburdened and was little effective in enforcing the city's regulations. Mayor Edward Koch had sought the new legislation as a way of providing the city direct control over enforcement and, by implication, over the whole gypsy and livery industry. Livery-base owners and drivers for their part saw the authorities' strengthened attempt to bring the industry under their regulation as undermining their existence. As Camacho put it, in the early and mid-1980s, base owners and drivers were forced to fight to try to save the industry.

The Committee for the Defense of Nonmedallion Cab Drivers was founded in the early 1980s to protect the interests of the livery bases and drivers. The Committee's first president was a Puerto Rican, Freddy Pérez; its two vice-presidents were Dominicans. And it had José Rivera and an African American who represented the taxi industry in Brooklyn as advisors. Camacho, too, participated from the start. In the first part of the 1980s, the Committee staged noisy mass protests over the city's taxi regulations outside City Hall. The livery industry demanded its own commission, bilingual tests, and a delay in registration. Among the documents Camacho had preserved in his Washington Heights apartment, I found newspaper articles and photos from New York's English- and Spanish-speaking press that documented a couple of the largest and most noisy protests that had been staged outside City Hall in those days. The articles included a set of photos of police officers and drivers in heated confrontation. These protests were headed by Freddy Pérez, state assemblyman José Rivera, and state senator Joseph Galiber (both elected by districts in the South Bronx with many Latinos and African Americans).

A cease-fire was agreed on in 1987. The terms were that the Taxi and Limousine Commission finally won jurisdiction over the city's livery vehicles; in 1987, car services were required to obtain a license, and to become licensed, they had to register with the Taxi and Limousine Commission. Legally livery drivers were not allowed to pick up passengers who hailed them on the street but could respond only to telephone calls to their licensed base station. But as we already know, in practice, the livery drivers continued to cruise for street hails. As Camacho said, in the mid-1980s the livery drivers tried to win the legal right to pick up people on the street; protests were staged for this right, but it was not conceded.[7] A part of what livery drivers do, picking up on the street (in addition to responding to calls to their base), is therefore illegal. This has preserved a situation replete with tensions and mutual mistrust. After 1987, all livery vehicles and drivers have been licensed by the Taxi and Limousine Commission. But part of what any livery driver does as his or her normal job is not legal.

In hindsight, it is easy to see how crucial the Puerto Rican contribution to the livery industry's collective struggle in the first part of the 1980s was. By the time scores of Dominican immigrants started to enter New York, Puerto Rican Americans had already built a community in the city (Sánchez Korrol 1994). Many had a New York City education, and many were bilingual. In the late 1970s and early 1980s, New York City Puerto Ricans controlled resources in a wide sense that made it possible for them to mobilize and incorporate Dominicans. Most importantly, after 1917, the Puerto Rican migration to New York was not about "immigration." New York City Puerto Ricans were not (illegal) immigrants; they were U.S. citizens who had rights. For their part, many of the Dominican newcomers in the livery industry in the early 1980s were without papers. They lacked rights, and spoke little English. Camacho said about these years, the early 1980s, that the regulations adopted by the city in this period "were a bit difficult. Many of the Dominican pioneers of this industry remained [undocumented] immigrants, right? Since they were undocumented, it was impossible to comply with the new rules adopted by the city."

Despite this, the Dominican control over the livery industry in northern Manhattan and the Bronx grew rapidly. Soon Freddy Pérez, who headed the Committee for the Defense of the Nonmedallion Cab Drivers in the first half of the 1980s, withdrew from the organization and the industry. In 1985 Jaime Vargas, a Dominican immigrant and owner of a livery base on St. Nicholas Avenue in Washington Heights, had become president of the association of livery-base owners and drivers in northern Manhattan. Each base had its representative who acted as channel of communication between his base station and the association's leadership. The leaders and representatives were most often recruited from the ranks of the base owners.

According to Camacho the few car services that existed to begin with, say, around 1980, were not cooperatives; each was owned by one person. The owner was most often a Puerto Rican. When I lived in Washington Heights, however, nearly all the Dominican-controlled bases in this part of the city were cooperatives. This happened because, first, those early bases with only one owner were afterward bought by a group of drivers together, and second, a series of entirely new bases were founded by groups of drivers together—typically by drivers who had left their base to try to improve their conditions by founding a new base. Camacho said,

> A cooperative is a union of a number of drivers—100, 150; they create a base which has about the same characteristics as the "mother" of the

new bases. For example, I may give you an example. Three new bases sprang up from this base [Camacho's base]. We founded this base in 1982. Subsequently, this gave birth to three new bases, in 1984, 1985, and 1986. All were cooperatives. During this period, [Dominican] cooperatives begin to emerge—they were created here in Manhattan, in the Bronx, and in Brooklyn and Queens. The drivers became owners of the bases.

One of the largest and most important Dominican-owned bases in northern Manhattan when I was carrying out fieldwork was Fort George. The Fort George base was transformed into a cooperative in 1984. In 2002, it had more than 300 drivers, among them Armando Ferrera. Then in his sixties, Armando had participated when the cooperative was founded in 1984. Born in La Vega, he had moved to the Dominican capital in 1960. In Santo Domingo, he had worked for many years for the state and had also worked for a private company as a truck driver. He moved to the U.S. in the early 1980s; his wife followed him in 1989. She had studied medicine in the Dominican capital, and, after learning English, she found a job in a hospital in Harlem. In 2002, they were divorced. Armando lived in a tenement a few blocks away from the base. In Santo Domingo, where he planned to spend his last years, he owned a house.

In the early 1980s, Armando said, Fort George Car Service had one owner, Vicente Castillo. In 1984, Castillo sold the base to a group of thirty drivers, who thereby became *socios*. One of the *socios* was Armando. The group split the amount it paid to Castillo evenly, and each *socio* paid $400. The price was low because what the group in practice bought was not much. The company did not own cars; instead, each driver owned or rented his own vehicle. Armando said the group bought just "a table, radio equipment, and two phones—we had two phone lines," but the *socios* built the business up through promotion, and two decades later the Fort George base station must have had over twenty phone lines. Its offices were computerized, and it used local radio and television channels to advertise.

Armando explained that the foundation had resulted from a conflict in another base. A group of drivers in the Amsterdam Car Service had decided to leave that company and establish their own due to deep disagreement with the owner. For his part, Armando had not been part of this group; he had not belonged to the Amsterdam Car Service. Before he took part in the foundation of Fort George, Armando had driven a gypsy cab. The owner of the vehicle had taught him the work, and Armando had paid him $125 a week to rent his car. Neither the owner of the car nor Armando had belonged to a car service; they had just picked people up. In 1984, one of Armando's friends had invited him to participate in a set of meetings held by the group of drivers that eventually had bought Fort George. The meetings had planned the deal, and Armando had joined the other *socios*. Some years later, in the early 1990s, a handful of the original *socios* had sold their shares and left, but the bulk of the group carried on. At that time, the number of *socios* was greatly expanded. A large group of new drivers—some fifty or sixty men—bought shares in the base. In this way, the base got fresh capital and new perspectives on how it should be run and developed. The drivers who headed and managed Fort George at the time of the fieldwork belonged largely to the cohort that had entered in the early 1990s.

Each Dominican-owned livery base elects a board each year. The electors are the base's *socios*, not drivers who belong to the base without being among its owners. In addition, the board members are chosen from among the *socios*, and the president of the board is the base's manager. He manages the base's affairs from his office in the base station. For his work, he is paid a salary by the base. For their part, the base's drivers are *not* regarded by the cooperative as "employees." On the contrary, all I spoke with emphasized, as a defining characteristic of these business enterprises, that the driver is not employed by the base, but, instead, works as self-employed or "independently." This was explained as follows. A livery base does not own vehicles. Instead, each driver is responsible for obtaining his or her own vehicle. Working hours are fixed by the drivers themselves. If a driver wants to work fifteen hours, he may do so; if he wants to take the rest of the day off after having worked half an hour, he is free to do it; if he does not want to work, it's his decision. Moreover, drivers do not even have to inform the base about their work decisions. Each week, the drivers must pay a fixed amount to the base. In Fort George in 2002, the amount was $50. This is considered payment for what the base sells to its drivers: the right to respond to the telephone calls by customers to the base station. If a person needs a cab and calls the base, he or she is connected with a driver who is in the vicinity; the customer and the driver thereafter negotiate the details, and the driver is paid in cash. Nothing of what the driver is paid goes to the base.

Armando once explained to me how he had obtained his first vehicle. The story is instructive because it shows how relatively little capital one needed to get started as a livery cabbie in the first half of the 1980s; almost anyone could do it. As already noted, at first Armando rented a car for $125 a week. After becoming a Fort George *socio*, he continued to rent. But soon a friend said to him, "You ought to buy yourself a car." The friends were almost relatives; they belonged to two Dominican families with longstanding mutual ties. But Armando did not think he had enough money. One day his friend said to him, "Look! I've seen your car!" He explained that he had seen a car for Armando in New Jersey. They went to have a look at it, and Armando bought it. This was in 1984, and the car was a Chevrolet 1978 model. The price was $1,500. His car insurance was $700 a year, and the radio equipment he needed in the car to be able to operate as a livery driver cost less than $300.

Just like working in a bodega, driving a livery cab used to be viewed by New Yorkers as one of the most dangerous jobs in the city. More than 30 cab drivers were murdered in the city in 1990; two years later, the number soared to almost 40.[8] The numbers then fell until a wave of killings of livery cabbies returned in 2000:[9] four were killed in the first two months of that year. After 2000, the numbers fell again until they hit a historic low in 2003 and 2004. In the almost two years from late January 2003, when two drivers were murdered while on duty, to early 2005, not a single livery driver was killed. Almost every livery base has at least one driver who has been killed, and the drivers who have been killed continue to be remembered by their bases. A driver's dispatch number is his or her identity: if your number is 37, you are "*Número 37.*" If a driver is asked his name, he often replies with the number he hears daily over the two-way radio; even close friends call each other by their numbers. If a driver is killed, his number is never given out by the base again. Once Camacho pulled out a roster sheet of the base's about 200 drivers and pointed to a few crossed-out lines on the sheet, saying, "Number 5, he was killed; number 9, he was killed; number 29, he was killed; number 60, he was killed. And this is just one base! Imagine the rest!"

As we have seen, liveries were the cause of large-scale negotiations of power and control from their inception. The emergence of livery bases in neighborhoods like Washington Heights formed an integral part of a wider battle, the struggle over rights, resources, and influence in New York City. In the light of this, the industry's capacity to make itself heard in the second part of the 1980s and most of the 1990s remained extremely weak. Base owners and drivers had their organizations and leaders, but their voices were barely listened to at the level of the city, and the livery industry remained politically divided, little coordinated, and fragmented. From the mid-1980s to 1996, Jaime Vargas headed an organization that represented the livery industry, La Asociación de Bases de Nueva York (or Livery Owners Coalition of New York). Most of the members were Dominicans and belonged to bases located in northern Manhattan and in the Bronx. The organization continued to stay in touch with representatives of other cab-industry bodies, like representatives of the Brooklyn-based black-car and livery industry run by African Americans. Vargas's organization staged protests against Taxi and Limousine Commission regulations and enforcements and cried out against the violence that hit livery cabbies. Above all, it attempted to demand what Dominicans in the livery-cab industry wanted most of all: social recognition and respect.

In 1996, Vargas left the organization, which thereafter was further weakened. In 1996, the Dominican political party that Vargas supported, the Partido de la Liberación Dominicana (PLD), won the presidential elections; as a reward, Vargas was given a four-year position in Japan by the new government. A new chapter in the history of the livery industry's fight to protect and enhance the rights of its members began in 1999, when a group of Dominicans founded a new organization, the New York State Federation of Taxi Drivers. The new organization's president was Fernando Mateo. Mateo, who grew up in modest circumstances in the Lower East Side as a son of Dominican immigrants and was a high school dropout, never drove a livery. Instead, he is a self-made wealthy businessman, has a home in Westchester, and is one of the most high-profile, best-known Dominican New Yorkers today. The State Federation and Mateo's leadership are dealt with in a later chapter.

At the time of my fieldwork, base owners and drivers in Washington Heights were bearers of a particular discourse. This discourse, which was historically produced, energized base owners' and drivers' forms of resistance and political practice and shaped their collective struggle. The core of this discourse was a deep sense of injustice. Base owners and drivers regarded themselves as hardworking, serious, and honest. What a livery driver did was to support his or her family—in brief, to do his or her duty. But, they claimed, instead of being treated with respect for what they had managed to do, they were often dealt with in disrespectful ways, exploited, and criminalized. They were deprived of both dignity and money. Drivers complained of having been treated in impolite, condescending, and incomprehensible ways by Taxi and Limousine Commission employees and police officers. Needless to say, a big part of the problem had to do with the language barrier. Few drivers understood and spoke English sufficiently, and the situation only worsened with uses of technical and juridical language and forms that had to be completed.

People also complained about the Commission regulations, enforcements, and license fees.

One of the most important sources of dissatisfaction was the ban on picking up passengers off the street. I met no one in the livery industry who supported this; on the contrary, all drivers did it, and, again, it was seen as necessary to be able to make a living. The outcome was, therefore, not only that drivers were dissatisfied but also that they were often fined by the police. This angered and frustrated base owners and drivers. Not only did people lose money, but they also felt criminalized for just working, for just being who they were. The continual ticketing represented a persistent attack on their dignity. Many tickets were primarily seen as unfair taxation; people claimed the city used ticketing of livery drivers to increase its income. Livery drivers also felt increasingly exploited by the insurance industry. In 2002, the annual insurance premium for a car used as a livery cab was no longer some $700, the amount Armando had paid for his first car in 1984; it had increased dramatically: the annual premium many drivers paid approached $7,000.

A History of Two Business Partners

Below I present two more stories derived from conversations I had with Dominican New Yorkers about their life histories. The two narratives—Chelo Ramírez's history and Fernando Mella's history—sketch features of the business careers of two *socios*, two men who at the time of my fieldwork together owned a Dominican restaurant in Marble Hill, an area that geographically is part of the Bronx but politically belongs to northern Manhattan.[10] The two histories are followed by a brief story of New York's Dominican beauty salons, with a goal of broadening the perspective. So far we have looked at the histories of three economic niches: the neighborhood bodega, the independent supermarket, and the livery-cab operation. The following histories present data on two other types of ventures that have been important among Dominican New Yorkers. As we shall see, Dominican immigrants have developed and operated these various forms of enterprise (the bodega, the supermarket, the car service, the restaurant and the beauty shop—and, for that matter, also other types of enterprises such as the car-repair shop and the travel agency[11]) in ways that show considerable overlap. Many have moved from one type of business to another. Some have simultaneously had stakes in both a cab operation and a bodega or restaurant. The most basic cultural forms and practices that Dominicans have put to use to develop small businesses have not differed much from one economic sector to another.

Chelo's History

I met Chelo Ramírez for the first time in fall 2002 in his Caridad restaurant, on Broadway on the edge of the Marble Hill neighborhood. Today, New York has a stream of popular restaurants that serve Dominican food at a modest price. They serve popular classics like *sancocho* (a Dominican soup), *carne guisada* (beef stew), *pollo al carbón* (roasted chicken), *chivo* (goat meat), rice and beans, green and sweet plantain, *ensalada de aguacate* (avocado salad), and so on. Most of these restaurants are small, with only six or seven tables, but some are larger, with twenty tables or more. They are open seven days a week from around seven in the morning until midnight or later; serve breakfast, lunch, dinner, and sandwiches; and offer take-out—many offer free delivery. In neighborhoods like Washington Heights and Inwood, the number of such places is especially high. The restaurants are owned by individuals—either by a man or a woman alone or by two or more *socios*. They have names like El Punto de Sabor (Place of Taste), Destiny, Dyckman Express, El Pollo Dorado (Golden Chicken), and El Conuco (Small Plot [of Land]). Some Dominican restaurants use the same name. Northern Manhattan has a handful of Dominican restaurants called Mambi, and a series of Dominican restaurants in New York uses the name Caridad. In 2002, the city had nearly twenty Caridad restaurants. With a couple of exceptions, the Caridads were similar, with plastic tablecloths, mirrored walls, and waitresses in black jeans and white blouses or shirts serving plates of Dominican staples. The Caridads served also food not classified as Dominican—a selection of dishes marketed as Latin, American, and International. Caridads usually advertised their products as Latin and International cuisine.

Chelo's Caridad restaurant was spacious, with a long counter and some thirty tables. He and I sat at one of the tables, sipping coffee and talking about the city's Caridad restaurants, his life history, and his plans. It was in the afternoon, a quiet moment of time in the restaurant. Before I was finally able to sit down with Chelo, I had for a time tried, without success, to track him down. I had read a few sentences about him in a printed piece produced for a 2001 New York City Dominican small-business convention. From what I read, I understood that Chelo's family had played a crucial part in the development of the city's many Dominican Caridads. I decided to attempt to find him and eventually succeeded, and thereafter continued to visit Chelo's and Fernando Mella's Caridad for a meal, a coffee, and a chat.

Chelo said that what he described as the original—or first—Caridad restaurant opened in 1976.[12] This restaurant, which was located in Upper Manhattan on 151st Street and Broadway and has since burned down, was started by Caridad Alvarez, a Cuban political refugee who learned the restaurant business as a dishwasher. With a $6,000 loan from her family, Caridad opened the tiny restaurant with six tables and named it after herself. In 1976, there were more Dominicans than Cubans in Washington Heights, so she cooked to please them. She put sugar in her stews and rice dishes instead of the cumin and *vino seco* beloved in Havana. In the late 1960s, there were Cubans living along the entire upper West Side of Manhattan from 135th to 207th Street, and relatively many were engaged in small business. Cubans operated restaurants, travel agencies, groceries, candy stores, and so forth, catering to the Spanish-speaking community (Cohn 1967: 6–8).

Born in Janico, a community in the Cibao, Chelo immigrated in 1981. In 2002, he and three older brothers and a sister owned and ran Caridads in New York. They are five out of fifteen siblings. The first members of Chelo's family who migrated arrived in New York in the late 1960s. When Caridad opened her restaurant in 1976, it became a hit. In 1978, Chelo's oldest brother, Alonso, offered to buy it. According to Chelo, Caridad then went to Miami for a while but returned and opened a new Caridad in Washington Heights, this time on 191st Street and St. Nicholas Avenue. After a couple of years, she sold this place also to Chelo's brother Alonso. After spending some time again in Florida, she opened a third Caridad, on 207th Street in Inwood; Chelo's brother also bought this. Then, Caridad started a fourth restaurant, on Broadway and 184th Street in the heart of Washington Heights. This restaurant was not sold to Chelo's family; instead, Caridad sold it to another family when she retired. In 1988, Chelo and his brothers established a new Caridad in Kingsbridge in the Bronx, copying and elaborating on the already established model. Fourteen years later, Chelo told me, he and his four siblings had owned fourteen Caridad restaurants: they had bought three, and started the rest themselves. Most of the Caridads were situated in the Bronx and Manhattan, but there were others in Queens and Brooklyn. They had sold many of the restaurants they had opened. When I met Chelo in 2002, the siblings owned and ran only three Caridads themselves. In nearly every case, they had sold to a Dominican who had worked for some time in one of their restaurants as a cook or a waiter and, therefore knew both the Caridad concept and Chelo's family well.

Chelo recognized that the family's claim to the name Caridad was disputed. The first restaurant that used the name was probably not the one opened in Washington Heights in 1976, but a restaurant called La Caridad 78 at 78th Street and Broadway. La Caridad 78, very different from the Dominican-owned Caridads, was started by Chinese Cubans in the early 1970s, serves Chinese and Cuban dishes, and was named after Caridad del Cobre, patron saint of Cuba.

Another restaurant that claims to be the only "real" Caridad is Caridad La Original No. 11 on Amsterdam Avenue at 89th Street. This restaurant is owned by Consuelo Alvarez, a daughter of the first Caridad.

In the late 1990s, Chelo said, fake Dominican Caridads run by people who had never worked for his family were tarnishing the reputations of the real Caridads, the places owned by his family and his friends. A confrontation with the owner of a new arrival, a Dominican who had started a restaurant called Silvio's Caridad in Parkchester in the Bronx, prompted Chelo to apply for a federal trademark in 1999. "This man had never worked for us," Chelo insisted, adding that the man had had no experience of the restaurant business. The application for a trademark was commented for opposition and received no opposition. In 2000, Chelo's family got a trademark. In 2002, Chelo said that the family had not yet started to sell the right to use the name, or to franchise, but the family was considering the possibility.

The siblings ran their businesses in cooperation. One was charged with administration, another with finance, a third with representation, and so on. After arriving in 1981, Chelo attended high school and simultaneously worked full time in a local pizzeria. Subsequently, he took courses in business administration at Baruch College. His brothers also took business courses after they had moved to New York.

Chelo said he used to raise capital with the aid of a German American private moneylender. He had also started to use bank loans. The family's restaurants received supplies on credit, particularly when they first opened. The Caridads employed immigrants from the Dominican Republic, Mexico, El Salvador, Peru, and other Latin and South American countries. Although the majority of the employees were Dominicans, their best cooks, Chelo said, were from Mexico and El Salvador. All the cooks had learned to cook in Caridad restaurants; they started as ordinary workers, for example, as dishwashers, and afterward were given training as cooks in one of the Caridads. Chelo described the Caridad concept in the following manner: "We offer good food at a modest price. We have Latin food [*comida latina*]." Is the Caridad food "Latin" or "Dominican"? I asked him. "I would say that it is Latin, since many dishes are Cuban, Puerto Rican, Dominican. I wouldn't say Dominican; instead, it is a combination—an international taste." It was true that all Dominican Caridads had a varied, rich menu, but most of their customers were served Dominican staples like fried salami, fried cheese, mashed plantains, roast chicken, bacalao, sancocho, red beans, and white rice.

Chelo had also opened a restaurant in the Dominican capital, a place for seafood at a modest price. Although its name was Caridad, it was not modeled on the family Caridads in New York; the menu and locale were different. When I met him, the family were spending much time on their latest project, their first Caridad in Westchester County, in Yonkers. Chelo said the siblings had bought an Italian restaurant in Yonkers and that the Caridad restaurant they were now opening there would constitute a new combination: it would serve Latin and Italian food, since, as Chelo put it, the neighborhood now had many Latinos and still a number of Italians.

Fernando's History

Chelo's *socio* in Marble Hill was Fernando Mella, a first-generation Dominican immigrant in his late thirties. Both Chelo and Fernando were informal and unpretentious, and the latter was an extrovert, too. He always treated me exceptionally kindly. Each owned 50 percent of the restaurant. While Chelo was on the road, moving from one place to another, Fernando worked long hours in Marble Hill and managed the business. He worked in the restaurant seven days a week, from around noon until midnight. Most of the time he was behind the counter or sat at one of the restaurant's tables. Sometimes he was in the office. When he did not work, he was at home with his wife and children. Chelo had recruited Fernando as his *socio* in 2001, about a year before I first met them. In 2001, the restaurant was already well established. But Chelo had needed a partner, so he called Fernando, an old friend, and proposed a deal. Fernando bought half the business from Chelo, and they became *socios*. Before that, Fernando had not worked in the restaurant business, but his dream, he said, had always been to run a restaurant. In spite of the extreme work load, Fernando did not complain. On the contrary, he was grateful for the chance he had been given by Chelo and for learning to operate a restaurant. According to Fernando, the Caridads were basically independent restaurants. With the exception of the three Caridads owned by Chelo and his siblings, the restaurants were owned and run by independent owners, and there was little or no direct cooperation between the different Caridads.

Fernando left the Dominican Republic in 1983, at nineteen. He arrived together with three of his siblings. His mother was already living in New York, so they migrated as part of a legal family reunion. Before he became one of the two owners of the Caridad in Marble Hill, Fernando accumulated a broad experience. Let us look briefly at his life between 1983 and 2001.

The first job Fernando found in New York was in a factory on the east side of Manhattan. Thereafter, he got a job in upstate New York, in a Jewish school in Georgetown where he and another Dominican immigrant were employed as maintenance men. The other's name was Hipólito Quintero, and the two became friends. Hipólito had a brother-in-law who owned a small business in Brooklyn. The brother-in-law had promised to assist Hipólito in raising capital so he could buy his own business. If he got the help he needed, Hipólito said to Fernando, he would hire him in his store. The bodega Hipólito and his brother-in-law bought was in Freeport, Long Island, and Fernando was given a job there. With this, Fernando began his career in the small-business sector.

Later, Fernando started to work in another store, now in a part of Brooklyn. The bodega belonged to another of Fernando's friends. An emergency forced his friend to travel suddenly to the Dominican capital. While he was in Santo Domingo, he was robbed in his home, and he then decided to remain some time on the island. Meanwhile, Fernando took care of the store—his friend now rented him the bodega. Fernando gave him a fixed weekly amount and paid the bills and taxes; in addition, he paid the rent to the landlord and the wages to the employees. The surplus belonged to Fernando. In this way, he managed to accumulate around $35,000. With these savings, he bought his first own bodega, a small store on Jefferson Street and Evergreen Avenue in Brooklyn. But things went badly. Fernando lost money and was forced to sell the store. According to Fernando, the bodega proved to be very "slow," with a small turnover. He then found a job as a manager of a combined bodega and butcher shop in Yonkers.

One day in 1996, his cousin called him saying a friend had told him that a deli in Co-op City, a cooperative in the northeasternmost corner of the Bronx, was for sale. Co-op City has shopping centers, an educational park, and a private security force on the premises. The deli, which was situated in one of the shopping centers, was owned by an Italian American. Fernando bought the business. He paid the owner a part of the total amount. The rest was a loan; according to the deal, Fernando was to pay the debt within five years. The deli had a good location, and Fernando increased its sales, selling, he said, a combination of Italian and Hispanic food. After five years, he had paid off the whole debt to the previous owner. When Fernando became Chelo's *socio* in Marble Hill, he had had the deli in Co-op City for five-and-a-half years. One day in 2001, he had had to make a delivery from his deli to a party in Marble Hill. He entered the Caridad restaurant to ask how he could find the party. As an old friend of Chelo, he had already been in the restaurant, but did not know the neighborhood. A week later, Chelo called to propose the deal that made Fernando his partner. Fernando then sold the deli to his cousins. But as he said, this was his cousins' first business, and they had not had much initial capital. They gave him only a small sum; the rest was a loan to be paid off weekly. In the meantime, Fernando remained the legal owner.

The Dominican Beauty Salons

Dominican women are represented in a wide range of New York City industries, in part as owners and in part as employees. First-generation female Dominican immigrants own and operate grocery stores, supermarkets, restaurants, travel agencies, sweat shops, and many other types of businesses. Even so, the majority of the Dominican bodegas and supermarkets are owned by men, and almost all the Dominican livery drivers are men. On the other hand, the women dominate one important sector: the Dominican beauty salons. In his quantitative, sociological study of Dominican businesses in New York City, Luis Guarnizo (1992) found that female Dominican entrepreneurs often chose beauty parlors as their niche: "One out of every five respondents is a woman. Unlike male [business] owners, however, women are clustered in a single sector: 60 percent of women own service firms (especially beauty salons and other personal service establishments) while only 25 and 15 percent of them own commercial or manufacturing firms, respectively" (121).

Today, there is an impressive number of Dominican beauty salons in New York. In Washington Heights and Inwood alone, there were over 145 salons in the early 1990s—or "a salon on nearly every single block" (Candelario 2007: 187–90). Harlem and the Bronx have large numbers of Dominican-owned salons also, as do certain areas of Queens and Brooklyn (Williams 1999). Some Dominican women have started and sold a stream of beauty salons. I heard of women who had opened between six and ten beauty parlors and then sold them—most often to female relatives (sisters and/or cousins).

The Dominican women who entered New York in the 1960s and 1970s typically used beauty shops owned by Cubans and Puerto Ricans, who already resided in Manhattan (Cohn 1967; Sánchez Korrol 1994). But in the course of the 1980s and 1990s, Dominicans established their own salons. In an article on the city's Dominican beauty culture industry, Ginetta Candelario (2000: 131) claims that "The post-1980 flow of Dominican women into beauty shop occupations—whether as owners, hairdressers, manicurists, shampoo girls, estheticians, or masseurs—reflects simultaneously changes in the New York economy from manufacturing to service industries, changes in the demographics of the Washington Heights area, and changes in Dominican beauty culture in the Dominican Republic as well." As she puts it,

> in the Dominican Republic beauty culture has come to be seen as a respectable and professional field. Although commercial beauty shops have existed in the Dominican Republic since at least the 1930s, they generally serviced the elite. The majority of Dominican beauty culturalists operated out of their homes until the 1980s. Typically these shops were located in a converted front room, patio, or garage space and consisted of an owner-operator and a young neighborhood assistant. Shop owner-operators and assistants alike were considered nearly at par with domestic workers, and thus were of low socio-economic status.... In the early 1980s, however, beauty culturalists began to professionalize, via the establishment of a professional organization, Asociación de Estilistas Dominicanas (Dominican Hair Stylists Association), the proliferation of beauty schools and certification programs, and a shift from the use of domestic and home-manufactured products to an increasing reliance upon hair-care products and technologies imported from the United States. Beauty shop work, in other words, has come to be viewed as a skilled profession one trains for and pursues. (2000: 132)

Most Dominican salons in New York City are in small locales. Music is typically playing at the shop, often merengue and salsa. Sometimes the television is turned on as well, and the blow-dryers are frequently working. The majority of the salons are run by their owners. From five to seven women (including the owner-operator) work in an average-sized shop. The bulk of the Dominican salons in New York are open seven days a week. They have a solid market: "Dominican women use salons for regular weekly hair care, not for intermittent haircuts and hair treatments. Therefore, there is a steady demand throughout the week, although Fridays and Saturdays are still the busiest days" (Candelario 2000: 134). The majority of Dominican women in New York City become beauty shop customers around the age of fifteen, while many Dominican men frequent beauty shops regularly.

A large proportion of the Dominican salons are still neighborhood institutions that primarily serve Dominicans and some other Latinas/os. But a growing number of the Dominican salons (especially if they are located, not in Washington Heights, but instead in Harlem, the Bronx, Queens, or Brooklyn) are now frequented also by African American and West Indian women. Much like New York City Koreans, who have made nail salons their business, Dominican women have increasingly made hair styling their niche in the city, as described in the *New York Times* in 1999:

> On this northern stretch of Broadway [in a part of Harlem, at 143rd Street], hair salons that are owned and operated by Dominicans are everywhere, and inside, black Americans are present in great numbers. The same scene is repeated throughout the city. . . . Not surprisingly, African-American salon owners and stylists accuse Dominicans of everything from incompetence to undercutting with shamelessly low prices. Yet Dominican stylists have increasingly been able to build up a varied clientele among African-American women—from bookkeepers to babysitters and writers to waiters—largely through word of mouth. (Williams 1999: B1)[13]

The same article points out the reasons for the Dominican success:

> Most Dominicans—many of whom are black or of mixed race and accustomed to handling black hair—set a client's wet hair in jumbo-sized rollers. When it's dry, they blow out most of the curl. This process, according to Dominicans, is less damaging to the hair than the typical method of washing and blow drying because less heat is used. . . . Another difference between black American and Dominican salons: Dominican-owned beauty parlors are by and large less expensive than African-American-owned shops. A wash-and-set at a Dominican salon might cost as little as $10 or $15, while an African-American salon on average charges twice that or more. (B1, B8)

* * *

In this chapter we have seen how the Dominican immigrants with whom I worked consistently incorporated their memories of how they and others had taken part in the creation and building of a network of Dominican small businesses in the city into a wider and more comprehensive history, a narrative of conspicuous economic, social, and demographic changes New York had witnessed over the past decades, particularly from the mid-1960s to the late 1980s. In addition, I have stressed that the Dominican migrants who have become business owners are very heterogeneous; most were part of the Dominican popular classes when they emigrated; a minority were professionals—they had graduated from a Dominican university before they left. In any case, almost all began their new life in the United States with little or no capital. Only a few arrived in the United States as part of a wealthy Dominican family.

In Chapters 3 and 4, I shift the focus to practices and activities at the time of the fieldwork. The main questions I deal with in these chapters are the following: How are the Dominican immigrants' businesses created—that is, established? How are they organized and run?

PART II

CHAPTER 3

From Bodegas to Supermarkets

So far I have described how informants accounted for the emergence of Dominican-owned businesses in New York City and how they emphasized that Dominican immigrants had used ties with kin and friends to raise the capital needed and to develop their own economic enterprises. In this chapter and the next, I look more closely at Dominican-owned businesses' characteristics, examining Dominican immigrants' enterprises as configurations of practices and relations. While this chapter looks at those businesses that are typically owned by a single man or woman, or by two or three or four individuals together (such as bodegas, restaurants, and supermarkets), the next chapter analyzes the Dominican car service. As mentioned, most Dominican-controlled car services are cooperatives.

The key structural factor in understanding why so many Dominican immigrants in New York have ended up in small business and forms of self-employment is what has been called the United States' segmented labor market (Sanders and Nee 1987; Mar 1991; Park 1997). Kyeyoung Park sketches this in the following way:

> workers are separated into two or more labor markets with different job characteristics and outcomes. Primary and secondary labor market segments are characterized by differences in human capital returns, job tenure, working conditions, wages, and promotional opportunities. There are two main sources of exclusion from the primary market, which tend to operate even if all other qualifications are equal. One is a gender disqualification strongly influencing the conditions of female employment; the other is a racial/ethnic disqualification. Therefore ... immigrants, particularly ethnic groups, are relegated to the secondary labor market. ... Jobs in the

secondary labor markets are shunned by native-born workers. (Park 1997: 43)

According to Park, the segmented labor market explains why so many first-generation Korean immigrants in New York City have gravitated to small business and self-employment. The same can be said about the Dominicans. The U.S. segmented labor market goes a long way toward explaining why so many Dominican immigrants in New York have ended in small business.

In addition, it is important to note three other factors. First, as we have seen in the foregoing chapter, first-generation Dominican immigrants often had little knowledge of English. If they were professionals with a degree from a Dominican university, their professional certificates were often not recognized. And even a person who had a certificate recognized usually had problems with the language. All this has made it difficult for most first-generation Dominican immigrants to obtain a job where they make significantly more than minimum wage. Second, for New York, the service sector was the major employer in the 1980s and 1990s; but most service-sector jobs have low wages and little security. Many in the service sector earn only the legal minimum wage or slightly more; many earn less than the minimum wage. And third, Dominican immigrants (like immigrants from Korea and a number of other countries) entered the city's small-business economy at a time when it was undergoing important change. During the 1960s and 1970s, many neighborhoods were losing their traditional retail businesses as white owners retired or moved away to the suburbs. But at the same time, the total population of potential customers in these same neighborhoods was growing. In *The Future of Us All*, Roger Sanjek has drawn a detailed picture from Queens:

> Immigrants arriving in Queens during the 1960s and 1970s found a borough losing its retail base as white American proprietors moved away or retired, and at the same time increasing its population of potential customers. While retail businesses fell by 1,200 during the 1960s—an average loss of ninety stores per community district—Queens gained 177,000 residents, and annual retail sales grew from $1.7 billion to $2.4 billion. The majority of immigrant-owned businesses in [Queens] were of the very types being abandoned by white Americans—gift and electronics shops, laundries and dry cleaners, newsstands and liquor stores, meat and fish stores, convenience groceries and fruit and vegetable stands, drugstores and florists, barbers

and beauty salons, furniture and pet stores, clothing and shoe stores—and they competed for customers of all backgrounds. (1998: 65)

Overall, the city was a profitable frontier for immigrant entrepreneurs. Among those who were willing to pioneer were Dominican immigrants. This chapter is divided into three main sections. First, I look more closely at the processes by which Dominican small-business owners obtain capital. Second, I examine aspects of the recruitment of labor and of the relations between owners and employees. In the third and last section, I discuss features of the everyday life in some representative Dominican-owned businesses—in a small, popular restaurant and in two bodegas, all three situated in Upper Manhattan.

Capital

Dominican immigrants who have obtained small businesses have used their own savings and borrowed money from kin, friends, and moneylenders. Most of those who have opened a store, a restaurant, or another form of business have, in addition, relied on receiving supplies on credit. Only a minority have borrowed money from banks.

Today, in immigrant neighborhoods in New York City, the private moneylenders (called "loan sharks" by some) may be said to constitute a mainstream institution, financing everything from tiny disbursements and airline tickets to bodegas and discos for the poor and the middle class alike. Dominican immigrants call them *los prestamistas*. While most *prestamistas* lend money at illegal interest rates, some compete more directly with ordinary banks. Among Dominicans in Washington Heights and the Bronx, they are usually said to be fast, reliable, and often flexible and understanding.

There are a number of reasons Dominican and other immigrants use *prestamistas* and not banks. Some people say that they are doing what is normal in the Dominican Republic, where the poor most often do not use banks. Some do not use regular banks because they are undocumented migrants. But by far the most important reason is that most Dominican immigrants take it for granted that it is extremely difficult to obtain a bank loan. Many Dominican immigrants with whom I talked had themselves been turned down for loans at mainstream banks, and many said they did not even bother to apply. Many people need only relatively small loans. As Granovetter (1995: 140) has said, many are not classified as creditworthy by big banks or formal lending institutions "because the investigation required to support small loans would be uneconomical." In other cases, Dominican immigrants are turned down for a loan because they are not able to provide a bank with all the documentation and information required.

New York law caps interest rates on most bank loans at 25 percent per year, 16 percent on person-to-person loans. At the time of the research, the going rate among *prestamistas* who lent money to immigrants in northern Manhattan and the Bronx was frequently 2 to 5 percent per week—about 104 to 260 percent per year. Nevertheless, Dominican immigrants did everything they could to fulfill their obligations. People would pay the interest rates because they wanted the access to credit. Their creditworthiness depended on their reputation. If a person had already shown that he or she was able to pay off a loan, his or her creditworthiness had been improved. I heard little about forms of intimidation and coercion to force repayment.[1]

Some alternatives do exist. Northern Manhattan and other areas with many immigrants contain a number of nonprofit groups. Some of these promote small-business development and make loans to owners of small economic enterprises. One of these organizations is the Audubon Partnership for Economic Development, an Inwood-based corporation created in 1996 that provides lending and development services for Dominican immigrants and others engaged in small business in northern Manhattan; it is headed by a Dominican immigrant. Another nonprofit organization in the area that makes small loans to businesses is the Washington Heights and Inwood Development Corporation. Entities like these represent an alternative both to the moneylender and to the mainstream bank. Some Dominican immigrants with small businesses have begun to use these nonprofits. But this is still like a drop in the ocean. Most Dominicans in Washington Heights and elsewhere in the city who need a small business loan still use the *prestamistas*. Although the latter charge high interest rates, they ask relatively few questions and deliver the loan fast.

Access to credit is conditioned by class position. Some Dominicans do not have to use moneylenders but get ordinary business loans through mainstream banks. The majority in this group are men and women who have been successful—people who started with little but now control resources. Some of these now use only bank loans. Others (like Chelo Ramírez, the Caridad owner, described in Chapter 2) continue to use their regular *prestamistas* in combination with bank loans. One reason may be that some *prestamistas* are willing to drop interest rates significantly for their best, most reliable, and loyal customers; in such cases, substantial loans may be made at a 20 percent annual rate or less.

A striking example of how social mobility improves access to credit and, hence, ability to raise capital may be seen among those Dominicans who have become owners of supermarkets. An important change took place in the city's independent supermarket industry in the mid-1990s. At that time, Chase Manhattan Bank (now JP Morgan Chase) started a lending program for independent supermarket owners in New York. The program was designed to provide access to capital for independent grocers who operated in low-to-moderate-income neighborhoods. A large proportion of those who have borrowed money through the program have been Dominican immigrants who were previously viewed as "nonbankable." They have borrowed money to obtain a new store, to purchase or upgrade equipment, or to buy the building that houses a store. The program started to operate in 1996, and it has since made Chase the dominant bank in this market. Between 1996 and 2003, Chase lent over $40 million to Dominican and other operators of independent supermarkets in the New York area.

Before 1996, the leaders among the Dominican supermarket owners would tell me, they had not obtained bank loans. "Nonbankable" Dominican supermarket owners had financed their stores through loans from two main sources: the owner's principal supplier (Krasdale Foods or Associated Wholesalers) and the *prestamistas*. The interest rates charged by Krasdale and Associated were high. With a bank loan instead of a loan from Krasdale or Associated, the supermarket owner saved money and also strengthened his or her independence. The relationship between an independent supermarket owner and his or her supplier may be of two kinds. If Krasdale or Associated has lent the owner money, the latter is less free to get significant parts of the supplies from other companies. If no direct loan is involved, the supermarket owner is freer to maximize profits in the market.

The discourse on the transition from being "nonbankable" to being "bankable" was used by Dominican owners of supermarkets in two different ways. They sometimes used it with reference to the Dominican immigrants who now owned supermarkets as a group—a collective. Used in this way, the discourse on having finally become bankable celebrated the economic success and strengthened recognition of people who had been able to take over an impressive part of an important industry. On other occasions, the speaker referred not to the past of a group but to that of an individual, describing his or her own transition from being nonbankable to being bankable. Two things were underscored in these situations: the shift to bank loans made it possible to save money and, hence, increase profits, and it secured enhanced autonomy.

This does not mean that Dominican-owned independent supermarkets are now financed only by means of bank loans. Far from it. Dominican immigrants who purchase a supermarket still use kin and friends to raise initial capital. Many continue to be "nonbankable"; they must, therefore, borrow from moneylenders and from Krasdale or Associated. The situation is especially difficult for those who attempt to obtain their first supermarket. In these cases, people usually have limited capital and fewer contacts in the industry; if they do not get a bank loan, they must pay high interest rates. In comparison, those who have already successfully operated a supermarket probably find it relatively easy to get a bank loan to purchase a second supermarket.

It would not have been possible for Dominican immigrants to obtain small businesses to the extent they have had it not been for their capacity to raise initial capital by mobilizing family members and friends. Usually, one first managed to save some money, then raised more with the aid of kin and friends, and finally got a loan from a moneylender. This was well illustrated by Luis Salcedo, executive director of the National Supermarkets Association, who said that to purchase an independent supermarket in New York in the 1970s, one would need just $100,000, but things had changed much since then; now (in 2002, the year we spoke) it was necessary to have at least $500,000. If you have half a million, you can go to the *prestamistas*, Krasdale, the bank, and so on. He then said, "Today it is very difficult for a person with a small bodega to put aside the amount of money one needs to obtain a supermarket.... As I said, the minimum amount is half a million. How can a person with just a small store save $500,000?" But relatives help; "Almost always. I'd say that 98 percent [of those who purchase their first store] have relatives [who help them]—brothers, cousins, sisters, wives.... Our traditions, the solidarity of the family and the importance of friendship—this is extremely important to be able to succeed."

When a Dominican—on the island or in the United States—speaks of the *familia* or family, he or she often refers to a large but loosely organized network of persons. Above the level of the household, the basis for construction of kinship is personal kindred. This personal kindred is individual-centered and bilateral by nature: that is, it consists of persons who are related to a particular individual on both the father's and the mother's sides. These personal kindreds are only apparent when mobilized. Historically, personal kindreds have become visible in connection with life-cycle rituals, especially funerals. They have also been among the most important building blocks when people have made, remade, and modified everyday life. Dominicans have drawn on their personal kindred and mobilized relatives when developing and organizing agricultural activities, trade, and businesses. The use of *la familia* has also played a crucial part of the country's political life. Kindreds have been put to use to shape and reshape leaderships, factions, political parties, and the public sector (Derby 2009; Krohn-Hansen 2009).

Many Dominican immigrants in New York have been able to raise capital with the aid of relatives and friends in part because they have had access to a considerable number of kin. Even though most Dominicans have been poor, access to a large family has in itself been a resource that has helped enlarge the action space and open possibilities. Let us briefly look at why a person's family has often included many people.

Population growth in the Dominican Republic has been high since official census taking began in 1920. The country's overall fertility rate was estimated at 6.8 in 1970. It declined substantially in the 1970s, and in the late 1990s was estimated at around 2.8. Many Dominican immigrants have had a significant number of brothers and sisters and often many uncles, aunts, and male and female cousins. Such relationships have been put to use. Luis Salcedo is the oldest of eleven children. He purchased his first personal business with a cousin in 1984. Six years later, he and the cousin bought a new store together, larger than the first one. Thereafter Luis obtained his first supermarket.

Chelo, too, worked together with his family. His older brother had developed the first Dominican Caridad restaurants. When I met Chelo, he and three older brothers and a sister, five out of fifteen siblings, ran most of their businesses together. When Fernando Mella, Chelo's *socio* in the Caridad restaurant in Marble Hill, sold his deli in Co-op City to become Chelo's partner, he sold to his cousins. Fernando's cousins, as mentioned in the previous chapter, did not have much capital, so they gave Fernando what they had, the rest being a debt that had to be paid off weekly; in the meantime, Fernando remained the legal owner. As he put it, he had so far only sold the store *de palabra*—based on a verbal agreement. But this gave his cousins the help they needed.

The fact that Dominicans' personal kindred often include many people should also be viewed in the light of hegemonic popular images of masculinity. Many ordinary Dominican men's relations to women are paradoxical (Krohn-Hansen 1996: 115–16, 2009: 134–38). On the one hand, a man is expected to be *mujeriego*, a womanizer, engaged in sexual conquest even when he is married or living in a stable union. An image of masculinity closely linked to that of the man as a womanizer is that of him as one who is always ready to party with his male friends, drinking, listening and dancing to music, and telling stories: dominant notions of masculinity say that a man should be a *bebedor* (drinker), a *bailador* (dancer), and *fiestero* (fun-lover). On the other hand, the man is also supposed to be a good husband and father, providing for his woman and children. Hence, ordinary men's negotiation of masculinity is caught in a tension between contradictory ideals. As a result, many men and quite a few women have children with more than one partner. When I lived in La Descubierta in the Dominican southwest in the early 1990s, it was not unusual for a man to have more than fifteen or twenty children with several different women. A few older men of some economic means maintained two or three households at the same time. Personal kindreds include also half sisters and half brothers. Some in addition maintain a tie to a stepfather or stepmother. We saw an example of this with Benito Paulino in the preceding chapter.

As noted previously, many grow up in a household headed by a woman. The number of households headed by women is significant both in the Dominican Republic and among Dominicans in New York (Walker 1972; Georges 1990; Gilbertson and Gurak 1992; Pessar 1995; Brennan 2004; Gregory 2007). The situation is a product of at least two factors—first, the political and economic processes that leave so many Dominicans with generally few resources and, second, Dominican vernacular images of masculinity and femininity. Often there is a flow of children between households. A woman who finds it hard to provide for her children may arrange for one or several of them to live for a time, or some years, in the household of a sister, a brother, or another relative. When I lived in La Descubierta, my landlady's household was regularly visited by three women in their early twenties who lived in the Dominican capital. They were my landlady's sister's daughters, but had been raised by my landlady in La Descubierta and continued to call her "mother" and their biological mother "aunt." For her part, my landlady had to send her seven-year-old son to the capital, where he was raised by her sister with the latter's children who continued to live in their mother's household. Two other children sent by kin came to live for a shorter period in my landlady's household during the time I resided in La Descubierta. Similar practices remain widespread.² The circulation of children between households often leads to enlargement of people's kin networks. And, finally, personal kindreds include also ritual kin—godparents, coparents, and godchildren.

Dominican immigrants in New York maintain and reproduce family ties in everyday life and ritual. Their use of such ties to raise capital and create businesses should be seen as rooted in other practices that tie the family together. Many send money to, and telephone frequently, one or more relatives in the home country, and many visit relatives on the island, for example, over Christmas or in the summer. If they have purchased a plot of land or a home or a small business on the island, they may have recruited a kinsman or kinswoman to look after it. Visits go in the other direction also. People who live on the island go to New York to spend time in the apartment of a relative. Often these persons have previously lived and worked in New York but have now moved back to the island.

Sometimes kinship ties are renewed and reinforced through large gatherings or parties. Hugo Cruz, who had immigrated from Puerto Plata in 1965 and, when I met him, was in his late forties and, together with his *socio*, owned two independent supermarkets in different parts of the Bronx, told me that he had an enormous number of relatives—aunts, uncles, cousins—in the United States. Most of them lived in New York and New Jersey, but some lived in Florida and Puerto Rico, even in California. He said that a large reunion was often held in a home or a park during the summer. Two years earlier, in 2000, Hugo had thrown a party where he had invited his family; 280 family members had been there, all persons who lived in the United States. In 2003, he said, he would invite the family to a reunion in the Dominican Republic. In this way, family members who lived in the United States and others who lived in the Dominican Republic could spend a day together. The reunion was scheduled to take place during the Christmas period on a farm situated near Puerto Plata. The farm had once belonged to Hugo's father, then to others, before Hugo bought it back in 2001; he had hired relatives living in the area to run it.

Three features of Dominican immigrants' family relationships may explain why many have been able to draw on these relationships to raise capital for development of small businesses. First, kinship ties can only be used efficiently for such purposes if they function in a climate in which exchanges are backed by mutual trust, or what Alejandro Portes (1995: 14) calls "enforceable trust." The kinship institution must be in a strong position; people must deeply identify with discourses and practices asserting that relatives ought to exchange favors and stick together. The Dominican Republic's political and social history in the twentieth century produced such a climate.

Second, Dominicans have obtained money through alliances with different types of relatives. Some have used brothers and sisters, some cousins, and some an uncle or an aunt. Others have got help from a half brother, a brother-in-law, or a sister-in-law. Dominicans' kin relationships are characterized by a certain looseness and by flexibility; this has, in turn, widened Dominican immigrants' room for maneuvering and creative action.

Third, many have had access to a considerable number of relatives. This too has helped broaden the space for action—for exchanges of services, shared savings, and efficient resource pooling. Aspects of the migration process have been significant too. The Dominican migration to New York has unfolded through "chains." A chain links one immigrant to another; people have either acted as pioneers and formed a new chain or linked themselves with an established chain. What has connected the members of a chain has, for the most part, been kinship. This helps explain why many Dominican immigrants not only have had a considerable number of relatives but also, increasingly, have had very many of these in New York. People have used the family both to organize and give form to the emigration process and to try to raise capital after they have arrived. Sometimes the two processes have almost become fused. One day while we sat in his regular restaurant in Inwood, José Delio Marte painted a vivid picture:

> If we analyze it, we see that our businesses, the sort of businesses we all do, go from hand to hand. [An example:] If you are my brother and I have a business and the business is good, and if you would like to obtain your own business, then—what I do—I say: "Well, let me give them a call, let me go to the bank and ask them to give my brother a loan." Or I say to my brother: "I sell you 50 percent of the business and keep the other half. You give me a sum weekly—you send it to me in Santo Domingo." In the Dominican Republic, there are hundreds of people like that, people who have retired and own 50 percent of a business here, or they own one third, and they are sent their money monthly. So, the last one who has arrived is the one who remains, he's the one who is here. And when he leaves, a new person begins. When he is finished, a new person comes, and that's how it is. The family—all the members of the family [left on the island] are dreaming. I have seen families in Santo Domingo—for example, in San José

de Las Matas I met a boy, he's fifteen years of age. When he is twenty-two, he will take over a bodega in New York. He said, "That's how we do it. Carlos has finished. He gave the bodega to Juan. Juan will give it to Francisco, who is now nineteen." Then Francisco must give it to the fifteen-year-old I met. Juan gave me my 50 percent. Francisco will give Juan his half. In Santo Domingo, there are businesses which operate that way.

Mark Granovetter (1995: 145) has claimed, "What we must look for . . . in understanding successful entrepreneurial activity, is some combination of social cohesion sufficient to enforce standards of fair business dealing and an atmosphere of trust, along with circumstances that limit the noneconomic claims on a business that prevent its rationalization." So far, I have sought to examine how Dominican immigrants use the mutual trust and solidarity that exist between kin to produce capital and obtain businesses. In the following, I look at Granovetter's second question: what prevents an "uncontrolled solidarity, which produces excessive noneconomic claims on an enterprise"? (1995: 137)[3]

Dominican businesses in New York do not employ overly large staffs. Nor do they seem to be eroded by excessive claims of relatives. How do we explain this?

Dominicans are used to private property. Land was turned into a commodity in all parts of the country during the late nineteenth and early twentieth centuries (Franks 1995; Baud 1995: 153–65; San Miguel 1997b: 199–220; Turits 2003: 1–114). Businesses and factories have been privately owned. Modern Dominicans emphasize family solidarity, but they also cultivate persons' right and ability to act autonomously—to be independent. Caribbean societies have often been said to value and maintain personal independence (Wilson 1969; Mintz [1974] 1989: 37–38, 155–56; Olwig 1993: 131–35). Based on the fieldwork I carried out in the Dominican southwest in the early 1990s, I have written elsewhere:

> A personal treasure guarded by men and women alike was the room for independence or autonomy. . . . In La Descubierta, men sought continuously to shape their own independence or autonomy as a kind of "free mobility" when they interacted with others. The formation of groups of men in the streets, in the park, and in the bars, was characterized by flow and considerable looseness. . . . A rule of these daily

encounters was articulated sharply one day in the park. With some twenty men, I was waiting for a car that would take us to the cockfight arena of a neighboring village. Along came a man with two others. One of my group called out his name and greeted him with a "Where are you heading?" The man's response to the salutation, expressed loudly at a few meters' distance, was that "Nobody asks me where I am going." (Krohn-Hansen 2009: 138)

When I asked Dominican immigrants why they had ended up in the small-business sector, it was striking how often people responded that it had been, or was, a means to—as they put it—*independizarse* (to become more independent): in contrast, many said, to being employed in a factory.

The familiarity with private ownership and the belief in persons' right to freedom have served as an ideological basis for Dominican immigrants' economic and social activities. People have taken for granted that enterprises belong to, and are run in a sovereign manner by, those who own them. There is a considerable overlap here between hegemonic U.S. values and the values of Dominicans.

Dominican businesses have also been shielded by Dominican small-business owners' ideas about what produces value—what produces money. Dominican small-business owners have, like other immigrants, worked hard. They know that the source of profit is labor. This has made it possible to create and maintain a boundary between those in the family who have contributed labor and those who have not. This boundary has been used to limit the extent of solidarity between kin. We may see an example in the story of Eligio Peña and his brothers. In 1978, they pooled their resources to purchase a large bodega in Queens. At the same time, they founded a family company. The brothers all bought shares in the company, but only some of them worked in it (or in the bodega). Only those who actually worked in the store received a regular salary; the others had only their respective stakes in the company. The same system has been used by the family to this day. We see another example in the history of the Caridad restaurants. At the time of the fieldwork, Chelo and three brothers and a sister cooperated. They started, operated, and sold Caridad restaurants. All worked in the family business and distributed tasks. The five had many more siblings, but, outside the group, the solidarity dropped sharply.

Two other circumstances have been important.[4] First, many enterprises have struggled to survive. Many have gone into bankruptcy. This has been recognized and has helped protect the businesses against excessive claims. Second, Dominicans who have succeeded—like Dominican owners of independent supermarkets—efficiently ward off claims by hiring employees according to the market. They mainly employ workers to whom no special allegiance is owed. Dominican owners of independent supermarkets employ Dominicans, African Americans, Mexicans, Ecuadorans, Puerto Ricans, and so on; they pay them based on the going wages in the labor market.

It is often said about economic history that "a rising tide lifts all banks." According to this argument, we would expect ethnic minorities' entrepreneurs "to have difficulty in hard times but to succeed during an economic boom" (Granovetter 1995: 153). Granovetter argues the opposite: that minority groups' entrepreneurial activity—if it operates relatively efficiently—finds its main advantage in a weakened economy. In "a highly favorable macroeconomic situation in which entry of firms is relatively easy, capital can be raised without difficulty, and profits have not yet been squeezed," established businesses will most often continue to do well. But with a weakened economy there is no margin for error; profit is reduced and credit gets tight. Under such economic conditions, enterprises based on kinship ties and other informal relationships may have an advantage (154–55). Granovetter also suggests that the advantage of such businesses is especially pertinent "in industries with low barriers to entry, and where trust rather than technical knowledge is the most valuable commodity" (155).

This is important for understanding why certain groups of Dominican immigrants who entered particular retail industries, like grocery stores and small and medium-sized supermarkets, in New York in the late 1960s, the 1970s and the first part of the 1980s were able to do so (relatively) well. As previously mentioned, in the mid-1970s the city was hit by a grave fiscal crisis. "Overall, the city budget shrank 22 percent between 1975 and 1983, and service cuts affected every aspect of neighborhood New York life" (Sanjek 1998: 93). In this economic and social landscape, immigrants from the Dominican Republic and other countries entered the city's retail businesses in great numbers. For this, they raised capital and developed enterprises with the aid of kinship. A few of those who entered the city's retail businesses during the 1970s and 1980s did strikingly well, while many just barely survived and yet others failed. Some of those Dominicans who did especially well during the 1970s and 1980s had entered food retail—or groceries and independent supermarkets. Food retail is an industry with low barriers to entry, where trust rather than technical knowledge is the most valuable commodity.

Another cornerstone of Dominican society has been friendship (Hoetink 1982; Georges 1990). Dominican immigrants who have sought to obtain money and develop businesses have done this not only through the kinship institution but also with the aid of friendship. The value of friendship is recognized in all strata of Dominican society—by women and men alike. Native discourse articulates the strength of the friendship tie in terms of the degree of *confianza* or trust. *Confianza* denotes "mutual readiness to engage in reciprocal exchange" (Lomnitz 1977: 4). Friendships have simultaneously political, material, social, and cultural elements—that is, they are simultaneously useful and emotional. Friends sometimes strengthen and cement their friendship by choosing each other as the *padrino* (godfather) and *madrina* (godmother) for their children; they thereby become *compadres* and *comadres*—ritual kin. Friendships occur both between social equals and between patrons and clients. Much of the political, economic, and cultural life in today's Dominican Republic is deeply shaped by the ongoing exchanges between patrons and clients (Krohn-Hansen 2009: 49–156).

One of the many Dominican immigrants in New York who have turned their ability to cultivate friendship into practical use is Fernando Mella, whose story we learned in the previous chapter.

Fernando himself had a clear understanding of how important his friendships had been to what he had become and had obtained. He said, "My businesses have come by chance—and owing to a series of things, like having friends, friendships, and being in the middle of things where one learns about things; I'm a guy who is very open, and I like conversation, I like people." Fernando said, "I've always had as a principle that I prefer that, if someone has to lose his property, it should be me, not the other. I always like to leave by the main entrance."

A term used by Dominicans and Dominican immigrants alike to express the degree of men's trustworthiness—and creditworthiness—as partners in reciprocal exchange, is *serio*, "serious."[5] A good man, Dominicans and Dominican immigrants say, should be *serio*: that is, he should meet his obligations, not cheat or steal. *Serio* is a fundamental category; it refers simultaneously to the moral, the economic, and the political. To claim that a man isn't *serio* is to imply that he is a *sinvergüenza*, or shameless.

These relationships between kin and friends have helped many. But it is important to understand that they have their rules. These ties involve constant give and take. They do not come easily. Above all, they demand considerable willingness to keep resources in circulation. Fernando expressed this also; he had sold his previous business, a deli, to his cousins. When I spoke with Fernando, his cousins still owed him the bulk of the purchase price:

> Sometimes in business one does things according to other norms—to do business isn't cheap, nor is it easy [*los negocios no son baratos, no es tan fácil*]. Almost no one here has money saved up—cash. Most often what one does is to make a deal where one trusts the other person's word; it is agreed that the business can be paid off weekly. You don't get the money right away.

Friendships may also be of use if one needs a loan from a moneylender, a supplier, or a bank. Dominican immigrants who already have established a good reputation often help their close friends by recommending them. Luis Salcedo gave an example. Previously, Luis stated, he had, like most others, to borrow from moneylenders, but now he uses only banks. When I first met him in 2002, he had just helped a good friend. The friend's supermarket was financed with loans from moneylenders at high interest rates. Luis called Chase (or JP Morgan Chase) and recommended the bank give his friend a loan. Chase lent the friend $1 million, and his loan service expenses dropped substantially.

Dominican immigrants who have achieved a good reputation as businessmen are often asked for advice by compatriots. In Washington Heights and Inwood, for example, many have over the years consulted José Delio Marte and men and women like him, regarded as skillful, experienced, and generous. Before purchasing a bodega or opening a new restaurant, for example, people have asked for José's views on the business's location and potential. Others have asked for a viewpoint on financing. A man who is frequently asked for an opinion by friends is Eligio Peña. Eligio is not only a pioneer and the most successful of those Dominicans who own supermarkets; he is also extroverted and cheerful and likes to be with others. When I was with him in late November 2002, he had just been consulted by one of his friends. I reproduce Eligio's story about this below because it shows the continued importance of these networks marked by *confianza* or mutual readiness to engage in reciprocity, even among Dominicans who have experienced a fair amount of mobility, and illustrates that these networks are transnational in nature—they connect people in New York and the Dominican Republic.

Sometime before we spoke, Eligio had been contacted by a friend who lived in Santo Domingo. Roberto Despradel, who had operated a considerable business in the Dominican Republic, had gone bankrupt. He had never lived in the United States and knew little English. In the Dominican capital, he had discussed his situation with Eligio's son. The latter had called his father and asked him to try to help. Shortly after this, Roberto went to New York where he met Eligio. After describing his financial situation, he asked his friend what he could do. Roberto owned a house worth $1 million and a commercial building worth around $300,000; Eligio said he should sell his house and invest the money in a business and, when Roberto refused, insisted, "Live in the present! Don't live in the past!"

Roberto then decided that he should move to the United States. Shortly afterward, he again consulted Eligio. Roberto wanted to purchase a supermarket in New York; the maximum price he could pay was $2.3 million. Eligio told Roberto that, since he spoke little English and was not familiar with the ways in which business was done in the United States, he should get a store that was mostly "Hispanic"—a supermarket with mostly Spanish-speaking customers. Eligio knew about a supermarket that might be suitable, in Rhode Island. "Do you want to live in Rhode Island?" he asked. Roberto said that he had a sister who lived there, that it sounded good. Eligio then asked him to call his sister. Roberto later called Eligio and told him that his sister knew the store well and liked it; her son worked there. Eligio knew the owner and called him, saying, "Look, I know you have two supermarkets and that it takes you three hours by car to get from one store to the other. Do you want to sell your store in Rhode Island?" The owner replied that he had not thought about it, but might consider it. Eligio said it was for a Dominican friend, a man who did not know English, adding that the two of them could meet and discuss it—and that he could pay the owner $1 million immediately.

After that, Eligio recommended that Roberto borrow $700,000; with that sum, he would have $1.7 million. The rest, he said, Roberto would have to negotiate with the owner. Thereafter, Roberto bought the store and moved to Rhode Island. Eligio said that his friend now got much help from his nephew—his sister's son who had already been employed when Roberto bought the business. This man, who had grown up in the United States, was fluent in English.

As we have seen, kin and friends who are business partners label each other *socios*. *Sociedades* or partnerships are essentially based on trust, not juridical documents (though some completed forms and other papers documenting the existence of the partnership often exist). We should view the *sociedad* form as a flexible, open form. The term *sociedad*, as it is used by

Dominican immigrants, refers to different types of arrangements. There can be a *sociedad* when two or three or four individuals own and run a small business together. The term is also used when a large number of cab drivers together establish a car service. Those who together own such an enterprise are called *socios* or partners; a car service may have over 50 *socios*. Finally, a *sociedad* may be a rotating credit association temporarily organized by a small group of relatives and friends, usually ten persons.

The history of one small business, a bookstore in Washington Heights, illustrates the *sociedad* institution's elasticity and adaptability. When I began the fieldwork in 2002, this small store was owned by two *socios*, Santiago Cepeda and José Muñoz. They sold books in Spanish and had mostly Dominicans and other Latinos as customers. The store had been established fifteen years earlier, not by Santiago and José but by Santiago and his brother. At the time of my fieldwork, Santiago was in his mid-forties. He had spent his first fourteen years in Santo Domingo, before moving first to Puerto Rico and then to the Bronx with his parents and siblings. He studied business administration at Baruch College and got a job in the Metropolitan Life Insurance Company (MetLife). In the mid-1980s, he and his brother started to buy books in Spanish from Spanish, Argentine, and Mexican publishers for sale in New York. They sold the books during their spare time, in the street, at Hostos Community College in the Bronx, during the Annual Dominican Day Parade in Manhattan, and so on. In 1987, they rented a location in Washington Heights and opened a bookstore. Santiago and the brother owned 50 percent each, and Santiago kept his job at MetLife. His brother took care of the store in the daytime five days a week, while Santiago worked there in the evenings and during the weekends.

Several years after the bookstore opened, Santiago's brother got a good job in the publishing business in Puerto Rico. He sold his part of the store to Santiago and moved. For some time, Santiago owned the store alone, but in the late 1990s, he recruited a new *socio*—José, a Colombian immigrant who lived in Queens and had spent over twenty years in the city. When he became Santiago's *socio*, José had a well-paid job in the Calvin Klein company. He and Santiago had been friends for over a decade and had common intellectual interests. In 2002, Santiago no longer worked at MetLife. His wife, a Salvadoran immigrant, had an office job. Santiago took care of the store in the daytime. José, who still worked for Calvin Klein, looked after the store in the evenings and during weekends.

Santiago said he had decided to recruit a new *socio* because the store needed fresh ideas, a new perspective. Also, Santiago wanted to expand. He had found a bookstore in Queens that he wanted to buy; it was well established and had a good location and a larger turnover than the store in Washington Heights. It sold books in Spanish and was situated in an area with different groups of Latinos—Colombians, Dominicans, Ecuadorans, and Argentines. The store's owner was old and wanted to sell. In this situation, Santiago needed José's help. The latter had lived in Queens for many years and was a Colombian; having worked for many years for Calvin Klein in the city's garment industry, he knew a number of Jewish and Italian moneylenders well. José raised over $300,000 with the aid of moneylenders (Santiago had already been turned down by banks), but the owner in Queens demanded $500,000 in cash as a first installment to sell. The negotiations dragged on, and finally Santiago and José gave up; half a million in cash, they said, was too much, so they refrained from buying. In the meantime, their bookstore in Washington Heights did badly in the recession of the early 2000s, even though it began to sell quartz stones and quartz decorations in addition to books.

In 2004, Santiago and José chose to sell 50 percent of the business to two new *socios*, Dominicans who lived in the neighborhood. The store now had four *socios*, each owning 25 percent. With four men who could work in the store, the partners extended the opening hours. When I visited them in August 2004, they also planned to make other minor changes to try to increase sales. At that time, Santiago did not spend much time in the store. Instead, he spent much of his time on two other projects: expanding another business that he had started previously and seeking to establish a completely new store. This was possible because he had got fresh capital by selling a part of the bookstore. The business he had started earlier was an enterprise that sold books in the street. It was operated by Santiago and a *socio*; they had recruited trusted persons who sold the books in the street in different places in the city. Santiago's other project was to rent a space and start a new store—for books and other products—in the heart of Washington Heights, in a commercially important part of the neighborhood. The rent that he and his three *socios* paid was relatively low. If he started a new store, the rent would be much higher, but he would be in a commercially more dynamic and attractive area.

Labor

This section examines the ways Dominican enterprises obtain and manage labor power. I first look at the norms that regulate co-owners' respective work contribution. I thereafter discuss a feature that characterizes nearly all these economic enterprises—namely, the owners' long working hours. I round off by examining the recruitment of employees and the working conditions of employees.

Dominican small-business owners told me that they preferred to have a *socio* rather than hiring a manager or worker. The fact that a *socio* has personally invested in the business secures a better result, they claimed. Santiago, for example, said,

> It is better to have a *socio*, someone who takes part [*comparte*], than having an employee. That is my philosophy. In a business, everybody should have a self-interest. You need to be a *socio*. If it is impossible for you to raise the money immediately, that's OK; but you obtain the money little by little. But you need to be a *socio* so that you feel responsible and want to sell. To have an employee is not the same thing as having another person who owns. This is especially the case in a small business. An employee is great, a great help, but for a small store it's not the same thing. Employees don't offer the same service to the customer. It's important to treat people well, and employees don't necessarily do that.

Santiago's view is representative. I am not saying that he is necessarily right but that his ideas form part of most owners' way of thinking.

As I have said, the relationship between *socios* is informal and based on mutual trust. But it is also regulated by conventions. One of the rules says that both partners—or all three or four—should do their share of the work in the enterprise. This may take various forms. Often two *socios* divide the day into shifts, one looking after the business in the daytime, the other the evening. In other cases, people do as Santiago and José did; one works on weekdays, the other evenings and weekends. After the bookstore of Santiago and José got two more *socios*, all four did their share, as Santiago also did. The latter now spent considerably less time in the store than he had done earlier, but he continued to work there a few hours each day.

The relationship between partners may contain latent and manifest tensions. These may arise from the partners' division of labor. One who made me see this clearly was Fernando. The division of labor between him and Chelo deviated from the norm. Fernando spent the whole day in the restaurant, seven days a week; Chelo stopped by but spent most of his time taking care of a multitude of other tasks in different places in New York City and Westchester. One night while I sat with Fernando in the restaurant, I asked him what he thought about the partnership. He said, "It's a bit complicated":

> According to the rules, one should work one shift and the other, another. But with Chelo, it's a bit difficult because he has got accustomed to doing a number of things simultaneously. Sometimes he wants to do too much, and he gets involved in too many things at the same time. But I got an opportunity. I knew him, his way of operating. But the partnerships with this type of person rarely last long. Not because he is a bad person—no! He's a—to me he's a great *caballero*, a gentleman. As a man and partner, he's a person with much integrity, very respectful, and very honest. Unfortunately, no one among us is perfect . . . unfortunately, it almost never lasts long, this sort of partnership, owing to that problem. For the right thing would be that we both took our shift so the business could work better.

Even so, Fernando was content: "Even with a break up tomorrow, I wouldn't regret anything." What he recognized and valued was that this partnership had given him the opportunity to learn how to operate in an industry where he had lacked previous experience.

In a few cases, *sociedades* are dissolved in anger. When I met Mario Solano for the first time in early August 2002, he operated a small bodega alone on the corner across the street from the Washington Heights tenement where I rented my room. I was often there, buying a sandwich or something else and chatting with him and customers. He had run the store alone for two months. Before that, he had operated it together with a *socio*. It was a story of a friendship destroyed. The first time he mentioned it to me, he just said laconically, "I had a *socio*. I had problems with him. I had to kick him out."

The partners purchased the bodega together in summer 2000, for $38,000. It was Mario's first own bodega. When they bought the store, it had just been shut by the police. The previous owners had been running a drug operation and selling drugs from the store. Mario and his friend had not hesitated to buy, though. They had figured, he said to me, that the neighborhood would soon recognize that the new owners did not sell drugs and give the store a chance. But Mario's *socio* liked to drink; he mixed looking after the business with drinking beer with friends. Mario and the partner repeatedly quarreled over this. Subsequently Mario found out that his *socio* had sold some illegal lottery tickets in the bodega without giving him his share of the profit. About two years after they had bought the store, Mario's mother was killed in an accident. After Mario left for Santo Domingo to help organize the funeral, his partner did not send him any money from the store. When he returned to New York, he asked his partner to leave. Yet Mario was poor. The store, which was bought on credit, barely survived. Ten months after he had asked his *socio* to leave, Mario still had not paid him for his part of the business.

As previously mentioned, all the Dominican entrepreneurs I met labored long hours, in most cases six or seven days a week. Dominican-owned stores, travel agencies, restaurants, and beauty shops are usually open seven days a week, from early in the morning until 8 P.M. or midnight or later. Some owners have the help of a *socio* or a close relative (like a spouse, son, or mother). All the same, they work extremely hard. When Benito Paulino and his stepfather (see Chapter 2, "A Story of Survival") bought a bodega in the Bronx, they opened it seven days a week. One week Benito and his mother opened it each day at seven; at two in the afternoon, his stepfather started his shift, and Benito went home to get some sleep. At four, Benito returned to the bodega, his mother went home, and he and the stepfather kept the store open until midnight. The next week Benito started to work at two in the afternoon, while the stepfather and mother opened the store, and so on. Such a rhythm is representative.

Even when they have employees, Dominican owners generally put in very long hours themselves. For example, in 2003, Diana Martínez and her husband Alejandro owned and operated four supermarkets. The husband operated one of the stores, their eldest daughter another, a friend the third, and Diana the fourth. The family's home was in New Jersey, but Diana's C-Town was on 116th Street in Manhattan. In addition to running one of the stores, Diana was responsible for keeping accounts for all four. Diana was tough. In her C-Town, there were several employees (African Americans, Mexicans, Dominicans, and so on), and she said of her relationship to these, "My employees respect me because I'm very strong. I like to talk once, and I like to deal with adults.... I mean, I'm willing to help my employees in whatever is necessary, but I do expect them to do—to conform to what they are supposed to do and to give me that in return . . . and if they don't wanna work with me, they have a problem working with a woman, they just have to take a walk, you know? They just have to leave, because this [C-Town] is my house and I run it my way." At the same time, she also continued to work long hours herself, five, six, or seven days a week. Her typical day in the C-Town in Manhattan began around 9:30 A.M. (after she had first seen to it that her youngest children got to school), and she spent most of the working day in her small office in the store, with piles of invoices and documents and phone, fax, and computer. Through a window in her office, she could observe what took place in the store. She stayed in the store almost until it closed—8:30 or 9 P.M. If she had an appointment or meeting somewhere or if she had to meet with one of her children who still attended school somewhere, she left the office earlier.[6]

Some owners said that they sometimes felt like a "slave"—or like a "prisoner"—in the small store. The store area was often very small, and it was often crammed. The work could be monotonous. To do an errand or simply leave the store for a minute or two was was usually impossible. Instead, they looked out on Broadway, Amsterdam, or St. Nicholas Avenue through the window—or while they paused to smoke a cigarette outside the entrance. One of those who said to me that it was as if her business had turned her into its slave was Juana Molina, a woman in her thirties who operated a tiny beauty parlor, "Salón Juana Unisex," in northern Manhattan. Store locales in Manhattan are often small, and those situated in Washington Heights are no exception. Juana's beauty shop consisted of a small rectangular room. On both sides were rows of chairs. One wall was covered by shelves with equipment and cosmetics, the other by mirrors. At the back of this main room were two tiny rooms that also formed part of the shop. Five women worked in the space, which in addition had to house the customers and friends who stopped by to chat. Juana opened the business herself around 9 A.M., six days a week. She stayed all day, and often closed around 10 P.M.. Monday was her day off, the day her business was closed. She used the day to do necessary errands and spend time with her mother. Juana's husband and two daughters, nineteen and sixteen, lived in Santiago in the Dominican Republic. She had bought the beauty parlor at a favorable price from her female cousin two-and-a-half years before I met her, only six months after she had immigrated.

Some, such as Mario, ran businesses completely alone. Some of these owners did nothing but be in the store and go home to sleep. Mario's street-corner bodega was very small. His two most important commodities were beer and soft drinks. The store consisted of one oblong room, with windows on two sides. At the back were refrigerators filled with beer and soft drinks and shelves with chips and other snacks. One of the long walls was covered with merchandise from floor to ceiling—piles of canned products (such as beans, ravioli, and Campbell's soups), rice, spaghetti, sugar, maizena, toilet rolls, soap, detergent, and so on. The shelves on another wall contained products such as shampoos, deodorants, and razor blades. On the counter was a pile of *El Diario/La Prensa* (a New York daily in Spanish), some large Dominican avocados (at least if it was August), and some empanadas and *dulces de coco*. Under the counter were salami, ham, cheese, tomatoes, lettuce, bread, and a variety of candy of mainstream U.S. brands. On the wall behind him, Mario had phone cards—some with names like "Dominicall," "Quisqueya Phonecard," "Mangú NY Phonecard," and "Sancocho Phonecard." In the evening, the bodega was filled with the loud, melancholy bachata, music many Dominican men like to listen to while having a beer. In the daytime, Mario often played merengue or some other music. The bodega was open seven days a week, and Mario did everything himself. He opened between 8:30 and 9 A.M. and closed between 10 and 11 P.M., sometimes midnight. To go to a bank or an office was difficult; he then had to get one of his most trusted friends to look after the store while he hurried to do his errand.

Before Mario left the Dominican Republic, he had worked for eleven years as a teacher in a high school in one of the capital's popular sectors. He left his wife and children on the island when he migrated. In New York, he lived with a new woman. It's difficult to live alone, he said to me. One day in October 2002, I stood with Mario outside the store while he smoked. There was no customer in the store. I was tactless enough to ask, "Do you like being a *bodeguero*?" He said, "The issue isn't whether I like it or not. I have to. I'm like a slave in this place. When you run a bodega that is profitable, that sells a lot, then you like it. But this isn't like that."

There are several reasons Dominican small-business owners work long hours. Since they have become owners by means of loans, they must work hard to be able to pay off heavy debts. If the owner loses creditworthiness, it becomes difficult to keep financially afloat and almost impossible to start a new small enterprise. The owner is no longer sufficiently trusted—that is, no longer viewed as fully *serio* or serious. Owing to the debt, it is impossible to employ much help. Most owners also see it as necessary to be around to keep an eye on things—from the cash register to employee performance. Sometimes store owners fear to leave their business for other reasons. A Washington Heights *bodeguero* explained to me that he did not like to leave the store to obtain supplies. While he was away, there was just one employee in the bodega. The store should be looked after by two, he said, since it could be robbed. Mario hired another Dominican immigrant to aid him in the bodega but got rid of him after just two weeks, saying he was of little help after all. While the man was there, Mario still hesitated to leave the store. I asked why; Mario said that the bodega let men and women consume beer inside the store and illegally sold lottery tickets, and he feared the police would suddenly show up on inspection while he himself was not there to handle it. The store was licensed to sell alcohol, but it was not licensed as a bar; the beer was supposed to be consumed elsewhere—not inside the store.

Most Dominican immigrants who have become owners of their own businesses calculate profitability in ways that resemble those often seen in peasant societies—or in societies in which the productive entities also are households (Gudeman and Rivera 1990). An owner rarely or never looks at his or her work in terms of payment by the hour. Instead, the owner's attention is directed to how much is left after he or she has paid all (yearly, monthly, and weekly) cash expenses (installments including interest on loans; rent; bills for supplies, energy, phone, and TV; wages to employees; taxes; perhaps a ticket fine; and so on). The expression used by many informants when they did this sort of calculation in conversations I had with them was *lo que (me) sobra/sobraba*—that which is/was left, or that which I have/had left. Given this way of figuring out usefulness and profitability, it may make perfect sense to keep the business open extra hours and do most or all the work oneself. Although the turnover during the extra hours continues to be modest or low, it is precisely this extra effort, with its accompanying sale, that secures that enough is left after the bills have been paid.

I have underscored that Dominican entrepreneurs have drawn on the family to pool resources, engage in mutual exchange, and maintain solidarity. But we know from studies across the world that the kinship idiom is used to construct and naturalize not only solidarity but also hierarchy and inequality, even exploitation (see, for example, Weiner 1988; MacGaffey and Bazenguissa-Ganga 2000; Graeber 2001; Yanagisako 2002). A number of Dominican immigrants who have owned a small store or other type of enterprise have had a spouse who has worked daily or temporarily in the business. Others have had a young son or daughter, a mother, or some other relative doing such work. The work may have been crucial to the enterprise's survival and profitability, but it has not been paid, at least not by an ordinary salary: instead, it has been understood as a contribution to the household or the family, as a form of self-help. At the same time, the business remained essentially controlled by the spouse, parent, or son. If it was sold, the owner kept the money the sale left. The point is that this type of unpaid "help" has in most cases been necessary and a contribution to a collective, household, or family; viewed in this way, it has in reality constituted a form of self-help—but it has also helped maintain and naturalize hierarchies based on gender and age. When Benito and his stepfather, for example, were *socios* and operated a bodega together in the Bronx, Benito's mother worked each day from 7 A.M. until 4 P.M. in the store. Her role in the division of labor was important, but she did not receive a wage. After the store was sold, Benito and the stepfather retained the surplus left after the sale.

If the owners' working conditions often are brutal, those of the employees are no better. In fact, those who are employed in Dominican-owned small businesses are generally paid low wages, work long hours, and have little or no job security.

Dominicans who own independent supermarkets hire African Americans, Puerto Ricans, Dominicans, Mexicans, and persons of other backgrounds, depending on the racial/ethnic composition of the store's neighborhood. When I lived in the city, most of these workers worked five, six, or seven days a week and were paid salaries that corresponded more or less to the U.S. minimum wage, which was $5.15 per hour. Many were paid about $5–6 per hour; some less than $5. Workers did not receive overtime pay. Dominicans who owned bodegas, restaurants, bakeries, laundries, hardware stores, record stores, and other small enterprises in Washington Heights often employed other Dominicans but recruited also Mexicans, Hondurans, Salvadorans, and other categories of recently arrived immigrants.[7] Dominican-owned travel agencies and beauty parlors in Washington Heights mostly employed Dominicans. The payment fluctuated around the legal minimum wage and was not seldom below it.

In fall 2002, Evelyn Lara (my landlady's niece) worked in a small supermarket. The store, owned by a Dominican, was located in Upper Manhattan. When Evelyn applied for a job some months earlier, the owner had already known her and her family for several years. In the store, she worked as a *cajera* or cashier. The store had departments for fresh meat and for fruit and vegetables, and a selection of groceries. Evelyn worked from 9 A.M. until 5 P.M., six days a week. For a few weeks in fall 2002, she worked seven days a week, since one of the other cashiers was ill. The pay was $5.15 per hour. With six working days a week, she made a little less than $250 per week; with seven, a little less than $290. Many employees in Dominican stores in Washington Heights made a similar amount—$200, $250, $300, or $400 a week.

A Washington Heights bodega I often visited during fall 2002 was located at St. Nicholas Avenue and 191st Street. In early 2002, the Dominican who had established it over twenty-five years earlier sold it to a nephew in order to retire. The nephew, a young man, then hired Socrates Vallejo to work in the store. Socrates was around fifty, had been in New York for seventeen years, and was from the same town in the Dominican Republic as the previous owner and the latter's nephew, San Francisco de Macorís. Before he began to work in the bodega, Socrates had had a low-paid job in a golf club in New Jersey. In the bodega, Socrates was something between an ordinary worker and a manager. The nephew, who also ran another business, did not spend much time in the store; instead, he stopped by a couple of times each day. In the meantime, Socrates in practice ran the bodega. He worked from 7:30 in the morning until 11 or 11:30 in the evening, seven days a week. He opened and closed the store, obtained supplies, and attended to customers. Two other employees worked with him in the store, one in the daytime, the other in the evening. Socrates ordered his food from a Dominican restaurant in the neighborhood and ate it standing behind the bodega counter. He was paid a weekly wage. I do not know the exact amount, but I know the rate was low. He had been promised a bonus if the bodega went well, but each time I was in the store he complained about the economic crisis in the city; it was evident that the bodega did not do well.

Socrates told me that he did not feel like a *bodeguero*, and that he did what he did only because he had to. He was often tired. One evening he said, "I don't live. I barely live" ("*Yo no vivo. Yo mal vivo*"). The man who worked the evening shift in the store with Socrates was Elvin Ocaña, a Dominican in his mid-forties who, like Socrates, lived in the neighborhood. Elvin put merchandise in order and attended to customers. Previously, he had worked in a factory in New Jersey and in another Washington Heights bodega. His shift started at 4 in the afternoon and he worked until Socrates decided to close; he worked six days a week. His salary was so low it made Socrates feel embarrassed.

Near the bodega, also on St. Nicholas, was a small Dominican restaurant. I used to visit it together with taxi drivers from a base located next door. The restaurant's name was El Sitio (The Place), and it was owned by a Dominican immigrant in his late thirties. Like the Caridads, it played merengue and other music and had plastic tablecloths and waitresses in black jeans and white blouses who served plates of Dominican staples. One of the waitresses who worked in the restaurant was Yesenia Valdez. In 2004, she was in her early or mid-forties. Raised in Los Minas, a popular sector of the Dominican capital, she had arrived in New York in 1992, on a tourist visa sponsored by a sister. At that time she was already a single mother of three. In 2004, her two boys had finished a college education and had begun to work. The youngest child, a daughter, was in the middle of her education but had had to interrupt her studies because she had just become a mother. They all lived together in the same household, headed by Yesenia.

In Santo Domingo, Yesenia had worked as a waitress in a restaurant. After she arrived in New York, a female cousin who worked as a waitress in a Dominican restaurant in Harlem helped her get a job in the same restaurant. After a while, she quit. The reason, she explained, was that the owner treated the waitresses badly. But with the experience she now had, she easily got a new job as a waitress, this time in a restaurant in Harlem owned by Cubans. Subsequently, her brother bought the place where she worked when I met her. At that time, it was just a tiny café. Yesenia was hired by her brother and started to work farther north, in Washington Heights. After a year, her brother sold the place to one of Yesenia's female cousins, the woman who had assisted her in getting her first job in New York. Her cousin transformed it into a restaurant and ran it for four years, then sold it to the Dominican who now owned it.

In 2004, Yesenia had worked there for seven years, under three different owners. She now worked four days a week, always the day shift from seven in the morning until four in the afternoon. Previously, however, she had worked seven, six, and five days a week—but always only the day shift. The owner paid the waitresses $25 per day. In addition came *la propina* or the tips, in this place usually around $25 per day. In restaurants in midtown and downtown Manhattan, a tip is regarded as obligatory and is 15 percent or more of the bill. In Dominican restaurants in Upper Manhattan and the Bronx, to tip is voluntary, and the 15 percent rule does not apply. Many give $1, some do not tip, while men who drink often give more, perhaps $5. With six working days a week, a waitress made about $300 a week; with four, she made $100 less. The evening shift was from 4 P.M. until midnight. Waitresses who worked in the evening earned roughly the same as those who worked the day shift. These were standard conditions for waitresses in Dominican restaurants. In most places, the owner paid $25 per shift; a few waitresses could make $30 or $35. The tips varied from one restaurant to another and one day to another.[8]

Yesenia was paid a little more than the $25 the other waitresses were paid, owing to her experience. In return, she had to train the new waitresses the owner hired. Yesenia said that most of the waitresses hired in this restaurant worked only for shorter periods—two or three years, some months, or even only a few weeks.

One of Yesenia's sisters was employed in a hotel in downtown Manhattan. She said her sister's job was better; it was a job with wages and rights based on unionized regulations. Those who work in Hispanic restaurants, she said, don't have rights and are not paid overtime. In conversations with me, she did not hesitate to use the word "exploitation" about her working conditions. "We're exploited (*explotadas*)," she said. Yesenia and the other waitresses ate in the restaurant, but the break was short, perhaps fifteen minutes, depending on the number of customers in the restaurant.

Since Yesenia had previously had a close relative as her boss (first a brother, then a female cousin), I once asked her about this situation. Her reply was clear: it's not good to work with kin. What they want, she went on, is to exploit the situation. When she worked for her cousin, it was good for the cousin, but not so good for Yesenia; she (Yesenia) was like a manager, she did everything, and that was good for the cousin, who came only to pick up the money. It's better, she concluded, to work for a *particular*, one who is not a relative.

In spite of these words, she did not seem bitter, just patient. She and the other waitresses often exchanged working days, which meant they had a certain flexibility. The owner saw this as a good thing; in this way the waitresses were more satisfied and less inclined to quit.

A couple of blocks farther up St. Nicholas was Juana's beauty parlor, described above. The women who work in beauty shops also have tough conditions. Juana's business offered all sorts of beauty work, including haircuts, and served women and men alike. Each service had a fixed price. Juana and four other women, all young Dominicans who lived in the vicinity, attended to the customers. The five women were in three categories. Juana was the *dueña* or owner. Three women worked *por comisión*: they had no basic wage and only earned money if they had customers. Juana kept 50 percent of what the customer paid; the rest belonged to the employee. In return, Juana covered all expenses (space, equipment, and cosmetics). The employees often started the day around eleven in the morning and ended between seven and eight in the evening. If there were no customers they went home earlier, but sometimes they worked longer. They worked four, five, or six days a week. Their income varied considerably from one week to another. It is, therefore, difficult to estimate how much these women employees made on an average, but the average weekly amount cannot have been high.

The fifth woman did not work *por comisión* but "rented space." She paid Juana a monthly rent of $600 for the right to use one of the two tiny rooms at the back of the salon. Juana's rent for the whole space was $1,700. The woman covered her expenses herself and kept 100 percent of what her customers paid for her services. Again, it is hard to estimate an average income. If she worked long hours and had many customers, she increased her income. If she worked less or if business was bad, her income dropped. Working conditions and business arrangements like these are found in many Dominican barbershops and beauty parlors in the city. One of the young women who worked *por comisión* for Juana had worked there for two years, another for a year and ten months. Given that Juana had owned the place for only two-and-a half years, her labor force had been relatively stable.[9]

When Dominican owners of small businesses recruit a new employee, they use their networks. The process is informal, and the criterion to which owners attach the greatest importance is the degree of *confianza* or trust that the candidate in question enjoys. Owners recruit relatives, friends, and neighbors. In other cases, they hire people recommended by persons they trust. Besides recommendations, owners attach importance to experience. All said it was easier to obtain a job if one already had had a similar job. In the restaurant business, some owners also give weight to the waitress's looks. One waitress in El Sitio said when I asked her how people are hired that most important is *experiencia*, but the other criterion an owner uses is whether *se ve bién*, whether she looks good—the owner believes many men come to the restaurant to look at the women, she said.

A worker in a Dominican-owned enterprise typically has a raw deal. He or she works hard but makes little money. But we would commit a grave mistake if we viewed this as essentially a product of Dominican owners' ideology—or Dominican culture. Dominican society has for a long time been heavily integrated into the world economy, but a large part of the Dominican people live in poverty. It is common in the Dominican Republic for people to be obliged to work for little, but this is not primarily a result of Dominican culture or values. On the contrary, it is basically an expression of the ways Dominican society has been, and continues to be, structured as an effect of its integration into the global political economy (see, for example, Gregory 2007).

More important, wages and working conditions in the Dominican small-business economy in New York mirror features of the wider U.S. society. Until 2007, the nation's minimum wage was just $5.15 per hour (the Fair Minimum Wage Act of 2007 raised the federal minimum wage rate to $5.85 per hour effective July 24, 2007, $6.55 effective July 24, 2008, and $7.25 effective July 24, 2009). Employees who earned $5.15 per hour and worked forty hours per week took home significantly less than $200 a week after taxes and transport expenses. Thousands of businesses throughout the United States regularly hire workers who do not even receive the minimum wage. The biggest U.S. employer, Wal-Mart, has long been known for its aggressive union-busting tactics and is, by virtue of its market position, pulling down wages and benefits at large and small enterprises across the country. Small wonder, then, that Luis Salcedo shuddered to think what might happen should the two stores he himself owned—two C-Towns—become unionized: "The unions were created for good reasons, but the small-business owner cannot let his employees unionize, because he can't. Economically, he simply can't."

It is, nonetheless, clear that the wages paid by many Dominican employers are conspicuously poor. In a comparative statistical study of Dominican and Colombian female workers in New York City, Greta Gilbertson (1995: 657) has concluded that employment in Hispanic-owned businesses "provides women with low wages, minimal benefits, and few opportunities for advancement." According to the same study, the average annual income for Dominican and Colombian female employees in Hispanic-owned businesses in northern Manhattan and Queens in 1980–81 was $7,795. In comparison, Dominican and Colombian women who did not work for a Hispanic owner but worked alongside other nonwhites made $6,765. A third category indicated that the ethnic composition of their workplaces was "predominantly white" and that the owner was not Hispanic. These workplaces had a high degree of unionization. The average annual income was $9,291, and women in this category made up about 15 percent of the sample used in the study (Gilbertson 1995: 661–62). Irrespective of these differences, all women in the sample earned very low incomes. Dominican and Colombian women in Hispanic-owned businesses earned $1,500 less per year than men (Gilbertson 1995: 662; see also Gilbertson and Gurak 1993).

In spite of the low wages and the minimal job security, Dominican immigrants continue to apply for jobs in Dominican-owned businesses. The data provided in this chapter show also that a number of those who are just employees in these businesses have already spent many years in New York. Many have worked for several years in the Dominican small-business economy; a number are U.S. citizens. Why do Dominican New Yorkers prefer to be employed in the Dominican small-business economy?

The best answer is that the economic alternatives are not much better, sometimes worse. Dominican women and men who worked as employees in Dominican businesses in Washington Heights said to me: I could work at a factory in New Jersey and earn a bit more than I do here—perhaps $6 or $7 per hour, but I would have to pay $5 or $6 for the round trip to the factory, and I would spend over an hour on the bus each day without being paid for it—it's not worth it.[10]

Those who prefer a job in the Dominican small-business economy to a factory job have other reasons also. Most Dominicans strongly dislike the surveillance and discipline in the factories. One Dominican woman in Washington Heights said in a 1999 *New York Times* article that the time when she and her friends were waiting for the van that would take them to the factory was the time to chat; at work, silence was the rule: "We're like mute people," she said. "Five-minute breaks, and 10 hours standing" (Kugel 1999). An employee in a Dominican restaurant or store may work in the daytime or evening. He or she may find a job where it is possible to work four, five, six, or seven days a week. Some owners agree to the employees exchanging shifts. The greater flexibility makes it easier to combine work with responsibility for a family. It also makes it easier to combine employment with an education; quite a few Dominicans who are employed in the Dominican small-business economy are also students. A number of these are single mothers in their twenties or thirties. Most of these women would not have been able to study but for (1) the relative flexibility their job situation ensures and (2) the help they receive from their family, in practice, female relatives, especially their mothers.

The case of Marisol Romero is typical. Marisol was a single mother in her late twenties who lived and worked in Washington Heights. In the evening, she attended classes. Marisol worked four days a week as a waitress in the small Dominican restaurant El Sitio; previously she had worked five and six days a week. Her shift started at 7 A.M. and ended at 4 P.M., and she had now worked in the same restaurant for seven years. Her sister was employed in the same restaurant. Both lived only a couple of blocks away, as did their mother. Each of the three had her own apartment, and Marisol's household consisted of herself and her seven-year-old daughter. She had arrived in the U.S. about eight years earlier.

Marisol had now studied for three years. She attended classes in English and computer science at City College of New York at 138th Street. The classes formed part of a special program for immigrants, and her goal was to complete this program and then enter one of the City College ordinary undergraduate programs to get a B.A. She studied five evenings a week. Four times a week she got up at 5:45 A.M. and made breakfast. At 6:45 she had taken her daughter to her mother's apartment; fifteen minutes later she began her shift in the restaurant. After 4 P.M., she did shopping and errands and spent time with her daughter and mother. She then took the subway from 191st Street to 137th Street. The classes lasted from 6 to 9 P.M., but because the teacher and his students had agreed not to take a fifteen-minute break, they finished at 8:45. After this, Marisol headed north again for her mother's apartment, where she fetched her daughter. In spite of her formidable schedule, Marisol enjoyed studying. She said it had got her new friends, not only other Dominicans but also immigrants from other countries, and she and her daughter (who had started school) could now do more things together, not least on the computer; and she had learned more about American society.

Ironically enough, a Washington Heights dead-end job can form part of a relatively calculated attempt to become more incorporated into the U.S. "mainstream" and achieve mobility. Marisol and the other women in the restaurant could exchange shifts. Her sister was employed in the same place and could help her, and the owner allowed her to work only four days a week. In addition, Marisol had reduced the time spent on transport to a minimum. She and her mother and sister lived on the same block. Her job was located only a few minutes away, as was her daughter's school. The subway ride to 137th Street took less than fifteen minutes. Marisol told that she had once lived in Washington Heights but been employed in a factory in the Bronx. That, she said, had been exhausting; she spent too much time traveling to and from work.

Finally, some begin to work in a bodega or beauty shop or travel agency because they hope to learn a business by practicing it. Many of those who have managed to start their own enterprise have first learned the business as an employee.

Practices, Relations, Structures

Thus far, I have maintained that Dominican immigrants who have developed small enterprises have drawn on their social networks. People have also found jobs with the aid of a relative, friend, or neighbor. In the rest of this chapter, I argue that many of the businesses, viewed as sites and sets of practices, themselves contribute to the production and reproduction of social networks—or social relations that, in turn, are used to develop enterprises and obtain employment. As I have previously claimed, Dominican migrants maintain kin relationships in different ways. Relatives trade information, exchange services, cook and eat together, go to a park together, and call each other. Some own a business together. Others are employed in the same place and are, consequently, work comrades. Likewise with friendships: Dominican New Yorkers who are friends exchange knowledge and services and call each other and spend time together in apartments or homes. Some own businesses and/or work together. The Dominican-owned small businesses form a part of this. Dominican restaurants, bodegas, bakeries, beauty salons, and so on are sites in which social relations are created and recreated. In these places, Dominicans make and remake neighborhood relationships, reproduce already established friendships, and develop new ones. Below, I seek to substantiate these assertions by means of ethnography. I describe a set of practices and activities drawn from three different places—a small popular restaurant and two bodegas, all in Washington Heights.

El Sitio, the small restaurant where Yesenia, Marisol, and Marisol's sister worked as waitresses, was in many ways a typical Dominican restaurant. It was located on busy St. Nicholas Avenue, a few blocks south of the 191st Street subway station. The nearest neighborhood is commercial but mostly residential. Marisol said the great majority of the restaurant's customers were *tradicionales*, regulars. Most of them stopped by El Sitio almost daily. Nearly all were people who worked; they were factory workers, employees in shops and institutions, and shop owners. In El Sitio, one got a big meal—a substantial breakfast, lunch, or dinner—for around $4 or $5. In addition, many left $1 as a tip. Most of the customers were Dominicans, but some Mexicans, Filipinos, and Chinese also used the restaurant.

One category among the regular customers was Dominicans who lived in the tenements in the vicinity and stopped by early in the morning to buy a large breakfast. These were on their way to their workplace, often a factory in New Jersey. The breakfast was a Dominican breakfast—for example, mashed green plantains and fried salami or cheese. They waited in the restaurant until it was ready, and took it with them. Some had coffee while they waited. Two other categories were Dominicans who worked in the stores near the restaurant or taught in a public high school a few blocks away. Most of these lived in the tenements near the restaurant or elsewhere in Washington Heights. They often bought lunch in El Sitio; some ate in the restaurant, at the counter or at a table, some ate in the workplace, and many did a bit of both, depending on the day. Another category of regulars consisted of employees in a large nursing home near the restaurant. Some nurses and nursing auxiliaries purchased lunch. In addition, El Sitio was used regularly by taxi drivers. One of the largest livery-base stations in Washington Heights was almost next door. Most of the drivers who were regulars lived in the tenements in this area of Washington Heights.

When the regulars entered and left the restaurant, they greeted the owner, the waitresses, and their friends. The regulars' interaction with the waitresses was personal. Marisol explained to me that one of the most important aspects of her job was to pay attention to the regulars' food preferences and habits and use this knowledge when serving them. Often she would suggest a dish. In most popular Dominican restaurants in New York, the food is on display in containers behind the counter. The waitresses, too, are mostly standing behind the counter. They prepare and serve while the customer watches. But regulars' meals are seldom identical, even though they may have ordered the same dish: sometimes a man says to Marisol while she is preparing the dish he has ordered, "And please add just a tiny piece of *guineo* (boiled green plantain)." Another may say, "And give me a small piece of yucca."

In El Sitio, one could hear news of the neighborhood—of persons, families, tenements, businesses, and events. The majority of the Dominican popular restaurants in the city function like El Sitio; they are neighborhood institutions where old friendships are recreated and new friendships are developed and strengthened through forms of ritual activity—mutual exchanges of greetings (accompanied by polite questions regarding the other's family) and common meals.

Another important neighborhood institution is the bodega. In a fine book on the Dominican Republic, *El Colmado* (1996), Gerald Murray offers a detailed investigation of a Dominican institution of great significance: *el colmado*. Colmado is a term used in the Hispanic Caribbean to designate a small neighborhood store that sells a bit of everything but mainly household supplies, such as food, beverages, toilet requisites, and cleaning products. Colmados are found across the Dominican Republic, in all hamlets, villages, and urban neighborhoods. As Murray (19) claims, the country's host of *colmados* is perhaps the most striking manifestation of Dominicans' will and capacity to start and operate their own small businesses. Dominicans on the island use also the terms *bodega* and *pulpería*. These terms are used in certain rural areas; *pulpería* is used only to designate a very small store, typically located in a hamlet.¹¹

Dominican immigrants have in a way replanted the typical Dominican *colmado* in New York. On the way, they have, of course, transformed the original *colmado*. But they have also changed those stores, originally bought from Irish, Puerto Ricans, and Italians. The outcome is the "Dominican" bodega in New York, a new type. But the differences between the Dominican *colmado* and the Dominican bodega in New York should not be exaggerated; in some ways, they are very similar. Dominican New Yorkers often mentioned four differences when I asked them. (1) The two stores do not look the same; they have dissimilar storefronts, and the bodega in New York is often located in a five-or-six-story building. (2) The bodega in New York is largely self-service; the *colmado* is not. (3) In the typical *colmado*, a customer may come in and say, for example, "Give me tomato sauce for ten cents" and receive a small amount of tomato sauce in a paper wrapping or ask for "sugar for fifteen cents" or "soap for twenty cents." Stores in New York do not sell things in this manner; in the bodega in New York, a person buys the whole can or the whole bag, or does not buy. (4) The store in New York keeps the food it sells better, since the authorities' demands and regulations are stricter, and some customers seem more preoccupied with hygiene.

But some of the more basic social and cultural features are almost identical. Like his colleague in the Dominican Republic, the *bodeguero* in New York typically greets a customer when he or she enters, often by using the customer's name. Many customers live and/or work in the vicinity; they are in the store frequently, if not daily. Since a number live in the neighboring streets, the *bodeguero* sometimes knows almost the whole family—the mother, the father, their children, aunts, uncles, nephews, and nieces. Sometimes he asks a customer, "And how's the family doing?" Among the most experienced *bodegueros* in Washington Heights was José Delio Marte, who had operated bodegas in New York for over thirty years. I once asked him to compare the *colmado* and the bodega in Washington Heights; he said, "Look, it is the same thing. It is the same thing. Physically, they are different. But the practice to greet the customer, to chat with him, to sell some of the same products that we have there [in the Dominican Republic], and the wish to sell—this shows that it is the same thing."

The bodega in which Socrates Vallejo and Elvin Ocaña were employed was located on St. Nicholas Avenue. Many of the customers were Dominicans who lived in the neighboring streets' tenements. Others resided in other parts of Upper Manhattan or the Bronx but worked in shops and agencies situated close to the store. Since the bodega was located in the middle of a shopping district on a busy avenue and near a subway station, a few customers were people who just happened to be in the area. (Mario Solano's bodega, for example, was smaller than the one on St. Nicholas and located in a less busy commercial area. While the only newspaper Mario sold was *El Diario/La Prensa*, Socrates and Elvin sold three: one in Spanish, *Noticias del Mundo*, and two in English, *New York Post* and *Newsday*.) Yet many of the customers lived or worked close to the store. A testimony to this was a poster inside the bodega. The poster, which was in Spanish and hung beside the cash register, said (to the store's regular customers): "If I give credit, I lose what I own. If I give, I go bankrupt. If I lend, I am a nuisance when I want to be repaid. To avoid all these difficulties: I don't give credit, and I don't give, and I don't lend." ("*Si fío, pierdo lo mio. Si doy, a la quiebra voy. Si presto, al cobrar molesto. Para evitar todos estos líos: Ni fío, ni doy, ni presto.*") Socrates said he sometimes gave credit, however.

While I hung out in the store, it was rare that a person bought for more than a very small amount. Most purchased only one, two, or three items. While I was there on a Friday in August 2002, for example, one customer bought two beers, another four bottles of water, a third a bag of Dominican biscuits, a fourth apples and a Snapple, and so on. On another day the same month, some children bought sweets, a man a bottle of shampoo, a woman washing powder and a beer, another man a sandwich, and a second woman a phone card. Those in the vicinity who used the store bought little each time but went there frequently. Some ate a banana or another snack inside the store. A few chatted for some minutes on the sidewalk outside the store. Many came to the store to purchase a phone card. One Dominican who worked in an office next door but lived in the Bronx said to me, many start the day by buying a new phone card in the bodega.

For many customers, the place where Socrates and Elvin worked was more than a store. People got and shared news and gossip from the neighboring streets, with their businesses, apartments, and families, and expressed views on politics, baseball, child rearing, and the prices of commodities. The constant encounters in the bodega helped convert the immediate vicinity into a community—a loosely organized system of shared pieces of information and meanings.

Mario's bodega was on a street corner, on Audubon Avenue. The area was mainly residential but had also a number of small shops and commercial establishments. Across the street from the bodega was a Dominican livery-base station. Almost all Mario's customers were Dominican immigrants; they rented apartments or rooms in a tenement close by or worked in the immediate vicinity. Mario greeted most of his customers by name.

A few of the activities in the bodega were very informal—not to say illegal. Mario allowed neighbors and others to post small papers with advertisements inside the store. Most people advertised a room for rent. One week Mario distributed advertisements for a fiesta organized by Dominican New Yorkers with ties to the Dominican community of Cotuí; although Mario had lived mostly in the Dominican capital before he came to New York, he had ties to Cotuí, and some of his close friends in New York were from that town.

A Dominican woman who lived in the vicinity made empanadas in her home and sold them to Mario. Another woman made *chicharones*. Mario sold the empanadas and the *chicharones* in the bodega. He himself prepared ham and cheese sandwiches in the bodega. A number in the vicinity did as I did—bought something to eat and ate it in the store. Sometimes several people ate there at the same time, for example, around lunchtime.

Mario's most important commodity was beer. As I have previously said, he also allowed customers to consume their beer inside the store, although he knew that this was prohibited and, therefore, constantly feared a sudden inspection by the police. If he was caught, he would be fined. If he was caught a second time the fine would be higher, and the third time he would lose his license to sell alcohol and tobacco. (In the bodega in which Socrates and Elvin worked, I never saw a person drink a beer inside the store.) In the evenings on weekdays and on Saturdays and Sundays, men from the neighborhood dropped in or gathered for hours at the back of the store to drink beer and listen to bachata. This was a time for cultivation of male friendship. Many Dominican neighborhood bodegas have this characteristic. They are locations where men in the immediate vicinity get together to chat, play dominos, drink, and listen to music (see, in addition, Ricourt and Danta 2003: 48–50).

Similarly, the typical Dominican beauty salon in Washington Heights helps sustain female Dominican networks. The women who work in a given salon are most often from the vicinity or from another area of Washington Heights—likewise with the customers, who live in a tenement situated in the neighboring streets or somewhere else in Upper Manhattan or the Bronx. While owner, employees, and customers are together in the salon, they have time to chat about all sorts of subjects—from beauty work and child rearing to education, jobs, and businesses.[12]

* * *

In this chapter, I have tried to make two points. First, it is best to try to understand Dominican-owned small businesses as connections between economic or material life and uses of kinship and friendship. Dominican immigrants who have developed their own small enterprises have drawn on their networks. Many of the businesses that have been developed have functioned as neighborhood institutions: they have helped produce and sustain the same kinds of informal ties—ties between kin, friends, and neighbors—that made it possible to establish them to begin with. In other words, if there has been a core in New York City Dominican entrepreneurship, it is this relationship between making money and making and remaking bonds between relatives, friends, and neighbors; one may say the construction and reconstruction of ties of kin, friends, and neighbors have been an aspect of the development of businesses. This way of putting things may seem unnecessarily cumbersome, but it helps us keep in mind the obvious: these enterprises *are, and remain, businesses*. They arise from social and cultural practices. But these practices remain material: the goal is to make money. Ultimately, the practices that shape these businesses are concrete, flexible, shifting, and pragmatic—or profoundly historical: in other words, associated with particular historical conjunctures and particular places.

To cater to their mostly Dominican customers, Dominican bodegas in Washington Heights displayed and sold commodities that reminded people of the homeland—products like Dominican sweets, Dominican biscuits, and Dominican *casabe* (bread from bitter yucca flour). As Socrates once explained to me, they had to have plantain in the bodega. If they didn't have plantain, he said, people (or his Dominican customers) would say that the store had nothing. Sometimes they even sold plantain at a loss just to be able to offer the product. But in other parts of the city, things were different. In large parts of the Bronx and in Queens, for example, a Dominican *bodeguero* knew that he had to cater to a far more mixed clientele: not only to Dominicans but also to Puerto Ricans, Mexicans, Colombians, and so on. In these other parts of the city, the relative significance of the Dominican preferences diminished. In return, it became more important to sell other products—specialties from Puerto Rico, Mexico, and Colombia. A Dominican who had operated two bodegas in the Bronx told me, "There [in Washington Heights] everybody is Dominican.... Here, it isn't like that. Here in the Bronx, it's mixed. Here there are many Puerto Ricans, African Americans, whites." He then added that to be a *bodeguero* had not been difficult, "for they [the customers in the neighborhood] come and ask for things. As soon as they ask for a product [that you don't have in the store], you have to write it down and order it, for he will be back [and ask for it again].... Or he says, 'Look, order this! I'll buy it.' The customer shows you where you have to go."

The last sentence is telling. A *bodeguero*'s practices are flexible and open. They are in the making. Above all, they are shaped by the surroundings. A *bodeguero* does what he has to do to sell.

I have also tried to underscore that to understand Dominican immigrants' businesses requires a perspective combining an interest in forms of agency with an interest in important structural forces. This type of perspective—or what the literature often has described as a practice-theory position—has been developed over the last four decades by a varied group of theoreticians, writers like Pierre Bourdieu (1977, 1980), Sherry Ortner (1995, 1996), and David Graeber (2001). Practice theory insists on the existence of a dialectical relationship between creative, social action, and social structure. It says that analysts must "both take account of major structural constraints ... and at the same time recognize the role of real actors—their intentions, desires, fears, dreams; in short, their 'agency'—in living within and/or against those constraints, and thus in both reproducing and/or transforming them" (Ortner 2003: 205).

The Dominican small-business economy in New York has been shaped by what Ortner calls real actors—immigrants of flesh and blood, or persons with aims, aspirations, and dreams. The whole analysis in this and the previous chapter documents this. But if it is right to say this, it is equally correct to maintain that the Dominican businesses in New York have been, and continue to be, a product of wider structural forces. The most important structural forces that have helped give form to the Dominican immigrants' small-business economy are those that have gradually, since the mid-1940s, altered the U.S. and New York political economy, transforming the region's production system, labor markets, and demography.

The effects of the wider political economy are not only real: they can also be merciless. As we have seen, scores of Dominican and other immigrants in New York City are forced to work for wages that are miserable, even though they are market-based and legal. Another central component of New

York's political economy is the property market. Roger Sanjek (1998: 32) has claimed, "Much New York City political history can be read as the jockeying for ascendancy of politicians, landowners and developers, and financiers and as competition and alliances among them. What ties them together is a common interest in Manhattan real estate and in profits generated by maintaining and increasing its value." The value of land in downtown-midtown Manhattan affects land prices, house prices, and rents for commercial sites and apartments in most parts of the city—northern Manhattan, Brooklyn, Queens, the Bronx, and Staten Island:

> As the Manhattan core of offices and luxury housing expands not only vertically but laterally, the land-value politics governing this process result in continuous pressure on neighborhood New York. Existing structures and neighborhoods are either "upgraded" as investment capital for new construction and renovation flows in, or "downgraded" by "disinvestment" in repairs and maintenance and an intensification of housing stock usage (that is, more crowding). In consequence, neighborhoods "change": either upper and upper middle classes begin to appear or immigrants, lower-paid workers, and poor persons start moving in. (Sanjek 1998: 34)

While I lived in Washington Heights, rents were on the increase. As already noted, in 2002, 2003, and 2004 the city's economy was in bad shape. The economic recession had started in the first half of 2001. With 9/11, the city's economy was badly hit.[13] Small business owners in Washington Heights complained about decreased sales. This, however, did not prevent landlords from seeking to increase rents. In November 2002, Socrates and Elvin lost their jobs. After operating for over twenty-five years in the same store spot, the bodega in which they were employed was forced to close. The monthly rent, which had been $3,500, was suddenly raised by over 40 percent, to $5,000. Socrates's and Elvin's boss could not afford it. The bodega was soon replaced by a chain store that sold sneakers and sports accessories. A bit further south, on Manhattan's 110th Street, a woman and her husband ran an independent supermarket, a C-Town. The two were first-generation Dominican immigrants and also owned another store in the city. I first met her in spring 2003. At that time, they were trying to renew the lease. The supermarket was in a tall apartment building on the edge of Central Park. She and her husband had established it many years earlier, in the late 1980s. When I met her, she was worried. The landlord wanted to double the rent and bring in a new face with a more upscale supermarket, a store adjusted to the now slightly more gentrified surroundings. She said this was common and was "forcing people to move out." When I returned half a year later, they had been forced out. The C-Town was gone and had been replaced by a new supermarket run by new owners.

This chapter has looked only at a part of the Dominican small-business sector in New York. The next chapter will examine another part of this sector: the Dominican cab operations.

CHAPTER 4

From Livery Cabs to Black Cars

The basic entity in the livery industry is *la base* or the base, the livery-car service operation that includes a certain number of drivers.[1] The bases have mainly been a means of survival. Groups of men have pooled resources and cooperated to secure a livelihood. A large part of the process has been network driven. Groups of friends have joined forces to create a car service. In turn, the bases have functioned as meeting places, helping sustain forms of friendship. A collectively owned base includes *socios* and *choferes particulares*. The *socios* or partners are the drivers who own the base. Each *socio* has bought a share in the base with its activities. Those drivers who belong to a given base without having purchased a share in it are simply called *particulares* or individual drivers. In most bases, there is an annual election in which the *socios* elect the base's board and leadership for the next year. Two of the *socios* are elected base president and vice-president. In addition, they elect a treasurer, an auditor, and a *presidente del departamento de disciplina* or president of the base's internal discipline. The base president manages and runs the base's commercial and other operations on a day-to-day basis.

The president works in the base station. Bases rent a small commercial site that functions as base station. In the base station, one finds the president, one or two secretaries, dispatchers, and a few drivers who have stopped by for an errand or a chat. As I have explained, legally livery cab drivers are not permitted to pick up passengers who hail them on the street but can respond only to phone calls to a licensed dispatch service. The persons employed by the base to respond to calls from people who need a taxi are called dispatchers. The president, secretaries, and dispatchers are paid salaries. A base does not own vehicles. Instead, each driver is responsible for obtaining access to a vehicle; each one owns or rents the car used as a cab.

Each week, the drivers pay a fixed sum to their base. The money is used to run the base (wages, rent, electricity, phone, etc.) and is regarded by base and drivers as payment for the base's product or commodity: the right to respond to telephone calls to the base station. A customer who calls the base is connected with one of the drivers. The passenger pays in cash, and the whole payment belongs to the driver. This system means that a base's income is limited. A surplus has to be divided among all the *socios*. Bases that operate as cooperatives are, therefore, essentially a means. The goal is to make it possible for each driver affiliated with the base to produce a sufficient livelihood, partly by responding to calls and partly by picking up people. Yet, as we shall see, a number of bases have expanded their commercial operations. Livery bases have bought restaurants, opened auto repair shops, entered the black car industry, and so on.

The bases with which I worked are located in northern Manhattan and in the western and southern Bronx and are owned and dominated by Dominican immigrants. In Washington Heights and Inwood, the bases are almost entirely Dominican but include also a few drivers from other countries (most often other Latinos). In the Bronx, the ethnic composition of the drivers is more varied. A base may be completely owned and run by a group of Dominican *socios* and have mostly Dominican drivers but also include a number of drivers who are immigrants from Colombia, Ecuador, Mexico, Pakistan, parts of West Africa, and elsewhere.

In the next section, I examine how a base is created. After that, I discuss the conditions of the drivers and look briefly at the roles of, respectively, the dispatchers and the secretaries. Thereafter, I examine leadership and internal discipline and bases' commercial operations and strategies. A base represents much more than an economic enterprise; toward the end of the chapter, I look at the Dominican livery car services as community institutions and as forms of making and remaking masculinity. Throughout the chapter, I seek to show that the base is both a network-produced and a network-producing process.

Establishment

One of my key informants in the livery industry was Silvio Tolentino, a first-generation Dominican immigrant in his mid-forties. When I met him for the first time in August 2002, he was president of one of the largest bases in Washington Heights. He had immigrated in the early 1990s and now lived in a tenement close by the base. Silvio was married and had five children. His oldest son had finished high school and obtained a good job in Verizon, the communications company. The other children were still in school. Before migrating, Silvio had graduated as an engineer from the Autonomous University of Santo Domingo and then worked for some years in the Dominican public sector. He spoke little English. In Washington Heights, he had joined the base he now headed. After working as an ordinary driver for about seven years, he had mostly worked administratively in the base station.

One day early in the fieldwork, I sat down with Silvio in his office. He tried to explain to me how bases are created. The description was generalized and underscored the part played by friendship. It went like this: Two or three friends who are all livery drivers see each other regularly. They have lunch together or go to the same café or restaurant and start talking about establishing or purchasing a base together. They invite friends—other livery drivers they know—to join them. Each of the two or three friends recruits three or four persons. If the group includes around ten drivers, they may contact a lawyer. With the aid of a lawyer, they manage to have the necessary paperwork done. Above all, they need the necessary licenses: a license to operate as a company, a license to run a radio dispatcher, and a license from the New York City Taxi and Limousine Commission to function as a livery-car service. After this, the group has to recruit more drivers. Again, this is done through personal networks.

Let us suppose that they are twenty men, Silvio said. Each of the twenty becomes a *socio* by buying a share, perhaps for $1,000. In this way, the partners have $20,000. The capital is used to purchase radio equipment, rent a location, and establish the base station with offices, phones, and the rest of what is needed to start working. The base now begins to operate. This is a critical phase. The drivers must advertise the new car service in the neighborhood and elsewhere. And the *socios* need to recruit more drivers, so that the base's income grows and the company gets big enough to survive. As Silvio said, many attempts to create and develop a new base fail; a newly established base must quickly grow and expand.

Silvio's own base was located on St. Nicholas Avenue a few blocks north of 181st Street and was one of the leading bases in Upper Manhattan. In 2002, this base had fifty owners and around 350 drivers. Nearly all the 350 were Dominicans, and all were Latinos. Everything in the base was carried out in Spanish. Half of the *socios* continued to be drivers in the base; the rest did other things (they had found another job, bought a bodega, moved back to the island, etc.). This base had also invested in the black car industry. It owned half of a company that furnished black car services to corporate clients with offices in downtown Manhattan; I shall return to this. In 2002, Silvio and the other *socios* had decided not to sell more shares in the base; their financial position was solid. But if one of the already existing *socios* wanted out, he had a right to sell his share. In this case, the share was sold to the base—or the remaining *socios*. Once in a while, a *socio* chose to sell.

Two decades earlier, in the 1980s, Silvio's base was individually owned. In 1984, the owner, a Puerto Rican, sold the base to a group of thirty drivers. The vast majority of these were Dominicans. Each paid $400 for a share. Less than ten years later, in the early 1990s, a large group of new drivers purchased shares in the base, which had lost some *socios* and needed a new start. It got this with the new capital and the new partners it secured then. Among those who bought shares at that time was Silvio. Some of Silvio's best friends in the base were men of this "generation"—the group of drivers who had joined the base at the same time as he had done. Those who headed the base when I conducted my research mainly belonged to this cohort.

Dominican immigrants either purchased an already existing car service or established a completely new base. In both cases, they most often ran it as a collectively owned entity.[2] The transformation of individually owned entities into collectively controlled enterprises had not ceased when I lived in Upper Manhattan. One base, Highbridge, owned and managed by a Puerto Rican-Dominican couple for over twenty years, was bought by fourteen Dominican drivers in late 1999.[3]

Many car services have been created by people collectively leaving another base. These drivers were dissatisfied with the way in which the base has been managed, or they simply wanted to become more independent through controlling their own base. When Silvio's base was transformed from an individually owned enterprise into a collectively owned car service in 1984, it was, as mentioned, purchased by thirty drivers. Many of these had belonged to another base in the same area of Washington Heights and decided to acquire their own company after a bitter conflict with those who ran this other base.

The story of the creation of Superb, a Dominican-owned base situated on Webster Avenue and 204th Street in Norwood, in the western Bronx, shows how precarious and full of difficulties such a process is in most cases. In 1990, thirteen drivers left Kiss, another Dominican base located in the same part of the Bronx, to establish a new base. In 2002, one of the founders said that they all had left because they wanted to have their own business and make decisions themselves. But the start was extremely difficult. Superb was at first located in a small repair shop. Ten of the thirteen partners were Dominicans; one was from Ecuador and two from Puerto Rico. They had not mastered English and were barely able to do the paperwork. Finally, they got the base registered and licensed with the aid of friends who knew English and how to fill in applications. After a while, the base rented space next to the repair shop. But things continued to be difficult. Soon, Superb was in deep trouble. The base did not make enough money to pay the rent, and the *socios* were getting tired. The landlord had already set a last deadline, and the phone and electricity companies threatened to cut service.

At that time, the Superb partners learned that between 30 and 50 drivers in their former base, Kiss, had been saving money; they had formed a group, and each member had paid $10 weekly to a shared pool of resources. The money was meant to provide security—if a driver had an accident or fell ill, he could receive assistance. After contacting the group, the *socios* in Superb found that the men also had discussed starting their own base. They invited the group instead to buy shares in Superb, which was already licensed and had its own base station. Superb now got 50 new *socios* and drivers. Each of the 50 paid $1,000. With the $50,000 and, more important, many more drivers, the base survived—and it started slowly to improve its situation. From around 90 drivers the number grew to 110 and then 120. In 1995, they moved into a new, larger, and better situated space, the one they had in 2002. They were lucky: the one-story building into which they moved had just been destroyed in a fire and had had to be rebuilt. The landlord agreed to a fifteen-year lease. Near the base were several hospitals; this secured passengers. Superb's passengers were ethnically diverse, and a great majority of them lived in the neighborhood. Most of the drivers were Dominicans, but there were others from Colombia, Honduras, Puerto Rico, and Pakistan. The base's leaders were Dominicans.

Livery car services situated in the same part of the city compete with each other for passengers, which has led to a certain rivalry between bases. An expression of this competition has been a gradual increase in investment in vehicles. Previously, in the 1980s, one could use any cheap car as a cab but not now. To attract and keep customers drivers began to purchase newer and better cars, and bases started to establish and apply rules, minimum standards for vehicles.

A veteran driver in Fort George told his story in the following manner.

(Fort George is the base Silvio joined in the early 1990s and now headed.) Another large car service in northern Manhattan is First Class. This base, situated in Inwood, was established by a group of Dominican drivers in the first part of the 1990s. The emergence of First Class in the early 1990s, this veteran said, had challenged the drivers who belonged to Fort George and other bases in the area. The first livery cab that he himself had owned had been a 1979 Chevrolet, which he had purchased inexpensively in the mid-1980s. In the 1980s, he said, the Dominican bases had not yet established minimum standards for the vehicles. These rules came in the 1990s. When First Class was founded, it soon established an internal rule that all the base's vehicles had to be models from the 1990s, preferably Lincoln Town Cars. If a driver only had access to a model from the 1980s, First Class's president turned him down, saying he should find himself another (less demanding) base. After this, the *socios* of Fort George held a meeting where they decided that the base's drivers had to obtain better vehicles. Many of Fort George's drivers drove Cadillacs and Oldsmobiles, and most of the base's cabs were models from the 1980s. The *socios* agreed that the base's drivers now had to acquire models from the 1990s and that the oldest model Fort George later would accept would be the 1990 model. Subsequently, many of Fort George's drivers began to drive Lincoln Town cars. When I started my research, virtually all the base's drivers used Lincoln Town cars, most often models from the years from 1995 to 2000, but a few from 2001 and 2002. A handful drove fairly new Cadillacs.

Relations with the authorities and competition for passengers have forced bases and drivers to develop and live up to a set of rules and norms. Yet, as we shall soon see, the newer and more expensive cars have also meant that it has gradually become more difficult both to get started and to make a living as a livery driver.

A driver who has helped establish a base is sometimes referred to as one of the base's *fundadores* or founders. To be among the founders secures a certain respect and authority among the base's *socios* and drivers. But the differences between *fundadores*, *socios*, and *particulares* are not great. *Fundadores* and *socios* are basically drivers; they make their living as drivers. Even a base's president was a driver before he became president. After serving a period as president, many continue to work as drivers. As one of Fort George's drivers said, "In the street, there's no difference. We all have to make our money in the same way, as livery drivers, picking up passengers."

Working as a Livery Driver

Dominican livery drivers are mostly first-generation male immigrants. Many entered the United States after having spent their childhood and youth in the Dominican Republic, some in their mid-thirties. A few had graduated from a Dominican university; they were engineers and lawyers and had worked for a while in their country as professionals before they emigrated. Others had relatively little education and had worked in agriculture and small business. Yet others were nineteen-year-olds who had just completed high school.

Some Dominican immigrant livery drivers are, however, bilingual. They grew up in Washington Heights or elsewhere in the city or moved to New York in their early teens and have gone to school there. Some Dominicans who drive a livery cab combine this with going to a university.

Many of the drivers with whom I worked had been livery drivers for several years—from three or four to more than twenty. Many had belonged to the same base for years. Armando Ferrera, Roque Hernández, Daniel Lugo, and Milagros López all drove for Fort George. Armando immigrated in the early 1980s; before he left the island, he had first been employed in the Dominican armed forces and thereafter as a driver in a large private company; in 1984, he was a part of the group that founded Fort George as a Dominican cooperative. Twenty years later, in 2004, he was in his late fifties and still drove for Fort George. For his part, Roque was in his forties and had been a Fort George driver for the last seven years. He had arrived in 1984 and thereafter done different jobs. From 1987 to 1990, he was a livery driver in Audubon Car Service, another base in Washington Heights. From 1990 to 1997, he was employed by a large company, Glenwood Management, as a construction worker, before he became a livery driver again. Daniel had been in Fort George since 1989. When he first arrived in New York in the second half of the 1980s, he was nineteen and had completed high school in Santo Domingo and thereafter spent a few months in the military. After some time as a truck driver in downtown Manhattan, he joined Fort George.

Nearly all those who drove for Fort George were men. One of the exceptions was Milagros, a Dominican in her early thirties, who had been a livery driver in Fort George for five years. Before she began as a livery driver, she had worked for six years in different factories in New Jersey. She came to New York when she was about twenty.

To operate as a livery driver, one needs a vehicle. Many drivers have bought their own cabs, while many others rent cars. Those who own their own cars frequently rent either the day shift or the night shift to another driver, typically another in the same base. If a driver rents, he or she has access to the cab for twelve hours each day or night, for example from 5 in the morning until 5 in the afternoon, or from 5 in the afternoon until 5 in the morning. Of around 350 drivers who drove for Fort George, some 75 or 80 percent had bought their own cars. Between ten and fifteen drivers owned more than one car, most often two or three. The remaining 20 or 25 percent rented. Of the four Fort George drivers described above, one drove his own car and three drove rented cars when I first met them in 2002.

As mentioned, to obtain one's own vehicle has gradually become more expensive. In the mid-1980s, a driver could buy his own car for $1,500 and spent significantly less than $1,000 a year on auto insurance. In the late 1990s, drivers purchased their used Lincoln Town Cars for from $8,000 to $12,000 each, and the price of auto insurance for livery drivers had increased dramatically—to between $6,000 and $7,000 annually by 2002. This lowered the profitability and enhanced the risk for many livery drivers. When I began my research, many in the industry complained that far too much money now had to be spent on vehicles and insurance, and some of those who owned their own vehicles were not able to make enough money to cover their combined car and insurance expenses and, therefore, risked losing their cabs or had already had to sell them. One of these was Roque. In 1999, he bought himself a new cab. He had sought a 1995 Lincoln Town Car, he said; the price had varied from $10,000 to $13,000. But instead of buying a 1995 model, he had decided to obtain a brand new vehicle. His capital was $13,000. After getting a bank loan, he paid $17,000 as a first down-payment; the rest would be paid off as regular installments. It was hard, he said, but he managed to pay. Thereafter began his difficulties. After the attack on the World Trade Center in 2001, he made less money. In fall 2002, he had not been able to pay the bank in almost half a year and had no insurance; therefore, he had to park his own cab. Instead, he rented a friend's cab so that he could work. He would most probably lose his car, and his economic situation had become a mess.

To reduce the risk of losing one's car, drivers borrowed from friends, or from each other, when they bought it. Many sought to avoid a bank loan. Daniel claimed that he had seen too many driver friends get in trouble after having purchased a new and expensive car with a bank loan. He said there was another way of getting a car, which he himself and others used. Instead of buying a car through an intermediary or a car dealer, he went to an auto auction where he paid in cash. After the auction, he owed no money to a bank or a dealer. If the car you want to buy costs $8,000 and you only have $5,000, he explained, you ask *un amigo de confianza* or a friend whom you trust for a loan. You pay him interest, perhaps high interest, but you know you won't have difficulties, or lose your car, for the loan is informal and flexible. If you don't have the money to pay him back, he can wait; you pay him the next week.

Many drivers borrow sums from each other, most from a friend in the same base. A few drivers have specialized in this. In almost every Dominican base, there are two or three men who make some extra money by offering small loans to others in the base.

In late 2002, a livery driver in Washington Heights or the Bronx who rented his or her cab for twelve hours a day, seven days a week, paid $250 a week. If the car was almost new, the rent was a bit higher, most often $275. If a driver rented a cab for twenty-four hours a day, seven days a week, the rent was about $350. The car was maintained and repaired by the owner; the person who rented only paid for gas and washing. The driver was handed a clean car with a full gas tank each day; when the shift was over, he or she handed back the same.

A driver may own more than one vehicle. Such drivers most often drive one of the cars, or one of the shifts, themselves. Daniel told me that the next week he would buy a new car, a 1999 or 2000 Lincoln. The cab he already owned was a 1995 Lincoln model. After he had purchased the new car, he would keep both. He would drive the day shift in the 1999 or 2000 model himself and rent the other shift to another driver for $275; he would rent the other cab to another friend for $350 a week. In this way, he explained, the other car would be preserved better, being used by just one driver.

Driving one's own vehicle and renting a shift to another driver may be profitable. But renting instead of owning is not necessarily viewed by drivers as unfavorable. Some of those who prefer to rent live a part of the year on the island. They drive a livery in New York for four, five, or more months a year and reside and work the rest of the time in the Dominican Republic. These men prefer to have as little economic responsibility in New York as possible. Students also rent cars; they regard being a livery driver as something temporary, as a means to finance their education, even though they may continue to drive for years. Others who prefer to rent are in other situations. Milagros lived in a tenement in Washington Heights and was a single mother with a nine-year-old daughter who attended school. She paid $250 a week for her day shift and said she preferred to rent. When she rented, she said, her responsibility was limited. When the shift was over and she picked up her daughter, she knew she would not suddenly have to leave her. If one was an owner and rented the other shift to another, she explained, one always risked receiving a call concerning the car, perhaps late in the evening or in the middle of the night; if something needed to be fixed, one had to take care of it.

Most bases want to have as many drivers who pay a weekly sum to the base as possible. If a new driver shows up and wants to drive for the base, the president will most probably ask few questions and welcome him, provided that the driver has brought the necessary documents. He must have a driver's license and be licensed by the New York City Taxi and Limousine Commission to drive a livery cab. If the driver owns his own cab, the president needs also to see valid auto insurance. The new driver is then registered in the base. In Fort George, the price for registration was $100. Thereafter, the driver must pay a weekly amount to the base. In return, he has the right to respond to phone calls to the base from customers. The weekly fee varies slightly from one base to another. In Fort George in 2002, it was $50.

Every base has a set of rules, adopted by the *socios*. The rules specify a driver's rights and duties and how he should behave toward passengers, other drivers in the base, and the base's dispatchers and administration. When a new driver has been registered, he is, therefore, informed by the base about the rules. Even so, each driver remains, to a striking degree, an independent actor—his or her own boss. A driver's situation remains largely under his or her own control—and extremely flexible. The drivers drive their own vehicles; if they rent, they rent not from the base but informally from friends. A livery cab has no meter; when a passenger pays for a ride, the payment is in cash, and the driver keeps all the money; the base receives nothing. A driver decides his or her own working hours. If a driver wants to work only day shifts or only night shifts or one day to stop working after just two hours and park the car, he or she is free to do so. When a driver has paid the weekly fee to the base, the base's administration knows that he or she works the week in question. But a driver has a right not to pay; this means that he or she does not work—having gone on vacation or traveled to the Dominican Republic or perhaps being ill or needing to repair a cab or having auto insurance that has expired. In 2002, Fort George had about 350 drivers registered; between 260 and 290 paid each week to the base.

Once, at the base station of Excellent Car Service (located in the western Bronx), I met with two drivers. One was a Dominican in his fifties who had arrived from the island the evening before. He had left his family on the island and come alone. His home was in a community in the Dominican Republic that lived by tourism; the high season was now over, and he had left for the United States to drive a livery. For almost twenty-five years, he said, he had gone back and forth and driven a livery in New York. He used to drive in this part of the city. The other man was a friend, a Puerto Rican who lived near the base. While the Dominican was in the city, he would live in his Puerto Rican friend's apartment. He told the secretary that he had worked for Excellent many times before and that he wanted to work again but needed to rent a car. The secretary found his name, address, and phone number in her computer and asked him if the registered information was correct. Then she checked his two licenses and other papers. He preferred to rent a car twenty-four hours, not for only twelve; and if this was impossible, he wanted the day shift, not the night. She replied that a twenty-four-hour shift was difficult to find and that most of those with a shift for rent now preferred to drive the day shift themselves. A few minutes later, she called three men in the base and asked if they had a car for rent. She was unable to find a twenty-four-hour shift but found a day shift. The recently arrived driver smiled. He and the owner of the car would negotiate the rest.

Most drivers work long hours. Many work on average about ten hours a day, six days a week. Some work a bit more. Roque, for example, drove a rented car and worked the day shift. His base was Fort George, but he lived together with his wife and children in an apartment in Queens. (This was unusual. Most of those who drove a livery in Upper Manhattan or the Bronx also lived in those parts of the city.) Roque got up about 4:15 in the morning; after a cup of coffee in his home, he began the shift at 5 A.M.; later in the day, he had breakfast in a Dominican restaurant. He ended the shift around 4 P.M., parked the car, and went home to eat. Armando now only drove the day shift, but had previously driven in the night. His night shift had started at 5 in the afternoon, and ended around 2 or 3 in the morning, sometimes later, around 4 or 4:30. He had worked seven nights a week. After some years, his wife and children had arrived from the Dominican capital, and he had subsequently begun to drive in the day, most often six days a week.

When I asked Dominican livery drivers how much money they made, I got two standard answers. Drivers said it could vary considerably from one day to another; on a good day, they could make $160 or $170, perhaps more, but they also had bad days with far less than $100. They also said that the goal for most drivers who worked ten or twelve hours a day was to make, as they put it, $100 "*limpio*" (clean) a day; $100 *limpio* referred to net income after payment for gas and car wash (and perhaps parking and a meal).

One afternoon in 2002, I sat in the Fort George president's office. With Silvio, I sought to estimate a driver's income and expenses. Let us assume, Silvio said, that a driver who works a ten-hour day on average makes between $90 and $125. This is gross income, he then said; it isn't *limpio*. From this figure, the driver has to subtract expenses. A livery driver who works ten hours needs about $20 for gas, and in addition must pay for a car wash, costing $5. Sometimes he needs to spend money on parking. These are daily or almost daily expenses. In addition, he continued, the driver has other expenses. A driver buys his own vehicle, or he pays rent. Those who own their own vehicles must pay for oil shifts, repair work, inspection of the car three times annually, and auto insurance. The auto insurance, he said, is now almost $6,500 a year. After a first down-payment, the driver pays monthly installments. The last expenses Silvio mentioned were the annual fees a driver has to pay to the New York City Taxi and Limousine Commission. At this point in the conversation, one of the drivers in the base entered and interrupted us. In answer to questions from Silvio, he said he worked twelve hours and, in that time, earned sums varying significantly, from $100 or less to between $150 and $170; his gas cost $25, insurance $6,350 for twelve months.

When a livery driver manages to earn enough, it is primarily because he or she works a lot. My assumption is that most drivers make between $450 and $700 a week (after subtracting for gas and car wash and possibly car rent), provided that they work six or seven ten-or-twelve-hour shifts. If a driver badly needs money, he or she can get some by deciding to drive particularly long shifts (if that is possible; it depends on one's family situation). As Daniel told me, a driver may go out determined to make $200. He does not stop driving until he has reached his goal, although he has to work twenty hours before the job is done. Some do this. But as Daniel also acknowledged, few can do this more than occasionally; it is too exhausting.

Milagros, as we have seen, was a single mother without a mother or other relative who could take care of her nine-year-old daughter; she rented her car. How had she organized her day? She got up around 6 A.M. and made breakfast. Sometimes she got a neighbor to take her daughter to school, but most days she did it herself. After this, she immediately began her shift. On most days, she started to cruise for passengers around 7:30. Around noon, she took a long break—one to two hours. She used this time for errands and shopping and for preparing and cooking food and eating in her apartment. The food was partly for the evening meal—in this manner, she and her daughter could eat sooner after the working day was over. Milagros paid a Dominican woman to take care of her daughter after school. The woman, who lived in the same tenement, fetched the child in the school yard and looked after her in her own apartment. When the shift was over, Milagros picked up her daughter, and she and the little girl were at home in their own apartment by 6 or 6:30. Milagros said that, because of her daughter and shopping, she was at a disadvantage compared with male drivers.[4]

Dominican livery drivers view their job as a survival strategy. All drivers with whom I talked maintained, however, that driving a livery was much better than being an employee or working in a factory. They underscored two factors: a livery driver made more money than most factory workers and had not lost his freedom: he remained his own boss.

Many of those I met in the industry continued to go back to the island for one or two weeks annually to visit their families. Some had bought houses or apartments or a piece of land or a part of a business on the island. A number had gone home for good. Others traveled back and forth, living and making money in two countries. But as we have seen, many remained livery drivers for years, even decades. They had children who were U.S. citizens and grew up in Upper Manhattan or the Bronx. Their children, as the drivers themselves put it, would never leave the United States. Some of these drivers invested in other forms of economic activity, for example, buying a share in a bodega, restaurant, repair shop, or insurance agency. Some continued as livery drivers while they sought to diversify their economic activities. They owned their own cabs and drove shifts themselves and also owned a part of a bodega or restaurant. Others gave up livery driving and became *bodegueros* or operated other small businesses.

Dispatchers and Secretaries

Dispatchers and secretaries are employed by the base and, unlike drivers, work in the base station. The dispatcher works in a small room with a window facing the street, responding to calls to the base and observing the traffic in the street and on the pavement outside the base station. A secretary has her desk or office behind the dispatcher's office.

A person who calls the base to ask for a cab first reaches a dispatcher. In large car services like Fort George and Superb, two dispatchers always work simultaneously. In a base receiving fewer calls, one is sufficient. The dispatcher notes the exact time of the call and the passenger's location. Then, he immediately announces the call over the radio, and a driver who happens not to be far from where the customer has called answers. The driver and passenger negotiate the rest alone, without the dispatcher as intermediary or listener. The dispatcher is in many ways a key figure. He not only responds to a stream of calls and advertises them over the radio, but he also replies to questions from the drivers over the radio and conveys information and messages from the base to all the drivers.

Most dispatchers are men, and many have themselves been livery drivers. A number combine the two roles; they both drive their own cabs and work shifts in the base station as dispatchers. A Fort George driver who had earlier worked also as one of the base's dispatchers explained that it was an advantage to have driven a cab. Often, he said, a driver who was unable to find a particular place would ask the dispatcher for help; a dispatcher who knew the city well could then reply based on his experience and did not always have to resort to a map.

A dispatcher's job demands concentration and patience and is monotonous. In Fort George, the dispatchers were paid relatively well, $16 per hour. This was necessary to secure a motivated and stable group. In the same base, a dispatcher worked six-hour shifts; therefore, for each day and night, Fort George needed eight dispatchers.

In 2003 Daniel only worked as a driver, but he had previously been one of the base's dispatchers. He underscored an important difference between the two jobs. A driver's job was flexible, but a dispatcher had little flexibility. His working schedule was set by the base's administration. When his shift started, he had to be there, no matter what. Every two hours while the shift lasted, he had the right to a ten or fifteen minutes rest outside the office.

In the Dominican-owned bases in Washington Heights and Inwood, the dispatchers used Spanish when they announced calls over the radio. In addition, they were forced to talk fast. To function as a driver in one of these bases therefore, it was necessary to master Spanish. Silvio told me that African Americans, Pakistanis, and people from different countries in the Middle East had come to his office and asked if they could drive for Fort George; they did not know Spanish, so he had had to say "no."

Most Dominican bases have hired one or two secretaries. The secretaries receive the weekly payment from the drivers. They write letters and certificates and take part in the base's running administration.

Most of these women are Dominican immigrants, often in their twenties or thirties. In spring 2004, Fort George's secretary decided to leave. To replace her, the base hired a new woman, Dabril Gómez, a single mother in her early thirties who lived in the Bronx. She had moved from the Dominican capital to New York twelve years earlier. Before she left, she had studied medicine for a year and a half. Her first job in New York had been at a McDonalds. Later, she had worked for three years in a doctor's office. When Dabril landed the job in Fort George, she had been unemployed for over a year but had just started to study business administration at Baruch College. Before that, she had had to improve her English; she had studied it for three semesters.

Dabril and the other secretaries in the Dominican bases worked from 9 to 5, five days a week. The payment was low. Dabril would not tell me how much Fort George paid her, only that her wage was low. She hoped for an increase after a while; meanwhile, she tried to do her best. Dabril described the last part of the week, Thursday and Friday, as exhausting—almost as "hell." On Thursday and Friday, Fort George's drivers came to the base station to pay the weekly dues to the base, and it was her job to attend to all the drivers who came to pay. The first part of the week, she said, was less busy. On Monday, Tuesday, and Wednesday, drivers stopped by to ask her to write letters of confirmation—documents that stated who they were and that they drove for Fort George. Drivers asked for these when they bought or renewed auto insurance or had appointments with the health authorities or another part of the U.S. bureaucracy.

Leadership and Discipline

Dominican livery bases reproduce many of the forms of voluntary associations formed by migrants in New York (Sánchez Korrol 1994: 131–66; Jones-Correa 1998: 132–36; Sanjek 1998: 290–99), including Dominicans who have created an impressive number of voluntary associations in the city (Georges 1984; Sassen-Koob 1987; Sainz 1990; Torres-Saillant and Hernández 1998: 80–85). Dominican New Yorkers call these associations "*clubes*" or "clubs." The Dominican Republic has for a long time had an enormous number of *clubes*. While some have been formed with a political purpose, others, even most, have mainly had social, cultural, or recreational aims. The origins of Dominican *clubes* in New York City can be traced as far back as the mid-1940s (Torres-Saillant and Hernández 1998: 80). With the heavy influx of new Dominican immigrants that began in the 1960s, the number of Dominican voluntary associations in the city skyrocketed. Like on the island, they often started as networks of friends, acquaintances, and families.

Many Dominican social and recreational clubs in New York City have a recognizable structure with common organizational features that have been imitated and adapted in the Dominican, collectively owned car services. Popular Dominican *clubes* in New York are mainly of two types. One is the regionally or locally defined club, established by and for Dominicans with common roots in the same region, town, or community in the Dominican Republic. The other is open to all and often recruits members from many different parts of the country but with particular activities (sports, cultural activities, and so on). The two types of clubs share some organizational features. (1) They usually begin as networks of friends, acquaintances and families. (2) After a club has been founded, the members are registered. The members are called *socios*, and they pay a small registration fee. Thereafter, each *socio* pays a certain amount—often a monthly sum—to the club. (3) With the aid of the money the club receives from its *socios*, it rents a space, where the *socios* meet and cultivate sports or other activities and organize ceremonies, dances, fiestas, and such for the *socios*' families and others. (4) The club has been founded by a group, not one person and is also administered by a group. Each year, or every two years, the club's *socios* elect a board; this is headed by the president and also includes a vice-president, a treasurer, and other positions. Those *socios* who are elected serve for a clearly defined period, usually a year. If they have done a good job, they may be reelected; but relatively often, the club gets a new president and a new board.

While I lived in New York, I used to go to a Dominican club in northern Manhattan, a bit north of Harlem; the club's name is La Hermandad Quisqueyana Community Center. I was registered as a *socio*. I ended up there because I had got to know Nelson Camacho, one of the veterans in the Washington Heights Dominican livery industry, who in 2002 and 2003 was the club's president; he invited me there initially.

The club was located in a large, rented basement that had served as a gymnasium and been remodeled by the club's members. The basement belonged to a six-floor tenement. From Sunday to Friday, the club members used the space to play dominos, pool, and ping-pong. Some participated in softball and basketball tournaments. In one corner was a bar; in another, a television. There was also a large dance floor. Each Saturday the club organized a dance or a fiesta. On these occasions, it was visited by whole families, men, women, and children. But most of the time—or from Sunday to Friday, mostly in the evening—it was mainly used by the club's male members. Almost all the *socios* were first- and second-generation Dominican immigrants. They came from all parts of the country. A few were immigrants from other countries—El Salvador and Colombia. The great majority worked in factories or the service sector (including the taxi industry and small businesses). Some were teachers or students.

In the same part of the city, there were several similar Dominican clubs. La Hermandad Quisqueyana had been founded by ten friends more than thirty years earlier. In the club, I met several of the founders. Thirty years after the foundation, the number of *socios* was several hundred. Some lived in Washington Heights, others in the Bronx or New Jersey. Many had been friends for years, even decades. After the club had been founded, it had first rented a small space on 157th Street. Subsequently, it had moved four or five times, always in the area between 157th and 184th Streets, before finding its present location. The club had obtained a seven-year lease and paid $1,600 a month in rent. Every new member paid a small registration fee. Thereafter, he or she paid a monthly sum to the club; in 2004, the sum was $10. Every year the *socios* elected the club's board and president. When I first met Camacho in 2002, he had been president only for a short while. In 2004, another member became president.

The elected board in a Dominican livery base typically includes a *presidente* or president, a *vicepresidente* or vice-president, a *tesorero* or treasurer, a *fiscal* or financial inspector, a *vocal* or board member, and a *presidente del departamento de disciplina* or president of the Discipline Department. The boards of the Dominican popular *clubes* have a similar composition, although the number and titles of board positions may vary a little from one club to another. La Hermandad Quisqueyana also had its own *departamento de disciplina*. This was responsible for seeing to it that the club's particular rules were respected and followed by the members. This overlap in organizational forms is not strange, however. The heart of the Dominican immigrant club is friendship, and this applies also to the typical Dominican-owned car service. The Dominican livery bases would not have existed but for the pooling of resources and the mutual aid among groups of friends. Like most of the Dominican clubs, the Dominican collectively owned car services remain short of money and are maintained and energized by networks of relatives, friends, and acquaintances.

When the *socios* in La Hermandad Quisqueyana elected Camacho president he had been a member of the club for years and already knew and was known by all the members. He was respected and viewed as *una persona seria* or a serious person, a person who was upright. He had also been a community activist and a grass-roots leader in Dominican Washington Heights for a long time. For nearly two decades, he had been active in the struggle to improve the conditions of the livery bases and the livery drivers. Those who are elected as presidents and board members in the Dominican car services have backgrounds resembling Camacho's (although the latter clearly had been more of a pioneer and a general neighborhood activist than most base presidents I met in the field). Those men who are elected have been *socios* and active in the base for several years and have earned sufficient respect and authority.

In 2002, Superb's *socios* elected Benito Paulino as their new president. Benito had been a driver and an active *socio* in Superb since the base was established. He was one of the base's founders but had never before been president. Before he began to work as president, he drove his own livery. Benito was in his mid-forties and lived in the Bronx with his wife and a son; he had lived in New York since 1984 and was mainly a worker, a man without university education.

Benito won the election in 2002 by a fairly narrow margin. He obtained only four votes more than his main rival, another base *socio*. But the number of *socios* in Superb in 2002 was only seventeen. Sometimes several *socios* in a base want to become its next president and mobilize their closest friends in the base to back them; these elections may be strongly competitive. To secure enough backing, Benito promised his comrades to work particularly on two projects. Part of the relatively large site that Superb rented was underutilized, and Benito promised if elected to try to use it better; it could have a cafeteria and a couple of other small businesses. After his election, he kept his promise and delivered results. He also kept another promise, that if he was elected Superb would organize a *sociedad* or *san* savings group, to help Superb's drivers assist each other to raise capital to buy newer and better cabs. Only a couple of months after he had been elected, the *san* started; forty of Superb's drivers participated, and each paid $50 a week. Every two weeks, the base organized a *rifa* or raffle after which one of the forty received $4,000. The first driver who received his $4,000 was a man who did not drive his own cab; he could now obtain his own vehicle.

Benito was the base's president for just one year. In 2003, another of the *socios* became president, and Benito once again became an ordinary driver.

Silvio became Fort George's president in late 1999. Fort George was a larger and more established base than Superb. Like Benito, Silvio was in his mid-forties and had been part of the base for years, since the early 1990s. Before he was elected president, he worked for a year as the base's treasurer. Before that, he was a driver. Unlike Benito, he had university training; he had graduated as an engineer and worked for some years for the Dominican state. Silvio was exceptionally hard-working and loyal. He fully dedicated himself to the base.

Earlier, Silvio told me, Fort George's election procedures had been different. A *socio* had voted for a whole board, with a name for each post, and often two or three complete alternatives competed. Now the *socios* voted separately for each board position and by ballot.

Fort George too saw competition for positions. In December 2002, Silvio had been president for three years and wanted to continue. About a week before the election, I was in the office of another base *socio*. While I was there, he passionately tried to persuade another *socio* over the phone to vote for Silvio. The latter, he insisted, had already proved he was good at the job, and to back him would be best for the base. In spite of this, Silvio lost to another *socio*. A majority voted for Danny Guillén. In the year that followed, Silvio worked a bit as a driver and continued to carry out administrative work for the base. Danny knew the base and industry but had little administrative experience; Silvio backed him and assisted him with advice. In December 2003, Danny did not want to continue—he had not liked the job—and Silvio became president again.

Fort George paid its president a weekly salary, $600 in 2003. As in other bases, the working hours were from 9 to 5, five days a week. A president often had to work significantly more than this, without extra payment.

Why do the bases change their presidents relatively often? At least three circumstances may help explain this. First, those who created the Dominican car services borrowed forms and practices from the Dominican clubs, and the clubs often changed their presidents. Second, the large group of people who together control the base as *socios* contains internal tensions—individuals and smaller groups compete for influence and control. And third, to be president means a large responsibility and considerable pressure but relatively low payment.

A base president is an intermediary, a head, and a manager. He represents his car service in dealings with the city's authorities, large and small companies, other bases, elected officials, and the community; and he runs the base.

He is the base's key decision maker. If the decision is important, he confers with others—the rest of the board and other leaders among the *socios*. A part of the president's responsibility is to operate the base economically. He negotiates contracts and monitors and manages the base as a business. Another responsibility is to run the base as an organization; he hires people and gives people orders. Often when I entered Silvio's office, I would find him with his secretary going through the latest pile of forms from the dispatchers' office. They carefully read through all the sheets with notes about each call to the base. Silvio did this to run the base commercially and organizationally in the best possible way.

Another obligation was to reply to letters from the Taxi and Limousine Commission and to spread the commission's information to the drivers. Each day a stream of drivers from the base would stop by the president's office. If a driver from the base has been stopped by the police and been fined, he often discusses the situation with the president; together they seek to find out what the base and the driver must do. On one day that I tried to contact Silvio, he spent the whole day in meetings. First he spent the time from 10 A.M. to 2 P.M. in meetings with representatives of the Taxi and Limousine Commission, in downtown Manhattan; when he returned to the base station, he held a three-hour meeting with Fort George's dispatchers. Such days are not uncommon.

All Dominican car services have a *departamento de disciplina*. One driver called this entity "*nuestra corte interna*" or "our internal court." The department is headed by a president. Those who fill this position are experienced drivers, men who know the industry and the base and enjoy respect. Some have earlier occupied other board positions, such as president. After being elected, the president of the Discipline Department recruits the other members; there may be eight to twelve members in all. He finds these among the base's full-time drivers; both *socios* and non-*socios*, and both older men and younger men, are picked. One of the members is picked to serve as the department's secretary. All these positions are nonpaid.

The livery industry is subject to the law and the New York City Taxi and Limousine Commission's regulations. In addition, a base has its own rules. Some of Fort George's own rules and norms are that drivers must be properly dressed and wear a tie; they should treat the customers well; the cars must wear the Fort George logo, and they should not be dirty; no gambling is permitted on the base's premises or on the pavement in front of the base. Other bases apply similar rules. The members of the Discipline Department are charged with seeing that the law and the rules are followed by the base's drivers. If a driver violates a less serious rule (for example, if he drives without the base logo or without a tie), the base suspends him for a period, maybe two to twelve or more hours, during which he is not allowed to work.

If a passenger calls the base with a complaint, the base follows a routine. Passengers may complain for several reasons. Some claim that a driver was rude, others that he laid hands on them or overcharged them for the ride or drove them to a wrong place. In Fort George, a passenger who calls with a complaint first talks with one of the secretaries. The secretary contacts the base's president or the president of the Discipline Department, and he calls the driver and asks about what happened. Sometimes it is an experienced driver with no previous complaint against him or her, and the president concludes that it is a complaint without sufficient basis; he calls the passenger and seeks to calm him or her down. On other occasions, the president is in doubt, and the driver is asked by the base to meet in front of its "internal court," the Discipline Department. The members of the department consider the complaint and listen to the driver's description of what happened. They then ask him some questions, before they rule "guilty" or "not guilty." If a driver is found guilty and in addition has previously violated rules, the base may expel him. In these cases, the president writes a letter to the driver, with a copy to the Taxi and Limousine Commission, where he informs the driver that he no longer is allowed to work for the base. Some drivers are expelled. One afternoon in August 2002, I met Silvio, who explained that he just had had to get rid of a *socio*. He drank too much and had treated a female passenger disrespectfully; Silvio had given him the money the other *socios* owed him for his share in the base and had then evicted him.

In early October 2002, two of Fort George's drivers were asked to meet in front of the base's Discipline Department following complaints; I was allowed to attend. Aurelio Guerrero, a Fort George veteran in his fifties, was the president of the Discipline Department and chaired the meeting. Beside him sat the department's secretary, another experienced driver. After the meeting had started, Silvio entered and presented the first complaint by a passenger; then the driver, a Dominican, was asked to describe the incident. The story that followed was told with many details and a lot of anger or exasperation. According to the story, the passenger, an old woman, had entered the cab and asked the driver to go to the bank on 181st Street. After a while, he had asked her which of the banks on 181st Street she was going to. (There were at least two or three possibilities.) Her first reply had been "Damn! These

Dominicans!" After that he had transported her back to the base station and asked the base to give her another cab, and she got furious. After discussion, Aurelio recommended that the driver work on his temper, to seek to become less aggressive: "In this job, it's essential to be able to control one's temper. A cab driver meets all sorts of people. If you want to stay in this business, you have to learn to be more patient."

The other driver facing the Discipline Department, also a Dominican, described the incident leading to the complaint with a lot of anger, and, when he had finished and the others asked him questions, he interrupted and was impolite. His version differed considerably from that of the passenger. A mother had not wanted to fasten her small daughter's seatbelt, while the driver had insisted it had to be done. In the car, the girl had played with her ball and disturbed him. The mother had done little or nothing to stop her. When the ride was over, she opened the door and stepped out, and he got the impression that she would leave without paying him. He had, therefore, guardedly seized her arm and asked for the payment—$5 (the minimum tariff for a ride). She then accused him of laying hands on her. Aurelio called on this driver, too, to work on his emotions and to seek to become less irritable and more patient, before thanking him for having come. After this followed a short break and then the judgments. All found the first driver not guilty. In the second case, the men were divided, but a solid majority and Aurelio found this man not guilty also. Why were they acquitted? Aurelio and the rest of the majority stuck strictly to "the law." They recognized that both drivers were too hot-tempered, that they lacked patience and could be impolite, and they acknowledged the two could have acted otherwise; but they did not accept that an important rule had been (gravely) violated.

After this, the men continued the meeting for a while. One of their duties was to keep a continual eye on the drivers. If a member of the Discipline Department sees a driver who works without the base logo or without a tie, he must report it. Aurelio praised one of the younger members present because he had just given him a small pile of reports, a set of notes about Fort George drivers he had seen break a rule somewhere in the city. The president asked the others to pull themselves together and do the same. Another said, that he sometimes chose to close his eyes. If he reported one of his colleagues, he had to come to these meetings and spend time on the complaint. He too had a family and needed the time to work to put food on the table. Around 6:30 P.M., Aurelio closed the meeting. It had lasted about three and a half hours.

The Discipline Department helps secure order by monitoring and sanctioning conduct, which is necessary, in a group with more than 300 men, to avoid losing customers and money and keep the business alive. Its activities also have an educative function. Those who head and operate the discipline departments in the Dominican livery bases possess considerable knowledge—not only about driving a cab but also about being a first-generation, male, Spanish-speaking immigrant in the United States. Sometimes they use their authority and experience to give a piece of advice. Like Aurelio, they tell a comrade what he ought to do not to get in trouble one day.

Economic Diversification

A large proportion of the Dominican-owned bases appeared during the 1980s and 1990s. They were built in order to run a car-service operation, and their sole source of income was what the drivers paid to the base each week. Yet since the early or mid-1990s, a growing number of the Dominican car services have begun to change. Some of the bases now manage more than just one source of income. A few have become property owners. Others have invested in the black-car business. Still others have established small enterprises, such as repair shops. The motives behind this economic diversification have been complex: in some cases, the *socios* have mainly sought to increase the base's income; in others, they have wanted to spread or reduce risk.

Below, I sketch some examples. I first look at two bases—Seaman and High Class—that have in common that they purchased real estate. Thereafter, I discuss Dominican bases with an involvement in the city's black car industry. These continue to run their livery operations, but have in addition expanded into the black car business. After that, I look at other strategies used by Dominican car services to diversify economically. The Dominican livery base continues to be a livery base, and only very rarely have Dominican car services been able to develop an important extra source of income. Still, the tendency is evident; many of the Dominican bases seek now to create additional businesses.

The first time I met Seaman's president, a Dominican in his fifties, was in a meeting in northern Manhattan, attended by around ten Dominican base presidents. Subsequently, I met him in Seaman's offices. The base is situated in Inwood and is owned by 45 *socios*, almost all Dominicans, while a couple are from Central America. In 2002, the number of drivers was around 100.

The president had only held the post for a year; before being elected, he had worked as a driver. He told me the base's history.

Seaman was founded by 100 drivers; each of the 100 *socios* paid $300. The base station is located in a six-floor tenement on 215th Street. At first, the *socios* paid rent. Subsequently, Seaman bought the entire building sometime in the first half of the 1990s. The building is situated next to a subway station, and the area is almost dead commercially. Seaman, therefore, obtained the building at a modest price. The *socios* financed the purchase by means of a mortgage. Each of the base's (at the time) 60 *socios* paid $500. This was necessary to be able to pay the first installment. After becoming owners of the building, the *socios* no longer had to pay rent.

In 2002, Seaman consisted of three firms—Seaman Radio Dispatcher (or the base), Seaman Realty, and Seaman Mechanical Services. All three were controlled by the *socios* and were headed and administered by the base's president. Seaman Realty, a property firm, had been created when the *socios* bought a second building, this time in a part of the Bronx. In this building, they established a car-repair shop. To be able to run this, they founded Seaman Mechanical Services. Seaman Realty managed the base's buildings. In the Bronx, Seaman had tenants, for example, other immigrants who operated small businesses. In Inwood, the *socios* had invested a significant sum in the base's offices. On the building's second floor, they had just opened a hall for ceremonies, fiestas, and seminars. The hall could be rented.

Of Seaman's 45 *socios*, about 20 continued to drive a livery for the base. The others had different jobs. Four had studied and later moved back to Santo Domingo where they now worked for the Dominican state; they remained *socios*. Many of the others had obtained their own small businesses in New York; a few had become owners of repair shops; others owned and ran parking lots. When a *socio* bought his own business, the base assisted him in obtaining a bank loan by helping him with documents and application.

In October 2002, Seaman had just sent off an application to New York City's authorities. Seaman wanted to purchase four or five buildings in a neighborhood in the Bronx. The buildings were owned by the city but were abandoned and dilapidated. The base offered to buy but demanded also that the city spend money on the buildings' remodeling and restoration. The goal was to be able to offer apartments in the buildings to *socios* and others and to hire out space for small-business development.

In 2004, High Class was owned by 97 *socios*, and consisted of three businesses—two car services and a car-repair shop.[5] High Class was created in 1995 when a large group of Dominican drivers founded a new base in northern Manhattan. Two years later, High Class's *socios* bought a building on Jerome Avenue in the Bronx. They financed the purchase with a loan. In this building, they opened another car service, High Class Bronx, and a car-repair shop. In 2004, the three entities employed 54 people. Each of the three had its own manager. The principal leader and administrative head of all three was the base's president, elected by the 97 *socios* every two years.

In 2004, High Class had already managed to pay off a large part of its debt; the rest of the loan would be paid off in two years' time. High Class's administration and *socios*, therefore, discussed whether they should make new, major investments. One of the options they considered was to buy another building. Another was to invest considerably more in the building they already owned, on Jerome Avenue. Later in 2004, the base would say "yes" or "no" to a business proposal. This proposal sketched a detailed plan for the construction of between twenty and twenty-six new apartments in the building on Jerome Avenue. If High Class decided to say yes, the plan would be to sell the apartments to some of the base's *socios*.

Another base that had managed to secure another source of income was Fort George. At the time of my fieldwork, Fort George was probably the only Dominican base to own a significant part of a company forming a part of New York's black car industry. The *socios* in Fort George controlled fifty percent of Nonstop Limousine, a black car company serving downtown and midtown Manhattan. Nonstop's manager was Pedro Heredia, a Dominican immigrant in his forties. Pedro came to be one of my best informants. He was bilingual, one of few in the Dominican livery community who spoke fluent English. He had moved from the Cibao to New York in his teens and had served in the U.S. marines. Before being hired as Nonstop's manager, he had both driven a livery and worked in the black car business. Pedro was also an activist and a grass-roots leader. At the time of the fieldwork, he headed a newly formed organization, the New York City For-Hire Base Group. Established to fight for improved conditions for livery drivers, this was backed by most of the Dominican bases in Washington Heights and Inwood and some in the Bronx. On the board were Pedro and a group of presidents of Dominican bases.

Fort George and Nonstop were separate companies, but they shared offices. At the farther end of the Fort George base station, Nonstop had two tiny offices. These offices housed Pedro and two others, Luis Zayas (a clerk) and Ivelisse Jiménez (a secretary), both Dominicans. Nonstop and Fort George shared a meeting room. Pedro and Silvio ran two different operations but saw each other daily and were good friends. They often discussed common affairs. Pedro was even a Fort George *socio*, one of those who had elected Silvio.

Nonstop would probably not have existed but for Pedro. In 1998, he stopped driving a livery and started to work as a driver for a black car company. He soon saw that he made more money in his new job than he had done as a livery driver. Like the rest of those who drove black cars, he now transported executives and employees in big companies who worked in Manhattan's financial district. The clients are the corporations, and their executives and employees pay by means of vouchers, not in cash. Having picked them up outside an office building located in downtown or midtown, Pedro drove them to another part of the city or to places like Long Island, New Jersey, and Connecticut.

Nonstop was founded a couple of years later, after Pedro had approached Fort George and another company with a proposal. Pedro went first to the *socios* in Fort George and explained that he wanted the new company to offer work to drivers from Fort George. He then went to a major player in the black-car industry, the Executive Transportation Group, owner of a series of New York's black-car companies. Together they created Nonstop. Fort George and the Executive Transportation Group own 50 percent each of Nonstop. Pedro was given the job as a manager. Three years later, in 2003, Nonstop had the following corporations as regular clients: Morgan Stanley, Lehman Brothers, Solomon Smith Barney, Deutsche Bank, Barclays, Goldman Sachs, and Merrill Lynch.

To begin with, Nonstop recruited a number of drivers from Fort George; in 2003, Dominicans who belonged to Fort George continued to drive for Nonstop. But most of Nonstop's drivers were immigrants from Asia, the Middle East, and West Africa. All these drivers arrived once a week or once every two weeks in Fort George's base station to deliver their vouchers to Pedro, Luis, or Ivelisse. On a normal day in the Nonstop office, it was almost as if one were in a part of the United Nations building. People from many parts of the world said hello and carried out their errands, before heading back to downtown's financial district.

Fort George's involvement in the black car industry had given the base a solid foundation. In 2000 a share in Fort George was priced at $6,000. In 2003, the price had gone up to $25,000: a *socio* who wanted to sell would receive $25,000 from the rest of the partners. In mid-2004, Fort George had taken a new step, renting a location in the Bronx; the plan was to use this to establish a carwash business.

Another Washington Heights base that had tapped into the city's black car industry was Highbridge. Highbridge, which was owned by fourteen Dominican drivers, remained a livery base. But Highbridge had managed to secure an extra source of income. One of its owners and leaders was Eduardo Aquino, who worked both as a manager for the base and as an ordinary driver. Like Pedro in Nonstop, Eduardo had earlier driven a cab in downtown Manhattan. Before he and his partners bought Highbridge in 1999, he had worked for twelve years in the city's black car industry, mainly for a company run by Russian Americans. After 1999, Eduardo used his contacts. Agreements were made with the same black car company for which he used to work; this company sometimes lacked drivers, particularly during rush hours, and Eduardo arranged for Highbridge to send some drivers downtown if the black car company needed it. Highbridge's drivers had been registered in the black car company and had the necessary documents. If they were needed downtown, they worked like any driver who drove a black car and were paid by vouchers; they got their cash a week or so after the voucher had been handed over to the company. For each voucher from a Highbridge driver the car company processed, Highbridge was paid a small percentage, and this strengthened the base's finances.

Eduardo and his partners also attempted something else: they opened a multiservice agency, located in Highbridge's base station. The goal had been to create a small business that did a bit of everything—from selling phone cards and processing remittances to offering brokerage and travel agency services. But when I began the fieldwork in 2002, this project was already rather dead. The turnover in the agency was very small, and Eduardo acknowledged that they had so far failed. He said the base had lacked sufficient capital.

Another base that made an attempt to diversify was Superb. Up to 2002, Superb was exclusively a livery base. After 2002, it tried to convert a part of its fairly spacious base station into spaces for three small businesses.

Superb's reconstruction of a part of its base station began in early 2003. The base's space was rented, but the base had a fifteen-year lease, and the location was good. When I left the city in January 2003, Benito (the president) had just taken the first step. When I returned to the base six months later, more reconstruction had been carried out. In mid-2004, the reconstruction had been completed, and Superb's address now housed four entities: the base station with its offices, a small coffee shop, a small barbershop, and a small multiservice agency. The barbershop had already opened; the Dominican-born barber hired his own people and paid rent to the base. The coffee shop and the multiservice agency would open soon. The base would not operate these businesses itself but would rent out the space.

A last example of commercial expansion and diversification should be mentioned. One of the large bases in Upper Manhattan is Kennedy Car Service, owned collectively by a group of Dominican drivers. In 2002, this base purchased another base,[6] which Kennedy remodeled and reopened with an inauguration ceremony and a street party on September 14, 2002. Kennedy gave this base, which is situated in the southern Bronx, the name Kennedy New City. The purchase and the remodeling cost Kennedy's *socios* over $100,000. Both bases were headed and run by Kennedy's president.

The diversification has produced a certain differentiation. Bases like Seaman and Fort George have managed to strengthen their economic position. But the vast majority of the Dominican car services continue to be like Kennedy, Superb, and Highbridge. They remain either wholly or almost wholly dependent on the weekly sums paid by their drivers, and they chronically lack capital and struggle to survive.

The cases of Seaman and High Class are instructive, though, not to say thought-provoking. These bases had bought property. When I carried out my fieldwork, both dreamed of being able to assist their *socios*, or some of them, in obtaining apartments, and perhaps small businesses, in the same tenement or set of tenements (in a part of the Bronx). Friendship continued to serve as the idiom for their activities and projects, even after the base had capitalized and improved its economic standing.

More Than Work: Ceremonies, Sports and Politics

Dominican drivers often refer to their base as "*la compañía*" (the company), and as one driver once put it, "the point of the company is, like in any company, the work," or making money. But as both this driver and the rest of those I met in the Dominican livery community acknowledged, *la compañía* is, nonetheless, also about something more than making a living. As the same driver explained to me, "The point is the work, but, well, we consist of various parts. . . . Me, for example, I've always had a passion for sports." He went on to describe how being part of a base and working as a livery driver had made it possible for him to continue to cultivate his passion. In the base, he and other drivers played softball and basketball regularly and organized and participated in tournaments. Sometimes he and his teammates from the base traveled to a city like Boston or Miami to meet another Dominican team or a team composed of Puerto Ricans or Cubans. Or they met a team on the island; as he reiterated, he loved this. It formed an important part not only of everyday routines but also of his feeling of belonging.

The Dominican car services are businesses—but businesses that mirror forms and practices in Dominican *clubes*. Just like Dominican voluntary associations, Dominican car services organize sports, social gatherings, and picnics. And just like the clubs, the bases have political functions. Many in the Dominican car services carry out political work.

The Dominican-owned car service resembles a "total" phenomenon (in the Maussian, or classic anthropological sense of this expression; Mauss 1923–24). The practices and processes that give the Dominican car service its characteristic shape should not be reduced to mere economics. They also have social, cultural, political, and recreational components. Anyone who seriously wishes to comprehend the Dominican livery bases, how they were able to emerge and how they are reproduced and transformed, must attempt to understand them in their complexity.

Many Dominican men are sports fans, and quite a few love to participate a bit themselves. The main sport in the Dominican livery community is softball. In most bases, there is a group of drivers who regularly play softball. The season starts each year in the spring and ends in the fall, and there is an impressive number of series. These series, which all have their own names (for example, "La Liga Porfirio Reyes" or "The Porfirio Reyes Series" staged by the Kennedy base), are organized by the bases themselves, sometimes in cooperation with others in the Dominican immigrant community (such as clubs or representatives of other parts of the small-business sector). In some of the series, the teams that play against each other are from different bases; in others, they are from the same base. Sometimes a series consists of teams in part from Dominican livery bases and in part from Dominican popular clubs. The games are played in the city's parks and sports grounds. Other sports and games in which Dominican car services in northern Manhattan are involved are basketball, football, and dominos.

Fort George in earlier years had participated in a softball series with teams from other bases, but, in 2002, it organized its own internal series. Around fifty drivers from the base formed teams that played each other. The series opened in May, and games were thereafter played each Tuesday between 10 A.M. and 1 P.M. in Inwood Hill Park, at the northern tip of Manhattan. Fort George had rented a part of the park's sports grounds from the city for the whole season. One of those drivers who participated was Daniel Lugo, who played on Fort George's basketball team also. When the softball season ended in the fall, the drivers began the basketball season. The team winning the softball series was given a prize by the base. The prize was a trip to meet a team from New Jersey or Florida or elsewhere; in 2002, the winner went to Washington, D.C.

The practice of softball and other forms of sport is accompanied by rituals. After the game in Inwood on Tuesdays, Daniel and other drivers from the base went to a cafeteria and shared a drink. When a new season opened in May, this involved a ceremony, which could be solemn. The following provides an illustration.

On May 18, 2004, Fort George inaugurated that year's softball series. The series included three teams, all from Fort George. Each team was sponsored by Dominican-owned small businesses located in the same neighborhood as the base station. One was supported by a Caridad restaurant, another by an auto dealer, and a third by an insurance broker. Fort George had declared that none of the drivers on the three teams had to pay the weekly dues to the base. The base had also paid for the players' uniforms and equipment and for the referees.

The inauguration on May 18 occurred in Inwood Hill Park and began with the entry of the three teams. A *madrina* accompanied each team; she was an employee in the business that sponsored the team. After the entry, the *madrinas* exchanged bunches of flowers as a token of friendly rivalry. The arrangement was headed by Silvio, Fort George's president. Two others who were present and participated in the ceremony were Guillermo Linares, the first Dominican-born person to win a seat on New York's City Council, and José Viloria, General Secretary of the New York State Federation of Taxi Drivers. Also present was a Dominican journalist, who subsequently wrote a piece about the event in *El Taxista*.

This year, Fort George's softball series was dedicated to the memory of the newly deceased Agustín Ortega. Ortega had been one of Fort George's drivers, "number 27." As part of the inauguration, his family (represented by his father, a sister, and a brother, who also drove for Fort George) was presented with a commemorative plaque by Silvio.

Sometimes softball games are accompanied by a picnic. Drivers who play bring their wives and children, and a large gathering eats and relaxes in the park after the game.

Ceremony and social gathering are always part of the events when a base hosts a team from another city or when a group from the base travels. In the fall of 2002, for example, Fort George hosted a softball team from Maryland, Los Bachatús. At the opening ceremony in Inwood Hill Park, Silvio formally welcomed the guests and a representative from Maryland expressed thanks for the hospitality. The teams played two matches, and the delegations shared food and drink and partied together.

On the walls in the Fort George president's office, there were framed photos of teams that had represented the base in softball tournaments over the years. The office also displayed trophies and premiums won by the base's teams. The display was a source not only of pride but also of memory and was far from uncommon. On the contrary, in many of the bases I got to know, I saw the same. On a couple of walls, there were pictures of the base's teams from various years and diplomas and trophies.

The sports activities in the bases, and the rituals accompanying them, contribute to the production of friendship. The practice of sports creates not only new friendships, but it consolidates and strengthens a multitude of already existing relations, ties between drivers, families, and bases, and between the bases and representatives of small enterprises, corporations, clubs, authorities, radio stations, and newspapers. Thus the *socios*' and drivers' making money can hardly be understood in isolation from the bases' cultivation of softball and other forms of sports.

The Dominican bases have also functioned as sites for neighborhood activism and politics. In May 2004, extensive flooding hit part of the Dominican Republic and Haiti. The area hardest hit in the Dominican Republic was Jimaní (in the southwest). In the wake of the disaster, Dominican New Yorkers organized massive collections of money, food, and other supplies. In northern Manhattan, the collections were led and coordinated by the Alianza Dominicana, the strongest of the voluntary associations led by Dominican New Yorkers. Many in the livery bases participated in the collections. In Fort George, for example, the drivers organized their own collection; they contributed money themselves and received donations. The food and other supplies donated were stored in the base station, before delivery to the Alianza Dominicana.

In other cases, a group of drivers supports an initiative or project in that part of the city where they work. This is logical: a large proportion of the drivers reside in the area, quite often with wives and children, as do many, if not most, of their customers; and the bases have, therefore, a strong vested interest in the quality of life in the neighborhood. In Silvio's office, there were certificates that Fort George had received from associations and institutions in the area; one, from a hospital, thanked Fort George's drivers for their contribution to a blood donation drive. In the fall of 2002, another Washington Heights base, High Class, backed an attempt to create a new library (Enver 2002).

In most bases, there are some drivers who take an active part in politics. Several support one of the large Dominican parties, particularly during periods when the Dominican Republic holds elections. Others back the city's Democrats. A number do both simultaneously—they take part in both the Dominican Republic's and New York's political processes.

A striking example was Camacho. Camacho was not just one of the most experienced in Washington Heights car services; he had for more than twenty years taken part in politics. In Upper Manhattan and the Bronx, he worked for the Democrats. On the island, he had always backed the Partido Revolucionario Dominicano (PRD). In New York, he had supported, and worked together with, Latino Democrats, figures like José Rivera, Fernando Ferrer, and Guillermo Linares. When the PRD's leaders arrived from the island to visit Washington Heights, Camacho lent a hand.

Driving a Livery, Negotiating Masculinity

This chapter has argued (1) that the Dominican car services have to be understood as network-driven processes, propelled and sustained by exchanges between friends and acquaintances, and (2) that the bases are products of a series of material and cultural practices—business activities, sports, social gatherings, ceremony, and politics.

The networks that have generated the bases are gendered. If it is correct to say that the Dominican car services resemble total phenomena, it is also necessary to recognize that these enterprises are massively male: simply because almost all those who own the bases, and drive liveries, are men. Only a few Dominican women are part of the livery industry. In earlier works, I have discussed the relationship between notions of masculinity and the construction of leadership and authority among Dominicans (Krohn-Hansen 1996; 2009: 49–156),[7] claiming that ideas about masculinity among the Dominican masses constitute a dominant discourse—a discourse that helps shape the socially and politically desirable and thinkable and the society's power relations—but also that they are nuanced. Many concepts and categories—or cultural images—are used in everyday life in Dominican society to give shape to, and assess, male conduct (like "independence," "courage," "generosity," "seriousness," and so on).

There is a considerable overlap between those vernacular ideas about masculinity that have for decades shaped society and politics on the island and those notions of masculinity that have given form to the Dominican car services in New York. Or to put it another way, the Dominican bases have been built through thinking about masculinity—and this comes from the island, though migration brings changes: the car services are products of change, and those who move to New York are forced to adapt.

Dominican men's male ideals may be roughly divided into five different groups of ideas (Krohn-Hansen 1996: 111–20). These ideas have been transported to New York. First, a basic image of masculinity on the island is that of the *hombre independiente*, the free, independent, autonomous man. This ideal says that a man should be able to make his own decisions. He ought to be sufficiently free, not a slave. Compared to a factory worker or a wage earner, a man who works as a livery driver is "free." He runs his own operation and makes his own decisions. Dominican livery drivers call themselves "*independientes*" or independent contractors. Time and again, those I met in the bases would tell me this. Another important and inseparable image of masculinity is that of the *hombre valiente*, the courageous man. A man has to be brave, not a coward. To keep his independence and dignity, he should be willing to fight, provided that it is necessary. I sometimes asked men in the bases why there were so few women livery drivers and often got this reply: in the 1980s and 1990s, many drivers were robbed; a high number were killed; to drive a livery is dangerous, so it is a job for a man, not for a woman.

Another set of ideas revolves around an image of the man as one who should *compartir*—spend time and share resources with his male comrades. The good man is generous. He is willing to do others a favor and cultivates reciprocity and friendship. Closely linked to this image is that of a man as one who dedicates himself to politics and/or sports. In the Dominican Republic, politics and sports are national passions. The country's political processes—and sports activities—are almost entirely based on patronage and clientage or mutual exchanges between friends. It is easy to see that these ideals have been important in New York also. The livery bases have provided Dominican immigrant men with an arena for production of friendship and comradeship between men. The base is a place where it is possible and necessary to *compartir*, to participate in reciprocity. But there is more. These sites, or these systems of reciprocity, have not just made it possible for many to survive economically: they have also made it feasible for many to take part in forms of sports and politics—quite simply to be a man.

Third, another central concept is that of the man as *serio*, that is, serious. As already said, the serious man is the man who enjoys enforceable trust. He is the man who fulfills his obligations, who does not take what belongs to another. To characterize a man's "seriousness" is to speak directly about his creditworthiness and capacity for reciprocity and friendship. In brief, discourses that produce differences between those men who are serious, or *serios de verdad* (really serious), and those others who are not sufficiently serious, *sin vergüenzas* (shameless), condense an entire political, economic, and social worldview. This worldview states that men should construct society—or businesses and other activities—by means of mutual exchanges, transactions between kin and friends. The label *serio* is probably one of the most frequently employed words in Dominican society and is also frequently used in the Empire City—because all these commercial activities have been network-driven, they have been created with the aid of (material and cultural) friendship.

Fourth, Dominicans sometimes claim about a man that he is eloquent, or skilled at using words. They say, for example, that *"Tiene un verbo fácil"*—he speaks easily. Important national leaders (like Joaquín Balaguer and Juan Bosch, two former presidents) have been intellectuals and prolific authors, and, time and again, authority in politics is explicitly related by ordinary people to evaluations of verbal skills. It would be a gross exaggeration to maintain that the Dominican car services are products of rhetorical abilities or eloquence. But as we have seen, these institutions have also been arenas for the exercise of power and authority. Some men in the bases have become leaders. In the political processes in the bases, verbal skills have played a part. Silvio, for example, knew how to speak. He was an engineer and had worked both for the Dominican state and as a teacher. He also knew how to represent the base and to stage ceremonies. This was recognized by the others in the base.

Fifth, as I have previously said, many Dominican men's relations to women reflect a paradox. On the one hand, a man is supposed to be a good husband and father, providing for his woman and children. On the other, he is expected to be *mujeriego* or a womanizer, engaged in sexual conquest even when he is married or living in a stable union. A good deal of Dominican men's constructions of male identity can be understood as continuous attempts to strike a viable balance between these two sets of ideals, and this applies also to Dominican men in New York. The situation in the bases reflected this. Some of those I met in the bases appeared to be loyal husbands and fathers. A large number were divorced. Some had new partners, and many had children with various women.

So far, I have mainly claimed that the Dominican livery bases embody a deep cultural continuity, that they mirror a set of well-worn Dominican masculine ideals, notions that for a long time have given form to economy, society, and politics on the island. Yet this is not the whole story. The Dominican bases also reflect change; the Dominican livery sector is an outcome of adaptations to the U.S. economy and society.

While friendship and an accompanying lack of formality have shaped transactions and practices in the bases, Dominican drivers know perfectly well that things work in a different manner in other parts of the city. Drivers often explained to me that, in the United States, the law was the law; it was applied. If they were fined by the police, they said, they knew that they had to pay. Likewise with the Taxi and Limousine Commission and the rest of the bureaucracy: drivers knew well that the paperwork had to be done and that they had to keep to the time limits. In the Dominican Republic, they said, this could be different: rules and regulations there were not always applied. One man, a driver in Superb, put it like this: "Let's say that I buy a car in my home country [the Dominican Republic]. I get auto insurance, pay it only once, and then forget about it. I return no more to the insurance agency. Here, it's different. Here, if you don't renew the insurance, you lose your license. Here, the city is well organized."

Many in the bases showed a striking discipline. They worked six or seven days a week, often between nine and twelve hours a day. Most of those I met in the bases believed that a man typically worked harder in New York than on the island. One consequence is that many drivers have less time to spend on their male friends, compared to (urban and rural) working-class men on the island. As an example of this type of self-discipline, one man in Fort George who was keen on softball and on partying after a game always drove some extra hours the day before he played, so that he did not lose work or money.

A number of authors have examined how Dominican immigrant women's regular access to jobs and wages in New York City has resulted in challenges to the traditional Dominican domestic code and the fashioning of more egalitarian unions (Pessar 1987, 1994; Grasmuck and Pessar 1991). Traditionally, Dominican women have been expected to place a high priority on marriage, motherhood, and dedication to family life, while men, as we have seen, have been expected to be providers and household heads. In New York, many Dominican women have jobs outside the household and make their own money. On the island, this is less common. In New York, more Dominican men are, therefore, forced to participate more in child rearing, cooking, and other domestic tasks; on the island, these are mainly female domains.

These processes may be observed also among those Dominicans who populate the livery bases. Often a Dominican livery driver has a wife or partner who also works. In these cases, the driver's everyday practices reflect this. One example is Miguel Peguero, a driver in Fort George. Miguel's wife, who was from the Dominican Republic, had her own job outside the household, and they had two daughters. The family lived in Washington Heights. Miguel began his work at 6 A.M. He drove until noon. At that time, he had a quick lunch before he continued to work. At 5 P.M., he picked up his two daughters, who both went to school, and drove them home. At home, he prepared dinner and looked after the girls. When his wife returned from work later in the evening, Miguel and his daughters had already eaten, and her dinner waited in the kitchen.

Yet we should not exaggerate the significance of such changes. Many, if not most Dominican men continue to take extremely little part in the work at home. On the contrary, they continue to expect a wife or partner to carry out the bulk of the domestic tasks, even when she has her own job outside the household. As already noted, the rate of separation and divorce among Dominican New Yorkers is strikingly high. Many of these separations and divorces seem to have their roots in the man's lack of will to adapt and change— or in conflicts between the parties over the division of labor and the decision making in the household.

* * *

I have argued that the Dominican-controlled car services have been created and constructed through particular images of masculinity. Dominican immigrant men who have worked in other sectors have perhaps not had the same opportunity to reproduce a powerful Dominican discourse of maleness. At least we ought to acknowledge that the Dominican bases, with their large collections of Dominican men, appear to have made it especially easy for many Dominican immigrant men to *compartir*—or spend time and share ideas, stories, resources, and fate—with other Dominican men, comrades and fellow countrymen.

But this needs a couple of qualifications. First, *most* Dominican immigrants (and both men and women) have made considerable use of friendship—and I have already shown that those friendships that they have especially drawn on have been with other Dominican immigrants. Second, the city has an abundance of Dominican voluntary associations. Many of these *clubes*—in particular, those that have devoted themselves to sports, social gatherings, and forms of community activism—have played a part overlapping with that of the livery bases. Both arenas have largely functioned as places where the men, not the women, have ruled.[8] Put another way, those Dominican immigrant men who have not belonged to a Dominican base have been able to *compartir*, or cultivate friendship, with other Dominican immigrant men in the *clubes*.

PART III

CHAPTER 5

Dominicans and Hispanics

As we have seen, a significant number of the Dominican immigrants in Washington Heights and elsewhere in New York are involved in forms of political activism, which is an important field. It acts as an intermediary between the everyday life of the bulk of the Dominican immigrants and the city's more formal political activities (such as the elections). New York's most prominent Dominican-born elected officials have had and still have strong links with grass-roots activists, clubs, and industrial bodies. Toward the end of this chapter and in the two that follow, I look more closely at the Dominican New Yorkers' forms of political activism and, especially the connections between specific forms of political activism and the emergence of important political leaderships.

But it is impossible to understand forms of activism in the Dominican community in New York unless we first have some answers to the following question: how have Dominican migrants in Washington Heights and elsewhere in the city identified racially and ethnically? The two sets of processes—the construction of political life and the production of race and ethnicity—are intimately interwoven. On the one hand, forms of activism and political processes are shaped by constructions of race and ethnicity. On the other hand, racial and ethnic formations are themselves products of society's power struggles—including those that are fought by means of activist and/or overtly political practices (Omi and Winant 1994; Wade 1997; Gregory 1998; De Genova and Ramos-Zayas 2003; Oboler 2006; Escobar 2008; Lazar 2008).

Most of the Dominicans settling in Washington Heights and Inwood continue to view themselves as "*dominicanos*" or "Dominicans." A few sometimes call themselves "Dominican American," but they too maintain a strong Dominican identity (see also Duany 1994: 33–34). This does not mean that

Dominican immigrants do not change; the vast majority adapt to their new homeland and become Americanized. But most continue to look at and represent themselves as Dominican, or possibly Dominican American.

Since about 1970, the United States has seen the gradual emergence of a new overarching identity—one termed "Hispanic" or "Latino" in English and "*hispano*" or "*latino*" in Spanish. The terms—Hispanic and Latino—are now used in the United States to refer to all people in the country whose ancestry is predominantly from one or more Spanish-speaking countries. As Suzanne Oboler observed, the label Hispanic/Latino "therefore assigns people of a variety of national backgrounds to a single 'ethnic' category. It encompasses great racial and class diversity, obscures gender differences, and even includes people whose primary language is not Spanish [such as Brazilians]" (1992: 22; see also Giménez 1989; Calderón 1992; Flores 2000; Dávila 2001; Suárez-Orozco and Páez 2002; Arreola 2004; Oboler 2006). The labels Hispanic and Latino were also used by most Dominican immigrants I met in Washington Heights and elsewhere in the city. People often spoke of themselves as *hispanos* and/or *latinos*. If they spoke English, they used the English categories. The most frequently employed term among Dominican New Yorkers was *hispano* or Hispanic, not *latino* or Latino. But a few preferred to use *latino*/Latino, and many employed both terms. I must emphasize that this new identity—Hispanic—did not at all replace the identity as Dominican (or Dominican American); rather, it functioned as an additional identity, one that could be used in everyday situations and in encounters with representatives of authorities and bureaucracies and could be mobilized by Latino (that is, Puerto Rican, Dominican, Mexican, Colombian, and so on) activists, organizations, and politicians. My informants had, and used, both these identities. They were primarily Dominican or Dominican American, but they also formed part of a much wider category of United States/New York Hispanics or Latinos.

Racial, ethnic, and panethnic identities are not best understood in terms of answers to abstract questions (like "To which race do you belong in the United States?" or "How do you identify yourself ethnically?"). Instead, we ought to see racial, ethnic, and panethnic identifications as results of myriads of social practices—as "productions." The practices that "fix" racial, ethnic, and panethnic subject positions within a given social order are outcomes of historical processes and imbued with power. In addition, they are many faceted—they are spatial, material, cultural, and political. They cross conventional boundaries between social domains or fields. They are a part of the everyday, of the economy, of the educational sector, of the family, of rituals and ceremonies, and so on.

In what ways did Washington Heights Dominicans produce and sustain their identity as Dominican? In what ways did they produce an identity as Hispanic? My goal in this chapter is to provide answers to these questions, to show how various practices and processes produced and gave form to two forms of belonging—the two identifications *dominicano/a* and *hispano/a*. The four sections are entitled (1) everyday life in tenements, households, and families; (2) racial classification practices; (3) political economy; and (4) forms of political action. The division is exclusively analytical; the practices and processes under each heading do not occur in isolation but are closely connected with the rest of the practices and processes the chapter examines.

Everyday Life in Tenements, Households, and Families

Dominican immigrants in Washington Heights claimed to be, and felt, Dominican. Take Miguel Peguero, for example, a livery driver around forty who had lived fourteen years in New York. Asked how he saw himself, he said, "Well, I'm Dominican. In my view, a person's nationality doesn't change a bit dependent on where one lives. You, if you live here, you have to comply with the laws of the United States. What happens? I'm a Dominican, because I feel Dominican—[but] I live here."

Or Marisol Romero, mentioned in Chapter 3. A single mother in her late twenties, she was a waitress at El Sitio, a Washington Heights restaurant, and attended classes in English and computer science at City College at 138th Street. We discussed her daily routines and her contact with her family on the island. When I asked her about how she identified herself, her reply came without a moment's hesitation: "Dominican."

Rather than assume that identity is a frozen entity, or a "thing," we ought to examine "it" as a reflection of specific, changeable processes. In the following, I argue that common everyday and ritual practices in Washington Heights tenements, households, and families helped produce and sustain a Dominican belonging.

In a sizable part of northern Manhattan, most tenements were mainly occupied by Dominicans when I conducted my fieldwork. This was true, for example, of most blocks east of Broadway between 170th and 193rd Streets, and a considerable part of Inwood, east of Broadway between Dyckman and

215th. South of 170th Street as well, many blocks and tenements were largely inhabited by Dominicans.

The use of Spanish was not only a part of everyday life but was also taken for granted. Spanish was used on the pavement outside the building, on the stoop, in the stairway, and inside the apartments. One could hear children and adults who (only, mainly, or sometimes) spoke English, but the language that prevailed was Spanish. Since most were of Dominican descent, people continued to speak Spanish in a Dominican manner—with accents, words, and expressions derived from the island. People did not use only the language of the native country; neighbors who resided on the same block exchanged memories and news both from the island and from the city's Dominican community.

In the tenement where I rented my room, a small group of Dominican men—all elderly and/or retired first-generation immigrants—often killed time together. They spent mornings and afternoons together on the stoop or in the stairway, observing and talking with each other and with others who resided in the vicinity. In the evening, others from the tenement—all Dominicans—spent a while on the stoop, greeting and conversing with neighbors. In the summer, neighbors often spent a part of the evening together outside the tenement. Some placed chairs on the pavement. Others played dominos. A number listened to merengue and bachata. A few had a beer or a shot of rum. Dominican children played on the pavement and in the stairway. This reminded first-generation Dominican immigrants of scenes in the native country. The buildings and the streets were evidently different, but those who occupied them, and a number of their activities, were similar.

To illustrate, I present an excerpt from one of my fieldwork diaries:

> *Thursday August 1, 2002.*—I spent around an hour of the evening sitting on the stoop, from nine to ten. No one but me from my tenement sat on the stoop or the pavement. A few yards away, on the pavement outside the next-door tenement, a woman sat in a chair. A young man sat next to her, also in a chair. On the stoop in front of them (they sat with their back to the street) sat three others, two women and a man. All were Dominicans and spoke Spanish. Denise [a Puerto Rican woman who had been a resident in the tenement where I now lived for several years and rented an apartment on the fifth floor] came home from work; she greeted the group on the neighboring stoop and sat down with them for about half an hour. Beyond this group, on the next

stoop, I saw another group of neighbors, observing, greeting neighbors, and chatting. Between us, some small Dominican children played on the pavement; a couple had bicycles. About half past nine, an ice-cream truck parked on the corner [a few yards from where I sat], and some neighbors bought ice cream.... The two Dominican bodegas I could see from where I sat were open and people from my own tenement and others in the vicinity entered and left. A group of Dominican teenagers, all boys, played basketball on the court situated on the other side of the crossroads; they spoke English and Spanish. As far as the eye could see, I saw cars densely parked on both sides of the street.[1]

Children of Washington Heights Dominicans who attended school usually spoke both English and Spanish, but at home with their mothers and fathers and other adults (grandmother and grandfather, aunts, uncles, and so on), they spoke Spanish. Another crucial identity source is the daily preparation and eating of food—the household's food habits; as has often been said, you are what you eat. Dominican households in Upper Manhattan prepared and consumed Dominican dishes, not least for lunch and supper. People mixed what they saw as Dominican food with other food—from Kellogg's Corn Flakes to Chinese takeout to McDonalds burgers and pancakes. But Dominican food prevailed in most households. The second generation, too, consumed Dominican food. This was natural. Not only had their parents been brought up on "rice and beans"—Dominican food—but many were, as we have seen, looked after by a grandmother or other female relative, or a woman who lived next door, and these women frequently prepared Dominican staples—rice and beans, plantain, yucca, *batata*, and *yautía*.

First-generation immigrants narrated stories from the island and from their adolescence. Many continued to have strong links with relatives on the island. They often spoke with them on the phone and sent them money. A number communicated via e-mail. Marisol, the Washington Heights waitress who attended evening classes, had a sister on the island, in Baní. She called her and sent her money; about once a week she sent an email.

In sum, a set of everyday and ritual practices in tenements, households, and families helped shape and reshape a Dominican identity—experiences of a Dominican belonging, awareness of the Dominican Republic as the family's and one's own native country. But other dimensions of the same tenements, households, and families produced something else also: experiences of being a part of the newer and wider panethnic category Hispanic.

Even in the heart of those areas that constituted Dominican Washington Heights, in practice, very few tenements contained Dominicans exclusively (see, for example, Duany 1994: 13–14). Quite a few contained one or two or more Hispanics of non-Dominican origin—especially Mexicans, Ecuadorans, and Puerto Ricans, but also Hondurans, Salvadorans, and others. This created and sustained what Ricourt and Danta (2003: 36) have aptly called a "potential for experiential panethnicity." Dominicans and Hispanics of other origins spoke a common language, Spanish. Most were relatively poor. If they lived in the same building or on the same block, they sometimes met and spoke; a few went farther and, using Spanish, exchanged gossip, information, and services. In brief, even in the heart of Dominican Washington Heights, a certain limited Hispanic panethnicity arose from everyday life in tenements, on stoops, and on residential blocks.

A study using marriage records from New York documented intermarriage patterns among Hispanic groups between 1975 and 1991 (Gilbertson et al. 1996). The researchers "showed that there was considerable intermarriage among all Hispanic groups with each other" (456). But the same data demonstrated also that the city's Hispanics were "far from a homogeneous group" (457). The city's Puerto Ricans and Dominicans had "distinct patterns of intermarriage, characterized by high rates of intermarriage with each other, lower rates of intermarriage with non-Hispanics, no intergenerational increase in intermarriage, and higher rates of nonmixed ancestry among the second generation." The study also concluded that the growing size of the Dominican population in the city had "contributed to the decline in intermarriage with non-Hispanics between 1975 and 1991" (457).

Nevertheless, the fact remains that some Dominican immigrants informally lived together with, and/or married, Hispanics of non-Dominican origin—as noted, often Puerto Ricans.[2] Partnership and marriage processes meant that a number of Dominican immigrants (and parts of their families) crossed Latino nationality lines. This helped nourish Hispanic panethnicity among the city's Dominicans.

Hispanic panethnicity was also furthered by television and newspapers. Magdalena (my landlady) and her daughters used to watch Univision and Telemundo, the principal U.S. Spanish TV networks. So did most others in the city's Dominican community. People watched news, soap operas, talk shows, documentaries, and advertising broadcast by Univision and Telemundo. As Arlene Dávila has shown in her *Latinos, Inc.: The Marketing and Making of a People* (2001), over the past few decades the U.S. Hispanic marketing industry in general, and U.S. Spanish-language TV networks in particular, have reconfigured and produced Hispanic/Latino panethnicity, culture, and identity. U.S. Hispanic media live by the idea of a common "Hispanic/Latino market." New York's principal Spanish-language newspapers produced Hispanic panethnicity and identity. Dominicans in Washington Heights and Inwood read *El Diario/La Prensa, Noticias del Mundo,* or *Hoy*; all three newspapers targeted New York's "Hispanics."

Racial Classification Practices

When Dominicans moved from the island to the United States, they simultaneously moved from one hegemonic symbolic system of racial classifications to another. Both the Dominican Republic and the United States grew out of a history of colonialism and slavery, but the two countries have had, and still have, clearly dissimilar systems of racial classification. This led to a racial-identity dilemma, even a racial-identity crisis, for migrants. When Dominican immigrants in Washington Heights and elsewhere in the city presented themselves as *hispanos* or Hispanics, which they often did, they frequently used the term as a racial-identity strategy.

The Dominican political and cultural elites who headed the nation-building project in the eastern part of the island of Hispaniola from the mid-nineteenth century onward seemed almost possessed by antiblack prejudice and a desire for whitening. A consequence was that the Dominican state discourse came to associate Dominicanness "with things Hispanic (referring to Spain), Catholicism, and whiteness" (Itzigsohn and Dore-Cabral 2001: 323). This discourse came also to characterize a considerable part of the population—or broad sectors of society (Krohn-Hansen 1995; Martínez 1997; Torres-Saillant 1998; Sagás 2000; Howard 2001; Derby 2009). In reality, those who lived in the eastern part of Hispaniola covered "the entire color spectrum from black to brown to white" (Duany 1998: 162). Thus, it was impossible for the Dominican nationalist discourse to define the Dominican masses as white—but it managed to define all (true) Dominicans as nonblack and reserved the category of black for Haitians. This racist discourse was reinforced and consolidated after 1930 under Rafael Trujillo and Joaquín Balaguer.

Accordingly, Dominicans, to a certain extent, deemphasize racial differences among themselves. Yet they continuously classify one another hierarchically in terms of skin color and race. The nineteenth- and twentieth-century

Dominican Republic produced a paradoxical dogma, which stated that the bulk of the Dominican masses were *indios*, but *indios* understood as *mestizos*—people of mixed heritage (Sommer 1991: 233–56), the light-skinned product of a supposed history of mixing of light-skinned native or Indian blood with the blood of white Spaniards. In the late 1930s, the Trujillo state adopted the category *indio* as a color classification for the registration of skin color on the compulsory official identity card (Incháustegui Cabral 1976: 6; Sagás 2000: 35, 67, 130–31). When I carried out fieldwork in the southwestern Dominican Republic in the 1990s, the majority of the population were either *trigueños* ("brownish-goldens") or *indios* (indicating the span from *trigueño* to *blanco* or "white"). The *indio* category is subdivided, so that people commonly employ *indio oscuro* ("dark *indio*") and *indio claro* ("light *indio*") for purposes of classification on the basis of skin color. Completely dark-skinned people were officially classified, euphemistically, as *morenos* ("browns"), but people often spoke pejoratively of them as *negros* or *prietos* ("blacks") or simply as *haitianos* ("Haitians"—even when they were born, and had always lived, in the Dominican Republic). The system was about the same in the whole country.

The use of the term *indio* has made it possible to maintain ideas about essential differences between the Haitians seen as blacks and the Dominicans seen as whites and light-skinned *mestizos*—or *indios* (Fennema and Loewenthal 1987: 28–30, 61–65; Fennema 1998: 211). But this Dominican concept of *mestizaje* necessarily presupposed ideas about the existence of different pure categories, as an implicit guarantee of its own meaning. The difference was viewed in hierarchical terms: the most important forces that had created Dominican society, it was believed, had been white, Catholic, and Hispanic (Krohn-Hansen 2001).

Today many Haitians continue to migrate to the Dominican Republic in search of temporary or more permanent work. Many of the worst-paid jobs in the country are carried out by impoverished Haitians. Itzigsohn and Dore-Cabral (2001: 324) note that "Haitians are physically indistinguishable from dark-skinned Dominicans," but "the former are referred to as black, whereas the latter are referred to as *indio oscuro*." Hence the Dominican system of racial classifications, with intermediate racial categories between white and black (of which *indio* is the widest, the one that contains most people) is different from the dichotomizing system of racial classifications that Dominicans encounter when they enter the United States.

The U.S. system "is based on two binary distinctions: a general one between white and nonwhite, and a more specific one between white and black" (Itzigsohn and Dore-Cabral 2001: 323). In both systems, the actors' classifications are based on a combination of phenotype with other elements. In the Dominican Republic, people mainly use skin color but also use other physical factors such as hair type and facial features, and elements such as language, religion, clothes, education, and economic position; in the United States, racial classifications are often based on phenotype in combination with national and family ancestry. Whereas many in the United States classify most Dominican immigrants as "colored" or black, Dominican immigrants tend to define themselves as light-skinned or white—and categorically reject being seen as black. To this day, to be Dominican has been not to be black.

As a result, most Dominican immigrants in New York experienced the definition and representation of their own racial identity as a deep challenge. Dominican historian Frank Moya Pons has maintained that "The most unbearable aspect of his [the Dominican's] existence in the United States is having to be treated as black..., after having spent most of his life believing, thinking and seeking to be exactly the opposite" (1986a: 248; my translation).

These social and psychological tensions are reflected in U.S. census data. In the 1990 Census, for example, 50.1 percent of Dominicans in New York City chose to classify themselves as "other," 25.2 percent "black," and 24.3 percent "white": almost 75 percent as "other" or white. With that, a conspicuous number rejected the binary racial system.[3]

The categorization in the United States today of Chicanos, Puerto Ricans, Cubans, and other groups from Latin America and the Hispanic Caribbean under the terms Hispanic and Latino is the outcome of a series of changes. It seems largely to have arisen from their use by the U.S. Census Bureau and other government agencies, the media, the advertising industry, and politicians on the federal level (Moore and Pachón 1985; Giménez 1989; Dávila 2001). But it is also constantly given shape through the use of these terms by all sorts of actors on the grass-roots level (Padilla 1985; Oboler 1992; Ricourt and Danta 2003; De Genova and Ramos-Zayas 2003).

The category Latino has been employed for quite some time by U.S. activist groups, though without implying "a separate ethnic identity" as the terms Hispanic and Latino do now in many contexts (Calderón 1992: 39). The history of the category Hispanic is different:

> In the 1960s, Chicano groups fought hard to popularize the word Chicano as a replacement for Spanish-American, which implied the

assimilation of the Chicano people into U.S. society, left out the Indian heritage, and implied that Chicano history had its origins in Europe. Whereas Spanish-American had been acceptable to the large society, Chicano (or even Mexican-American) was viewed as militant.... When the term Spanish-American fell into disuse, the U.S. Census Bureau and other government agencies, with the blessing of various Latino politicians, replaced it with the term Hispanic. (Calderón 1992: 39–40)

The activity of the U.S. Census Bureau has been key, as Dávila has noted in *Latinos, Inc.* (2001: 40). In the 1970s, the U.S. Census institutionalized Hispanic as a new category for all populations from any Spanish-speaking country, even Spain. After this, the category became a widespread nationally used category[4] whose use reached a peak in the 1980s (40).[5] In the 1980 and 1990 Censuses, gathering and reporting data on race and ethnicity were guided by standards embedded in an official 1977 document, laying down four mutually exclusive single-race categories—white, black, American Indian and Alaskan native, and Asian and Pacific Islander—and two ethnicity categories: Hispanic origin and not of Hispanic origin. Under new federal standards issued in 1997 and used in the 2000 Census, there were five categories of race—white; black or African American; American Indian and Alaska Native; Asian; and Native Hawaiian and Other Pacific Islander—and a sixth category, "Some other race."

A second, perhaps more profound change allowed people to identify themselves as belonging to one or more categories. On the 2000 Census race question, respondents were asked to mark all races that applied to indicate their racial identity. People of Hispanic origin could be of any race and were instructed to answer the question on race by marking one or more of the race categories on the questionnaire. Hispanics were asked to indicate their origin in the question on Hispanic origin, not in the question on race, because in the U.S. statistical system ethnic origin (or ethnicity) remains a separate concept from race.

With these changes, the Dominican migrants in New York were offered a second chance, or a new opportunity, not available with the earlier U.S. binary system of racial classifications. At the time of my fieldwork, many Dominicans in Washington Heights and elsewhere in the city produced and sustained distinctions between three categories—"the Hispanic" (called "*el hispano*" or "*el latino*"); "the white" (called "*el blanco*" or "*el americano*" or "*el anglo*" or [more rarely] "*el gringo*"); and "the black" (called "*el moreno*" or "*el prieto*" or "*el africano americano*"). These distinctions were often shaped by means of the term *hispano*—and it was clear that the person who spoke saw himself or herself as part of the Hispanic category and saw this as a racial category.

This worked much more effectively if people represented themselves as Hispanics, not as Dominicans (or *indios*). Why? Because the term Hispanic was easy to use and present. It was now an official, widespread, and more and more important term, employed throughout the United States. A set of ideas about race (derived from the homeland), and the political and social climate in the United States, made Dominican immigrants often describe themselves as Hispanics rather than as Dominicans. For many, the intermediate racialized category *hispano*/Hispanic paralleled the Dominican Republic's intermediate racial category *indio*.

Was the Hispanic category employed in this manner in Upper Manhattan? Did many of my informants in practice racialize it? When I look at my data from observations and conversations, the answer to both questions is "yes."[6] For example, at a meeting in the Fort George car service's discipline department, after examination of a complaint by a Dominican woman in her late twenties who seemed clearly to have been a difficult passenger, Aurelio Guerrero, the chairman, said,

> Those who are difficult are we. It's the Latinos [*los latinos*] and the African Americans [*los africanos americanos*]. It's not the American [*el americano*]. What does the American do? He enters the car, says "Good morning!" and then where he is going—to 42nd Street. Thereafter they sit quietly, reading the paper. It is the same with small children. Americans place their child in a seat belt immediately—but not we. One has to remember that we have something to learn. This country became civilized a long time ago.

The consciousness of being excluded from the category white was a reality. Dominican migrants often described forms of discrimination practiced by whites (called *americanos, anglos, blancos,* or *gringos*) against Hispanics in general and Dominicans in particular. In addition, they produced and reproduced a division between themselves (or the Dominicans/the Hispanics) and the African Americans or the blacks. The division was hierarchical. This helps throw light on a finding in the academic literature: that the racist and anti-Haitian ideas on the island so far seem to have been little influenced by Dominican transnationalism and return migration. Indeed, they are described as worsening by Peggy Levitt in *The Transnational Villagers* (2001), a study of the social and political connections that have arisen between Miraflores, a town in the southern Dominican Republic, and Jamaica Plain, a neighborhood in Boston (107, 111).

But Dominican migrants' ideas and practices associated with race obviously did change. On the island, they had called themselves *trigueños*, *indios*, and *blancos*; in the United States, they chose instead to sometimes call themselves *hispanos* or *latinos*. But the new category Hispanic renders it easier for Dominican and other immigrants from the Hispanophone Caribbean and Latin America to continue to reproduce the central elements of a racist ideology that historically has been used to legitimate and naturalize whitening. As Dávila, for example, has demonstrated, the advertising industry's dissemination of generalized ideas about *el hispano* was ultimately based on "the self-image, class background, and experiences of Hispanic marketers" (2001: 59). At first, the industry was dominated by well-educated Cubans. These pioneers constructed and spread an image of the U.S. Hispanic "as a family-oriented, catholic, traditional, conservative, and immigrant Spanish-speaking individual," an image that remains dominant (60).

So the U.S. panethnic category Hispanic has effectively laid particular stress on the category's Hispanic and Catholic and, by implication, white origins, at the expense of the other possible stories of origins. The hegemonic production of Hispanic panethnicity—or a new people—in the United States has been dominated by fear of blackness and longing for whiteness. The fact that most Dominican New Yorkers appear to use the term Hispanic more often than Latino should be viewed in this light. When they used *hispano* or Hispanic more often than *latino* or Latino, they seemed to stick to their roots. The term *hispano* evokes images of Spain, at least of Spanish-Hispanic roots. The competing term *latino* is less evocative of origins in Spain.

In sum, Dominican New Yorkers continued to identify themselves as Dominicans, but they also defined themselves as Hispanics or Latinos. In either case, they produced and sustained a set of ideas about race. Because they tended to racialize their own nationality and ethnicity, they often categorized themselves as Hispanics or Latinos/as, rather than as Dominican.

The Political Economy

In factories, Dominicans work together with persons of different nationalities. Superiors and co-workers speak of them and treat them as Hispanics, and a panethnic identity—or the category Hispanic/Latino/a—is thrust on them. But work in factories also sustains simultaneously a Dominican belonging. Most Washington Heights Dominicans who worked in a factory in New Jersey went to and from the job by bus. These buses (or minibuses) functioned largely as Dominican places. A number of the drivers were Dominican, and the bulk of the passengers were Washington Heights or Bronx Dominicans employed in New Jersey factories.

Dominican small businesses contributed considerably to the maintenance of a strong national identity—a Dominican belonging—among the city's Dominicans. But they also contributed to building Hispanic panethnicity. The Washington Heights Dominican car-service industry is a case in point. Many of the passengers were not Dominican, and the drivers picked up passengers in a large part of the city. Many passengers treated the drivers as representatives of the Hispanic category, and the drivers often preferred to present themselves—for example, in conversation with a passenger—as Hispanic or Latino.

In choosing names and signs for storefronts, Dominican business owners in Upper Manhattan seemed most often to use the national—or Dominican—identity. Quite a few business names and storefronts employed the word "*dominicano*" or "Dominican." Others used the name or logo of a Dominican product, the name of a Dominican place, or the Dominican flag. But even where a storefront exploited the word Dominican, or a Dominican symbol, it usually advertised in English as well as Spanish. The result was that the typically "Dominican" streets—or storefronts—in northern Manhattan were replete with mixtures of Spanish and English, with a Dominican name, image, or flag in between. But the Dominican Washington Heights and Inwood contained also a few businesses that had chosen another strategy: they had storefronts using the terms *hispano* and *latino*.

The Santo Domingo Candy Store, for example, was located on Broadway near 175th Street. A few blocks away, on the corner of Audubon Avenue and 175th Street, was Sto. Domingo Grocery, a bodega. A famous street in the Dominican capital is El Conde, and at the corner of Broadway and 175th Street, or close to the candy store, was El Conde Steak House Restaurant. A large bodega, the Tenares Supermarket, was at the corner of

Audubon Avenue and 174th Street. A green banner bearing the characteristic Presidente logo decorated the storefront; Presidente is one of the Dominican Republic's most popular brands of beer. Next to the bodega was a Dominican travel agency, Quisqueya Tours, which advertised on the front, "*Pasajes—Seguros*—Accounting—Immigration—*Notario*—Income Taxes—*Traducciones—Divorcios*" (Tickets—Insurance—Accounting—Immigration—Notary—Income Taxes—Translations—Divorces). Six blocks away, on Audubon Avenue and 181st Street, was Esmeraldo's Bakery. In addition to the name, one could read, "*Bizcocho dominicano—Todo tipo de dulce—Especial* [sic] sandwiches" (Dominican cakes—Sweets of all kinds—Special sandwiches).

All these enterprises were in the heart of Dominican Washington Heights, between 174th and 193rd Streets. Many more businesses in the area had chosen to market their products and services by exploiting, selling, and (re)producing a national belonging—or a Dominican or New York City Dominican identity. Other storefronts located in the same area built Hispanic panethnicity. At the corner of St. Nicholas Avenue and 185th Street was the Viva Pharmacy, whose front was decorated by two signs: "Viva Pharmacy. *Farmacia Hispana* [Hispanic Pharmacy]. Cosmetics—Perfumes—Vitamins," and "Viva Pharmacy. *Latina como ninguna. Productos dominicanos*" (As Latin as Anybody. Dominican Products). On the other side of the street was a small family-run Dominican restaurant; its sign read, "*El Pollo Dorado*. Fried Chicken & Restaurant. *Especialidad en comida típica dominicana & hispana*" (The Golden Brown Chicken. Fried Chicken & Restaurant. Specializes in Typical Dominican & Hispanic Food). About eight blocks farther north, at the corner of St. Nicholas and 193rd Street, was a Dominican bodega and butcher's shop whose sign read, "Food and Meat Town. *Carnicería Hispana*" (Hispanic Butcher's Shop). Next to this business was the Dominican restaurant La Tierra: "Mi Tierra Restaurant. *Especialidad en Comida Latina y Americana*" (Restaurant My Land. Specializes in Latin and American Food).

However, the Dominican or the Dominican American identity was used most prominently. In June 2002, I gathered data on the storefronts in a few selected parts of Washington Heights and Inwood. For example, on the left side of Broadway between 174th and 175th Streets (when you walk northward), I registered two six-story apartment houses. On the ground floor were fifteen businesses—two neighborhood bodegas; one laundromat; one dry-cleaning store; three restaurants; one bicycle repair shop; two travel agencies/multiservice operations; one enterprise that sold phone calls; one 99 Cents Only store (part of a chain); one florist's shop; one beauty parlor; and one shoe store. Three of the fifteen marketed themselves as Dominican. One of the restaurants was named after a street in the Dominican capital, and each bodega was decorated by a green Presidente banner. Only one of the fifteen storefronts contained the term *hispano*, and none the term *latino*. One of the restaurants was owned by Salvadorans; that sign read, "*Comida Típica Salvadoreña e Hispana*" (Typical Salvadoran and Hispanic Food). A bit farther north, I mapped the storefronts on the right side of St. Nicholas Avenue between 186th and 187th Streets. I noted four five-story tenement buildings, with a total of twelve businesses on the ground floor—one record shop, one shoe store, one beauty salon, one barbershop, two travel agencies/multiservice operations, three bodegas, one 99 Cents Only store, and two stores selling clothing. Three of the twelve marketed themselves as Dominican. The record shop and one of the travel agencies/multiservice operations had names that included a Dominican identifier, and one bodega was equipped with a large Presidente banner. None of these twelve storefronts contained the term *hispano/latino*.[7]

These small-scale (or strongly localized) marketing practices differed from the marketing organized and staged by big companies like Colgate-Palmolive, Johnson & Johnson, Goya, and AT&T. Washington Heights small businesses, or their fronts, communicated and produced both a Dominican or Dominican American and a Hispanic or Latino identity, but big companies, with their advertising practices, bombarded northern Manhattan and the rest of the city and the country with posters that gave form to and constructed a Hispanic or Latino panethnic identity above all (Dávila 2001). Subway trains and subway stations—and buses, buildings, and streets—were replete with messages marketing commodities and services (in Spanish and English) to "Hispanic" and "Latino" consumers.

Local shopping reflected and produced two forms of belonging also. When my landlady and her daughters shopped for food and other products in Washington Heights, some of the commodities they inspected and purchased were regarded as "Dominican." Mario Solano's bodega, for example, sold "*aguacate dominicano*" or Dominican avocado. Like other *bodegueros*, he sold phone cards, of which a number had names including a national—or Dominican—identifier. People also bought Dominican biscuits, Dominican sweets, Dominican magazines, and Dominican books.[8] Other commodities sold in the neighborhood's stores contained messages and images that targeted the Hispanic market—rice, beans, juice, and a stream of other items.

These three areas of social action—everyday life in buildings, households, and families; making and remaking of race; and economy—are three social fields in which identities in the urban United States are formed. Practices and processes in these fields produced two important forms of belonging or identity among northern Manhattan's Dominicans—one "Dominican" and one "Hispanic." Below, I look at a fourth field: political history—or a set of power struggles.

Forms of Political Action

The oldest surviving clubs formed by Dominicans in New York date to the early and mid-1960s (Sainz 1990: 67–82; Torres-Saillant and Hernández 1998: 80). During this early phase of Dominican mass migration to the United States, relatively few voluntary associations were created. A fine early study notes that these were generally elitist and small (Georges 1984: 15). As time went by, the number grew rapidly. In 1984, there were more than 125 Dominican associations of all types throughout New York; most, more than 90 were in northern Manhattan (9, 20). After this, the number continued to multiply. Many were primarily recreational or social clubs, but as early as the early 1970s there were a few organizations formed to further community development, advocacy, and counseling (Torres-Saillant and Hernández 1998: 81). Over time, Dominican immigrants began to create more and more associations of this type—goal-oriented organizations that sought to eliminate obstacles to economic and social progress of Dominicans in New York.

Many of the associations had almost exclusively Dominican members, and not a few cultivated specifically Dominican interests. Some came into being to commemorate important Dominican historical dates. Others were cultural groups that preserved and propagated an interpretation of a part of "Dominican culture"—music, dance, or literature. Still others were *clubes regionalistas*, place-based associations—formed by, and for, people originally from a particular province, town, or barrio in the Dominican Republic. But this does not mean that Dominicans who belonged to voluntary associations in New York conformed to a widespread stereotypical image of such ethnic activities. As Georges (1984: 7, 12) has convincingly shown, creating or joining a club did not signify a "no" to integration; most Dominican association members with whom she worked had first chosen to form or join their group after several years of residence in the city,[9] and they as a group showed better average adjustment to the United States society than nonmembers.

After 1965, the New York City Dominican community included many people who had left the homeland primarily for political, not economic reasons. They had supported Juan Bosch or had fled the U.S.-backed Balaguer regime's repression. Some of these had considerable political and organizational experience from the island (Georges 1984: 16–20; Hoffnung-Garskof 2008: 97–131). By the mid- and late 1970s, there were in addition a growing number of young Dominican New Yorkers who had been raised in the United States from an early age and were bilingual. This led to changes in the Dominican clubs and associations, which came to contain new types of leaders and activists and became socially and politically more varied.

In 1991, Guillermo Linares was elected the first Dominican New York City councilman. He represented District 10 (in Washington Heights and Inwood) and kept the seat for the next decade. Before the 1991 elections, the lines of District 10 had been reconfigured to mirror its Dominican majority and shape a district in which Dominicans might more readily win (Graham 1997). In 1996, Adriano Espaillat became the first Dominican to serve in the New York State Assembly, after unseating John Brian Murtaugh who had held his post in Manhattan's 72nd District (in Washington Heights and Inwood) for sixteen years. When Linares was term-limited out of the City Council in 2001 after ten years, another Dominican, Miguel Martínez, replaced him as northern Manhattan's councilman. Martínez served until July 14, 2009, when he resigned abruptly from the City Council and two days later pleaded guilty to stealing $106,000 from his council office and two nonprofit groups financed by the city. He was sentenced to five years in prison.[10] All three— Linares, Espaillat, and Martínez—ran with the Democratic Party. (In northern Manhattan, like several other parts of the city, an overwhelming majority were Democrats.)

In sum, when I began my research in 2002, many of the city's Dominicans were incorporated into a historically constituted complex web of informal and formal political-social relations. These networks crossed, and linked up, various domains; they connected Dominican immigrants' households, tenements, blocks, small businesses, clubs, and associations and elected political representatives—and helped integrate the city's Dominican community into a far more comprehensive power structure, that of the United States and beyond. Thus many Dominican New Yorkers functioned as political actors.

In the late 1970s, there were several attempts at integrating and unifying the growing number of Dominican associations in the city. One outcome was the 1978 foundation of the Federation of Social Clubs, a left-wing organization that unified around two dozen Dominican clubs, mostly in Upper Manhattan (Georges 1984: 30). Another was the establishment of an official annual Dominican Day. The Dominican Day Parade Committee was founded in 1981; the second parade down Audubon Avenue in Washington Heights, in August 1982, "attracted approximately 100,000 people and included participation by a broad spectrum of associations and the Dominican population in general; it was officially recognized by the mayor and governor, who took the opportunity to declare an annual Dominican Day" (31).

The parade became in many ways a milestone, a striking expression of the fact that the city's Dominicans had now become many and had improved their collective bargaining position in the new homeland. Since the start in the early 1980s, every year (on a Sunday in August), well over 150,000 people have gathered in midtown Manhattan to celebrate Dominicanness and display many of the Dominican immigrants' traditions and activities. After this, such massive Dominican gatherings have proliferated, for example, those in the Bronx and in Haverstraw, New York, as well as equivalent annual gatherings in New Jersey and Connecticut (Torres-Saillant and Hernández 1998: 102).

The everyday and ritual activities of the many Dominican clubs and associations were not only political; they also helped give form to, and construct, identity. It is the same with the activities of the grass-roots leaders and elected officials. Doing full justice to the complexity and variety embedded in this field (the activist-political field) looks like an impossible task.[11] In the remainder of this section (and this chapter), my goal is more limited. Rather than trying to be exhaustive, I shall present a case, looking in detail at a set of political-social events and processes and examining just how voluntary associations, community activists, and politicians helped forge forms of New York City Dominican belonging and Latino panethnicity.

A key symbol among Dominicans, both on the island and in New York, is the historical figure of Juan Pablo Duarte (1813–76). The hegemonic Dominican discourse has canonized Duarte; it has transformed him and his life into an image—a myth with accompanying rituals. Today most Dominicans describe him as the most important of *los padres de la patria—the* founding father of the Dominican Republic as an independent nation. The formal creation of the Dominican Republic as an independent entity, proclaimed on February 27, 1844, took place through a separation from Haiti—according to the Dominican nationalist discourse, from a Haitian barbarian tyranny.[12]

The Haitians' first public decision, once they held Santo Domingo in 1822, was to decree the abolition of slavery in the former Spanish colony and offer land to all the freed men. But after 1844 these and related facts were mostly forgotten. Instead, the new republic generated, as we have seen, a set of ideas about itself and its own population that were conspicuously anti-Haitian. Thus, being Dominican largely came to mean *not* being Haitian or, worse, being anti-Haitian. Duarte was, and remains, *the* incarnation of the Dominican national project. Two years after the Dominican Republic commemorated the centenary of Duarte's death, President Joaquín Balaguer published his *El Cristo de la Libertad: Vida de Juan Pablo Duarte* (*The Christ of Liberty: The Life of Juan Pablo Duarte*) ([1978] 1987); a sculpture of Duarte's face decorated the front cover. The face of Duarte is well known throughout the country. The story of his heroism has been used in the state school system. Streets and squares have been named after him. The heart of La Descubierta—the community where I conducted research in the early 1990s—was the park in the village nucleus; in this park, there was a sculpture of Duarte.

New York's Dominicans have kept the memory of Duarte alive and invoked him to express and maintain a Dominican American identity. Today in Washington Heights and elsewhere in the city, Dominican immigrants continue to use the nation's memory of Duarte to give shape to, and construct, belonging. This history documents in a clear manner that the production of identity has to be viewed as a political process—as a component of a wider field of power relations and power struggles with accompanying cultural processes. This history would have been unthinkable if it had not been for the activities of a set of Dominican clubs and associations. Other important actors have been some of northern Manhattan's political activists and elected officials.

A key figure in all this has been Guillermo Linares, who served for a decade—1992 to 2001—on City Council, was appointed city commissioner of immigrant affairs in 2004, and in 2010 was elected state assemblyman for northern Manhattan's 72nd District, replacing Adriano Espaillat who the same year was elected to the State Senate. Linares has not only been a pioneer and for many years a leader who has wielded a significant influence in the Washington Heights and Inwood Dominican community; he has also been a highly active supporter of building and consolidating a new collective Dominican American identity—through the memory of Duarte.

The two oldest surviving formal clubs or voluntary associations of Dominican New Yorkers are the Centro Cívico Cultural Dominicano (founded in 1962) and the Club Cívico Cultural Juan Pablo Duarte (1966) (Sainz 1990: 69–72; Hoffnung-Garskof 2008: 128–30). The former was founded to promote and maintain Dominican culture in the United States, the latter to preserve the memory of Duarte and spread his political and social thinking. Sainz (1990: 72) writes that the Club's president in the late 1980s had explained to him that the club's founder "would walk in Central Park and he would see the statues of Bolívar, San Martín, José Martí and would question the fact that Juan Pablo Duarte was not represented.... Then he decided to form the Club." Many of the founders were intellectuals, and all were Dominicans (73–74). Since 1988, following a suggestion made by President Balaguer, the official name is the Instituto Duartiano of New York (Torres-Saillant and Hernández 1998: 80). The mother entity is located on the island; Santo Domingo has for a long time housed an institution with the name Instituto Duartiano.

Today Lower Manhattan has a thirteen-foot bronze statue of Duarte made by an Italian, Nicola Arrighini. The statue, on Duarte Square, a brick triangle on the north side of Canal Street at Sixth Avenue, was a gift from the Dominican state, that is, the Balaguer regime, in the mid-1970s. To the members of the Instituto Duartiano of New York (and to many other Dominican New Yorkers), the statue and square were important, a source of ethnic pride. The members of the Club played a key part when the statue was erected, and the square was used for an annual ceremony. Each year on January 26, a number of Dominican New Yorkers commemorated the birthday of *el padre de la patria* in a ritual on Duarte Square. Other dates the Instituto Duartiano of New York annually marked with ceremonies were February 27 and July 15 and 16; February 27 is Dominican Independence Day, July 15 the anniversary of Duarte's death, July 16 the anniversary of the day Duarte and his closest allies created La Trinitaria, a secret organization for the liberation of the territory that in 1844 became a new nation.

The most important of these days was probably Duarte's birthday. Each year since the beginning in the 1960s, the Instituto has celebrated this date with a solemn meal or a banquet. The ceremony has been held in a Latino or Dominican restaurant in Washington Heights or Inwood, and those present have been leaders and members of the Instituto and a number of others who have wielded influence and/or enjoyed respect among the city's, and especially Upper Manhattan's, Dominicans—representatives of the small-business community, of clubs and associations, and of political parties. An Upper Manhattan Dominican businessman usually paid for the banquet. At the time of my fieldwork, this man used to be José Delio Marte, whose life history and business career in Washington Heights and Inwood I sketched in Chapter 2.[13]

The Instituto's basic task has been to contribute to the reproduction and spreading of ideas—forms of knowledge. It has done this in various ways. Some of the members have visited clubs and associations in Upper Manhattan to give talks on Duarte or on a part of the Dominican Republic's history. Others have organized more formal seminars and conferences, sometimes with speakers from the island. In addition, the Instituto has collaborated with a set of public schools. Most of these are elementary schools in Washington Heights and Inwood, with a high proportion of children of Dominican immigrants. This collaboration has ensured that the children have been told the classic story of the nation's birth. Some of the schools have in addition asked their Dominican children to write a short story about the life of Duarte.

The Instituto Duartiano has in some ways been small and conservative. The number of members has been limited, always fewer than a hundred—and the institution has claimed to be unpolitical, to operate on a level above politics (Sainz 1990: 74–75). In spite of this, it has been important. Some of the members have had a large circle of acquaintances. A few have also worked in politics. The Instituto's president in 2002 was Bienvenido Lara Flores, one of the institution's veterans; he worked for Miguel Martínez, Washington Heights's Dominican member of the City Council.[14]

At the time of my fieldwork, the cult of Duarte had become a part of everyday life. Each year in January (before Duarte's birthday), Spanish-language magazines and papers distributed and read in New York's Dominican community contained a stream of small and large messages with texts about and pictures of Duarte and other national founders. It was the same in February before Dominican Independence Day. These messages—which sometimes could fill an entire page—had a double function. On the one hand, they paid homage to Duarte and *la patria*. On the other hand, they were advertisements. They marketed a Dominican business (everything from a Caridad restaurant to a travel agency), a Dominican political candidate (from Miguel Martínez to Adriano Espaillat), or a Dominican entity or organization (from the Dominican state to the Dominican Consulate to La Alianza Dominicana).[15]

Business offices, too, testified to the worship of *el padre de la patria*. As previously mentioned, the Dominican-controlled National Supermarkets Association had its headquarters in an office building in Queens. One of the walls in the waiting room documented a part of the Association's history; it displayed photos of the Association's former presidents and of George W.

Bush and New York mayor Michael Bloomberg together with some Association members. The most important office in the headquarters was that of Luis Salcedo, the executive director. On the wall behind Luis's desk were two enormous portraits, of George Washington and Juan Pablo Duarte. This type of adornment was common: a collection of framed photos documented part of the business's or organization's history and signaled a mixed, Dominican American identity; a picture of Duarte was often part of such decorations.

When I lived in Washington Heights, one of the area's largest public schools had been named after Duarte, as had one of the main streets. P.S. 132 was renamed in the early 1980s. The man who, in a board meeting in New York City School District 6, proposed that P.S. 132 be renamed was Guillermo Linares, and the new name was P.S. 132 Juan Pablo Duarte.[16] Several years later, Linares proposed yet another name change. In 2000, the New York City Council approved that the stretch of St. Nicholas Avenue from 162nd to 193rd Streets should be called Juan Pablo Duarte Boulevard, one of Washington Heights's most important and most commercial streets.

To Linares and his supporters, these name changes were part of a political project. The ability to rename was important; it signaled and celebrated the growing strength of the Washington Heights and Inwood Dominican community. To put it another way, *el padre de la patria*, and that which he had created and continued to create, had now conquered part of the United States.

Linares's path to New York's political scene began in the north coast town of Cabrera in the Dominican Republic. The oldest of nine children, he arrived in the United States in 1966 to live with his parents in the Bronx. When fifteen-year-old Linares came to New York, he spoke no English and had no experience outside his rural hometown. After completing high school, he attended City College in Upper Manhattan from 1970 to 1975, where he trained to be a teacher, while driving a gypsy cab at night. In 1975, he married and began to teach in a public school in Washington Heights. His wife was a Puerto Rican, and the two were a team. Like him, she had studied at City College and had been active in left-wing student politics. And like him, she started to teach in a school in Washington Heights. I interviewed Linares (in English) in a quiet café in Inwood in 2003. He said about the years at City College,

> Those years [1970 to 75] were, for me, critical, in terms of how I defined what my role was going to be as an immigrant in New York City, and it was during those five years that I worked as a taxi driver during

the evening. I was exposed to other challenges at the same time while I was going through my schooling and became active and influenced by the civil rights movement of the 60s and early 70s, and so when we landed in Washington Heights I came to be a teacher, and that put me in a very unique position to connect with families. My wife was also a teacher.

Teaching in northern Manhattan during the 1970s, Linares and his wife Evelyn witnessed the influx of Dominican immigrants who would change the face of the area. To help the new arrivals now flooding into Washington Heights, the couple, along with a group of Dominican friends, began to work out of churches and Dominican clubs. The group taught people English and provided GED tutoring and immigration counseling. They also helped register thousands of new voters to advocate for new schools in the overcrowded district. In 1980, the group started a nonprofit, the Community Association for Progressive Dominicans, which coordinated the group's activities. Linares and his wife volunteered their time with the Association while continuing to work as teachers to support their children.

The Association provided Linares with a springboard into political life. In 1983, he was elected to the local school board—School District 6. This was a time when practically everything that had to do with the organization of northern Manhattan's—and the city's—public schools was intensely politicized. Linares and others demanded that the city build more schools and fought for more bilingual education and programs for recently arrived immigrant families.[17] In 1982, Linares's local school district got a Latina, a Puerto Rican woman, as its district superintendent. This was the first time School District 6 had a Latino or Latina as superintendent. After he was elected to the school board, Linares collaborated with this new superintendent. As he saw it, the two had together managed to "open" the area's schools to a broader audience, to the neighborhood's families. They had opened the public schools to some of those newly arrived Dominican immigrants who badly needed to be taught some English. Schools were used after the normal closing time, so "while we used to have five or six or eight classes before [for parents], now we could have easily forty, fifty classes in different schools," Linares recalled.

In 1983, Linares proposed that one of the district's schools should be named after Duarte. P.S. 132 was selected for several reasons. The school was in the center of Dominican Washington Heights. A large proportion of the children were Dominican, and the principal was a Latino, a Puerto Rican.

And many of the parents who had most actively backed Linares and his comrades (or the activities of the Community Association for Progressive Dominicans) belonged to this school. Some of the white members of the school board voted against the name change. As Linares recalled, "It was felt that it was inappropriate to name a school after a foreigner. Because a school should be named after someone in the context of being an American"—and there were some racist reactions also—but "we were able to win that fight."

Linares was reelected to the school board first in 1986 and then in 1989.[18] Two years later, he won for the first time a seat on City Council, a seat he kept up to 2001. One year before he ended his City Council career, he (with many other Upper Manhattan Dominicans) convinced City Hall to name a strip of St. Nicholas after Juan Pablo Duarte. The official procedure for adding or changing a New York City place or street name is a multistep process. The Department of Transportation requires that the new name honor a cultural or nonprofit entity or a person or event of historical significance. The subject has to be dead and to have had a link to the neighborhood or block where his or her (or its, in the case of an institution) name is to appear. Those sponsoring a new name propose it to their community board. The board votes on the proposal, and, if approved, the name goes to the Parks Committee of the City Council. If approved there, the proposal is presented to the full City Council, which votes and passes the matter along to the mayor. With the mayor's signature, the Department of Transportation is asked to make and install the sign.

The City Hall approval in 2000 to rename a stretch of St. Nicholas represented the end of several years of political struggle. The problem had been that the proposal had lacked the necessary majority in the local community board (CB 12—representing Washington Heights and Inwood). But in the late 1990s, Linares and his group finally got the majority and formal support they needed. In an interview, he said, "It took me about eight years to get control of the local community board to get a critical number of members."

After City Council had said yes to the proposal, Washington Heights and Inwood Dominicans celebrated this achievement with a local "carnival"—a parade accompanied by ceremony and festivity. The parade took place on St. Nicholas Avenue/Juan Pablo Duarte Boulevard in Washington Heights on a Sunday in late July 2000. What was meant to be a one-time event became an annual tradition. El Carnaval del Boulevard, as the celebration is officially called, is now held each year on a Sunday in late July. It is a day when northern Manhattan Dominicans take control of, and govern, El Boulevard. A number of corporate sponsors annually participate to demonstrate their support for the New York City Dominican community. But what makes El Carnaval a New York Dominican celebration is something else. For weeks young and adult Dominican New Yorkers—many of whom live in Washington Heights tenements—have been preparing costumes and masks to display at this event. Groups of residents have united to present Dominican folklore and culture—forms of music and dance.[19] Thus, forms of Dominican immigrant identity become objectified and anchored—inscribed in the city's landscape.

Duarte has been used by the Dominican state to produce a nationalist discourse that has been, and remains, anti-Haitian. In many ways Duarte has represented and symbolized not only the will to independence but also the necessary will to maintain an absolute distinction between the island's two populations—or between the Dominican Republic and Haiti. Duarte has represented freedom. But this freedom has largely been understood as the freedom to live in separation and security from the other side's (eternal) savagery. Relatively little has so far been done in Washington Heights and Inwood to revise or change this narrative. The activities of the Instituto Duartiano have essentially helped reproduce the hegemonic myths of Duarte created in the homeland. Of fifteen works I found in an online catalog search under "Juan Pablo Duarte" at the Washington Heights branch of the New York Public Library, as far as I could ascertain not a single one represented a significant deviation from the dominant discourse on the island.

Saying this is not to say that things do not change or that Dominican New Yorkers are, and express, just one thing. New York City Dominican political elites cooperated sometimes with Haitian leaders and activists. A number of Dominican immigrants had Haitian friends they had met in a factory, an evening class, or college. Some Dominicans saw themselves as blacks, and a tiny minority cultivated a form of Afro-Dominican belonging. But the dominant story of Duarte seemed little changed if we compare it to the corresponding narrative on the island.

There was no contradiction between building and maintaining a Dominican identity by means of the Duarte symbol and becoming, or being, American—far from it. Even those Dominican New Yorkers who described themselves as "Dominican American," not just "Dominican," needed their own symbolic resources (or their own symbolic weapons); they needed a story of roots of their own. This is strikingly evident from my interview with Linares. I asked him (rhetorically) if he believed the use of symbols was important. Had the use of the figure Duarte been politically important? He replied,

Of course. Of course.... 50 percent of the game is about how people interpret things, and that dictates the extent to which things are legitimated and become real, so, um, symbols are very important . . . , and for someone that is relatively powerless [in today's United States] and has little control over the means of projecting points of view, um, that becomes even more challenging.

He explained that, after the events of 1965,

We created this nonprofit [the Community Association for Progressive Dominicans], struggling to preserve the perspective that I had, that we were now a minority, a national minority in the United States, here permanently, and to forge our future here, in every respect, while there were those [among us] who were looking—who looked at the United States as an imperialist country and brought this concept from the left that they were here temporarily, but they were going to go back, you know. I left that perspective, and, in fact, I had confrontations with that perspective within the left, and when I—that other perspective was against my running for the school board, and we struggled.

C: What does Duarte mean to Dominican Americans in Upper Manhattan today?

L: Pride, heritage, that everyone respects because there is—everyone, regardless of what corner of the world you came, you can't dissociate yourself from your heritage, your background, you know, and the strength of those people that came before you and the sacrifice they made. That's a universal notion.

C: This was about much more than renaming a street?

L: Yes it was. You know what I did? [This is how I see it:] When you have the people who represent the city [i.e., City Council members] embrace the concept of the contributions that Dominicans have made to the city of New York, when they vote enthusiastically [for the proposal]—they are giving a voice to this latest group that had now become the largest immigrant group in the city, and who had brought life to many neighborhoods.

In looking at three social "fields"—everyday life in tenements, households, and families; racial classification practices; and the economy—I have argued that their practices and processes produced two forms of belonging among the city's Dominicans: Dominican (or Dominican American) and Hispanic also. I have also looked at forms of political action that contributed to the building of two identities. Now I support this with some brief examples.

In many of the Dominican clubs and associations, almost all the members were of Dominican descent, but there were non-Dominican ones (often Puerto Ricans, but also Ecuadorans, Colombians, Central Americans, and so on) (see, for examples, Sainz 1990: 79–140; and Torres-Saillant and Hernández 1998: 83). The club in Washington Heights that I used to visit, La Hermandad Quisqueyana Community Center, had almost all Dominicans as members, but at least a couple of the men who used to frequent this club to relax and have a game of dominos were from El Salvador. The Dominicans I met there seemed proud of the fact that the club now recruited, and retained, non-Dominican (but nevertheless Hispanophone) members.

New York Dominican leaders and politicians often cooperated strategically with representatives of other minority groups, mostly Puerto Ricans and African Americans.[20] Linares's wife Evelyn is a Puerto Rican, as previously mentioned. As they continued to work politically in the 1980s, they also continued to enter into agreements and alliances with non-Dominicans:

> We began to look for alliances in nonprofit organizations and other types [of organizations], and it was, you know, it became more than Dominican. It became part of a broader movement that was Latino in nature because we were looking at defending bilingual education.... So that dimension put us in contact with a broader movement, a movement that was Latino and minority, by the way. The minority dimension was actually [important].... [For example,] in 1984, we were approached—because we were being observed now by some dimensions that were connected to the [Democratic] party, and my wife was asked to run for to be a delegate to the national convention under the candidacy of Jesse Jackson, and the man who established the contact was David Dinkins, who then later became [the city's first African American] mayor and so forth.... They [the Jesse Jackson people] were looking for a Latino. Actually, a Latina, because... you need to have a balance within the structure of the party, so Evelyn became the natural Latina.... She got elected, and she went to San Francisco to the convention. Um, so that's how we began to establish [cooperation with one of the two large parties, the Democratic Party].

Two decades later, Washington Heights and Inwood had elected two other Dominican Democrats to represent this part of the city. Both Adriano Espaillat and Miguel Martínez had huge networks, and both cooperated often, not to say daily, with Puerto Ricans, African Americans, Asians, and whites.

This chapter has shown that an overwhelming majority of my informants viewed themselves both as *dominicanos* and as *hispanos*. Most Dominican immigrants I met wore both hats. As we have seen, this did not mean that Dominican New Yorkers were not leading transnational lives, nor that many, or most, were not adapting to the United States.

Identity is not a "thing," something given and unchangeable, but, instead, as Stuart Hall (1990: 222) has said, a production "which is never complete, always in process." This means we should seek to understand identities as outcomes of concrete forms of social activity, specific social practices. The Dominican immigrants' constructions of own identity in racial and ethnic terms mirrored, and were anchored in, a myriad historically constituted social activities.

CHAPTER 6

Up Against the Big Money

Politically, the city's Dominicans are still a relatively weak group. As Torres-Saillant and Hernández concluded as late as the late 1990s, the New York City Dominican community "suffers from a political invisibility that is hardly justifiable in light of the great size of the Dominican population" (1998: 96). But that does not mean that the community's lack of political visibility has remained unaltered. On the contrary, since the mid-1980s (and particularly since the early 1990s), the Dominican immigrants have become more and more visible. Several circumstances may explain this. First, the Dominican community has continued to increase conspicuously in size. Second, with that growth, more and more Dominicans have spent a considerable part of their lives in the United States; many were raised and attended school in northern Manhattan or in other parts of the city, and some obtained U.S. college training. In the early 1980s, the New York City Dominican community, therefore, began to house new types of activists and leaders, persons who were bilingual and bicultural.

Third, it was only in the 1980s that the Dominican voluntary associations with their activists and leaders began to become seriously involved in U.S. politics at the local level. Before that decade, during the 1960s and 1970s, Dominican immigrants created, as we have seen, a network of clubs and voluntary associations, but, as Eugenia Georges has put it, while these clubs and associations clearly

> provided the foundation for strong ties and internal cohesion within and among some segments of the population, they remained [relatively] inward-looking, lacking links beyond the immigrant population to sources of political power and information on the political process, bureaucratic decision-making, resource allocation at the city,

state and federal levels, etc. In other words, while ethnic associations provided the potential for organization of the Dominican population, they remained almost completely separate from the political process in the U.S. (Georges 1984: 37–38)

This changed during the 1980s and 1990s. Guillermo Linares, for example, worked at first without a tie to the Democratic Party or another U.S. party. It was only after some years, in the early or mid-1980s, that he and other members of the Community Association for Progressive Dominicans began to develop links to important New York City Democratic leaders (figures like Charles Rangel, Ed Koch, and David Dinkins) and gradually to a large part of the Democratic Party apparatus in the city.[1]

Yet New York's Dominican immigrants were gradually able to increase their visibility and achieve some political results, no matter how limited, for another reason. Before 1990, the Dominican small business community showed extremely limited ability to act collectively. There were many attempts to create some interest organization or business association, but all these associations remained weak. When I began the fieldwork in 2002, the picture remained mainly the same, but with a couple of clear exceptions, to which I shall return. In brief, the 1990s saw (1) the inception of generally stronger collective organizing among those Dominican New Yorkers who ran small businesses and (2) the emergence of at least two relatively high-profile and influential interest organizations anchored in the Dominican small-business sector.

This latter development was important. It furnished Dominican political activity in the city with a broader and stronger economic and social foundation. Dominican elected officials and representatives of the Dominican business community have had close contact. Those who owned businesses have needed the politicians' help when they sought amendment of an act, lower taxes, lower rents, lower energy bills, better protection against crime and harassment, and so on. For their part, the politicians have needed votes and economic contributions to election campaigns.

By the 1990s the proportion of Dominican immigrants who worked in, or were dependent on, the city's small-business economy had clearly been on the increase, while the proportion of Dominicans who were factory workers had been falling dramatically. This gave the small-business field—and those forms of political practice and collective organizing contained in this field—an extra significance; it had transformed itself into a political force.[2]

As already mentioned, most Dominican small-business associations were weak. Many were mainly one-man shows, with a leader and his close friends, a name, a phone number, and a business card, but little beyond this. But there were exceptions. The most important was the National Supermarkets Association, by far the strongest Dominican small-business association when I started my research and up to the present. Another was the New York State Federation of Taxi Drivers, which was headed by a Dominican American, successful businessman Fernando Mateo, and mostly had Dominican livery drivers as members. I study these in the present chapter and the next.

The National Supermarkets Association was started in 1989 by a handful of Dominican supermarket owners. The New York State Federation of Taxi Drivers was founded in 1999 by a group of Dominican drivers and Mateo. Irrespective of the names, both organizations were still entirely controlled by New York-based Dominicans. I wish to sketch the ways Dominicans who ran independent supermarkets and livery bases acted politically and the high degree of contact between representatives of both groups and a number of New York's politicians, not least those of Dominican origin (such as Linares, Adriano Espaillat, and Miguel Martínez), but also several others. Thus, I use ethnography to demonstrate the significance of a set of networks that connected, and interwove, two spheres: New York as an economy (or a business world) and New York as a political system.

The following two sections study the emergence of the National Supermarkets Association, as told by its representatives, and political battles that were fought in New York during the years from the early to the late 1990s. In 1992, the Dinkins administration announced a plan for megastore development, to bring giant supermarkets, furniture outlets, and discount warehouses to New York City's neighborhoods. After Rudolph Giuliani's 1993 mayoral victory, these efforts grew in strength. The new mayor intensified the attempts to bring a series of enormous stores (of up to 200,000 square feet, equal to five football fields) to the city's inner areas. In April 1998, the supermarket chain Pathmark opened a megastore, a 50,000-square-foot grocery store, at 125th Street and Lexington Avenue in Upper Manhattan. This was the first major supermarket chain to open in Harlem (in the whole of Manhattan north of 120th Street, for that matter) in thirty years, and the opening occurred after a bitter political fight. The Dominican supermarket owners were active in these struggles. The National Supermarkets Association fought against both the Dinkins-Giuliani megastore development plan and the Pathmark at 125th Street and Lexington. The Dominican supermarket owners' opposition to a Pathmark in Harlem became particularly heated.

When I began my research, the story of the association's defeat in the struggle against the building of the Pathmark at 125th Street had acquired mythic features. The narrative of these events contained and condensed a message of the necessity to stand up and fight for equality and justice, and to stand together, as I describe below.

The National Supermarkets Association also organized and backed a set of social and cultural activities. Each year it organized a ceremony—a large banquet—in downtown Manhattan. In the last two sections of the chapter, I discuss some of these other activities. Throughout the chapter, I seek to answer these questions: What was the Dominican supermarket owners' thinking? What was their central discourse? What drove them to act politically?

The Emergence of the National Supermarkets Association

I heard first about the National Supermarkets Association in late June 2002, in the office of Alfredo Placeres, a Cuban American lawyer and president of the New York State Federation of Hispanic Chambers of Commerce. Hugo Díaz, an Argentine immigrant in his fifties who was Placeres's right-hand man and federation vice-president, supplied information about the city's Dominican business associations and recommended three or four small-business leaders and organizations for more information. The association, he went on, is *una organización de verdad*, a real organization, not like the others; it is an organization with resources. It is headed by an elected president and a board but has hired an executive director and a secretary who work in the headquarters and are paid salaries to run the organization.

But like other small-business associations, this one began on a small scale. The man who is considered as the association's creator is Eligio Peña. Eligio was the man who got the idea and took the first initiatives. (For an outline of Eligio's life, see Chapter 2.) Eligio got the idea in 1989. He first presented it to his brothers and sister and then to a group of friends. The first informal meeting was held in a Dominican restaurant in Washington Heights. More meetings followed before the National Supermarkets Association was formally founded. Some say the founders numbered seven men, but others say eight or nine. At any rate, all were first-generation Dominican immigrants, and all owned at least one independent supermarket. At least four of the founders owned and operated stores in Brooklyn; another ran a supermarket in the Bronx. In 1989, Eligio owned two stores, one on Knickerbocker Avenue in

Brooklyn and another on St. Nicholas in Upper Manhattan. After the organization was created, the number of members grew. To be able to become a member, a person had to own at least one store, which had to be a supermarket, not just a large bodega. According to the association's informal rules, a supermarket was a store covering at least 6,000 square feet. The association employed the same criterion thirteen years later when I began the fieldwork.

Recruitment of new members was through personal networks. A member invited a relative or friend to join the association, provided that the latter already had become owner of a supermarket. The association's executive director and spokesman Luis Salcedo had been a member since 1991. He said about recruitment of new members in the early 1990s, "At that time we even had the tough rule that you needed to be invited by a member. You could only come to the meetings if you were invited by a member, and then, basically, before you were allowed to join the organization, you had to come to three meetings, before they would make a decision, 'yes,' because . . . we wanted to make sure."

According to Eligio, the organization had been, and remained, 100 percent Dominican. But the organization was, in principle, open to anybody, provided that he or she owned a supermarket. When the members founded the organization, Eligio claimed, they had asked a couple of Puerto Ricans to join them, but these had declined.

When I asked Luis why the organization was created, he went straight to the point: "I think it was a vision that Eligio had, that if we were gonna grow, that if we were gonna be owners of all this business, small business—all kinds—we needed to be organized in order to fight the political forces." The goal was to make money; to create a collectivity was a means. Eligio's answer was far more detailed and specific. He told me the following story to explain *why* the organization had been created. In the late 1980s and early 1990s, Eligio and the others who wanted to open an independent supermarket in the New York area had a problem. The source of this problem, Eligio claimed, was an injustice—or a form of discrimination: the authorities in practice treated supermarkets that belonged to chains (or big companies) in one manner and independent supermarkets in another, creating unfair competition. What was the problem? The bulk of the independent supermarkets were located in parts of the city where many people were poor. A relatively high proportion of the households were dependent on forms of welfare. If the supermarket was to manage, it had to be able to accept food stamps and WIC coupons as payment from some of its customers.[3] But to be able to do this, a supermarket had first to obtain the necessary licenses; this was the problem. A chain store, explained Eligio, got the licenses immediately. When it opened, it already had the licenses it needed. But an independent supermarket had to wait for months—sometimes up to a year—before the authorities licensed it to accept food stamps and WIC coupons. In the meantime, the store lost money because those in the neighborhood who received food stamps and WIC coupons were forced to spend their benefits elsewhere. Eligio and his colleagues were of the opinion that the authorities obstructed them—that, in practice, they worked against those in New York who sought to develop independent supermarkets. To solve this and other problems, Eligio believed it was necessary to create an organization. The outcome was his initiative in 1989. In his own words,

> We who owned and operated independent supermarkets—well, if we wanted to open a new supermarket, we had to wait up to twelve months for the license to accept the customers' WIC coupons as payment. It was the same with the food stamps—three and four months, and up to six months, to get licensed. But what happened? All these stores were located in poor neighborhoods, in areas where perhaps some 40 percent of the customers of our supermarkets were dependent on food stamps and WIC coupons. If I lacked a license, these customers went instead to a chain store. The chains got their licenses when they opened, straight away—but not we.... As an owner of independent stores, I fought considerably to get these problems solved—but I was like a voice in the desert. Then I found a solution. Ever since I was very young, around twelve years, I have belonged to groups, been taught to found and organize groups—youth clubs [*clubes de jovenes*]. So I said to myself, "Oh, here is the answer." So we created an organization, an association of owners of independent supermarkets—so we could demand, and fight for, our rights.

Some three years later, in 1992, Eligio had meetings with those in charge of the food stamp and WIC program in Washington. He secured these meetings, he explained, through a friend who knew a lobbyist in Washington with strong links with the first Bush administration. After meetings, Eligio claimed, the problem was solved; those who opened independent supermarkets in New York got their licenses without having to wait.

Eligio was association president from 1989 to 1993. From 1993 to 2005, five others followed (Mariano Díaz, Pablo Espinal, William Rodriguez, Nelson Eusebio, and Paul Fernández). All were Dominicans, and each served a three-year term. In 2000, the organization obtained its present location in Queens and appointed Luis Salcedo executive director. According to Luis, the organization had in late 2002 approximately 125 members, who owned around 300 independent supermarkets, the great majority in New York. These figures mirrored a social fact—that an impressive proportion of New York City's independent supermarkets were now controlled by first-generation Dominican immigrants. In Eligio's words,

> The majority [of New York City's independent supermarkets are owned by Dominicans]—yes. At the moment, as far as I know—and I'm pretty sure about this—there are two Puerto Ricans—owners of supermarkets. There is a group of Arabs—owners. I don't know from which part of the Arab world, but Arabs; they operate in Brooklyn and a part of Queens—they're not many. There is a small group who have come from Venezuela—they're Spanish-speaking Arabs [presumably of Lebanese and/or Syrian descent], from Venezuela. Well, these are doing all right. They operate under the name Trade Fair—there are around ten Trade Fair supermarkets in Queens. There is another small group that operates under the name Dynasty. I don't think this name is so good—nor Trade Fair, but they have done all right.... And a few Italians continue to be in the business, running some Key Food stores—and a few Associateds and some Met Foods and Pioneers, some of them cooperate with Krasdale, others with White Rose—but [these are] very few. The great majority here, the strong group, are the Dominicans.
>
> C: About how many independent supermarkets do we find in New York?
>
> E: Around 600, and around 500 of these are owned by Dominicans.

The last two figures may well have been too high, but Eligio's general picture was probably not far from reality.

The association worked politically (in a wide sense of this word). The goal was to defend the members' economic interests. As Luis put it in his typical manner:

> We are basically an advocacy group. That's what we are. We are an advocacy group, a nonprofit organization that is here to stop bad

legislation that can affect our members from happening—that's the political aspect. At the company [or business] level, we try to—we bring companies here, you know, and we show them: "Look, our membership buys for $20 million from your company a year!" And we do our [annual] banquet, which is a major event, to raise funds for the organization to run the operation.

The organization used its strength to obtain collective agreements with corporations. In this way, members were able to lower their costs—by paying less for energy, deliveries, and so on. The association was also represented at hearings in City Hall. One day when I had an appointment with Luis, he had just attended a hearing organized by City Council. Another who had been present at this hearing was Sung Soo Kim (whom Luis just referred to as "Mr. Kim"), founder and leader of the Small Business Congress of New York City. Sung Soo Kim is a Korean immigrant who began his political work in the city in the early 1980s. At that time, he was hired as executive director by the Korean Produce Association, a small-business organization that oversaw the interests of almost a thousand of New York City's fruit-and-vegetable-store owners. Subsequently, he founded the Korean American Small Business Service Center and, in 1991, the multiethnic Small Business Congress of New York City—an umbrella organization that, in the early 1990s, represented almost fifty small-business associations from all parts of the city (Sanjek 1998: 346).[4] Korean greengrocers and Dominican owners of independent supermarkets often had common interests. Sometimes they joined forces and struggled together (346–47). The relationship between Sung Soo Kim and Luis was, therefore, excellent. The National Supermarkets Association also had links to other small-business organizations and was a member of the New York State Federation of Hispanic Chambers of Commerce, which represented in 2002 around thirty Hispanic chambers of commerce and small-business associations.

The National Supermarkets Association did not back particular politicians or a particular party. If one of its members wanted to sponsor a particular politician, he or she was free to do so. But as an organization, it could not do this; on the contrary, it had established an internal rule that prohibited political support. In this sense, it was politically neutral. At the time of my fieldwork, this was being debated internally in the organization. Some of the association's leaders believed that it now should begin to play a more active part politically—that Dominicans with businesses and money now had to strengthen their political engagement. Others were more conservative; these wanted to continue as before. One of those who most strongly favored a more directly political role was Luis, the organization's executive director. One day in the headquarters, he spoke very straightforwardly—without any political correctness:

> We're obviously now discussing the fact that we need to become political because the true power is the economic and political put together.
> C: Of course.
> L: You have the money, but if you don't have the political connections . . . —and I, for example, use the Jewish people very often as an illustration. And I use the—I tell my people sometimes, "Look at what's happening." I use the following formulation—"When something happens in Israel, Washington starts shaking."
> C: Yes.
> L: And, uh, not to get into personal political views, but the fact of the matter—this is because the Jewish people [are] a very organized people.
> C: Yeah. No, you're . . .
> L: And they have the political power, and as strong as the U.S. is, I think it's not in our best interests to—Israel is the only friend that we have in that region of the world, but, nevertheless, I can guarantee that it has a lot to do with the economic power, so who has guts enough in Washington to say, "You know what? Screw Israel!" No, we don't do that, and it's not only that—they are our friends in the region so that it's a two-way street.

Yet despite continuing internal discussion about political involvement among some of the leaders of the Association, the organization at that time had already acquired considerable political experience. In 2002, the Dominican owners of independent supermarkets had already been through several controversies. In the next section, I look more closely at the association's political activities in a critical period from approximately 1991 to 1997.

The National Supermarkets Association at War

These years show with exceptional clarity that those Dominicans who ran independent supermarkets did not operate in political-economic isolation. On the contrary, they formed part of an intricate large-scale power structure. During this period, the association was "at war" with powerful groups. The two most important targets were New York City's mayor and a set of interests representing some of the big U.S. corporations and chains—that is, big business.

In the eyes of the Dominican supermarket owners, they belonged to a group that had been attacked for more than two decades. But in the last five years, the situation had become relatively quiet. Luis, for example, said to me, "We've been attacked from left and right politically. But now it has calmed down a little bit, because now a lot of politicians know who we are."

From the 1970s to the 1990s, the city's newspapers published a host of articles describing what they saw as the miserable state of inner-city food retailing. There were exceptions, but they were few compared to those that reproduced the dominant perspective. According to this perspective, the independent supermarket was an incarnation of urban neglect—a symbol of the tragic conditions of the city's low-income areas. The city's independent supermarkets, it was claimed, sold poor products, were cramped and dirty, and charged prices higher than those paid in a national chain store in the suburbs.[5] In Luis's words, the media saw the store owners as "exploiters, ripping off the poor with high-priced, poor-quality goods sold in unsavory surroundings." And, in 1991, the New York City Department of Consumer Affairs published a report titled "The Poor Pay More . . . for Less." This report, which contained a study of grocery shopping in New York City's low-income neighborhoods, not only reiterated most of what the newspaper stories had been arguing but also provided this discourse with an official seal. "The Poor Pay More . . . for Less" opens in the following manner:

> New York City's poor—already beleaguered by the problems of crime, housing, and inadequate medical care—also contend with dirty, cramped food stores that charge more than stores in middle-class areas. . . . Almost thirty years after David Caplowitz wrote his classic book, *The Poor Pay More* [1967] revealing how the poor are taken advantage of by furniture and appliance stores, we have found that the poor also pay more than they should for the most important and frequent of consumer purchases—groceries. (1)

Another paragraph in the introduction reads as follows:

> *Major supermarket chains have abandoned poor neighborhoods.* Our analysis of supermarket locations in Manhattan, Brooklyn, and the Bronx revealed that, with a few exceptions, none of the region's major supermarket chains, such as D'Agostino, Shop Rite, Waldbaum's, King Kullen, Sloan's or Grand Union, do significant business in poor neighborhoods. They have relegated poor neighborhoods to (often inferior) independently owned stores belonging to "voluntary cooperatives," [*sic*] such as C-Town, Key Food and Met. (2, italics in original)

After this, the push for the big chains' return to those parts of the city they had left in the 1960s and 1970s grew in strength. A series of actors—from local activists and community-based organizations to business interests, professional lobbyists, and top politicians—had almost only one thing in common: they worked diligently to attain this end. At the same time, the newspapers continued to produce and disseminate critical stories about the city's independent supermarkets.

The National Supermarkets Association sought to repair the damage, although this was difficult. Its representatives sent letters to editors and had meetings with editorial boards. According to the Dominican supermarket owners, almost all that had been spread through the press and the report "The Poor Pay More... for Less" drew a false picture. Most important, they claimed that it was completely incorrect that their prices—or the prices in an independent store in the inner city—were higher than those in a chain store in the suburbs. Who was right? It is hard to say. But it is far from certain that the Dominican owners of supermarkets were the most mistaken. Nine years after the New York City Department of Consumer affairs published its report came a new study: in 2000, Cashawn Richburg Hayes, an economist, published "Do the Poor Pay More? An Empirical Investigation of Price Dispersion in Food Retailing" (Richburg Hayes 2000). Richburg Hayes received her Ph.D. in 2000 from Princeton University, and this article was based on her doctorate research.[6] Her findings supported the views of the independent supermarkets' owners:

> Whether the poor pay more for basic food items has been a source of bitter empirical controversy for several decades. This paper contains the results of the first comprehensive empirical analysis of this issue

based on a representative, national sample of data from the [U.S.] Bureau of Labor Statistics' primary sampling frame for construction of the Consumer Price Index.... I find that the poor pay up to 6 percent less than their more affluent counterparts.... Further, I find that poor, predominantly white (non-Hispanic) neighborhoods and poor predominately Hispanic black neighborhoods experience price discounts up to 9.9 and 18.9 percent, respectively, while poor predominantly black (non-Hispanic) neighborhoods face the going price in affluent white (non-Hispanic) neighborhoods. (Richburg Hayes 2000: 1, 2–3)

Many in the city chose to oppose the megastore plan—not least the majority of New York's small business owners. Neighborhood groceries, clothing stores, pharmacies, and others feared that city-subsidized giant stores would make it impossible for them to survive. A leading force in the fight against the megastore plan was the previously mentioned five-county, multiethnic Small Business Congress. Sung Soo Kim claimed that the megastore plan was unethical. His message was "The big supermarkets abandoned the city in the 1970s, leaving a vacuum that immigrant businesses filled. . . . Now they want to come back, but only on their terms and with a host of unfair subsidies. This is not free competition" (quoted in Sanjek 1998: 348). Many in New York's neighborhoods sided with small business and against Mayor Giuliani: "The mayor's proposal received negative votes from twenty-eight of the thirty-eight community boards that contained manufacturing-zoned land [to be rezoned for megastores] and was rejected by all five borough boards. In December 1996 the city council voted down the megastore plan" (348). The plan was rejected for various reasons. Some of Giuliani's critics maintained that elimination of New York's existing zoning regulations and subsidizing of megastore development would in practice function as generous gifts to a part of the city's rich—that is, to representatives of the city's real estate industry or to New York's big real estate owners and developers. Others stressed that megastores paid poor wages, so that any policy to facilitate them would be detrimental to the city's labor market. Yet others argued that the proposed development would be damaging to the city's small-business owners (see, for example, Holloway 1994; Firestone 1996; Soto 1996).

To fight against the megastore plan, the Dominican owners of supermarkets—and the National Supermarkets Association—supported and collaborated with Sung Soo Kim and his allies; they formed part of the loosely structured, broad, multiethnic coalition of small-business associations Sung Soo Kim had helped create and led, the Small Business Congress of New York City.[7] Many in the city contributed to the fight against Giuliani's plan—some far more than the Dominican supermarket owners, who, however, did play a part. Luis said, "The battle over the megastore plan was an important turning point for the independent supermarket owners. We had fought back and won."

A significant incident, as the National Supermarkets Association saw it, occurred as late as November 1996—that is, only one month before City Council voted down the entire megastore plan. In an attempt to demonstrate the benefits of megastores, the Giuliani administration released the results of a survey on November 24, 1996, that it said showed New Yorkers could save as much as 30 percent on Thanksgiving dinner if they shopped in a food superstore instead of small, neighborhood stores (see Holloway 1996; Liff and Allen 1996). Giuliani, accompanied by José Maldonado, the commissioner of consumer affairs, and other officials, announced the results of the survey at a news conference at a Pathmark supermarket in Chinatown. Among other things, the mayor claimed that fresh turkey had been found on average to be 22 percent less expensive in large stores than in small groceries and that the frozen variety had been double the price in small stores. Small-business owners and others fighting the city's megastore plan, for their part, maintained that the City Department of Consumer Affairs had used bogus prices for the survey and that the announced results, therefore, were wrong. Many of the Dominican supermarket owners were furious; as they saw it, the city was again spreading lies. The National Supermarkets Association, therefore, organized its own press conference. There Luis sought to demonstrate why the association rejected the city's claim. He recalled later, "With bulletin boards filled with Thanksgiving circulars and actual food purchased in three different supermarkets, we convincingly exposed the price-gouging lie. After that, well-known columnists like [for example] Ray Kerrison [in the *New York Post*] leapt to our defense."

Although a majority in City Council voted down the megastore plan in December 1996, this has not prevented some enormous supermarkets from opening in those parts of the city that previously had none. Since the early 1990s, a limited number of megastores have opened under—or in spite of—New York's existing zoning. Each of these giant stores has been subjected to political examination and approval before it has in the end been built. In the last twenty years, the big chains have, therefore, to some extent, returned to those parts of the city that they left in the 1960s and 1970s. Big chains have opened giant supermarkets in Queens, in Brooklyn, in the Bronx, and on Manhattan. As a result, most small and medium-sized supermarkets in the inner city have faced tough competition.

In April 1998, the supermarket chain Pathmark inaugurated a 50,000 square-foot supermarket at 125th Street and Third Avenue in East Harlem. As previously mentioned, this was the first major supermarket chain to open in Upper Manhattan in three decades. It was built after an intense political fight. The final decision was made at a Manhattan Borough Board meeting on April 27, 1995, where a narrow majority voted for the Pathmark project in East Harlem. The Dominican supermarket owners, for their part, fought vigorously against the project but lost the fight. Three years later, Pathmark opened the new store. The story of the political battle over the opening of a Pathmark at 125th Street and Third Avenue is instructive. Through collective struggle, small-business organizations and others in the city managed, as we have seen, to put a stop to the megastore plan—the authorities' massive attempt to favor and stimulate big business—but they could not stop more and more megastores being built.[8] The story of the Pathmark project illustrates this clearly. There is no reason to be naïve or romantic. In New York, as in most of the rest of today's world, money rules—and the National Supermarkets Association and other small-business organizations in the city remain only "small fish"; they represent groups that have strictly limited political and economic influence.

The 1995 vote for the Pathmark project marked the end of a long struggle. Since the 1960s, or for around three decades, one of East Harlem's community associations, the Community Association of East Harlem Triangle, Inc., had been fighting to bring a major supermarket to this part of the city. The site—that is, 125th Street and Third Avenue—was owned by the city and had been barren and underdeveloped for the past twenty years.

The majority that voted to support the project approved a plan for the city to sell the site to the East Harlem Abyssinian Triangle Corporation, a joint venture between the Community Association of East Harlem and the Abyssinian Development Corporation (an offshoot of Harlem's Abyssinian Baptist Church); this joint venture would, thereafter, rent the land to Pathmark. Before the decisive vote in the Manhattan Borough Board in late April 1995, the East Harlem Abyssinian Triangle Corporation had managed to bring together a diverse group of participants from the public and private sectors and had, thus, raised $12.5 million, which it planned to use to leverage funds from federal and state agencies. A sizable number of ordinary citizens in East Harlem and beyond signed petitions in support of the East Harlem Pathmark, and a large proportion of the clergy in East, West, and central Harlem backed, and prayed for, the project. In addition, important elected officials worked for the project, including Congressman Charles Rangel, Manhattan Borough President Ruth Messinger, and several City Council members. The East Harlem Pathmark project was also supported by the Community Food Resource Center, Inc., a nonprofit organization dedicated to ensuring that poor people in New York have access to reasonably priced and nutritious food. Those who backed the project maintained that the new supermarket would provide better and less expensive food, create 200 new jobs in the area, and stimulate economic revitalization of this part of the Harlem and New York community.[9]

Among the project's most vocal opponents were some of El Barrio's small-business owners and the National Supermarkets Association. Some of the association's members ran stores in this part of the city—that is, not far from 125th Street and Third Avenue. There were other vocal opponents among New York's elected officials, including City Council members Adam Clayton Powell IV of East Harlem and Antonio Pagan of the Lower East Side, and state senator Olga Méndez of East Harlem.

Small-business owners in El Barrio and the National Supermarkets Association saw the project not only as a threat (to their livelihood) but also as an injustice—a violation of the rules of the game. According to them, the Pathmark project violated the rules of fair economic competition. They typically maintained the following argument: No one gave us anything—yet the city gives away public funds to big chains like Pathmark; public subsidy dollars should be used for small and medium-sized neighborhood businesses, not giant corporations (see Vega 1995a; Serant 1995b; Gonzalez 1996a).

When the authorities in 1995 voted yes to Pathmark's plan to build the East Harlem store, they also approved a loan and tax abatement package worth $6.2 million. Pathmark's store received a $1.5 million low-interest loan and a 22-year tax abatement from the city. The store was estimated to cost $12 million to build.[10] As East Harlem's councilman Adam Clayton Powell IV put it, the issue was not whether East Harlem wanted Pathmark. "I too want more Red Apples, more Associateds, more Grand Unions, and more supermarkets so that I can have more choices," Powell emphasized. The key issue, he said, "was that Pathmark was coming to the community with public money and not theirs" (Browne 1995). Alfredo Rodríguez owned and ran two independent supermarkets—two Associateds—not far from 125th Street and Third Avenue. He said, "They don't want to come [to the community] unless one gives them something in order to come. No one gave us anything" (Vega 1995a). The National Supermarkets Association's president at the time was Pablo Espinal, who said in an interview that the National Supermarkets Association was now fed up with the city's lavishing huge tax breaks on giant supermarket chains, while its members got crumbs (Serant 1995b).

In the Pathmark fight in East Harlem, the Dominican owners of independent supermarkets were represented by Richard Lipsky, a New York lobbyist, whom the National Supermarkets Association had hired to fight the project and defend the interests of the organization's members. Though the Dominican supermarket owners in the end lost this battle, Lipsky had considerable experience. He held a doctorate in political science from the City University of New York, and, in the mid-1990s, he had already been involved in eight major supermarket fights in various parts of the city, winning half (see Nossiter 1995; Gonzalez 1996b).

In the vote in the Manhattan Borough Board on April 27, 1995, seven board members voted for the project and five against. The meeting took place in a tense atmosphere. One member, Manhattan Borough president Ruth Messinger, normally abstained from voting (to be able to maintain a certain neutrality), but, on this occasion, she voted, and she voted for. Another who voted for was Guillermo Linares, Washington Heights and Inwood Dominican City council member. This came as a surprise; in addition, the vote he cast was decisive. Linares switched sides at the last moment, during the last forty-eight hours before the vote. Before he cast his vote in the meeting, Linares provided an explanation. He claimed that he was still concerned about the consequences the enormous new supermarket would have for those businesses already in the area, but, that during the last forty-eight hours, he had got "an answer to this worry." He also said that the big corporations had not invested in East Harlem for a long time and that to turn them down was not the best solution. Finally, he maintained that he was preoccupied because the battle over the Pathmark project had left an image of a racially divided community—a New York and Upper Manhattan community where Hispanics or Dominicans (who owned, ran, and depended on neighborhood groceries and other types of small businesses) and (Harlem's) African Americans fought each other. "I never opposed the Harlem community, and by this term I refer to blacks, Latinos and whites," Linares said, before he concluded, "I've decided to vote in favor."[11]

Linares's surprise vote made the opponents of the project furious. In the words of Adam Clayton Powell IV, "Linares sold out. He betrayed the small businesses in East Harlem through his vote" (Browne 1995). Four days after the vote by the Borough Board, more than a hundred people participated in a protest against Linares in front of City Hall in downtown Manhattan. Many were small-business owners from El Barrio and other parts of the city; they called Linares a "bandit" and a "liar" and accused him of "having sold his fatherland"—of being a national traitor (Castaño 1995).

Among those who felt most let down were the Dominican owners of independent supermarkets and the National Supermarkets Association. As Alfredo Rodríguez, one of the organization's members, put it, "During three years Linares was against the building of the [East Harlem Pathmark] supermarket. But he betrayed the community at the last moment" (Castaño 1995). About two weeks after the decisive vote, or in mid-May 1995, Linares sent a four-page letter to the National Supermarkets Association stating he would break off the connection with the organization unless it dissociated itself from the insults against him by a number of its members. The organization reacted negatively; Mariano Díaz, who had just ended his term as president, described it as "arrogant," before adding, "The one who should publicly offer an apology is he. . . . Linares never was the person we used to discuss our affairs with and the only time we asked him for help, he betrayed us." Pablo Espinal, who had taken over the job as president after Díaz, declared that he did not intend to "be at war with politicians" but that the association in any case "did not owe the city councilmember anything" (de la Cruz 1995). The Dominican supermarket owners saw Linares as "family" and thought he should have stuck together with them because they were Dominicans—compatriots. A number of years later, when I resided in New York, the Dominican supermarket owners remained bitter. Luis, the organization's executive director, told me that after what Linares did in 1995 "I know for sure that a number of our members, well known and with a certain power, campaigned against Linares. There is no doubt about this."

When I interviewed Linares in 2003, he admitted that the 1995 vote and subsequent conflict with the National Supermarkets Association had hurt him politically. In spite of this, he was reelected in 1997, before he was term-limited out of City Council in 2001, after ten years representing Washington Heights and Inwood. In 2002, he attempted to win a seat in the State Senate but lost the Democratic primary to incumbent Eric Schneiderman, a white liberal. Before the 2002 election, Schneiderman's Upper Manhattan district had changed and now housed a Latino majority. The day after Linares's defeat in the primary in 2002, I found myself in Adriano Espaillat's (a Dominican New York State Assembly member) headquarters at Sherman Avenue in the heart of Dominican Inwood. Three women in the waiting room, all Dominican from the neighborhood, chatted about why Linares had not won. Their views varied, but at least one emphasized that many remembered Linares's "treason" in the mid-1990s, in the Pathmark fight.

Schneiderman beat Linares by a solid margin due to a series of factors, not just the struggle over the supermarket plan; but the narrative and the memory of the Pathmark fight continued to play a political part among the city's Dominicans. The problem, as that woman in Espaillat's waiting room and several others in Washington Heights and Inwood saw it, was that, on that occasion in 1995, Linares had not shown sufficient loyalty to his own community—"the Dominican immigrants"—or, more exactly, a pivotal component of this community, its small businesses. This argument rested in turn on a (mostly unarticulated) assumption: that the relatively few Dominican immigrants who had managed to buy their own independent supermarkets could be viewed as representatives of the city's Dominicans, or at least of the Dominican small-business owners. This discourse glossed over the significance of the economic and social inequalities, or class differences, among the Dominican immigrants and pictured the Dominican owners of supermarkets as if they all (still) just owned one or two street corner bodegas—extremely small stores. On the other hand, it remained a fact that the typical Dominican supermarket owner had begun with little, usually by working as a low-paid employee, so quite a few Dominican immigrants could identify with them.

In this section, I have sought, first, to demonstrate that those Dominicans who had become owners of independent supermarkets actually practiced politics, that they, in fact, constituted a political force; the National Supermarkets Association during these years acted, negotiated, and struggled politically in a multitude of ways and had some achievements. Second, I have underscored that the Dominicans who ran supermarkets in New York were part of a large-scale power structure. This structure contained economic and political forces (or actors) that were far more powerful, far more influential, than the National Supermarkets Association (and the rest of the city's small-business associations, for that matter).

The political activity of the Dominican supermarket owners came to be important for Linares, or perhaps one should say for the political life in Upper Manhattan and more generally for the city's increasing number of Dominican elected officials. This is the third point I want to emphasize. After the vote by the Manhattan Borough Board in April 1995, Linares ended up in a sharp conflict with the National Supermarkets Association, and this weakened him politically: a good many Dominican supermarket owners began to work against him. Another of the city's prominent Dominican politicians, Adriano Espaillat, won his first election in 1996—the year after the decisive vote in the fight over the Pathmark at 125th Street. Since then, Espaillat has represented northern Manhattan politically, first in the State Assembly, and then (from 2011 onward) in the State Senate. Espaillat was a quick learner: at any rate, he never challenged or went against the Dominican supermarket owners. On the contrary, he has often backed and cooperated with them.[12]

Business, Pleasure, and Ceremony

What made the Dominican owners of supermarkets act as a group? In which ways did they produce and reproduce their spirit of community?

My first, and most important, answer is that the capacity to act in concert was an expression of awareness of common economic interests. When the National Supermarkets Association was founded, this was already clear. Eligio and the rest of the organization's creators understood that they had to build a collective to be able to reach their goal—to protect and improve each member's business terms and profits. The National Supermarkets Association used its collective bargaining strength to secure common arrangements with companies; through these each member—or store—paid lower prices for supplies. One member, Diana Martínez, gave an example of this:

> We buy—we all decide to buy from this company. [While she talks, she shows me an invoice from one of her suppliers, Woodlake.] This is Woodlake—they supply eggs. We buy eggs through them, so they give the price to the association, and the association gives us the list of the prices that they're supposed to charge. We buy every day, and, uh, they will fax a price list for the week, and then we have something to go by, you know? We have a price list—this is the price that they gave the association, you know? They arrange a price and they have to follow through.

Likewise with the other supplies—from energy to canned meat to beer and bread.

But the National Supermarkets Association's strength—or the Dominican supermarket owners' ability to stand together—was not only based on awareness of common economic interests; it also mirrored something else, something broader and deeper: namely, their production and reproduction of a form of identity, a form of belonging. Many members of the association saw themselves as members of a fellowship, a community. How had this spirit of community been generated, and in what ways was it upheld? Again, the Dominican supermarket owners' everyday life maintained an awareness of common material interests: each member benefitted from the association's ability to secure collective economic arrangements and reduced costs. Yet the spirit of community and the solidarity also arose from a set of other activities, as much social and ritual as economic and political; their common feature was that they helped produce and sustain social ties and comradeship—and a common identity among New York's Dominican owners of independent supermarkets. In the remainder of this section, I sketch and discuss some of these "other" activities.

The National Supermarkets Association organized informal gatherings or meetings for the members at association headquarters in Queens. Those who came were offered something to eat and drink and discussed common challenges. The association used these meetings to shape strategies and plan activities.

In addition, the association organized excursions and trips. A group of members visited a company or a set of companies or a congress together. For example, in 2001, a group of Dominican supermarket owners traveled to Chicago, where they participated at the Food Marketing Institute's convention. In 2002, a group went on a tour to the Dominican Republic, visiting Dominican companies and factories. The same year, another group visited a Nebraskaland Food Distributors warehouse. The year after, a number of Dominican supermarket owners and a group of executives and employees from Pepsi-Cola spent a day together at Shea Stadium; after playing three games of softball, the two groups enjoyed a barbecue.

In 1997, the association started a college scholarship program. It organizes an annual ceremony in Manhattan where a number of students are awarded scholarship checks; from the program's inception in 1997 to 2003, the organization had awarded around $500,000.[13] The recipients are mostly Latinos and African Americans, and they live in those parts of the city where the Dominican supermarket owners have their stores. Present at the annual ceremony are a number of the association's leaders and members. To raise money for its scholarship program, the association each year organizes a golf outing to Mansion Ridge in New York. Those who participate are members (that is, Dominicans in New York who own independent supermarkets) and people who work for big companies (representatives of Goya Foods, Porky Products, Stroehmann Bakeries, Entenmann's, etc.).

The organization has also supported cultural activities. In 2001, for example, the National Supermarkets Association celebrated Dominican Independence Day by inviting a Dominican scholar, Orlando Inoa, to New York; he delivered a lecture on the history of the island of Hispaniola. A couple of years later, the association cosponsored a concert by the Dominican Symphony Orchestra at New York's Lincoln Center.

If, then, a certain spirit of community existed among a number of Dominican owners of independent supermarkets, it was because this spirit in practice was produced and sustained through a series of activities; these were not exclusively of an economic nature: they were also political, ritual, cultural, and moral. Those supermarket owners had been able to act together because they, at least to a certain extent, constituted a group, a social network with its own history, its own practices, and its own collective identity.

The most important manifestation of the Dominican supermarket owners' unity was the National Supermarkets Association's annual banquet, which gathered around 1,200 persons representing various sectors and parts of the city. While I conducted my research, the banquet occurred on a Saturday in October or November in a fashionable hotel in the heart of Manhattan—the New York Marriott Marquis Hotel at Broadway and 45th Street. The annual banquet had various ends. The organization used it to raise funds and manifest political strength. In addition, the annual banquet was a party, organized to strengthen the Dominican supermarket owners' spirit of community. I once asked Luis why they organized the banquet. He said,

> We do our banquet to raise funds for the organization to run the operation.... [It is] the most important event that we have, and we do it to raise funds—and also that's how other organizations and politicians and corporate America learn that there is a Dominican group that is very, very strong. And I assume that the reason for which a couple would mention the organization is because we now have become the strongest group of Dominican business people in New York [and we use our banquet to demonstrate this].

On Saturday November 15, 2003, I was present at the National Supermarkets Association's annual banquet in the Marriott Marquis Hotel. Luis had put me on the guest list. The banquet began on the fifth floor at 7 P.M. On the fifth floor, I left the elevator with a woman in her thirties, a Latina. After first asking me in English if I was heading for that banquet, she asked, "Which company?" I said who I was, and she explained that she represented the company Nebraskaland. The formal program and the dinner did not begin until 9 P.M., in a hall on the sixth floor. Before that, there were drinks from a set of bars and tables with snacks; people greeted one another, formed small groups, and mingled, while one of the hotel's bands played Caribbean, mostly calypso, rhythms.

A large proportion of those present were of Dominican descent. Many supermarket owners had brought family members—wife or husband, grown-up sons and daughters, cousins, and/or other relatives. The founders, and the current leaders and board members, of the National Supermarkets Association wore black tuxedos, while most other male guests wore suits and ties. Luis, in a tuxedo and with a wireless transmitter, constantly moved around and directed and oversaw everything.

A poster at the entrance showed the seating for the formal program and the dinner. The participants were divided into four categories: "Companies," "National Supermarkets Association Members," "National Supermarkets Association Guests," and "Press." The first category included 65 companies; each company was assigned one or more tables for its representatives. I found my own name under "Guests" and under "Table number 95." Others who had been placed at this table were Kim Sung Soo, the Korean American who for more than two decades had struggled so formidably and so impressively for New York's Korean and other small business owners; José Fernández, a Dominican New Yorker in his thirties who headed a small association of bodega owners; and the latter's Dominican wife, who worked for a pharmaceutical company in New Jersey. Another in the guest category was Alfredo Placeres, president of the New York State Federation of Hispanic Chambers of Commerce. Others were among New York's most important Dominican and Puerto Rican politicians: the two state assemblymen Adriano Espaillat and José Peralta, City Councilman Miguel Martínez, and Bronx President Adolfo Carrión, Jr.

The formal program lasted for a couple of hours. The association's founders and current leaders and board members sat enthroned on chairs on the stage; others who had been awarded seats on the stage were a handful of representatives of the banquet's main sponsors and a few prominent guests. The rest of us sat at over a hundred tables in front of the stage. Two large flags could be seen, one on each side of the stage: the flags of the United States and the Dominican Republic. Luis began by formally welcoming us, then introduced the program's hostess, a Dominican journalist from Univisión. At her request, all rose to sing the two national anthems, first that of the United States and then that of the Dominican Republic. The two-hour show contained speeches, entertainment, and prize awards—and not least, many praises of, and advertisements for, the banquet's and, consequently, the association's sponsors. While we watched the program, we were served a three-course dinner. At 11 P.M., the show was over, and the light was thereafter softened, while Los Toros Band, a merengue orchestra that had been flown in from the Dominican Republic, took over the enormous stage. The merengue filled the room, and soon many of the banquet's participants had entered the stage and transformed it into a steamy dancing place. Finally, the fun started.

As Luis said, the association organizes the annual banquet to raise funds. In 2003, the main sponsor—or "platinum sponsor"—was the Miller Brewing Company. Four corporations had donated sums that made them the banquet and organization "silver sponsors": Coca-Cola, Entenmann's, Goya Foods, and Cibao Meat Products (a company created and built by Dominicans). After these came nine "bronze sponsors": Carolina Rice, JP Morgan Chase, Iberia Foods, Kraft Foods, Krasdale Foods, Altria Corporates Services, Budweiser, Porky Products and Frito Lay. In addition, a long list of other companies had supported the event and the association with smaller sums. Each sponsor was individually thanked from the stage while the company's logo was projected on large screens. A representative of Miller extended greetings and best wishes to all members and friends of the National Supermarkets Association and applauded what he described as the Dominican supermarket owners' "strong entrepreneurial spirit," before adding, "While you have a proud record of accomplishments, you have an even greater future ahead of you." Then he showed us a brand new Miller TV commercial. Miller had also been the banquet's main sponsor in 2001 and 2002.

The association's banquet is also political; it serves political functions. The annual banquet is a testimony to the Dominican supermarket owners' ability to mobilize collectively—to their resources, networks, and bargaining strength. In addition, it is a place where the association's leaders step forward and are acknowledged. As mentioned, some of the city's Latino—or Dominican and Puerto Rican—elected officials choose to be present. Each year the organization produces a program for the occasion; this is distributed at the banquet. The 2003 program was a glossy publication of more than sixty-five pages; the programs for 2001 and 2002 were similar. The program contained advertisements, information about the National Supermarkets Association's activities, letters from the organization's leaders, and, not least, homage to sponsors and the year's winners of scholarships and prizes. Also this publication documented, and testified to, the organization's resources. One of the first pages of the 2002 program showed a signed letter—or a greeting—from Mayor Michael Bloomberg, next to a photo of Bloomberg. The mayor welcomed "all those attending the banquet of the National Supermarkets Association" and expressed his "best wishes for an enjoyable event and for continued success in all of your endeavors." The year after, in 2003, the program contained a similar greeting, this time from New York governor George Pataki.

The banquet functioned in addition as an economic and political workshop, that is, as a place where small groups of guests gathered for a while in a part of the adjacent areas to discuss and resolve particular economic and/or political issues. When I was there in 2003, I saw Alfredo Placeres, Adriano Espaillat, and Adolfo Carrión, Jr., to only mention a few, absorbed in conversations in the corridors.

The annual banquet helps build and sustain the Dominican supermarket owners' union. This event (or secular ritual) is by far the most important celebration of the existence of this fellowship. The banquet gives form to, and helps reproduce, a discourse of identity, ideas about belonging. This discourse says that an overwhelming majority of the National Supermarkets Association's members are Dominican American; they have become American, at least Americanized, but remain nonetheless Dominican: they are Dominican American.

Many features of this ceremony expressed, and emphasized, an identification with the United States—the land of opportunity, the nation of immigrants. The place where the celebration occurred was virtually an American symbol—a hotel located on Broadway next to Times Square, in the center of New York. The ceremony would not have taken place without the conspicuous support from corporate America. As we have seen, a considerable part of the event consisted of a celebration of ties uniting first- and second-generation Dominican immigrant entrepreneurs and a series of representatives of corporate America. The main language used on the stage was English.

But the main thing was that this ritual, the annual banquet, efficiently reproduced a hegemonic story, a narrative of creation, transformation, and identity—the American immigrant success story. As Phyllis Pease Chock has put it,

> "Naturalization" is the provocative word that Americans use for the transformation of immigrants into citizens. It refers to a legal change of status that is overseen by an agency of the state, the Immigration and Naturalization Service. But the word evokes more than the law. It suggests, for example, that it also has to do with "nature." As David Schneider [1969: 120] pointed out, nature and law may define both kinship and nationality in American culture.... This is because "naturalization" is accomplished not just through legal processes but also through such cultural practices as talking about, telling and re-telling,... immigrant success stories. These stories are told widely in settings that Americans call "family" or "community," where they comprise "family history"; they also are told in scholarly works, in curricula, in mass media, in legislatures, and elsewhere. Immigrant success stories reiterate national mythic themes of rebirth, of opportunity, and of nationality. (1995: 239)

These stories are about a heroic (usually male) immigrant "who is an active protagonist who transforms himself into an American and a success" (ibid.); on his way to Americanness and success, he works hard and receives little or no help from anyone except his family and trustworthy friends. Telling an immigrant success story functions as a ritual (in the classic sense of this term); it helps transform social identity. By talking about and displaying, representing and "consuming" one's own transformation, one confirms one's authority to do so, asserts one's (changed) identity.

The whole banquet embodied and told an immigrant success story. In a way, it *was* an American immigrant success story. The ceremony testified to, and told about, these Dominican immigrants' upward mobility and success. Several of the evening's speakers directed our attention to these Dominicans' hard work, vitality, creativity, and success. The evening's hostess, the Dominican journalist from Univisión, was exemplary. After she was introduced by Luis as the evening's hostess, her opening words to the audience were, "As a Dominican, I feel honored and proud! Proud, because it's fantastic to see how many who have come so far!" Her first act was to highlight and applaud these immigrants' success.

Every year the National Supermarkets Association honors one of its members with a prize—the "National Supermarkets Association Member of the Year" prize. It is awarded at the banquet, and a photo of the member and the member's family history are printed in the program. A twenty-nine-year-old woman was awarded the prize in 2003. Mary Díaz, who had been raised partly on the island and partly in the United States, was married and a mother of three children. She owned and ran her own independent supermarket in New York together with a brother and a sister. Mary's family history, as it was rendered in the printed program, was a true immigrant success story. The narrative described the family's setbacks, struggle, and determined work on its way to success. The programs for the two preceding banquets contained similar stories. In 2001, another woman, Carmen Taveras, was selected as member of the year. Her family story, too, was rendered as a real immigrant success story. In 2002, three brothers—Juan, Corino, and Tony Guzmán—were together awarded the prize; they were first-generation immigrants and had little formal education, but now together owned and operated two supermarkets in Brooklyn.

The discourse of belonging that had given form to the National Supermarkets Association's banquet was complex: it denoted a combined Dominican and American belonging. Present at the banquet in 2003 as one of the guests of honor was Amelia Vega, who was that year's Miss Universe and represented the Dominican Republic. She addressed the audience in Spanish and as a Dominican. No one, it appeared, received a louder or more enthusiastic applause that night than the one Amelia got.

As we have seen, the Dominican supermarket owners' ability to act in concert rested on a fairly broad foundation. These entrepreneurs' everyday lives produced and sustained an awareness of common interests. Each member of the National Supermarkets Association profited from the organization's capacity to secure collective arrangements. But their team spirit was an expression of more than this. This fellowship had also been forged and maintained through other types of activities, including political meetings and political struggles; business trips and excursions; golf outings and softball matches; cultural events and ceremonies; dinners and lunches; and the organization's annual banquet. It was the sum of all this—in other words, the sum of all these activities and practices—that gave the Dominican supermarket owners their collective strength, their spirit of community.

Race and Justice

These Dominican entrepreneurs and "success stories" were bearers of a political and economic thinking, a set of ideas about society, the state, and the economy. This thinking caused many of them to criticize specific features of the U.S. social order. The National Supermarkets Association was, for example, critical of several aspects of the last decades' economic and social changes in New York. All the same, these Dominican immigrants embraced their new homeland. We have already seen that their annual banquet, to a striking extent, gave form to and articulated an experience of a double attachment—a Dominican American belonging. These first- and second-generation immigrants identified with the strength, productivity, and destiny of the United States. A great majority of the Dominican supermarket owners expressed and practiced political and economic ideas supporting central elements of the hegemonic American project as we know it. The Dominican supermarket owners' political and economic discourse produced and reproduced notions of hierarchy and equality, of exclusion and tolerance, of inequality and fairness. Two of the themes this discourse dealt with were the production and reproduction of the United States—or their new homeland—as a racial hierarchy and how a nation best secures and reproduces a healthy economy.

Like the other Dominican New Yorkers I met, those who had become owners of supermarkets maintained a profound awareness of the United States as a society very much structured in terms of ideas about race. These people were far from naïve. For example, I asked Eligio (the founding father of the National Supermarkets Association and now owner of a series of stores) how he explained that so many of the Big Apple's independent supermarkets had ended up as Dominican-owned. Why Dominicans and not others? His answer, which came fast, was replete with references to thinking about race. He said that a person has to take into account two factors. First, the Dominican immigrant arrived at the right moment, and he knew the (Spanish) language and the (Latino) culture that increasingly came to mark many parts of the city. Second, the Cubans arrived in the city more or less at the same time—that is, in the early and mid-1960s. What happened? The majority of those Cubans who entered the city differed from the Dominicans. They were educated, they were white, and since they were political refugees, they received some help from the authorities. They did not have to work like "we" (Dominicans) did; they weren't forced to survive, or go through what Dominicans had to go through. "We Dominicans," he ended (a bit steamed up), "received nothing, nothing, nothing, nothing! On the contrary—obstacles! The Dominican was forced to work hard. The Dominican isn't white—he is of mixed descent [*mezclado*]."

The Dominican supermarket owners cooperated systematically and routinely with representatives of corporate America, and many of the latter were white. Even so, the National Supermarkets Association's members remained without illusions. They knew perfectly well that the U.S. racial hierarchy made it impossible for them, in practice, to secure what Rosaldo (1994: 402) described as "first-class" (cultural, social, and political) citizenship.

On the other hand, those who live in the Dominican Republic, too, view classification of race as natural (as literally a part of nature), as something inevitable. Like the United States, the Dominican Republic is a direct outcome of a history of slavery and its aftermath.

An implication was that those Dominican migrants who had obtained their own supermarket(s) remained *dominicanos* and *hispanos*. The members of the National Supermarkets Association saw, and marketed and sold, themselves as Dominicans. At the same time, they viewed themselves as a part of the rapidly growing Latino population in the United States (with its accompanying market). Those New York City politicians who participated in the organization's annual banquet were, as we have seen, Dominican and Puerto Rican—Hispanics or Latinos. While I waited for Luis or another person in the National Supermarkets Association's headquarters, I used to kill time by reading magazines like *Supermercados USA: Serving the Hispanic Retail Community Nationwide* and *Hispanic Market News*.

The Dominican supermarket owners believed in the value of a strong market economy. In their view, the market forces were economically and socially fair and beneficial. The role of the authorities was, they maintained, to ensure that the market's supposed inherent competition and strengths were not weakened but, on the contrary, nourished and preserved. The National Supermarkets Association's resistance to expansion of megastores owned and run by chains should not mislead us. The Dominican supermarket owners were convinced capitalists and were not against what they saw as fair competition. What they opposed was not the creation of new stores but the fact that these new megastores were opened with the aid of subsidies—money derived from the taxpayers. This was, they insisted, an injustice, a violation of the rules of the game. In brief, the argument was that politico-economic elites (meaning politicians and representatives of big business) and the city's authorities worked against, and undermined, the market.

In June 1995, Pathmark had already six stores in Brooklyn, but, even so, the chain wanted at that time to open two more stores in this part of the city, one in downtown Brooklyn and another in Williamsburg. A Dominican in his thirties, Moises Esdaille, owned and operated a C-Town in Williamsburg; his store was situated three-quarters of a mile away from the site where Pathmark planned to build a new supermarket. Esdaile said to a journalist from the *Daily News*, referring to the tax incentives that lured Pathmark and other national retailers to the city, "I'm not afraid to compete with them. They [the city] are putting me to swim a race with Pathmark and they get all the breaks.... I'll challenge any store to see who is cheaper. Pathmark is not going to cater to Spanish [*sic*] clients like I do." Pablo Espinal, president of the National Supermarkets Association at the time, said to the same journalist about the project in Williamsburg, "Obviously, there's not much we could do to stop the project. We don't agree with the type of subsidy using taxpayer money. If they want to open a store, let them do it themselves" (Serant 1995a).

Less than a year later, Luis was interviewed by the *New York Times*:

> We want a level playing field. I will not put down Fairway at all as a business. The question is how someone got away with violating the law while others can't.... [In the 1970s and 1980s,] We came in aggressively and financed it privately. Now the big supermarkets see us thriving in here [in the inner city] and they want to come back. But they need special zoning and benefits we don't get. I don't think that's American. (Gonzalez 1996a)

One could go farther. These immigrants, or the Dominican supermarket owners, operated their stores completely without unions. Their political-economic practices and views made them resemble what could be called a set of "neoliberalists." This should not surprise us, though. As noted, post-1975 New York City became increasingly a neoliberal world—or pushed to its logical conclusion, "The politics of the Reagan administration of the 1980s became 'merely the New York scenario' of the 1970s 'writ large'" (Harvey 2005: 48).[14] A large proportion of those Dominicans who migrated to New York came to know the city from the 1970s onward. They adapted to, operated in, and were shaped by the political, economic, and ideological surroundings Harvey refers to. Small wonder, perhaps, that successful Dominicans, like the supermarket owners, were hard-nosed capitalists and had confidence in the power of market forces.

CHAPTER 7

In Search of Dignity

The previous chapter examined forms of political culture and activism in a part of New York's Dominican community. The objective of this chapter is the same, but it will focus not on the Dominican supermarket owners but on those Dominicans who belong to the city's livery industry, examining forms of political activity and collective action among Dominican livery drivers in the years from around 1998 onward.

In this chapter, I want first to document that Dominican livery-cab drivers have remained politically active. I have previously shown that Dominican livery drivers took part in a set of political struggles in the city in the 1980s; they participated in organized resistance against the authorities' attempts to obtain stronger and more efficient control over the industry. After 1998, New York's livery industry saw the emergence of two new interest organizations. Both fought to improve the working and living conditions for the city's livery cab drivers, and both were headed and controlled by Dominicans: the New York State Federation of Taxi Drivers (the more visible and high profiled) and the New York City For-Hire Base Group. While a large proportion of the federation's members were Dominican drivers who belonged to livery-cab operations in the Bronx and Brooklyn, the New York City For-Hire Base Group was almost exclusively based in Upper Manhattan and a few pockets of West Bronx. After 1998, New York's Dominican livery drivers strengthened their political position; they managed more than before to make themselves heard—in brief, they came to a greater extent to constitute a political voice in the city.

Second, I want to show the strikingly high degree of contact that existed between leaders and representatives of the Dominican livery sector and a number of New York's elected officials. This chapter, thus, continues to employ ethnography to document the existence and the significance of a set of political processes and networks that helped connect two parts of the city: New York as an economy and a labor market and New York as a political world.

In addition to functioning as a political force, the activism in the Dominican livery cab community was also a cultural force that helped produce and give form to experiences of fellowship. It helped build ethnic and panethnic identity—belonging as "Dominican" and "Hispanic." The third main purpose of the present chapter is to demonstrate this.

After analyzing the creation of the New York State Federation of Taxi Drivers and the New York City For-Hire Base Group, I shall discuss more closely below the ways in which the political culture and political activism in the Dominican livery-cab sector contributed to the construction of experiences of fellowship and ethnic and panethnic identity. I seek to answer the following questions: What characterized the political and moral discourse of the Dominican livery drivers? What drove Dominican livery drivers to act politically?

A Struggle to Be Heard

When I started the fieldwork in the summer of 2002, the New York State Federation of Taxi Drivers had formally existed for about three years. It had established itself as a relatively important organization, a political actor in the city. After the federation emerged, those who worked in the city's livery-cab industry had become more visible. In the last years before the federation was founded in 1999, those who represented and defended the interests of the livery-cab operations and the livery-cab drivers had been nearly invisible—they were hardly seen or listened to, or taken seriously, by those who governed New York.

The president of the New York State Federation of Taxi Drivers was Fernando Mateo, who continued to head the organization up to 2007. Mateo, a successful self-made businessman, grew up in modest circumstances in New York City on the Lower East Side. His parents were first-generation Dominican immigrants. In 1999, he was forty and already wealthy. Mateo had never been a cab driver. His right-hand man was José Viloria, a Dominican immigrant who had worked several years as a livery driver in the Bronx, before helping create the federation. Viloria knew the industry from A to Z and was in charge of the organization's office (on the Southern Boulevard in the

Bronx) and most of its day-to-day activities. But the organization's undisputed head was Mateo.[1] In the following, I look more closely at (1) the emergence and development of the New York State Federation of Taxi Drivers, (2) aspects of the organization's structure and political activities, and (3) features of Mateo's political leadership.

I met Viloria many times, in the federation's office in the Bronx or somewhere in Dominican Washington Heights—for example, together with drivers in some livery-cab base, in a Dominican restaurant, or at some event. Viloria, who was in his mid-forties, was always very accommodating toward me. He was friendly, energetic, and well dressed. He spoke little English; we always spoke Spanish.

In a conversation in November 2002, Viloria explained to me how he had become acquainted with Mateo and how the federation had then been created. Shortly before the federation was founded, Viloria and some other Dominican livery-cab drivers from the Bronx had failed in an attempt to organize a strike to improve the conditions in the industry; the drivers had little collective strength, but an overwhelming majority in the industry thought the city treated them arbitrarily and disrespectfully: both the bases and their drivers felt pushed around by everybody—the Taxi and Limousine Commission, the police, and those who controlled the city's yellow-cab industry. In September 1998, Viloria and a number of other Dominican drivers attempted to organize a strike among many of the city's (or at least among many of the Bronx's) livery drivers, but the strike brought no result. No one cared; nobody listened to their demands. In Viloria's own words,

> [In those days] we were a small group of persons who had studied at the university, who knew a little, and we began worrying about the situation, and we tried to get heard, and we attempted to organize our first strike. On September 8, 1998, we sought to organize a labor strike, so that the Taxi and Limousine Commission would listen to us and receive us, so that we could discuss the rules of the game—for we tried [each day] to survive [in the street], but we didn't know the rules. That is to say, we didn't know when we violated a law or a rule and when we didn't. If we don't have any documents to read, well, then we don't know when we break the rules. In brief, we wanted to organize things, but it was impossible, above all because no one listened to us. In those days the city didn't want to understand.... When we organized that strike on September 8, 1998, we paralyzed the area [of the

city] which we wanted, but we saw that this, in reality, didn't hurt the city because the authorities didn't worry at the time about what could happen in these parts of the city, in the poor, marginalized areas. It didn't matter to them in those days if the population went to work, or if it didn't go to work. The only ones who got annoyed were those to whom we didn't offer transport. Those who used the yellow cabs, that is, the population in midtown and downtown Manhattan, met with no difficulties. . . . Well, we started to get desperate, and a group of drivers believed that what was needed was a little bit more political power, and it was then that some proposed [we go and see] Fernando Mateo. When Fernando Mateo was suggested to me, I said, "Fernando isn't a taxi driver. How on earth can a guy who doesn't know our problems be our representative? Well, perhaps he can assist us. He can lead the way while we—but I don't think that a person who doesn't know our difficulties may be the president of any organization." Well, at first I didn't accept it.

The man who first proposed the group should attempt to get in touch with Mateo was Armando Peralta, a first-generation Dominican immigrant who, since the foundation in 1999, had been the federation's treasurer. In 2002, Peralta worked in the organization's office in the Bronx. Like Viloria, he had arrived in New York as an adult and had worked in the Bronx as a livery driver. He was older than Viloria and spoke little English. Finally, Viloria, Peralta, and their friends decided to contact Mateo. Why him? Mateo was, and is, a real American hero. Above all, he is a prosperous entrepreneur, but he is also a community activist and a politician. Dropping out of Manhattan's Seward Park High School at the age of fifteen, Mateo began to work. By the time he was eighteen, he was operating his own store—Carpet Fashions Inc. on Avenue A. A few years later, he had built his small floor covering business into a multimillion-dollar operation. When I interviewed Mateo on March 13, 2003, he characterized himself in the following (self-satisfied but all the same instructive) manner:

I get things done, and that has to do with who I am. That has to do with me not having a dime, dropping out of high school, being married at 17, and having a child to support. That—you know, and not having any excuses for failure. I don't believe in failure. Failure is an excuse, and everyone that fails has an excuse, and that's blaming somebody else. When things go bad for me, when they have gone bad for me—'cos it always hasn't been rosy—I blame myself. I don't look to say the white man is prejudiced against me and that's why I didn't succeed—no. I say, "I've gotta be just as good, or better, than the white man in order to get what I want." I can't be less smart than you and expect to get a better job than you, see? I don't believe in—I believe that racism exists, but I don't allow it to penetrate me.... What I had was a lot of heart and a lot of desire to succeed, and I always believed that I didn't want anyone to tell me what to do, so in order for me not to have a boss I had to work harder, so when people talk to me about how hard they've worked, it bores me because no one's worked harder than me. I learned how to lay floors when I was 15, and I worked no less than 18 hours a day.

Mateo has been shuttling between two countries since he was born. His immigrant mother flew back to her homeland so he could be born a Dominican. After that, his childhood was split between the Lower East Side and the Dominican capital. A dual citizen of the United States and the Dominican Republic, he is fluent in English and Spanish. When the federation was founded in 1999, he was forty. Five years earlier, he had gone into a new business—the money transfer business. In 1994, he started Mateo Express, a money-wiring company serving the Dominican Republic. In the late 1990s Mateo Express had 200 agents throughout New York City and transferred some $40 million a year (Sontag and Dugger 1998). Mateo and his wife and their three children had now moved to a suburb, the Westchester County suburb of Irvington. His wife, who had previously worked for an accounting firm, now ran a small construction company.

Mateo began his career as a community activist and political player in the late 1980s. In 1989, he started a program to help poor people in prison. In 1993, he created the "Toys for Guns" program; owners of illegal guns in New York City were encouraged to bring them in to the local police station in exchange for a $100 gift certificate at their local "Toys 'R' Us" store. The "Toys for Guns" program got a tremendous amount of coverage in the press and made Mateo famous. He went on the *Oprah Winfrey Show*, became a darling of Spanish-language television, and met Bill and Hillary Clinton. Through his minor renown in New York, Mateo was able to assert himself as an actor in the Dominican Republic's politics. In 1996, the Dominican Republic adopted constitutional reforms that recognized dual citizenship. Shortly after that, Mateo together with others in the Dominican community in New York started and headed a campaign to secure for emigrants the right to vote from the United States. This was granted in December 1997 by the Dominican Senate and Congress, so that New York had the second-largest concentration of votes in any Dominican election, after Santo Domingo.

Less than a year later, Viloria, Peralta, and a group of other Dominican livery-cab drivers from the Bronx decided to get in touch with Mateo. Mateo, recalling his first meeting with them (I repeat that Mateo's descriptions are evidently marked by some conceit, not to say self-praise, but I find them nevertheless useful),[2] said that they spoke of the problems drivers faced from the authorities and from criminals, and he replied,

> "Listen, guys, I really don't—I don't have the time. I don't have the experience. I don't know what I can do." They said, "Please! We're not gonna leave here until we have a commitment from you." They stood there. [I] said, "Look, guys, I'll look into it." So I called my lawyer and I called my accountant, and I started to understand a little bit more about what the industry was about, and we started to have meetings. The meetings started to grow. It showed that there was a problem in the industry, so I said, "OK, I will take on this responsibility, but I'm gonna need the support from you guys." I said, "I'm not a cab driver, you're the cab drivers. What I can do is present your problems, study them, and try to make changes."

The New York State Federation of Taxi Drivers was established during the first half of 1999. Before that, Mateo had picked Viloria as his right-hand man, and the latter and his allies had supplied Mateo with abundant information on their everyday lives as livery-cab drivers. Not only Mateo but also a few of his regular collaborators—for example, a lawyer and an accountant—attended some of these preliminary conversations and meetings and asked the drivers questions to obtain the best possible overview of this part of New York's economy.

Mateo has in a certain sense operated as a mediator and a broker—as an interpreter between social and cultural spheres or between two different parts of the city. Most of the Dominican livery-cab drivers speak almost only Spanish. The authorities' language is English, and few of New York's politicians understand Spanish. Mateo, for his part, is bilingual and familiar with both worlds—United States society and Dominican society. I asked

Mateo if he believed that his leadership in the federation had something to do with his language qualifications. He replied, "I think so. I mean, I grew up here, so I know the city well . . . Language definitely—language and [my] reputation."

Mateo was also wealthy and independent, and he had political contacts and was loved by the press. This made him suitable for the job as head of the new organization. Mateo, for his part, also benefitted from the arrangement. He had already established himself as an activist and a leader, but, with the establishment of the New York State Federation of Taxi Drivers, he got himself a new position in the city. As spokesman and advocate of the city's thousands of (Dominican and non-Dominican) livery-cab drivers, he could continue to take political and social initiatives—and with this gain increased respect and authority and, ultimately, consolidate and reinforce his (pan-)ethnic political and social leadership.

In 2003, the New York State Federation of Taxi Drivers claimed to have around 18,000 members. Between 2002 and 2005, this figure (or a similar figure, for example 13,000, 16,000, or 20,000) was often used by the press. Nearly all the members were Spanish-speaking livery-cab drivers who belonged to bases in the Bronx and Brooklyn. According to Viloria, around 75 percent of the members were Dominicans. Each member had to pay a $5 weekly fee to the organization. But only a small minority of the members did this in practice; Mateo estimated that perhaps 2,000 or 3,000 paid. The payment from the drivers was used to run the organization. The federation office in the Bronx was open for members and nonmembers five days a week; a member who had a question or a problem could stop by the office to get advice or help; if a driver needed assistance from a lawyer, the federation paid the bill (provided the five-dollar fee had been paid). In Mateo's words,

> That five-dollar fee is used to give the members lawyers in the courts. They don't pay for lawyers any more. We supply them, for five dollars. Any legal advice—I mean, not legal, but [for example] any translation, any problems, any abuse, anything that has hurt their chances of working, we have our door open to them, and we have a staff that we have to pay, and we have phones that we have to pay, and electricity. So we provide the service and a lot of times they've come in when they have a problem, and then, when you look 'em up in the computer you realize they haven't paid in six months, but they come now—"Oh, I'm a member. Look, they took my car away!" "You're a member?" "Yeah,

yeah! No problem!" "You're a member, pal, but you haven't paid your dues in six months, so you have to get a—catch up to date, and you pay for the lawyer this time, but what we pay." So, lawyers usually charge $200, $300. They charge us [in the federation] about $125, $150, so we give them the discount, but if they're up to date and they have a problem, we cover the $125, $150, so, in essence, the federation isn't a money-making organization. If 3,000 [members] pay, 2,000 pay, then we have just enough to cover the overhead.

The Bronx neighborhood where the federation rented its locale forms part of a working-class area of many Spanish-speaking immigrants from the Caribbean, Mexico, and Central and South America, with slightly smaller numbers from Asia, Africa, and Europe; there are also African Americans and white Americans. The federation's office was surrounded by small businesses—car-repair shops, dry cleaners, small restaurants, beauty parlors, and grocery stores. Each time I visited the office, I ran into drivers who had come to ask for some practical and/or legal assistance. In 2002 and 2003, five people worked permanently in the office, all Dominicans. Three women were employed as secretaries and bookkeepers; the two others were Peralta, the Federation's treasurer, and Viloria, the organization's and the office's administrative head. The language used in the office was Spanish. All five helped those who entered with various problems; some had questions concerning motor insurance, while others had been fined by the police or summoned by the Taxi and Limousine Commission.

When Viloria was not in the office, he went to see bases and drivers and attended meetings, hearings, press conferences, and ceremonies. Each base where a number of the drivers belonged to the federation had a *delegado* or representative. In addition, there were four *delegados*, each responsible for a borough, the Bronx, Brooklyn, Queens, and Manhattan. Almost all the delegates had so far been Dominican drivers; a handful had been Ecuadoran or Mexican. Every week the representatives stopped by the federation's office to exchange information with Viloria.

Being a livery cab driver in New York City in the 1980s and the 1990s was dangerous. Many were robbed, and an alarming number was murdered. A high proportion of the robberies and killings occurred in neighborhoods generally shunned as unsafe by the operators of the city's yellow cabs. The situation worsened in 1992, when 39 livery drivers were murdered; the next year, 37 were killed. But as New York City's crime rate fell sharply in the

1990s, so did the number of livery cab killings; in 1999, the total was 11, but that was still far too high.

Immediately after the federation was founded, Mateo and Viloria, therefore, defined increased safety for the drivers as the new organization's foremost goal. Viloria told me in late 2002, "On average 25 livery drivers were killed each year—on average. There were years where the number mounted to 39, but we had also years where the total was 15. Well, this became our main focus." So efforts were made to put pressure on Mayor Rudolph Giuliani; the federation demanded that the city made some moves to try to improve the safety for New York's thousands of livery drivers. Earlier requests to discuss the lack of safety and other problems had, according to Viloria, never received a reply.

The year 2000 started dreadfully; nine livery driver murders during just the first four months of the year once again had drivers fearing seriously for their lives. Mayor Giuliani had made cutting crime the cornerstone of his administration, and the city's politicians and police were alarmed. In this climate, Mateo decided to act, to intensify the pressure on the Giuliani administration. As a part of this, he used his access to the press. During the first six months of 2000, Mateo was repeatedly quoted in the city's newspapers—in everything from the *New York Times* and *Daily News* to *El Diario/La Prensa* and *Noticias del Mundo*. For example, on February 25, 2000, after a livery cab driver was shot in Brooklyn during a $170 robbery, Mateo angrily called on Mayor Giuliani to "take responsibility for these ruthless killings." He added that "if the mayor can take credit for all the good in the city, then it's time for him to explain how the city plans to protect the hardworking livery cab drivers."[3]

The sixth livery driver killed in the city that year was Luis Francisco Perez, a Dominican immigrant. About twelve hours after the shooting, Perez's widow and Mateo gathered at Whitlock Avenue and Aldus Street in the Bronx, the site of the killing, for a news conference. Mateo said the federation had met with the mayor less than a week before to discuss livery-driver safety and had called for safety partitions, security cameras, and tracking devices for livery cabs, as well as for increased police patrols aimed at thwarting taxi robberies. The news conference ended abruptly when Perez's widow began sobbing and then fainted as she spoke to the crowd of reporters, photographers, and television crews. She was taken away in an ambulance. Before she broke down, she talked briefly about her husband. "He was a good man, he was a happy man," she said in Spanish, with Mateo translating. "I lost it all. I have nowhere to turn."[4]

In an attempt to protect the livery drivers, the city adopted a series of measures. Mayor Giuliani created a $5 million program to provide independently owned and operated livery and medallion cabs with safety partitions and security cameras. The city offered free mobile phones to drivers, authorized a $10,000 reward for information, and established a relief fund for the murdered drivers' families. The mayor and police commissioner Howard Safir created a livery task force of more than 300 officers, and issued rules that made it easier for officers to stop livery cabs and initiate a search. In addition, the police set up safety zones in each borough, where drivers with suspect passengers could go to find officers and increased the number of decoy cabs on patrol.[5] After the first months of 2000 livery cab murders again fell. Not one murder of a livery driver occurred for the rest of 2000, and the numbers have remained low ever since. Two were killed on duty in 2003, none in 2004, one in 2005.

Between January and June 2000, Mayor Giuliani, Police Commissioner Safir, and other city officials met several times with Mateo, Viloria, and others who represented the federation to discuss ways to improve safety in the industry. At these meetings, the federation's views were clearly listened to. Viloria acknowledged that his view of Giuliani had changed and that the situation had started to change during spring 2000. Up to then, the mayor and the city had ignored the livery drivers, he said; they had not been interested in the industry. With nine livery drivers killed during just the first four months of 2000, things became different. But it was not just that the political climate in the city changed as a result of the murders. Crucially, the livery cab drivers now had someone like Mateo to speak for them. Mateo had some resources, and it was politically impossible to disregard him.

Mateo and Viloria both described how the federation had threatened the Giuliani administration with staging protests. After the body of the seventh livery cabbie to be slain in 2000 had been found, Mateo had told Giuliani that they would get seven caskets, one for each murdered driver and, as a symbolic action, leave them on the doorsteps of City Hall. At the same time, they would organize a large demonstration. In Mateo's own words, "I went to the mayor and I said to him . . . we were gonna close down the city because we were gonna come in from all the bridges and all the tunnels, and there are 30,000 cars. That's a lot of cars, so the mayor sat down with me, and he says, 'Fernando, what's the problem?' 'The problem is that you have no eyes,' and I said 'And your police commissioner doesn't care,' and I said, 'Your first deputy [mayor] is a liar.' I said, 'They promised me things. They don't deliver.'"

Mateo's account was evidently one-sided—and both lively and exaggerated. But there is no doubt that the federation during this period attempted to apply vigorous pressure to the authorities. After listening to the above story, I asked Mateo how his relations with Giuliani had been before 2000; he replied, "We were very good friends. After that, we were not friends any more. After that, they told me they don't want to deal with me any more." Mateo got a call on his birthday from Giuliani's first-deputy mayor, Joe Lhota, at 8 o'clock in the morning, saying, "Fernando, I want you to know that this administration wants nothing to do with you. We don't want you to call us. We don't want you to bother us. We don't want you to consider us your friends . . . Fuck you, Fernando!" to which Mateo replied, "You know what? Joe, if that's the way you feel, that's your problem." Mateo went on to explain to me,

> I was forceful. I was tired. The mayor would never, had never come to a funeral for the drivers. You know what it is to see two drivers being murdered in four weeks, two every week straight and do nothing and don't say something? If you get two people murdered a week in Central Park, he'll be the first there—one murder in Central Park! If you get seven cops murdered, the city would be in an uproar, but because they were cab drivers, it didn't matter. They didn't care. It was that simple. But these people never had anyone that [has] a voice that can represent them, that can do a press conference and have media come, because the media gave us a lot of support. Without the media, we would have never gotten to where we're at.

Mateo and the federation not only knew how to handle the press. The former had also good relations with Governor George Pataki. The two collaborated; Mateo supported the governor politically and spoke favorably of the Pataki administration's activities and initiatives in the media, and, in return, the governor backed the federation's work. For example, in mid-2000, he signed legislation to toughen penalties for crimes committed against livery drivers.[6] The same law also made it easier for the New York Crime Victim Board to grant compensation to the families of livery drivers killed as result of a crime; established a task force to investigate ways to increase the availability of Workers' Compensation coverage for livery cab drivers; created an advisory committee to examine initiatives to help improve livery driver safety; and established a safety training program for those drivers.

The governor's measures were applauded by Mateo, who said in early

2001, "This is the first administration that has supported our industry and has cared about our people. We're honored by the Governor's help and support and we will be for ever thankful" (Office of the Governor for the State of New York, George E. Pataki 2001b). That same year, Mateo began his second term as federation president. The event was marked by a small ceremony, and Mateo had asked his friend Governor Pataki to preside. At the event, the governor stated, "I am proud to be part of this ceremony, which demonstrates the courage and faith of every member of the Federation of Taxi Drivers. Driving a cab is the first job for many new arrivals to our City and State, and can be a dangerous and difficult job. These hard working men and women are the future of New York and America. They have already risked so much to live here, they should not have to choose between their lives or their livelihood in order to strive for the American dream" (Office of the Governor for the State of New York, George E. Pataki 2001a). Obviously the governor's goal was to win votes. Pataki saw Mateo as a high-profile representative and advocate of an important part of the rapidly growing Latino population.

Many difficulties that Dominican drivers and owners of cab operations in New York's livery industry experienced were due partly to their not mastering English. The New York City Taxi and Limousine Commission, for example, operated exclusively in English; Commission employees spoke English, and its rules and regulations were in English. These were complicated, and often, when a Dominican or Latino livery driver got a fine, it was because he or she simply lacked sufficient knowledge of those Taxi and Limousine Commission rules and regulations. Livery bases, too, were fined because their owners lacked an adequate knowledge of English.

Viloria and Mateo acknowledged that most of those who worked in the industry needed more knowledge. In May 2002, the federation published a booklet of approximately 90 pages called *Reglamentos de TLC para la Industria del Taxi* (New York State Federation of Taxi Drivers 2002). The booklet contained the first edition of a translation from English into Spanish of chapter 6 of the New York City Taxi and Limousine Commission's Rules and Regulations. This is the part that concerns the livery industry. Eighteen small businesses helped finance the translation and the publication. The firms, operating in various areas of New York City, ranged from insurance brokers and livery-cab operations to auto repair shops and money transfer firms; almost all were run by Dominicans and Latinos. A large number of Spanish-speaking bases bought piles of the booklet. The bases paid the federation $2 for each copy; the drivers received the booklet free from their bases.

The emergence of the New York State Federation of Taxi Drivers meant a change. Through its creation, Dominican and Latino livery cab drivers strengthened their bargaining position. Non-Dominican and non-Latino livery cabbies also gained. The change was a result of at least three factors. First, the federation would not have emerged without the informally and loosely organized Bronx-based network of Dominican base owners and drivers led by Viloria and Peralta; this network produced the group that sought out and recruited Mateo. Second, Mateo's contribution was decisive: the federation would not have obtained the results it did but for him. Mateo had resources and access to the media, and he was resolute and had a will to act; with him, the federation was able to apply some pressure to the authorities. Third, the social and political landscape had shifted. Leading politicians in New York now eagerly courted the Latino and the Dominican vote. This made it slightly easier for a man like Mateo and an organization like the federation to bring pressure to bear on city and state authorities.

In 2002, Mateo founded and headed a new organization, Hispanics Across America (HAA). This is defined as a not-for-profit think tank and civil rights advocate committed to advancing the educational, social, and political interests of Hispanics throughout the United States. In addition to being a self-made businessman, a frequently consulted spokesman of the city's Dominicans, federation president, and an advocate of U.S. Hispanic panethnic consciousness raising, solidarity, and activism, Mateo was also a militant Republican. In 2002, he vigorously backed Pataki when the latter was reelected as New York governor. Two years later, he was a significant fundraiser for President George W. Bush's 2004 reelection campaign. The same year he was invited to represent the Hispanic community of New York City as a delegate and speaker at the Republican National Convention, which in 2004 took place in the center of New York, at Madison Square Garden.

In the New York City Dominican livery-cab community, Mateo's leadership was definitely contested. Many Dominican drivers supported him, but others regarded him as an outsider, as someone who had never been part of the livery-cab industry; they maintained that he did not know the business and lacked sufficient authority and legitimacy at the grass roots—among base owners and drivers. Yet others viewed him as an opportunist, not to say a cynic; as these saw it, Mateo used his position as federation president mainly to advance his own interests and career. The absence of support for Mateo and the federation was especially conspicuous in the heart of the Dominican community in New York—that is, in the Dominican parts of northern

Manhattan. Among Dominican livery base owners and drivers in Washington Heights and Inwood, Mateo and the federation had, in practice, little support. In these areas, Dominican base owners and drivers founded a new, rival organization in late 2001, the New York City For-Hire Base Group, to be described in the next section.

Politics at the Grass Roots

During summer 2002 to winter 2004, I often spent time in the office of Nonstop Limousine, a black car company. As previously said, the Dominican livery-cab base Fort George owns fifty percent of Nonstop Limousine. The Fort George base is located in the center of Dominican Washington Heights, and the offices of Nonstop and Fort George are next-door neighbors. The manager of Nonstop was Pedro Heredia, a first-generation Dominican immigrant who had previously driven a livery cab for Fort George. Two others were permanently employed in the office; both were Dominicans, and both had earlier worked for Fort George. The office, which was very small, housed three desks, three computers, a copier, and a couple of extra chairs for visitors. Some framed photos hung on two of the walls. A couple of these showed Pedro together with a group of representatives of the Dominican livery-cab industry in Washington Heights and Inwood; the representatives were base presidents and drivers. Others showed Pedro together with, respectively, Assemblyman Adriano Espaillat, Councilman Miguel Martínez, and Matthew W. Daus, chair/commissioner of the New York City Taxi and Limousine Commission.

Pedro was president of the New York City For-Hire Base Group, the new organization that had been established by a number of representatives of the Dominican livery-cab sector in Upper Manhattan. Through visiting the office of Nonstop, I, therefore, gathered information about many things. I learned more about the city's taxi industry and more about everyday life and the political processes in Washington Heights and Inwood. Pedro belonged simultaneously to two different parts of the taxi industry. His job was to run Nonstop; as Nonstop's manager he was paid a fixed salary. But politically, he worked for the Fort George base and for the livery-cab industry. Fort George was owned jointly by a large group of Dominican livery-cab drivers; Pedro was one of the owners.

When I started my research, the New York City For-Hire Base Group was less than a year old. It had been created in late 2001 by a group of livery-base presidents. All were Dominicans, and all represented bases dominated by Dominicans. The total number of bases that belonged to and actively supported the organization was around twenty, of which the great majority were in Washington Heights and Inwood. All the largest and best-known bases in Dominican Washington Heights and Inwood supported the organization, such as Fort George, Kennedy, High Class, First Class, Seaman, Highbridge, and Audubon. The other bases that backed the organization were in the western Bronx, not far from Washington Heights and Inwood.

Another who supported this attempt to build a new organization was Walther Delgado, a Dominican who had since 1996 been executive director of an Inwood-based nonprofit, the Audubon Partnership for Economic Development. The Audubon Partnership was a local economic development organization serving Washington Heights and Inwood by providing lending, development services, and business advocacy for the area. In 1998, the federally financed Upper Manhattan Empowerment Zone (which was awarded to New York City for a ten-year period in 1993) provided Delgado's Audubon Partnership with a $750,000 revolving loan to fund commercial development in this part of Upper Manhattan.[7] Delgado had for a long time been a community activist and a political player in northern Manhattan. From 1998 to 2002, he was the chair of Community Board 12 (serving Washington Heights and Inwood).

The Audubon Partnership assisted Pedro and the other leaders of the New York City For-Hire Base Group in a number of ways. Delgado gave them advice and practical assistance, and he lent them a part of the Audubon Partnership's premises when they needed a place for a meeting or a workshop.

Among those who headed the New York City For-Hire Base Group, Pedro was the only one who was bilingual. Pedro's first language was Spanish, but he was also fluent in English; with me, he used both languages, frequently switching back and forth while we were speaking. None of the others spoke good English. This was an important reason that the organization had elected Pedro as president. The organization's vice-president was José Vargas, who represented Junior, a livery base in the Bronx. The other members of the organization's board were base presidents in Washington Heights and Inwood.

The new organization had a good start; it was immediately taken seriously. In December 2001, Pedro and other representatives of the New York City For-Hire Base Group met for the first time with Matthew Daus, chair and commissioner of the Taxi and Limousine Commission. In March 2002, the organization sent a group to Albany. The delegation was headed by Pedro and included some twenty base presidents and activists from Washington Heights and Inwood and the western Bronx. In Albany, the group met with Adriano Espaillat and other Latino and African American members of the State Assembly. In addition, the delegation had a meeting with Puerto Rican Ray Martinez, commissioner of the New York State Department of Motor Vehicles. The same spring Pedro and José testified before the Livery Operators Workers' Compensation Insurance Task Force, a committee that had been established to make recommendations to the governor concerning Workers' Compensation coverage for livery-cab drivers. In June 2002, Pedro testified before the City Council Transportation Committee.

Why did representatives of the Dominican livery industry in Upper Manhattan and part of the Bronx choose to establish a new organization in late 2001? Why did Pedro and his comrades not support the federation? Why was the city's Dominican-dominated livery cab community disunited? Let me attempt, in four stages, to provide some answers to these questions.

First, it is clear that many in the Dominican livery-cab industry in Washington Heights and Inwood lacked confidence in Mateo. Many viewed him mainly as an "interloper." As they put it, he had never been a cab driver and did not know the business—and before the New York State Federation of Taxi Drivers was created, he had never fought politically on behalf of New York's livery-cab operations. As we have seen in an earlier chapter, representatives of the livery industry had already struggled politically for a long time. For most of the 1990s, Dominican and Latino livery base owners and drivers were represented through the organization La Asociación de Bases de Nueva York,[8] which was anchored in Washington Heights and Inwood and in areas of the western Bronx. The organization's leaders and activists belonged to livery-cab bases located in these parts of the city. In the second half of the 1990s, La Asociación de Bases became somewhat weakened; in turn, this paved the way for the creation of a new organization, that is, for the establishment of the federation and the leadership of Mateo. But, as has been said, several owners and drivers in the Dominican-controlled bases in northern Manhattan and in the Bronx remembered earlier political activism and struggle on behalf of bases and drivers, in which Mateo and those who had established the Federation had not participated.

In the Dominican community on Manhattan north of Harlem, Mateo remained an outsider also for another reason: he had never been a part of the Dominican community in Washington Heights and Inwood. He grew up in another part of the city and had never belonged to an association or an organization in the area. Critics acknowledged that some of Mateo's political results were impressive, but, even so, they had no faith in him. A veteran in the Dominican livery-cab community in Washington Heights said, "The federation was created by a guy who never was a cab driver. Mateo is an opportunist who likes publicity. He uses us—the city's Dominican and Hispanic livery drivers—as a platform, a stepping stone. He uses us for his own advantage, to promote his own interests."

Second, Pedro and his allies wanted another type—a new type—of organization. Those who created the New York City For-Hire Base Group wanted an organization with a different way of working and a different style from those of the federation. The federation was in practice entirely hierarchical. Most of its decisions were taken by only a handful of individuals at the top. So base owners and drivers in Washington Heights and Inwood felt that the organization was too little democratic, that they were too little listened to, too little respected. The style of the new organization was different. The New York City For-Hire Base Group was in reality a loose network. Those who belonged to the network were from the same areas of the city. The board consisted of a group of base presidents; each had for years been a combination of base owner and driver. The organization was a grass-roots organization. Its perspectives and decisions reflected ongoing conversations and discussions among owners and drivers at the base level.

Third, Mateo was a Republican, while an overwhelming majority in the Dominican community in Upper Manhattan (and in the rest of the city, for that matter) continued to support the Democrats. Yet the scramble in New York City for the Latino vote had become considerably tougher. In 2002, for example, a Latina state senator, Puerto Rican Olga Méndez in El Barrio, switched from the Democratic Party to the Republicans. Meanwhile, both Governor George Pataki and Mayor Michael Bloomberg had visited Santo Domingo; on the island, both had been accompanied by Mateo.[9] Pataki had even begun to learn some Spanish.[10] The heightened competition between Democrats and Republicans for the Latino vote may have strengthened the wish in parts of Washington Heights to start a new organization—to create an organization like the New York City For-Hire Base Group—and to have it under Democrat control, not Republican, not Mateo's control. On the other hand, we should not exaggerate the significance of the party rivalry in what took place. As one driver and community activist in Washington Heights's Dominican livery-cab industry said in late 2002, "This [the emergence of a new organization, Pedro's New York City For-Hire base Group] has nothing to do with the division between Democrats and Republicans. Why? Because, after all, around here, in Washington Heights, we're all Democrats. No, this is due to the style of Mateo, the leadership of Mateo."

Fourth, we ought to remember that, in 1999 and 2000, Mateo and the federation attacked the mayor and the Taxi and Limousine Commission vigorously a number of times through the media; one result was that Mateo made some enemies in parts of the Giuliani administration. So his activities and style resulted in a certain acrimony in at least two places: in parts of the Dominican Upper Manhattan and in parts of the Giuliani administration.

The New York City For-Hire Base Group came into existence in this climate. A central figure when Pedro's organization emerged was the president of Fort George. Silvio Tolentino and Pedro were friends; both had been a part of the Fort George base for a number of years. Silvio was among my best informants in Dominican Washington Heights (see Chapter 4). On a hot Sunday in August 2003, he told me more about what had occurred almost two years earlier, in late 2001, when the new organization had been established. According to his account, in the summer of 2001, Matthew Daus was appointed by Mayor Giuliani and the New York City Council as the new Commissioner/Chair of the Taxi and Limousine Commission. According to Silvio, Daus knew Delgado, the director of the Audubon Partnership. Both looked on the part Mateo now played with disapproval; both feared the influence the federation had achieved. Both wanted to see the federation weakened. Silvio, for his part, so he told me, had at the time nothing against the federation, but he disliked Mateo's style. Daus phoned Delgado and asked him to do something. After that, Silvio had received a call from Delgado, who called on the Dominican livery-cab community in Washington Heights and Inwood to mobilize collectively, to attempt to create a new organization, and offered Silvio and his colleagues practical assistance. The rest is known. After hearing his story, I questioned Silvio about Delgado's being a Democrat, while Daus is a Republican. The question was naïve, and Silvio smiled. His reply was cynical: Delgado has become director of a local development organization; he needs projects; he needs grants from the authorities and others; he needs to keep alive and run his organization, the Audubon Partnership.

The New York City For-Hire Base Group and Pedro cooperated closely with City Councilman Miguel Martínez. The latter and Pedro and Silvio had known each other for many years. Like Guillermo Linares before him, Martínez had himself worked as a livery driver in northern Manhattan while he studied; thus he knew the business inside out. His base had been Fort George; both Martínez's father and Martínez himself had driven for Fort George. Martínez frequently asked his friends and allies in the industry for an expert opinion. For example, one day Silvio received a fax from Martínez's Washington Heights headquarters to Pedro in Nonstop, asking Pedro and his comrades for an opinion. A colleague of Martínez, councilman John C. Liu, who chaired the Transportation Committee, wished to propose a law to establish a set of fixed livery-cab stands in each of New York City's boroughs; Liu had invited Martínez to join him as a prime sponsor of the law proposal, and the fax contained a copy of Liu's draft law proposal.

Martínez and the New York City For-Hire Base Group were preoccupied with a range of issues. In late August 2002, Pedro explained that, during the past few months in particular, they had been absorbed by three projects on which they addressed the authorities—especially the Taxi and Limousine Commission. First, they demanded that the Taxi and Limousine Commission produce a driver's handbook for the city's livery-cab drivers. He explained:

> Look—[let's suppose that] you say, "Well, I want to begin to work as a livery-cab driver." You have your photo taken, and you fill in all those forms, and you bring the money, and the only thing that those who work at the Taxi and Limousine Commission care about is to channel the money, to give you a license, and it doesn't matter to them if you're sufficiently prepared and have enough knowledge of the job, if you know the rules and regulations that you have to know as a taxi driver, and all the rights that you have. So we want that they produce a book—and it ought to be published in Spanish, in English, in Chinese, you see? In this way everybody would know that, when the Taxi and Limousine Commission provides a man or a woman with a license to drive a cab in the city of New York, this person knows what is expected of him or her as a driver—all the drivers in the business would know the rules and the restrictions, and all their rights.

Their second demand, Pedro went on, was that the city establish a new (official) entity, what he called a Complaint Review Board. As he put it, this entity should be

> a place, a complaint review board, to which all the drivers and base owners can convey complaints—complaints against the conduct of

a representative of the Taxi and Limousine Commission, against the conduct of a policeman, and so on. Why do we need this? If you want to lodge a complaint against a taxi driver, you always have a phone number that you may use, but if a driver wishes to make a complaint against somebody in the industry, he doesn't have a place to call, he doesn't have a place to approach on the matter, you see? We want to be certain that there is an entity that defends, that protects, the interests of the driver and those of the owners of the bases.

A few months earlier, in May 2002, Councilman Martínez had presented a resolution where he formally proposed the creation of a Complaint Review Board for the New York City Taxi and Limousine Commission. His proposal was supported both by other City Councilmembers and by the Commission itself. On June 20 the proposal was the object of a hearing of the City Council Transportation Committee. One of those who testified in favor of the proposal was Pedro, who stated, among other things,

> As we say in the business, "One happy driver equals one happy passenger." ... One way we can ensure a level playing-field [in the taxi industry] is if the Complaint Board would be comprised of representatives of the black-car industry, of the yellow-cab industry, and of the livery-cab industry. This has to be a collective effort between the city and everyone licensed under the Taxi and Limousine Commission. Our organization, the New York City For-Hire Base Group, wishes to work hand in hand with this Transportation Committee and Taxi and Limousine Commissioner Daus in the creation of this complaint board.[11]

A little over a year later, in fall 2003, the City Council and Mayor Bloomberg agreed to establish the Complaint Review Board for the Taxi and Limousine Commission. Pedro and the rest of the livery-cab industry in Washington Heights and Inwood saw this as a victory.[12] The law that established the new entity stated that it should consist of fourteen members; three should represent the different parts of the city's taxi industry—the yellow-cab sector, the black-car business, and the livery-cab industry.

Their third demand, Pedro finished, was simple:

> Our last project is to try to ensure that all the hearings [in the Taxi and Limousine Commission] take place with the doors open. We

wish that the sentences of the Taxi and Limousine Commission are passed with the doors open [i.e., not with the doors closed like now]. Why? Because the judges are not appointed by the state. They are not appointed by state or federal authorities. Instead all the judges are appointed by the Chair of the Taxi and Limousine Commission. So, what happens? Well, a series of [special] interests influence the result. So what happens? Another problem that we have is that the judges of the Taxi and Limousine Commission are replaced often—they do not last long. Do you know why? We [for our part] have already understood that judges that don't produce [enough] money [through their fining activity] get fired. They get fired, you see? Because of this we demand that the judgments are delivered with the doors open so that anybody can enter the locale and be present and see if the rights of the drivers are respected—sometimes they don't even get a translator.

The political claims and activities of the New York City For-Hire Base Group reflected and articulated a moral economy, a form of thinking about (a lack of) fairness. An overwhelming majority in the Dominican livery industry felt that they lacked basic rights, that they lived and worked without experiencing enough human respect and dignity. The sense of constantly being subjected to indignities was striking. In Pedro's words,

The taxi driver lives as if he trusts nobody. The taxi driver—do you know what happens? That almost everybody arrives looking to find out how they may screw the taxi driver, even the police. We know, for example, that the police have to produce a certain number of fines per month. So what happens? When the month is drawing to a close they know that they must [intensify their production]—let's suppose that they're expected to produce 50 fines or 100 fines per month and that the month is coming to an end, well, that week they say, "Well, I don't have enough money. I haven't—this month I haven't produced enough fines." And they begin to stop livery-cab drivers, livery-cab drivers, livery-cab drivers, and since you're a person who doesn't even speak English they sometimes give you two or three ticket fines simultaneously! "See you in court!," do you understand? As a result of this the taxi driver develops his characteristic indignation against the authorities.

He added that drivers, because of some bad experiences, could become defensive toward passengers also. That is, they and the Dominican base owners almost completely lacked trust. They saw themselves as exploited. As they understood it, the authorities, and especially the Taxi and Limousine Commission and the police, had for a long time treated them in a profoundly arbitrary and highly unfair way.

After the New York City For-Hire Base Group had been created in late 2001, Pedro and his comrades continued to work closely with the Audubon Partnership for Economic Development. On August 29, 2002, at Audubon Partnership's locale on 207th Street in Inwood, I attended a small informal three-hour workshop on "Workers' Compensation Issues in the For-Hire Industry." Also present at the workshop were Silvio and nine other base presidents from Washington Heights and Inwood, Pedro, and three lawyers, in addition to Delgado and one of his employees. The lawyers represented the Manhattan-based the Legal Aid Society and had been hired by Delgado's organization to plan and run the workshop.

The U.S. Workers' Compensation system is designed to ensure that employees who are injured or disabled on the job are provided with medical and disability/wage benefits. In exchange for giving up the right to sue an employer in court, employees receive Workers' Compensation benefits irrespective of fault. In New York City, Workers' Compensation is regulated by New York State law, and this requires that every employer must obtain and keep in effect Workers' Compensation insurance coverage from an insurance carrier. But the livery-cab bases had never procured insurance coverage for their drivers, for two reasons. First, the bases maintained that the relationship between a base and a driver was different from that between an employer and an employee; the drivers were not "employees" but *"independientes"*— independent contractors—in charge of their own time. Second, the bases lacked resources. Many were a form of cooperative. Those who made the money were the drivers, not the bases.

In 2002, a number of bases owed money; some a considerable amount. These had been sued in court by one or more drivers and had lost. In these cases, the court had concluded that the driver in question had been an employee. In other cases, the court had ruled in favor of the base, and the driver had lost.

As noted, in mid-2000 Governor Pataki signed legislation to establish a task force to investigate ways to increase the availability of Workers' Compensation coverage for livery-cab drivers. In 2002, the task force was still at work.

In the meantime, the Workers' Compensation Board had requested that the Taxi and Limousine Commission suspend enforcement of its requirement that livery base owners provide proof of insurance coverage as a condition of obtaining or renewing a base license.

This formed the background of the workshop. A set of intricate Workers' Compensation issues challenged the livery-cab bases' viability. As mentioned, the three lawyers were in charge. Two were white men in their thirties, who spoke English. The ten base presidents were Dominicans, none of whom spoke much English. The third lawyer, a Latina in her thirties, had grown up in the neighborhood and was bilingual; she translated back and forth. After some discussion, the lawyers gave a general overview of New York Workers' Compensation Law. The rest of the time was set aside for questions, conversations in smaller groups, and a concluding plenary discussion. Pedro and the base presidents already knew a lot about the workshop's subject before they arrived. My impression was that the lawyers had underrated their knowledge, and that the event therefore became of limited value. Toward the end of the plenary discussion, Pedro summarized the base owners' challenge in the following manner: "In 90 percent of the cases, the base is able to document that the drivers are not 'employees,' but many bases spend annually $8,000, $10,000, and so on on these cases. And sometimes the base loses the case; in these cases, the owners of the base are sentenced to pay an enormous sum."

Nevertheless, Pedro and his friends were definitely not against Workers' Compensation coverage for the city's livery-cab drivers. On the contrary, all were completely in favor. All the ten base presidents who took part in the workshop wanted a change; they and the rest of the industry wanted Workers' Compensation coverage to be available for the drivers. The problem was that the politicians and the industry had not yet found out quite how it could be done without ruining or hurting the bases. Why did not only the drivers but also the base owners want a change? Why did practically everyone want the Workers' Compensation coverage to be available? The answer is simple. Such a reform would mean strengthened security and enhanced dignity for about everybody. One of the base presidents who took part in the workshop, the president of the High Class car service, spoke for all during the discussion when he said, "It is essential to recognize that we who are 'presidents' most often also are 'drivers.' Before we became presidents, we worked as drivers; and after having ended our term as president, we perhaps return again to just being an ordinary driver. That's why we're interested in finding out how we can obtain Workers' Compensation coverage for the drivers. But this has to be done in a manner that doesn't destroy the bases."

In addition to working closely with Councilman Martínez and Delgado's Audubon Partnership, Pedro's group was in communication with Assemblyman Espaillat. The politicians with whom the New York City For-Hire Base Group primarily had contact were Espaillat and Martínez, the Upper Manhattan Dominican community's two leading elected officials. Espaillat spent a considerable part of his time upstate in Albany, but he also spent much time in his district, among the people of Washington Heights and Inwood.

On March 19, 2003, in a basement on 211th Street in Inwood, belonging to the First Class base and normally used as a Dominican club locale, I attended a meeting of the board of the New York City For-Hire Base Group; Pedro, nine Dominican base presidents who were his fellow members of the board, Espaillat, and I (who was invited by Pedro) were there. Before the meeting, Pedro had told me that the board would discuss Workers' Compensation. He was worried, he told me; some livery-cab bases had recently been sentenced to pay large sums; they now owed $40,000 to $80,000. For his part, Espaillat sought to reassure the group: the whole issue of Workers' Compensation for the livery-cab industry remained politically unresolved, but, in the meantime, no base would lose its license, or be shut down, for owing money because of this issue.[13]

Another topic for discussion that evening was the funding of the organization. How could the New York City For-Hire Base Group be financed? How could the new organization get money so that it could rent an office, pay a secretary, and start and run activities? Espaillat urged the group to apply to the state for funds. He described how state authorities frequently granted money to unions and unions' projects, and he explained what an application should contain. He said they could get Delgado and the Audubon Partnership to help them with the application.

After that, Pedro's group applied to the state for $100,000, and in the summer of 2004 the state authorities awarded the New York City For-Hire Base Group $40,000 to run the organization's activities. With this grant, it got a small office in the basement of the Fort George base and hired a secretary.

On June 11, 2003, thousands of New York City livery-cab drivers met at City Hall and protested what they described as the Taxi and Limousine Commission's and the police's abusive fines. That day the two organizations, the federation and Pedro's group, joined hands. Pedro told me later about how he had met with Mateo at six o'clock in the morning that day in Washington

Heights, before they led the protest together. During May 2003, police tickets and Taxi and Limousine Commission fines for drivers multiplied. In addition to the regular fines, drivers received summonses from the commission to prove that they were insured. Mateo and Pedro said they had no problem with the insurance requirement, but they claimed the commission had rejected paperwork for minor omissions or that insurance companies failed to provide the requested information within fifteen days—earning drivers $200 fines. "That's wrong, and it must stop," stated Mateo to the press (Colangelo and Saltonstall 2003). The demonstration culminated in a march to the Taxi and Limousine Commission headquarters. Dominican, Puerto Rican, Cuban, Haitian, Salvadoran, Colombian, Guinean, and African American drivers attended. The protest received support from several City Councilmembers and political leaders, and Councilman Martínez spoke against the commission's violations. "The Taxi and Limousine Commission uses unfair tactics to generate income for the city. Drivers should have the opportunity to appeal these fines and prove that they sent the correct documents in a timely manner," Martínez said in front of the drivers. "We have to stop this 'cash cow' for the city," Mateo said to the drivers. He calculated that the fine blitz could produce up to $8 million for the Bloomberg administration.[14]

From the late 1990s onward, the city's Dominican livery-cab drivers strengthened their bargaining position to some degree. They came to constitute a political voice in the city more than before. A group of Dominican base owners and drivers in the Bronx united with Fernando Mateo. Together they created the New York State Federation of Taxi Drivers. In northern Manhattan and the western Bronx, representatives of the Dominican livery-cab community collaborated with elected officials like Espaillat and Martínez and with a Dominican-operated local nonprofit, the Audubon Partnership for Economic Development. Together these actors, or forces, built the New York City For-Hire Base Group.

The Dominican base owners' and drivers' political activities were complex. We should especially notice four circumstances. First, the political activists in the Dominican livery-cab industry had strong links with representatives of New York's more formal political sector. Both the federation and the New York City For-Hire Base Group worked together with political leaders and elected officials. Dominican base owners and drivers who challenged, protested against, struggled against, negotiated with, and collaborated with representatives of New York's authorities and elected officials were far from operating in an enclave.

Second, both the federation and the New York City For-Hire Base Group were entirely dominated by Dominicans. This mirrored the fact that Dominicans now controlled important parts of the city's taxi industry. Yet this did not mean these organizations attended only to the interests of Dominican immigrants and drivers. On the contrary, a large part of the work in both organizations aimed to improve working conditions for all in the industry. Large demonstrations and protests did not gather only Dominicans, although they were in an overwhelming majority; Puerto Ricans, Salvadorans, Mexicans, Haitians, and others participated also.

Third, the political activities and practices that could be observed in the Dominican livery-cab community were anchored in, and formed by, the base owners' and drivers' everyday life. The political activists in the Dominican bases were preoccupied with relations with the police and the Taxi and Limousine Commission. They spent most of their time on issues connected with fines, licenses, motor insurance, Workers' Compensation coverage, and language problems; in brief, they sought to improve their working conditions and their everyday lives.

Fourth, the Dominican base owners and drivers were bearers of a moral economy, a form of collective awareness that expressed a concrete idea of social justice.[15] The great majority of the owners and drivers in the Dominican car services were convinced that the city had treated them, and continued to treat them, arbitrarily and unfairly. The Dominican base owners' and drivers' political practices and strategies rested on, fed on, and reproduced this discourse. Basically, then, their forms of political action expressed a search—and a struggle—for more dignity, more respect.

Making Money, Politics, and Identity

So far, I have been content to look at the political activism in New York City's Dominican livery-cab community as expressions of political action. But this activism was not just a political force; it was also a cultural force. The political activism anchored in the city's Dominican cab industry helped produce and give shape to experiences of community.

I have already shown that the Dominican livery-cab industry produced and sustained a strong Dominican identity. Dominican drivers worked together with other Dominican drivers, and the language in the Dominican car services was Spanish. Small groups of base owners and drivers usually had breakfast or lunch together, often in a popular Dominican restaurant in the vicinity. In addition, Dominican base owners and drivers practiced sports together. But as we have seen, they had also adopted the Hispanic or Latino/a category. Most of those I met in the business identified primarily as Dominicans, but, in addition, they described themselves as *hispanos*. The political activism in the Dominican car services mirrored, and helped reproduce, this situation. Consider, for example, Pedro Heredia and Silvio Tolentino. Both preserved a strong Dominican belonging, but both often referred to themselves as *hispanos*. Pedro was a U.S. citizen, but his first language was Spanish, and he was proud to be Dominican. Every day he had lunch in his office, bought in a Dominican restaurant in the neighborhood. He and his wife and a daughter visited his native town, La Vega, in the Dominican Republic several times a year, and he had bought a house there.

Silvio's oldest son had obtained a good job in Verizon. The son was in his early twenties and now had his own apartment in the neighborhood. The other children still attended school. Silvio and his wife had moved to New York after they had reached thirty, and they still spoke little English. They lived like a Dominican family in a tenement in Washington Heights. Silvio and his family returned to the island frequently, usually a couple of times a year. That people like Pedro and Silvio had a twofold sense of belonging is logical; they were first-generation immigrants, and many of them continued to shuttle back and forth between the United States and the Dominican Republic.

The activities of the Federation of Taxi Drivers and the New York City For-Hire Base Group helped sustain this complexity, these experiences and discourses of intricate belonging. The political culture and activism in the Dominican car services helped maintain a strong, nationally defined belonging—a form of Dominican, or one might say New York City Dominican or Dominican American, identity. But the activists' practices had other effects at the same time. The social and political activities in the Dominican livery-cab sector contributed also to the production of a New York City Latino panethnic identity—and they kept rubbing in the fact that the Dominican base owners and drivers and their families (and most others who belonged to the industry) were immigrants. In the following, I attempt better to substantiate these claims, by investigating more closely two sets of processes—or two arenas (for cultural, political, and economic production).

When I conducted my research, the New York City Dominican livery-cab community had created two publications, which I shall now look at briefly:

the free paper *El Taxista*, with the subtitle *Vocero de la Industria del Taxi*, and a magazine, *New York City Taxi Magazine*.

Every year Dominican base owners and drivers attend a set of ceremonies and events. At the time of the fieldwork, the most important annual event in New York's livery-cab community was El Día del Taxista, or Livery Cab Drivers Day. El Día del Taxista was celebrated on a Sunday in late August; the event, which took place in a park in Upper Manhattan, was organized by the federation. After first looking at the contents of *El Taxista* and *New York City Taxi Magazine*, I sketch and discuss the celebration of El Día del Taxista. My goal is particularly to underscore the interrelation of two social processes: the practice of politics (including forms of political activism) and the making and remaking of forms of belonging.

El Taxista is a Spanish-language newspaper of 40 to 50 pages that appears monthly, during some periods twice a month. It is free, financed by advertisements. The founder and editor is José Rodríguez, a first-generation Dominican immigrant who lives and works in Upper Manhattan. He started the paper in 1998; before that, he worked in the restaurant business and as a journalist.

El Taxista serves Dominicans and other Spanish-speaking immigrants attached to New York's livery-cab industry. In Washington Heights and Inwood, the paper was distributed through the bases. Every month (or twice a month) during my fieldwork, each base received a pile of papers. Base owners and drivers got the paper in their base station. In Upper Manhattan, one could also get *El Taxista* elsewhere—for instance, in certain stores and in the headquarters of the area's elected officials. The paper was also handed out in other parts of the city, that is, in the Bronx, Queens, and Brooklyn. *El Taxista* was read by many in the industry; Pedro read it, Silvio read it, and so did the other activists in the Dominican livery-cab community.

A part of the paper consisted of articles and interviews. The articles covered the industry, events in the Dominican community in New York more generally, and political and cultural processes in the Dominican Republic. A few articles dealt with other topics. Some focused on U.S. immigration policy, others discussed processes among U.S. Hispanics or Latinos, while yet others covered a part of Latin America. Those interviewed were almost exclusively Dominican New Yorkers—drivers, base presidents, owners of small businesses, political leaders and elected officials. A number of those I met in the business (Pedro, Silvio, José Viloria, and others) had been interviewed by, and/or had themselves written a piece in, *El Taxista*. Another part of the paper was called "*Vida Social*" or "Social Life." It showed photos from family ceremonies and political and cultural events among the city's Dominicans. The last part of the paper consisted of articles on sports, mostly softball. These pages covered interbase competitions and matches and often contained a series of photos of the various bases' teams.

Take, for example, one of the editions from 2003. The front page of *El Taxista* of October 2003 was dominated by a large photo of Councilman Miguel Martínez surrounded by five other men, all elected officials or political activists; two of the five were Pedro and the Junior base's president. The photo, which showed Martínez and the others in front of City Hall immediately after City Council had agreed to create a Complaint Review Board for the Taxi and Limousine Commission, carried the heading "*Una gran Victoria*." Rodríguez's editorial also celebrated this victory for the city's Dominican livery-cab community.

The October 2003 edition contained five pages with articles on, respectively, the Mexican migration to the United States, protests and demonstrations among immigrants against new forms of U.S. immigration control, deportations of immigrants, the Catholic Church, and the retired boxer Muhammad Ali. Some thirty pages dealt with issues and events in the livery-cab industry and in the city's Dominican community more generally and on the island. A series of articles discussed political processes and election results in the Dominican Republic.

The *New York City Taxi Magazine* was created by José Viloria, Fernando Mateo's right-hand man and the federation's general secretary. It appeared for the first time in summer 2003 and then every other month. It was printed on glossy paper with a fancy layout, a magazine, not a newspaper. It was edited and run by Viloria; this was his enterprise, not the federation's.

In spite of its name, the *New York City Taxi Magazine* was published in Spanish. A few isolated articles were presented in both Spanish and English, but most of the magazine was only in Spanish. The magazine was financed through advertisements. The bulk of the advertisers were Dominicans who owned and operated small businesses in the city—everything from insurance agencies and livery-cab operations to car-repair shops and restaurants. The magazine was marketed and distributed through Viloria and the federation's office.

The actual contents of the magazine mirrored, and helped produce, experiences of a complex belonging. A good example is number 11, published in the fall of 2004. In his editorial in this number, Viloria wrote about the city's cab industry. So did Mateo in a brief article. The front page showed the faces of George W. Bush and John Kerry. In a seven-page article, this edition of the magazine dealt with the forthcoming presidential election. A set of other articles in this number dealt with subjects like the nationality of the Dominican baseball star Alex Rodríguez, the life of Che Guevara, the international oil market, the life and work of Pablo Neruda, blood donation, the music of the Dominican salsa star José Alberto, and the life and music of the Mexican singer Gloria Trevi. The last five pages of this edition were devoted to a series of pictures of Dominicans in New York City. Some had been taken at an inauguration in the Bronx; others showed cab operations' softball teams.

The production, spread, and use of *El Taxista* and *New York City Taxi Magazine* helped sustain forms of Dominican identity. Dominican base owners and drivers were Dominican, but they were also Hispanics and immigrants—and they were people who traveled back and forth between New York and the Dominican Republic; they formed part of a binational social reality. Everyday and ritual life, and political activism, in the Dominican livery-cab industry contained and expressed a cultural force. The Dominican bases helped produce and sustain experiences of belonging. The making and remaking of community and identity gave shape, in turn, to the building of the bases, or the cab operations, and to the base owners' and drivers' political activities. The making of money (or the building of businesses and the production of capital), the shaping of identity, and the practice of politics were interwoven.

El Día del Taxista or Livery Cab Drivers Day was celebrated in New York City for the first time in 2002. This annual event took place on a Sunday in late August in Riverbank State Park, one of Upper Manhattan's large parks. Riverbank State Park is a park much used by Upper Manhattan Dominicans. Rising around 70 feet above the Hudson River, it is located on the Westside Highway from 137th Street to 145th Street. The celebration of El Día del Taxista began around 11 A.M. and ended in the early evening, between 6 and 7 P.M. In the first half of 2002, New York's authorities—first the State Assembly and then the City Council—approved the annual celebration of the Livery Cab Drivers Day in New York City, to honor the city's livery-cab drivers' contribution to the New York society. Among those who put forward the proposal were Washington Heights's two Dominican elected officials, Assembly member Adriano Espaillat and City Council member Miguel Martínez.

The celebration was in practice completely dominated by Dominicans. Those who organized and led the event were Dominican, as were most of those who participated. This event was an expression and display of Dominican strength. It celebrated the Dominican base owners' and drivers' material and social contribution to the city's economy; it also celebrated the existence of a form of popular New York Dominican community and identity; and it underscored and applauded this community's and this identity's increased (even if still limited) political recognition and significance. That is, the ritual represented and made visible a set of connections, those mentioned above. The annual event in the Riverbank State Park staged and displayed, or packaged and offered, the connections between the building of a set of small businesses, the production of forms of identity, and the practice of politics.

I attended the event twice, in 2003 and 2004. The main features remained the same. The organizer was the New York State Federation of Taxi Drivers. José Viloria led and oversaw most of the preparations. A large stage was installed in the park for the occasion. Those who led the show on stage were Dominicans; in 2003, for example, the show was hosted by three men; two were Dominican New Yorkers who worked as journalists, and the third was a Dominican New Yorker who had previously worked as a livery-cab driver. The three spoke exclusively in Spanish. In addition, they seemed to take for granted that most of those present were Dominicans.

The event was made possible with the aid of sponsors. Among those who supported the celebration of El Día del Taxista in 2003 were Latino Mix 105.9 FM (a New York-based radio station); *Noticias del Mundo* (one of New York's Spanish-language daily newspapers); New York Life (an insurance company); Aeromar (a Dominican airline); Lipsig, Shapey, Manus and Moverman (a Manhattan-based law firm); four smaller insurance brokers (of whom at least two were Dominican); and eleven Dominican livery-cab bases. Many of these were among the sponsors in 2004 and 2005 also. The sponsors' logos decorated the stage. In addition, most of the firms had representatives in the park. The sponsors' representatives distributed business cards, brochures, buttons, T-shirts, soft drinks, and balloons. In 2004, a number of TV sets and a flight for two to the Dominican capital were offered as raffle prizes; these things had been donated by some of the sponsors.

To greet the participants in 2002, especially the drivers and their families, was New York State governor George Pataki. The following year, El Día del Taxista was visited by Mayor Bloomberg and one of New York's two U.S. senators, Democrat Charles Schumer. The latter was also present the year after, in 2004. Both Bloomberg and Schumer addressed those present as mainly Dominicans (although both spoke English). Bloomberg told the audience that he had just visited the Dominican Republic accompanied by, among others, Fernando Mateo: "It is a wonderful country," he underscored. For his part, Schumer opened with some words in Spanish, before he switched to English: "*Quiero aprender español*" (I want to learn Spanish).

In 2003, El Día del Taxista was also visited by Washington Heights City Council member Miguel Martínez and state senator Ruben Díaz, a Puerto Rican who represented a district in the southwestern Bronx. Mateo introduced the guests and thanked each of them for what they had done to support the livery-cab drivers and the city's Dominicans. He switched back and forth between English and Spanish, depending on which of the special guests he was presenting to the audience. Each guest then delivered a brief speech where he emphasized that he would continue to back the livery-cab drivers and their families.

There was also free distribution of Dominican food. Many of those present, including, for example, Mayor Bloomberg and Senator Schumer, received a free *almuerzo*, or lunch, of popular Dominican food—*arroz con pollo*, or chicken accompanied by rice and beans and a salad. The meal was sponsored, and handed out, by one of the car services that supported the event, the Washington Heights-based Fort George base (the base where Silvio was president). A number of those present had brought food from home; they used the park to picnic.

But the most important component of El Día del Taxista was the music. The event was dominated by live music. All the bands played a form of Dominican, or New York City Dominican, music—mostly merengue or bachata. One of the bands that played in 2004 asked the audience during one of its breaks between two songs, "Merengue or bachata?" A few of the artists were based on the island, but most of the groups were based in New York City. Among the singers on stage in 2003 were "El Gato" Joseph Portes, Raffi Burgos, and Richie Cepeda; among the bands were Mere N-Voice, Sin Duda, and Dominica Y Su Combo.

The total number of visitors was difficult to estimate; it fluctuated during the day. A conservative estimate is that it may have been between two and four thousand. Those present were people of all ages, including many children. More than anything else, this was a hot Sunday out in the park with friends and family.

Conclusion

The Dominican base owners and drivers correspond in many ways to the stereotypical image of a marginalized group. They lack resources and command of English, the dominant language. But it is one thing to acknowledge that a specific group has been and continues to be politically and socially almost "invisible," quite another to say the same group has been politically inactive or passive.[16] As I have sought to show, quite a few in the Dominican car services took part in forms of political activity. These demanded, and fought for, increased rights and enhanced dignity for those who belonged to the industry. Representatives of the Dominican taxi community struggled politically and collectively as early as the 1980s. Representatives of the Dominican base owners and drivers continued after that, albeit to shifting extents and greatly varying degrees of success, to take initiatives and act politically on behalf of the business and those who worked in it.

To understand the political activities and strategies in the Dominican livery-cab sector, it is necessary to see them as a part of a more comprehensive phenomenon, or set of phenomena—a specific migration history. The Dominican taxi drivers' forms of political action were intimately connected with a couple of other processes: their makings and remakings of a set of economic niches, or small businesses, and their constructions and reconstructions of forms of community. Three social processes were interwoven: recreation of cab operations, everyday and ritual production of identity, and forms of political action.

During the years from 1998 to 2002, New York's livery-cab industry saw the creation of two new interest organizations. Both aimed to help improve the working and living conditions of the city's livery-cab drivers, and both were controlled and run by Dominicans. The more visible was the New York State Federation of Taxi Drivers; the other was the New York City For-Hire Base Group, the Upper Manhattan-based network. During these years, the Dominican livery-cab community strengthened its position to some extent (although it remained both vulnerable and weak). From the late 1990s onward, Dominican base owners and drivers managed to make themselves heard more than before; they became more visible in the city's political landscape. The authorities' official creation of a new annual ritual, Livery Cab Drivers Day, or El Día del Taxista, was a testimony to, and a symbol of, this change.

Some will perhaps claim that this shift mostly was due to Fernando

Mateo—that the change was essentially a product of his ability to pressure on the city by drawing on his political and economic resources and media contacts. There is no doubt that Mateo played a significant part. But as I see it, two other circumstances were ultimately of greater significance for the change. As we have seen, a series of actors fought to improve the situation for the city's livery-cab drivers. The great majority of these belonged to the industry; they were base owners and drivers. Others were neighborhood activists, yet others were among New York's elected officials. The change resulted from the activity of many; it was a collective product. Second, some large-scale demographic and social processes were important. The relative size of the Dominican population in the city had continued to grow. In the New York City of the late 1990s, an increasing number of politicians realized that they needed, or would soon need, a larger proportion of the votes of the city's Dominicans. In New York City's Dominican community, the livery-cab industry was important, many Dominicans depending on it. This had created a political climate in the city where it was now, relatively speaking, somewhat easier, or at least more feasible, for the Dominican livery-cab community to be heard.

Conclusion

The history of the Dominicanization of New York is not primarily a history of the extremes—of flagrant failures and striking successes, dramatic defeats and great victories. It is, rather, marked by many shades of gray, but also by a good deal of hope, not to speak of patience. It has above all been created through forms of work and leisure, forms of household and family life, through forms of schooling, and forms of politics.

In the 1960s and 1970s, a significant proportion of the Dominican immigrants in the city found work in industry—but far from all were factory workers. Subsequently, the proportion working in industry declined. Instead, a growing proportion sought to survive partly through wage employment in the service sector and partly through forms of entrepreneurship, that is, running one's own business. But even after the 1990s, or the year 2000, a good many were still employed in New York and New Jersey factories. In any case, the great majority of the city's Dominicans have, like so many others in the post-1960s United States, made only modest sums. Ordinary wages have been, and continue to be, low or miserable. (Yet, as Ramona Hernández wrote some years ago, "What Dominicans [on the island] know for sure is that the adventure of emigrating, whatever the perils involved, represents the possibility of hope. For them, the potential to improve their lot is likely to be more appealing than staying home, where the alternatives for socioeconomic progress are slim"; 2002: 183.) Dominican New Yorkers who have run their own businesses have typically not made big profits but, rather, have primarily managed to survive. A tiny minority have experienced fabulous economic success. Not a few have failed spectacularly. A number have ended in the underground economy or become criminals. Some—after 1996, an increasing number—have been deported to the Dominican Republic.[1] But many Dominicans have gradually become Americanized, and a growing number have become Americans, obtaining U.S. citizenship.

In his *Black Corona*, Steven Gregory seeks with success to examine and write about the lives of a group of African Americans in a part of New York

City without apparently emptying their lives of "ordinary" or "normal" (everyday and ritual) activities. Gregory attempts to get rid of an often employed image, the image of the "black inner city" isolated from the American "mainstream." At the beginning of his book, he writes that all too often in public policy debates, the mass media, and academic research,

> the concept of an "inner city" isolated from the American "mainstream" and plagued with escalating rates of welfare dependency, crime, and teen pregnancy has served as a dominant trope for representing urban black experience in the post-civil rights era. . . . Narratives of black urban life in the mass media and scholarly research have tended to focus on poverty and its impact on the culture and social organization of the black poor. In pursuing this line of inquiry, investigators have addressed an extremely narrow range of social behaviors and relations: crime, teenage sexuality, family disorganization, and "ghetto street life" have dominated both the research agendas of academics and the imagery of the mass media. History, political organization, work and leisure, and other ["normal" or "ordinary"] everyday dimensions of urban life that de rigueur have guided and informed the research of social scientists working elsewhere fade from view within the epistemological frontiers of the black inner city. (1998: 5)

The challenge Gregory refers to is anchored in a deeper, or more general, difficulty. Too often minorities, or representatives of minorities (be they blacks, young dope hustlers, immigrants, or other categories), are described in ways implying that they live outside the "ordinary" United States, like islands in society (ghettos, enclaves, inner-city landscapes, or territories).[2] The discourses of population groups that live in isolation are mystifying. They prevent one from conceptualizing and seeing the groups in question precisely as minorities—as parts of something far larger, namely the historically constituted structures of power and social hierarchies of the United States and global society. In this study, I have sought to examine some Dominican migrants' economic practices, daily life, and struggles for respect, rights, and belonging. In so doing, I have tried to contribute to understanding of the many-faceted and shifting interrelation of race, class, and political practices and negotiations in today's American society—that is, of key processes in a piece of the (for want of a better word) ordinary United States.

In my opinion, two circumstances make it important to devote sufficient academic and ethnographic attention to the Dominicanization processes in New York. First, the Dominican migration to the city has been substantial. Second, there is a widespread inclination to overlook or disregard the specific and unique features associated with this history. In today's United States, there is a set of strongly homogenizing discourses on the country's Hispanics, turning them into a seamless, unproblematic entity. One effect is obvious: many histories are silenced—for example, that of New York's Dominicans. In 2002, a prominent Dominican American intellectual, Silvio Torres-Saillant (professor of English at Syracuse University and former director of the City University of New York Dominican Studies Institute), said the following about the construction partly of a U.S. Latino identity and partly of U.S. Latino studies, and about the fate of the U.S. Dominican community's history:

> A disdain for Dominican knowledge is evident in several of the interviews, surveys, and compilations that purport to cover holistically the history, culture, and contributions of Latinos in American society. Because such panoramic vistas are normally penned or coordinated by authors who belong to the Latino subgroups that enjoy greater socioeconomic and political empowerment, it makes sense that they should either omit any mention of the Dominican portion of the Latino experience or dispatch it briefly and superficially. (2002: 439)

He continued:

> The reiterative musings about borderlessness, hybridity, and transnational dynamics that pervade recent scholarly production on the Latino experience have ostensibly celebrated diversity. The exclusionary ideological structures that lie at the core of corporate identity formulations in the community remain virtually unchallenged. The academia, the media, and the consumer market for the most part have rallied around the consensus that promotes the notion that U.S. Hispanics constitute a seamless unit. (441)

Torres-Saillant exaggerates slightly—the picture is not quite so little nuanced. But in my view he is essentially right. We need a vigorously strengthened interest, in society in general and among scholars, in the variety and the dissimilarities embedded in the histories, practices, and forms of the many different subgroups that make up the United States' growing Latino population. Today, we have a fairly comprehensive academic literature on various components of the history of the Dominican community in New York City (see, for example, this book's bibliography). But few have so far, as I see it, written detailed ethnography drawn from everyday life in Dominican immigrants' tenements, small businesses, and small-business organizations. That history needs to become more visible, less muted: hence, this study.

An important circumstance to which I have sought to direct attention in the preceding chapters has to do with our understanding of the Dominicanization in New York as a power process. The Dominicanization has been shaped by, and has developed by means of, forms of politics. It is frequently said that immigrants take little part in the political processes in their new homeland. This may undoubtedly be the case sometimes, but often it is not so at all. On the contrary, many international migrants across the globe fight daily, politically, for improved social conditions and enhanced tolerance in their new environment. In any case, the question of political participation has to be examined empirically in each case. In this book, I have especially sought to document the need for a particular interest: in international labor migrants' small-business associations. Most of the Dominican immigrants belong to New York City's popular social strata or working class. But as Hardt and Negri (2005) have argued, this is not the working class as we used to understand it, but the urban masses or the city's underprivileged. With the last decades' deindustrialization and neoliberal restructuring, the economic and political condition of New York's masses has gradually changed. At the same time, these changes have also created new forms of economic and political action and new (neoliberal) collectivities—such as the Dominican-dominated organizations in the livery industry.

The Dominicanization in the city from the late 1970s onward has been tied to, and interwoven with, particular forms of political work. A part of this work has been carried out by hardworking activists, informal networks, and more formalized collectivities in the Dominican small-business field. Of particular significance has been the political mobilization among two groups or in two economic niches: (1) the Dominican owners and operators of small and medium-sized independent supermarkets and (2) the Dominican livery drivers. As the foregoing has fully shown, the city has already for a long time seen a series of close links between leaders and representatives of these groups and some important elected officials.

The Dominicanization has also operated as a production of culture, or of meanings. Dominican New Yorkers have had, or been forced, to seek to answer the question "Who, and what are we?" That is, they have made, remade, and modified particular concepts of selfhood and identity. The inquiry into notions of identity and belonging ought, I have attempted to show in this study, to be anchored in some basic assumptions. The production of culture, including concepts of identity and belonging, is wholly historical—and intimately connected with the organization of the relationships of power. The organization of political and economic power is never external to the shaping of concepts of selfhood and identity. On the contrary, political and economic power is always implicated in identity formations. Finally, it is imperative, as I see it, to recognize fully that the study of identities should be a study of practices—of forms of social action. Gendered, racialized, ethnic, national, and other kinds of identification are most fruitfully understood as reflections or outcomes of myriads of practices. The practices that constantly "establish" identities within a given social order are always complex; they cross conventional boundaries between social sectors or domains. Put another way, they are typically a part of everyday life, of the economy, of household processes, of family and kinship relations, of political activities, of rituals and ceremonies, and so on. In brief, they have to be discovered and studied ethnographically.

It is precisely these relations between the everyday and the ceremonial, between the small scale and the large scale, and between history, culture, economy, and politics that we need to explore more thoroughly if we wish to better comprehend the last decades' Dominicanization processes in New York City. In this study, I have sought to work based on this fundamental idea. Much more needs to be done.

NOTES

Introduction

1. Some words are in order here on the use of names and pseudonyms in this book. I have used real names of politicians and high-ranking functionaries in New York, and of political and economic leaders and familiar political activists in the Dominican community in New York. All other names of persons, including "ordinary" Dominican immigrants in New York, have been changed. I have used the real names of organizations, associations, and, not least, Dominican and other New Yorkers' small enterprises and car services—but in a handful of cases I have changed the name of a business or a car service to protect informants' anonymity.

2. Espaillat kept the seat right up to 2010. In November 2010, he was elected state senator for the 31st Senate District (which encompasses parts of the Upper West Side and northern Manhattan, including Washington Heights and Inwood, and a few sections of the southwestern Bronx, including Riverdale).

3. Based on data supplied by the U.S. Census Bureau.

4. After 1965 a new flow of immigrants arrived in the United States (Foner 2000, 2001). The U.S. Immigration Act of 1965 loosened in practice restrictions on immigration from regions beyond Europe, and since then Latin America, the Caribbean, and Asia (but also the Middle East and Africa) have supplied the majority of new immigrants. By the early 1980s Europeans constituted only 11 percent of U.S. immigrants (Sanjek 1998: 62). The 1965 Act "set an annual maximum quota of 20,000 per country within an overall Eastern Hemisphere immigration ceiling of 170,000. Spouses, unmarried minor children, and parents of U.S. citizens were admissible above this ceiling, as were designated groups of refugees.... Latin American and Caribbean immigrants were treated less favorably in the 1965 Immigration Act. Within an annual ceiling of 120,000, Western Hemisphere immigrants could apply only for occupational visas. The per-country limit of 20,000 did not apply, however—mainly to placate Mexico, supplier of the majority of New World immigrants before 1965. As with Eastern Hemisphere immigrants, the spouses, minor children, and parents of U.S. citizens were admitted above the annual ceiling. And in addition to the annual Western Hemisphere quota, 370,000 Cuban refugees entered the United States between 1965 and 1979" (1998: 62–63).

5. The existence and significance of this type of female reciprocity networks among New York's first- and second-generation Spanish-speaking migrants (Puerto Ricans,

Dominicans, Colombians, Ecuadorans, Mexicans, and so on) are relatively well documented in the scholarly literature (see, e.g., Sánchez Korrol 1994: 85–117; Pessar 1995: 54; Ricourt and Danta 2003: 24–92; Smith 2006: 94–146).

6. For their part, MacGaffey and Bazenguissa-Ganga (2000) are inspired by the work of Bruno Latour and John Law. They write, "[Our] approach draws on the work of Bruno Latour and John Law. Starting from a structuralist base, they look at relations, and location in sets of relations, and at how relations are mediated through objects" (2000: 14). For more on the ideas of Latour and Law, see, for example, Latour (1991) and Law (1992).

7. For two fine studies of New York City that have devoted considerable attention to the phenomenon of international migrants' small-business associations, see Park (1997) and Sanjek (1998). Both argue that immigrants' small-business economy is an important political as well as economic phenomenon. That is, both examine the practices and strategies of immigrants' small-business associations as expressions of significant political activity.

8. Graeber observes that the size of the U.S. border patrol has almost tripled since the signing of the North American Free Trade Agreement (NAFTA) (2002: 1226n3). For more on global migration patterns in the nineteenth century, see Mintz (1985: 70–72; 1998: 119–24).

9. The population data in this paragraph are derived from U.S. Census data.

10. As the author I here quote recognizes, "This does not mean that all Cubans who came to the United States after the 1959 Cuban revolution were white and upper class. This is testified in the growth of predominantly working-class Cuban communities such as West New York and the Cuban enclave in Union City, New Jersey" (Laó-Montes 2001: 42n52).

11. For more on the New York City fiscal crisis (particularly on the roots and the effects of the crisis), see Sanjek 1998, esp. 83–101.

Chapter 1. From Quisqueya to New York City

1. Dominican and Haitian immigrants in New York City have mostly settled in different parts of the city. The Haitians have typically settled in predominantly black neighborhoods, and many live in areas of Brooklyn (Foner 2000: 50, 56, 149–60; Kraly and Miyares 2001: 59).

2. For works on the political, economic, social, and cultural history of the Dominican Republic, see Sharpe (1977); Hoetink (1982); Georges (1990); Mateo (1993); Baud (1995); Betances (1995); Martínez (1995); Austerlitz (1997); San Miguel (1997a); Hartlyn (1998); Moya Pons (1998); Roorda (1998); Torres-Saillant (1998); Sagás (2000); Howard (2001); Turits (2003); Brennan (2004); Candelario (2007); Gregory (2007); Hoffnung-Garskof (2008); Derby (2009); Krohn-Hansen (2009); Simmons (2009). For works on the organization of the Dominican migration to the United States, see Hendricks (1974); Georges (1990); Grasmuck and Pessar (1991); Pessar (1995); Levitt (2001); Hernández (2002);

Hoffnung-Garskof (2008). For works on aspects of the Dominican immigrant community in New York City, see Hendricks (1974); Georges (1984); Lowenstein (1989); Portes and Guarnizo (1991); Duany (1994); Pessar (1994, 1995); Graham (1997); Guarnizo (1997); Torres-Saillant and Hernández (1998); Ricourt (2002); Aparicio (2006); Candelario (2007); Hoffnung-Garskof (2008).

3. For more on the background of the U.S. occupation of the Dominican Republic from 1916 to 1924, see Calder (1984); Hoetink (1986); Franks (1995); Moya Pons (1998).

4. By the mid-1930s, around 200,000 Haitians dwelt in the Dominican Republic's border areas and elsewhere in the country (Fiehrer 1990: 11). Haitian currency was in normal use in significant parts of the country. This Haitian presence was "anathema to Trujillo" (Moya Pons 1990: 517). There is considerable uncertainty about the number of Haitians killed in the massacre. Estimates range from 5,000 to 25,000 (Turits 2003: 161–62, 316–17n90).

5. This does not mean that the Dominicans do not have a much longer history in New York. Some Dominicans settled in the city in the nineteenth century; others arrived in the 1930s, the 1940s, or the 1950s—but the numbers remained small: "In the 1930s, 1,150 Dominicans immigrated to the United States. Another 5,627 joined them in the 1940s, followed by 9,897 in the 1950s" (Hoffnung-Garskof 2008: 69): "a fairly good number of the Dominicans who resided in the United States prior to the 1960s were government agents, diplomats, adventurers, entrepreneurs, or students from wealthy families. But probably a larger number was made up of political exiles and expatriates who opposed or had incurred the enmity of the ruling structure in the homeland" (Torres-Saillant and Hernández 1998: 109).

6. In his *A Tale of Two Cities* (2008), Hoffnung-Garskof has done a brilliant job in documenting in detail the intricate ways U.S. economic and military imperialism in the Caribbean in the twentieth century helped shape ordinary Dominicans' conditions, opportunities, and strategies. In a key paragraph in the book, he maintains the following:

> Conventional wisdom in U.S. history holds that the boom in new immigration from the Third World in the 1960s resulted from the passage of the Immigration Reform Act in 1965. The 1965 act is usually seen primarily as its liberal sponsors intended, as a repeal of national origins restrictions originally put in place in the 1920s to keep out "undesirable races." The reform granted a set number of immigrant visas to the Eastern and Western Hemispheres, without discriminatory national origin quotas. This change in policy spurred the transformation of New York into an archipelago of new ethnic neighborhoods, home to hundreds of thousands of migrants from the Third World and former Soviet Bloc. New York's largest group of newcomers after 1965, Dominican migrants led this remarkable ethnic explosion. But the Immigration Reform Act does not help to explain the sudden jump in Dominican migration. The immigration restrictions of the 1920s exempted the Dominican Republic, like all the republics of the Western hemisphere. While often imagined as a removal

of restrictions, the 1965 reform actually placed the first numerical restriction on the number of visas that could be granted to Dominicans and other Latin Americans. In any event, the legislation passed in 1965 could not have been a condition for the explosion in Dominican migration. By the time the reforms were enacted in 1968, Dominicans' colonization of New York was already well under way.

A shift in international politics, not the reform of immigration laws, produced the sudden opportunity for migration and a massive displacement of Dominicans to New York. To be precise, the sudden surge in Dominican international migration began as Washington stepped up its intervention in Dominican affairs after the death of dictator Rafael Trujillo. The intricacies of this opening reveal much, not only about the nature of migration to the United States in the period after World War II, but also about the nature of U.S. imperialism. (2008: 69–70)

7. The year 1978 may be said to give the first example of a peaceful transfer of power based on elections in the nation's history. Even so, the transfer of power in 1978 was highly irregular: Balaguer left office and thereby transferred the presidential power to the winner, the PRD's Antonio Guzmán, only after open pressure by the Carter administration in the United States.

8. Guzmán put an end to the repression (Hartlyn 1998: 146–49). Through personnel changes, he dismantled "the Trujilloist military machine that Balaguer himself had restructured in 1966 and kept in power since then" (Moya Pons 1990: 534). After Balaguer's return to power in 1986, the daily military repression that had characterized his first twelve years was not resumed. Yet this victory was achieved at a certain price. The Dominican military officer corps won a reputation as one of the most blatant participants in the use of public office for personal gain (Kryzanek and Wiarda 1988: 97).

9. In 1996, Dominicans elected Leonel Fernández to the nation's highest office. Fernández, who had been brought up in the United States and represented the Partido de la Liberación Dominicana (PLD), a party Juan Bosch founded and built after he broke with the PRD, secured more than 51 percent of the votes through an alliance with Balaguer. Before the election, Fernández worked to move the PLD toward a less radical or more "centrist" position, advocating economic liberalization and privatization of state enterprises. Four years later, the PRD's Hipólito Mejía won the presidency, before Fernández and the PLD returned to power in 2004.

10. As noted, the U.S. Immigration Act of 1965 in practice opened the door to new groups—to people from Asia, Latin America, the Caribbean, the Middle East, and Africa. After 1965, the major source of immigration to the United States shifted to countries outside Europe.

11. Falsified documents include, for example, (1) titles to forms of property on the island (such as land or a business), (2) documents verifying employment in a job on the island paying well over the minimum wage, and (3) documents confirming a

long-standing bank account with sufficient means to cover vacation expenses in the United States.

12. All the figures presented in this and the next paragraph are derived from Limonic (2008), which exclusively uses data produced by the U.S. Census Bureau.

13. For more on the recent history of the Corona area (including the area's settlement history), see Sanjek (1998); Gregory (1998); and Ricourt and Danta (2003).

14. All the information in this and the next three paragraphs is derived from Bergad (2008)—a brief statistical report on demographic, economic, and social changes in Washington Heights and Inwood in 1990–2005, which exclusively uses data from IPUMS (Integrated Public Use Microdata Series) for 1990, 2000, and 2005 for PUMA 3603801 derived from the U.S. Census Bureau and prepared as Steven Ruggles, Matthew Sobek, Trent Alexander, Catherine A. Fitch, Ronald Goeken, Patricia Kelly Hall, Miriam King, and Chad Ronnander, Integrated Public Use Microdata Series: Version 3.0 [Machine-readable database] (Minneapolis: Minnesota Population Center [producer and distributor], 2004: http://usa.ipums.org/usa/.

15. Puerto Ricans accounted for 8 percent of the Washington Heights-Inwood area's total Latino population in 2005, Ecuadorans 6 percent, Mexicans 4 percent, Cubans 3 percent, and Colombians 2 percent (Bergad 2008: 5).

16. There were dramatic differences between major racial/ethnic groups: in 1990, 39 percent of the Washington Heights and Inwood area's non-Hispanic whites twenty-five and over had a B.A. or higher degree; this increased to 53 percent in 2000, and an impressive 73 percent in 2005 (Bergad 2008: 16–17).

Chapter 2. Origin Stories

1. The bulk of this chapter focuses on Dominican-owned grocery stores, supermarkets, and taxicab operations. My discussion of Dominican-owned restaurants and beauty salons is far less detailed. This is because, first, Dominican immigrants have developed these various types of economic venture (the bodega, supermarket, car service, restaurant, and beauty shop) in ways that show striking overlap (as we shall see, the most basic cultural forms used by Dominicans in small-business development have not differed much from one economic activity to another); and second, I have fewer data on the histories of these two other types (the New York City Dominican restaurant and the New York City Dominican beauty shop).

2. Rotating credit associations are spread widely over the world and have received attention from ethnographers and social scientists (see, for example, Geertz 1962; Ardener 1964; Granovetter 1995). They take different forms, but as Clifford Geertz once argued: "[The] basic principle upon which the rotating credit association is founded is everywhere the same: a lump sum fund composed of fixed contributions from each member of the association is distributed, at fixed intervals and as a whole, to each member of the association in turn. Thus, if there are ten members of the association, if the association meets weekly, and if the weekly contribution from each member is one dollar,

then each week over a ten-week period a different member will receive ten dollars.... If interest payments are calculated ... the numerical simplicity is destroyed, but the essential principle of rotating access to a continually reconstituted capital fund remains intact" (Geertz 1962: 243).

3. In the Dominican Republic, even the authorities and some large companies have organized *sanes*. Previously, the authorities sometimes donated a set of building sites to a group of households. The families then built the houses themselves; they built all the homes together, for each household in turn. Large companies have sometimes provided a group of their workers with building sites and the workers have thereafter built homes together, for each family in turn.

4. See in addition Hoffnung-Garskof (2008: 176–78).

5. For a richly documented study of first-generation Mexican immigrants and their children in New York and Mexico, see Robert Courtney Smith's brilliant *Mexican New York* (2006).

6. In 2004 New York City had over 600 livery bases. Two decades earlier the number was still small.

7. What took place in 1987 was the outcome of a complex history. Beginning in the mid-1960s, some yellow-taxi owners (mostly owner-drivers) formed radio associations and started to serve customers by telephone prearrangements, as well as by traditional street hail. The number of radio taxis increased steadily. "As of 1979, 25% of radio cabs' overall time was devoted to serving business accounts and 12% to cash-paid radio calls.... The growth in radio work created a problem for passengers trying to hail cabs from the curb. Since the number of taxis was capped, hailers grew increasingly frustrated at lines of cabs passing by with their roof lights indicating 'on radio call.' To address this problem, the Taxi and Limousine Commission first allowed and then mandated that radios be moved from medallion [or yellow] to nonmedallion cars. The first radios were transferred in March 1982 in two companies, Intaboro and Dial. The transition of radios out of yellow cabs was completed by March 1987" (Schaller Consulting 2004: 26). In turn, this led to a dramatic expansion of the black-car industry: "In converting to nonmedallion radio cars, [yellow-]taxi owner-drivers generally bought and drove luxury black cars. They either leased their medallion cabs to other drivers or sold the taxicab license. To serve the booming business community in the 1980s, the original black car companies grew and additional companies were formed as offshoots of existing companies or from scratch. By the early 1990s, about 8,000 cars were licensed to 45 black car companies. In 2004, there were 9,900 black cars operated out of 65 bases" (26).

8. The source for the data on killings of drivers in this paragraph and the next is Martínez (2005).

9. The vast majority of the cab drivers killed have been livery drivers. Since 1994, no yellow cab drivers have been murdered.

10. Marble Hill became an island in 1895 when the Harlem River Ship Canal was dug, connecting the Hudson and East Rivers. Several years later Spuyten Duyvil Creek, at what is now 230th Street, was filled in, attaching Marble Hill to the Bronx. But old

habits are hard to break. Marble Hill residents vote for Manhattan political candidates but have a Bronx zip code and receive city services from the Bronx. The New York City Council member from Council District 10 in Upper Manhattan represents Marble Hill (in addition to Washington Heights and Inwood).

11. Today's New York has a multitude of Dominican-owned travel agencies. Most of these businesses have been established since the beginning of the 1980s, particularly since the late 1980s and early 1990s. The father of one of my informants was among the first Dominicans in the city who started a travel agency, and this man began to operate on Dyckman Street in Inwood in the mid-1970s. (Down to the mid-1970s, most Spanish-speaking travel agents and insurance brokers in New York City were Cubans.) The bulk of these Dominican travel agencies are multiservice operations that mainly function as neighborhood institutions. They usually offer a wide spectrum of services: from help with writing formal letters and photocopying, to aid with official forms, bookkeeping, and taxes, to booking flights and transferring money. Often a travel agent operates in addition as a real estate agent or auto insurance broker. Most, if not all, transactions are conducted in Spanish, and many clients are regulars—fellow Dominican immigrants (or other types of Latinos—Puerto Ricans, Salvadorans, Hondurans, and so on) whom the owner has assisted for years. Most of these enterprises are owned and run by two categories of Dominican New Yorkers: first- and second-generation Dominican immigrants who attended school in the United States and, while not college graduates or professionals, are bilingual and familiar with U.S. institutions and U.S. culture, and first-generation Dominican immigrants who are *profesionales* (professionals) with a degree from a Dominican university. The latter group immigrated as adults, but could not find work in the United States fitting their academic qualifications. Often, their English was poor when they immigrated. Instead of remaining factory workers or employees, they learned some English and started their own businesses; in this way, they obtained independence, could make more money, and could maintain or regain a certain respect and class position. An example was the owner of the venture Quisqueya Tours, located in a rented space on Audubon Avenue not far from where I lived, in the center of Washington Heights: a multiservice enterprise that among other services assisted Dominican store and restaurant owners in applying for licenses to sell tobacco and alcohol legally. The agency, which had four or five women employees, conducted most of its transactions in Spanish. Nearly all the clients were Dominican immigrants. The owner was a first-generation Dominican immigrant of around forty. Plácido Rodriguez held a *licenciatura* or master's degree from the Autonomous University of Santo Domingo. In 2002, he spoke English well, but with a heavy accent.

12. Sources for the following brief history of the Caridads include also conversations I had with others besides Chelo and a newspaper article by Liza Rodriguez (2000) "Faith, Hope and Caridad. A Name That Rings Bells for Dominican Diners Has Proliferated to the Point of Confusion."

13. Some Dominican beauty parlors now also have some non-Latino and nonblack customers, including a few white males.

Chapter 3. From Bodegas to Supermarkets

1. In April 2001, a *New York Times* article instructively portrayed a few *prestamistas* who operated in Washington Heights and the Bronx (Dexter Elkins 2001, "In Some Immigrant Enclaves, Loan Shark Is the Local Bank"). The article called one of them Tony. This loan shark (moneylender) active in Washington Heights said that he and his two partners had lent millions of dollars to mostly Dominican customers to help start area businesses. Tony dealt only in cash and usually charged 5 percent a week. He said he did not use coercion to force repayment from defaulting customers. Instead, he said that much like a bank, he and his partners secured collateral to seize if the loan failed—often property the borrower was trying to lease or buy. Tony said that was usually accomplished by holding the title of the property until the loan was repaid. "We're not going to break any legs," Tony said in the article, "but we have taken property back." According to the same article, a study by a nonprofit group concluded that Washington Heights alone had at the time a local market of $10 million a year for business loans under $10,000, one met almost entirely by *prestamistas*.

2. For a fascinating article showing that such practices remain important among Dominican immigrants in northern Manhattan and the Bronx, see Chen and Polgreen (2002).

3. The fact that businesses may be undermined through "uncontrolled solidarity" has been brilliantly shown in a classic ethnographic study of entrepreneurial activity, Clifford Geertz's *Peddlers and Princes* (1963: 123).

4. I owe the contents of this paragraph to Granovetter (1995: 146).

5. The meanings of *serio* or "serious" that I discuss here apply only to men. The classification of a Dominican woman as *seria* (serious) or *sinvergüenza* (shameless) is focused on the issue of sexual/marital fidelity. This is not the case for men.

6. To avoid possible misunderstandings, it should be stated that, as noted, Diana was tough, but also she adapted to the inevitable, or a part of "nature"—the inequality between the genders. Diana and her husband formed a team. They owned their businesses together, and she controlled the finances. Both had backed the activities of the Dominican supermarket association. But Alejandro was a man. He had been on the association board. Diana said, therefore, "There are other [Dominican] women who work in the supermarket area. It's not only me, you know? There are more women who work in the supermarket area, but their husbands, they work behind their husbands. They let their husbands lead, and they do—it's part of being a Dominican man, you know, to lead and to be in the front and to be the center of the attention and to be the macho man. Uh, but, um, there's a lot of women that do a good job and are behind their husbands and run the husband and run the business, actually, but the man gets the credit." Or to put it another way, both those Dominican immigrant women who belonged to the working class and those who were considerably more privileged (like Diana) had to put up with, and adapt to, the effects of the gender hierarchy.

7. In the 1980s, the flow of immigrants from Mexico to New York accelerated

considerably. New York now receives significant numbers of (often undocumented) Mexicans, Guatemalans, Hondurans, Salvadorans, and Nicaraguans who are willing to work for low wages (Ricourt and Danta 2003; Dávila 2004; Smith 2006; Limonic 2008).

8. In 2004, a cook in a Dominican restaurant who worked six days a week could perhaps earn around $450 per week. An auxiliary cook could earn $250-300 per week.

9. For more on typical working conditions and business arrangements in the Dominican beauty shops in Upper Manhattan, see Ginetta Candelario's fascinating ethnography in *Black Behind the Ears* (2007: 177-220, esp. 191-214).

10. As we have seen, many of those who work as employees in Dominican small businesses are women. A number of these are single mothers with small children. As Patricia Pessar (1994) has shown, even a job in a unionized factory was typically a worse alternative than employment in a Dominican-owned business in Washington Heights or elsewhere in the city for these women until the mid-1990s. Pessar's article narrates the story of Altagracia, a Dominican immigrant with two children and without material support from a husband. Altagracia was contacted by a union representative who had located employment for her, but she chose not to take the job. Instead she preferred to continue to combine welfare with sewing "off the books" in the neighborhood. Altagracia explained her decision to Pessar in the following manner: "I sat down and made a calculation of how much I would make in the factory, including the taxes and union dues they subtract, versus how much I could make by combining to receive my welfare checks and food stamps and working off the books in a small neighborhood shop. Well, there really was no choice; I figured I would make at least one-third less working in the [unionized] shop than by combining welfare and sewing *por debajo de la mesa* ('off the books'), even though the boss takes 5% off my pay for, as he says, 'assuming the risk of letting me work off the books'" (Pessar 1994: 134). In 1983, Altagracia's weekly wage was $80; she received $135 in welfare. Had she taken the job in the unionized factory, her net weekly wage would have been around $150. Before President Bill Clinton signed legislation in 1996 significantly restructuring U.S. welfare policy (see below), many Dominican female heads of households were forced to think like Altagracia. Since they were poor single mothers, they were eligible for government assistance—Aid to Families with Dependent Children (AFDC) payments plus food stamps. Supplementing assistance with salaried employment was prohibited; factory work was automatically reported, but wages earned in Dominican beauty shops, restaurants, and other sorts of small businesses went unreported. Those who in practice were subsidized by the government through this system were not the mothers and children but, instead, Dominican and other business owners who paid poor wages and did not comply with the law. As Ginetta Candelario and Nancy López (1995: 19) have put it, labor market problems left welfare mothers "with only two real options: work all the time and not have enough money, or receive welfare payments." The 1996 Personal Responsibility and Work Opportunity Reconciliation Act—commonly referred to as "welfare reform"—replaced the AFDC program with a completely new system, Temporary Assistance for Needy Families (TANF); TANF requires that women work to receive benefits for their children. The

Clinton welfare law, however, also created a series of new difficulties for the country's poorest, hurting low-income women and their children in particular. For more on these consequences, see, for example, Morgen and Maskovsky (2003); Pear (2010); and Shaw (2010).

11. In the rural southwestern region where I carried out fieldwork in the early 1990s, people used the term *colmado*.

12. For more on the social life in the Dominican beauty shops in Washington Heights, see Candelario (2007: 191–220).

13. Unemployment figures for the city as a whole were depressing; see, for example, Gandel and Gold (2003).

Chapter 4. From Livery Cabs to Black Cars

1. Some Dominican immigrants drive a livery cab without being affiliated with a base or car service; they just pick up persons in the street. But this is illegal. The vast majority of Dominican livery drivers belong to a base.

2. A few Dominican-owned bases are owned by just one man. The basic economic and social conditions of drivers are not different from those in bases owned by a group of *socios*.

3. Until 1999, the owners of Highbridge were a Puerto Rican and his Dominican wife, and many of the drivers were Dominicans. The base station was situated a couple of blocks south of 181st Street, on Amsterdam Avenue. Many of the base's regular customers were white, mostly Jewish. The latter lived on the western side of Washington Heights, in parts of the district that have the best housing stock and highest property prices. When they needed a cab, they would call Highbridge. Highbridge's Jewish customers continued to use the base after it changed hands in 1999. They constituted the bulk of the base's customers (a circumstance that made this base unique among the Dominican-controlled bases in Upper Manhattan). The dispatcher answered the phone in English. But most of the base's drivers, around 90 in 2002, were Dominicans, and most of these spoke only poor English. In addition, the base had ten to fifteen drivers from the Middle East, India, and West Africa.

4. Even so, Milagros was clearly pleased with her job. Previously, she had worked for six years in a factory in New Jersey and had spent two hours each day in transport, one hour each way. She said her current job was much better. She made more money, and, just as important for her as a single mother, working as a livery driver gave her far more flexibility.

5. The source for this and the next paragraph is an article in *El Taxista* (Manhattan-El Bronx-Queens-Brooklyn), by the paper's editors, Rodríguez and Rodríguez (2004).

6. The information in this paragraph about Kennedy's purchase of another base is derived from an article in *El Taxista*. Cruz Tejada (2002).

7. See, in addition, Derby (2000, 2009: 173–203); de Moya (2004); Alonso (2005, esp. 39–44); and Gregory (2007: 40–49).

8. Saying this is not to claim that Dominican immigrant women do not play a part in the *clubes*. Far from it (see, for example, Sainz 1990; Ricourt and Danta 2003: 95–147). Some voluntary associations have been organized, and are controlled by, Dominican immigrant women. And even where the club is mainly under men's control, women may have significant roles and perhaps occupy one or two board positions. But see Jones-Correa (1998: 157–60) on Latino immigrant men and voluntary associations (including Dominican ones) in New York City: Jones-Correa maintains that Latino immigrant men in New York "tend to form and lead ethnic organizations whose focus is the country of origin"; leadership positions in these associations, he goes on, "are almost entirely filled by men" (159).

Chapter 5. Dominicans and Hispanics

1. The excerpt has been translated; I wrote my field notes in Norwegian.

2. "In 1975, 24.6 percent of Dominican grooms married Puerto Rican brides; in 1991 this had increased to 34.1 percent. In 1975, 19.8 percent of Dominican brides married Puerto Rican grooms; this increased to 28.0 percent in 1991" (Gilbertson et al. 1996: 454).

3. For a similar history about New York's Puerto Ricans, see Rodríguez (1996); Flores (2000); Duany (1996, 2002).

4. This is not to say that the term Hispanic had not been used in the United States earlier; it has been around for a relatively long time. But what took place in the 1970s was decisive. For more on this, see Dávila (2001: 39–40).

5. For more on the 1980 Census and its changes in the categorization of Hispanics, see Tienda and Ortíz (1986).

6. The same conclusion has been drawn by Itzigsohn and Dore-Cabral (2001: 328).

7. For data on stores and storefronts among Latinos (including Dominicans) in Corona in Queens, see Ricourt and Danta (2003: 39–50).

8. See also Purnima Mankekar's "'India Shopping': Indian Grocery Stores and Transnational Configurations of Belonging" (2002). Mankekar's article shows how Indian-owned grocery stores in the San Francisco Bay Area enable the making and remaking of India and Indian culture in today's United States.

9. As Georges herself points out, "The major exceptions are the Dominican political parties, in which party loyalties are brought over with the migrant" (1984: 11).

10. When Martínez resigned, another first-generation Dominican immigrant, Ydanis Rodríguez, replaced him as northern Manhattan's city councilman. Rodríguez won the District 10 seat through the general election in early November 2009 and took office in January 2010.

11. In addition, it looks like an almost meaningless task: the researcher would have risked presenting a form of catalogue of the many different Dominican clubs, associations, and leaderships, instead of promoting an argument.

12. For more on this, see, for example, Moya Pons (1986b); San Miguel (1997b); Torres-Saillant (1999).

13. As explained earlier, José Delio Marte ran small businesses and operated as one of the Washington Heights and Inwood Dominican community's informal leaders for over twenty years. He financed the Instituto's annual banquet on Duarte's birthday for a number of years.

14. The political headquarters of Miguel Martínez was located in the heart of Washington Heights, and were visited each day by a stream of ordinary people. Many were Dominicans. They sought help and advice, often related to practical issues (the rent, the job, documents, and so on). Bienvenido and a number of others who worked on a daily basis for Martínez received people, listened to them, and tried to help. Bienvenido did not speak English, but he had spent considerable time in the Washington Heights Dominican community and knew a host of people.

15. For a few examples, see *Ecos Duartianos* (2002); *El Universal* (2002); *El Taxista* (2002).

16. This was not the only public school named after a Dominican historical figure. When I lived in the city, other northern Manhattan public schools were named after Gregorio Luperón, Salome Ureña, and Hermanas Mirabal (all central Dominican historical figures).

17. For a fine, instructive analysis, see Georges (1984). See, in addition, Linares's own paper, "Dominicans in New York: The Struggle for Community Control in District 6" (1989).

18. For data on the tremendous power struggles that marked Community School District 6 in northern Manhattan in the second part of the 1980s, see Linares (1989).

19. For more on El Carnaval del Boulevard, see, for example, *Manhattan Times* (2002): 1, 4–7, 10–11, 15, 17.

20. This is not to say that these groups were without ethnic rivalry or competition—such a thing would clearly be foolish, but rather that grass-roots activists, politicians, and top leaders from these groups—the city's African Americans, Puerto Ricans, and Dominicans—were often in touch with each other and from time to time formed clear alliances and cooperated.

Chapter 6. Up Against the Big Money

1. The information is drawn from an interview I had with Linares on March 22, 2003.

2. A still better example is the history of another of New York's "new" immigrant groups, the Koreans. See, for example, Park's monograph *The Korean American Dream* (1997) and Sanjek's instructive analyses of collective organizing and political activity among the city's Korean small-business owners (Sanjek 1998: 217–18, 295–98, 346–55).

3. The Food Stamp Program is the nation's largest nutrition program for low-income families. Recipients spend their benefits to buy eligible food in authorized retail food stores. The Special Supplemental Nutrition Program for Women, Infants, and Children (WIC) serves to safeguard the health of low-income women, infants, and children up to

age five who are at nutritional risk, by providing nutritious food to supplement diets and information on healthy eating. Both programs are administered at the federal level by the Food and Nutrition Service (FNS), an agency of the U.S. Department of Agriculture. State agencies administer the Food Stamp Program at state and local levels.

4. This umbrella organization, the multiethnic Small Business Congress of New York City, was founded by Sung Soo Kim together with two others, Steve Null and Alfredo Placeres.

5. For a couple of good illustrations, see the newspaper articles by Mitchell (1992) and Hays (1994).

6. Richburg Hayes's Ph.D. dissertation, "Do the Poor Pay More for Food? Three Essays on the Existence of a Poor Price Differential," won the National Economic Association's 2002 Rhonda M. Williams Dissertation Award.

7. For a far more detailed analysis of the Small Business Congress of New York City's activities and opposition to the city's megastore plan, see Sanjek (1998: 344–48). See also Park (1997: 155–82) for a more general treatment of Korean New Yorkers' small-business organizations and political activities in the 1970s and 1980s.

8. For documentation see, for example, Serant (1995a).

9. The sources for the information in this paragraph are Ancker (1995); Vega (1995a); Castaño (1995); and Jump (1995).

10. Serant (1995b). Such a loan and tax abatement package was far from unique. A series of new giant stores were, as I have previously mentioned, built in various areas of New York City during the 1990s, and several of these received a loan and tax abatement package from the city (for more concrete examples from the mid-1990s, see, for instance, Serant 1995a).

11. Vega (1995b). For more on race as a part of the fight over the East Harlem Pathmark, see, for example, Nossiter (1995).

12. To illustrate, when I resided in Washington Heights, Espaillat collaborated closely with two Dominican American brothers, the Fernández brothers, who owned and ran four or five independent supermarkets in Central Harlem. Not long before I began my fieldwork, the Fernández brothers had fought for the opportunity to build a new gigantic supermarket at 145th Street in Harlem; Espaillat backed their efforts politically. But the Fernández brothers lost this political fight; the Pathmark chain secured the right to build at this site also, its second supermarket in Harlem. For more on this, see Pristin (1999a,b, 2001); Egbert (2002).

13. I do not have the figures for the years after 2003, but the program has continued more or less unaltered until now.

14. Harvey's quotations are derived from Tabb (1982: 15).

Chapter 7. In Search of Dignity

1. When Mateo began more and more to withdraw from the federation and its activities in 2007, he handed over the organization's presidency to Viloria. When I returned to the field on a short visit in late August and early September 2007, Viloria had been appointed president of the New York State Federation of Taxi Drivers, and he continued to occupy this position in 2008, 2009, and 2010.

2. As previously mentioned, I interviewed Mateo on March 13, 2003. The excerpt is drawn from this interview. The interview was done in his headquarters, and we spoke English. Viloria was present during the whole interview, listening while we talked.

3. See Noel (2000).

4. See Rashbaum (2000).

5. See Rashbaum (2000); Chivers (2000).

6. The legislation signed by Pataki in mid-2000 provides that when the victim of certain crimes, such as robbery, assault, and manslaughter, was operating a livery cab or black car at the time the crime was committed, the defendant faces a sentence three to five years longer than he or she would have ordinarily received. According to Pataki and those who support this law, this enhanced penalty more appropriately punishes those criminals who prey on drivers of livery cabs and black cars.

7. For more on the organization and activities of the Upper Manhattan Empowerment Zone, see, for example, Dávila (2004: 97–127).

8. This organization is known under various names. Some in Washington Heights called it "La Asociación de Bases de Nueva York"; others called it "La Asociación de Bases y Choferes de Nueva York" (The New York City Association of Livery Bases and Drivers). The English-language New York press in the 1990s called the organization The Livery Owners Coalition of New York. Yet others called it El Comité Pro-Defensa de los Taxistas Sin Medallón (The Livery-Cab Drivers' Defense Committee); this name was especially used in the 1980s but also later.

9. See, for example: Archibold (2002); Bernstein (2003).

10. See, for example, Navarro (2002a, b).

11. Pedro gave me a copy of what he had said before the Transportation Committee; the excerpt is from this copy. I was not myself present at the hearing.

12. See, for example, Miguel Cruz Tejada's article "Junta de querellas, Una gran victoria," *El Taxista* (Manhattan-El Bronx-Queens-Brooklyn), 5, 101, October 2003, 1, 3.

13. About five years later, in 2008, the issue of Workers' Compensation got a form of political solution (although, in practice, it hardly removes all difficulties for the involved parties [the bases, drivers, and authorities] regarding Workers' Compensation). During spring 2008, the New York State Assembly and Senate passed a new Workers' Compensation Law—Assembly Bill A.11759 and Senate Bill S.8715. On July 25, governor David Paterson signed the bill into law. The new law has two important components. First, it establishes a set of rules meant to determine unequivocally whether a livery-cab driver in New York is an independent contractor or an employee of a livery base. Second, it calls

for the creation of a new fund to give independent contractor livery drivers and their families Workers' Compensation benefits in cases of severe injury or death. The fund will provide greater benefits to the drivers than if they were completely independent contractors, while the bases will pay less than if the drivers were full employees. One of the central leaders when the new law was passed was Upper Manhattan's Adriano Espaillat. Others in the State Assembly and Senate who were strong advocates of the new law were Assembly members José Peralta, Vito López, Rubén Díaz, Jr., Hakeem Jeffries, and Michael Cusick, and Senators Rubén Díaz, Sr., and Serphin R. Maltese. After the measure had been signed into law, U.S. representative Charles Rangel said, "This law is long overdue. These cab drivers—most of whom are immigrants who in the tradition of so many others work nonstop to give their families a shot at the American Dream—deserve some sense of security as they ride the streets night and day." For his part, Adriano Espaillat maintained, "This historic legislation will finally bring relief and much needed benefits to over 40,000 livery drivers and their families." (For the quotations from Rangel and Espaillat, see Office of the Governor for the State of New York, David A. Paterson, 2008.) Others were more critical, voicing concerns that the new law did not accomplish what it was originally meant to accomplish. Among the sharpest critics was Pedro Heredia, the former leader of the New York City For-Hire Base Group. He and a number of base owners and drivers belonging to the industry in Upper Manhattan maintained that the legislation began with good intentions but got derailed along the way. "The industry supports the premise of providing benefits to the drivers, but not this way," said Pedro in late July 2008. "This law will hurt the drivers [because they will pay higher dispatch fees to finance the new fund] and the riding public who will pay more to offset the new fees required by the fund."

14. The data on the protest on June 11, 2003, are from Colangelo and Saltonstall (2003) and Llanes (2003).

15. On the concept of "moral economy," see Thompson (1971, 1991) and Scott (1976, 1985).

16. To be politically almost "invisible" and to be politically idle are, as many have demonstrated, not necessarily two aspects of the same thing. See, for example, Price (1983, [1979] 1996); Scott (1985, 1990); Gregory (1998, 2007); Ricourt and Danta (2003); and Escobar (2008).

Conclusion

1. In 1996, the United States enacted a series of anti-immigration legislative measures, including the Illegal Immigration Reform and Immigrant Responsibility Act, Anti-terrorism and Effective Death Penalty Act, and Personal Responsibility and Work Opportunity Reconciliation Act. These contributed to the striking growth from 1996 on in numbers of immigrants converting from legal permanent resident to citizen. In addition the numbers of deportations increased.

2. For a stimulating, relevant discussion based on rich data on young dope hustlers in Detroit, see Bergmann (2004, particularly 10–39).

REFERENCES

Alonso, A. M. 2005. "Sovereignty, the Spatial Politics of Security, and Gender: Looking North and South from the US-Mexico Border." In C. Krohn-Hansen and K. G. Nustad, eds., *State Formation*, 27–52. London: Pluto Press.

Ancker, J. 1995. "Proposed Supermarket Development on 125th Street and Third Avenue to Revitalize an Underserved Community." *New York Beacon*, 2, 60, 31 March, 4.

Aparicio, A. 2006. *Dominican-Americans and the Politics of Empowerment*. Gainesville: University Press of Florida.

Appadurai, A. 1996. *Modernity at Large*. Minneapolis: University of Minnesota Press.

Apter, A. 2005. *The Pan-African Nation*. Chicago: University of Chicago Press.

Archibold, R. C. 2002. "Dominicans Defend Pataki After a Comment by McCall." *New York Times*, 13 August, B6.

Ardener, S. 1964. "The Comparative Study of Rotating Credit Associations." *Journal of the Royal Anthropological Institute* 94, 2: 201–29.

Arreola, D., ed. 2004. *Hispanic Spaces, Latino Places*. Austin: University of Texas Press.

Austerlitz, P. 1997. *Merengue: Dominican Music and Dominican Identity*. Philadelphia: Temple University Press.

Balaguer, J. [1978] 1987. *El Cristo de la Libertad: Vida de Juan Pablo Duarte*. Edición especial. Santo Domingo: Editora Corripio, C. por A.

Baud, M. 1995. *Peasants and Tobacco in the Dominican Republic, 1870–1930*. Knoxville: University of Tennessee Press.

Bergad, L. W. 2008. "Washington Heights/Inwood Demographic, Economic, and Social Transformations 1990–2005 with a Special Focus on the Dominican Population." Latino Data Project Report 18, December. City University of New York, Graduate Center, Center for Latin American, Caribbean and Latino Studies.

———. 2011. "The Latino Population of New York City, 2009." Latino Data Project Report 43, April. City University of New York, Graduate Center, Center for Latin American, Caribbean and Latino Studies.

Bergad, L. W., and H. S. Klein. 2010. *Hispanics in the United States: A Demographic, Social, and Economic History, 1980–2005*. Cambridge: Cambridge University Press.

Bergmann, L. J. 2004. "Owners, Occupants and Outcasts: Young Drug Hustlers in Detroit, Making Money, Time and Space." Ph.D. dissertation, University of Michigan, Department of Anthropology.

Bernstein, A. 2003. "Bush's New Buddy Fernando Mateo Raises a Fortune." *New York Observer*, 24 August. http://www.observer.com/node/47984.
Betances, E. 1995. *State and Society in the Dominican Republic*. Boulder, Colo.: Westview Press.
Black, J. K. 1986. *The Dominican Republic*. Boston: Allen & Unwin.
Bourdieu, P. 1977. *Outline of a Theory of Practice*. Cambridge: Cambridge University Press.
———. 1980. *The Logic of Practice*. Stanford, Calif.: Stanford University Press.
Bragg, R. 1994. "New York's Bodegas Become Islands Under Siege." *New York Times*, 20 March, B1, B39.
Brennan, D. 2004. *What's Love Got to Do with It?* Durham and London: Duke University Press.
Brodkin, K. 1998. *How Jews Became White Folks and What That Says About Race in America*. New Brunswick, N.J.: Rutgers University Press.
Browne, J. Z. 1995. "Powell Disappointed over Positive Vote for 125th Street Pathmark." *New York Amsterdam News* 86, 18, 6 May, 4.
Bryan, P. E. 1985. "The Question of Labor in the Sugar Industry of the Dominican Republic in the Late Nineteenth and Early Twentieth Centuries." In M. Moreno Fraginals, F. Moya Pons, and S. L. Engerman, eds., *Between Slavery and Free Labor*, 235–51. Baltimore: Johns Hopkins University Press.
Calder, B. J. 1984. *The Impact of Intervention: The Dominican Republic During the U.S. Occupation of 1916–1924*. Austin: University of Texas Press.
Calderón, J. 1992. "'Hispanic' and 'Latino': The Viability of Categories for Panethnic Unity." *Latin American Perspectives* 19, 4: 37–44.
Candelario, G. E. B. 2000. "Hair Race-ing: Dominican Beauty Culture and Identity Production." *Meridians: Feminism, Race, Transnationalism* 1, 1: 128–56.
———. 2007. *Black Behind the Ears: Dominican Racial Identity from Museums to Beauty Shops*. Durham, N.C.: Duke University Press.
Candelario, G. E. B., and N. López. 1995. "The Latest Edition of the Welfare Queen Story: An Analysis of the Role of Dominican Immigrants in the New York City Political-Economic Culture." *Phoebe: An Interdisciplinary Journal of Feminist Scholarship, Theory, and Aesthetics* 7, 1/2: 7–22.
Caplowitz, D. 1967. *The Poor Pay More: Consumer Practices of Low-Income Families*. New York: Free Press.
Caro, R. 1975. *The Power Broker*. New York: Vintage.
Cassá, R. 1976. "El Racismo en la Ideología de la Clase Dominante Dominicana." *Ciencia* (Santo Domingo) 3, 1: 61–85.
Castaño, J. 1995. "Protestas contra Linares: Ataques contra el concejal por votar a favor del Pathmark." *El Diario/La Prensa*, 2 May, 2.
Chen, D. W., and L. Polgreen. 2002. "When Home Is Here, and There, and There." *New York Times*, 16 August, D1, D3.

Chivers, C. J. 2000. "For Beleaguered Officers Now on Livery-Cab Duty, Gratitude." *New York Times*, 22 April, B1.
Chock, P. 1995. "'The Self-Made Woman': Gender and the Success Story in Greek-American Family Histories." In S. Yanagisako and C. Delaney, eds., *Naturalizing Power*. London: Routledge.
City of New York, Department of City Planning. 1993. "Socioeconomic Profiles: A Portrait of New York City's Community Districts from the 1980 and 1990 Censuses of Population and Housing." New York: New York City Department of City Planning.
———. 1996. "The Newest New Yorkers, 1990–1994: An Analysis of Immigration to NYC in the early 1990s." New York: New York City Department of City Planning.
City of New York, Department of Consumer Affairs. 1991. "The Poor Pay More . . . For Less." New York: New York City Department of Consumer Affairs.
Cohn, M., ed. 1967. "The Cuban Community of Washington Heights in New York City." A Report Prepared by Students in the Anthropology Workshop sponsored by the Brooklyn Children's Museum and the National Science Foundation. Occasional Papers in Cultural History 12. New York: Brooklyn Children's Museum.
Colangelo, L. L., and D. Saltonstall. 2003. "Thousands Protest Tix Blitz: Cabbies, Restaurant Owners Take Gripes to City Hall." *New York Daily News*, 12 June.
Comaroff, J., and J. L. Comaroff, eds. 2001. *Millennial Capitalism and the Culture of Neoliberalism*. Durham, N.C.: Duke University Press.
Conquergood, D. 1992. "Life in Big Red: Struggles and Accommodations in a Chicago Polyethnic Tenement." In L. Lamphere, ed., *Structuring Diversity*. Chicago: University of Chicago Press.
Cruz Tejada, M. 2002. "Inauguran Kennedy New City en el Bronx." *El Taxista* (Manhattan-El Bronx-Queens-Brooklyn) 4, 89, October, 1, 2.
———. 2003. "Junta de querellas, una gran victoria." *El Taxista* (Manhattan El Bronx-Queens-Brooklyn), 5, 101, October, 1, 3.
Dávila, A. 2001. *Latinos, Inc.: The Marketing and Making of a People*. Berkeley: University of California Press.
———. 2004. *Barrio Dreams*. Berkeley: University of California Press.
De Genova, N., and A. Y. Ramos-Zayas. 2003. *Latino Crossings*. New York: Routledge.
de la Cruz, E. 1995. "Sigue la controversia en el caso Pathmark." *El Diario/La Prensa*, 18 May, 5.
de Moya, E. A. 2004. "Power Games and Totalitarian Masculinity in the Dominican Republic." In R. E. Reddock, ed., *Interrogating Caribbean Masculinities*, 68–102. Kingston: University of the West Indies Press.
Derby, L. 2000. "The Dictator's Seduction: Gender and State Spectacle During the Trujillo Regime." In W. Beezley and L. Curcio, eds., *Latin American Cultural Studies: A Reader*, 213–39. Wilmington, Del.: Scholarly Resources.
———. 2009. *The Dictator's Seduction*. Durham, N.C.: Duke University Press.

Domínguez, V. 1973. "Spanish-Speaking Caribbeans in New York: 'The Middle Race.'" *Revista/Review Interamericana* 3, 2: 135–42.
———. 1978. "Show Your Colors: Ethnic Divisiveness Among Hispanic Caribbean Migrants." *Migration Today* 6, 1: 5–9.
Duany, J. 1994. *Quisqueya on the Hudson: The Transnational Identity of Dominicans in Washington Heights*. New York: CUNY Dominican Studies Institute.
———. 1996. "Imagining the Puerto Rican Nation: Recent Work on Cultural Identity." *Latin American Research Review* 31, 3: 248–67.
———. 1998. "Reconstructing Racial Identity: Ethnicity, Color, and Class Among Dominicans in the United States and Puerto Rico." *Latin American Perspectives* 25, 3: 147–72.
———. 2002. *The Puerto Rican Nation on the Move*. Chapel Hill: University of North Carolina Press.
Ecos Duartianos: Organo de difusión del Instituto Duartiano de New York. 2002. 1, 1 (January).
Egbert, B. 2002. "Businesses Not Sold on Chain Lease." *New York Daily News*, 28 February, Suburban Section, 1.
Enver, R. 2002. "Ponen en Marcha Campaña para la Cultura." *Manhattan Times*, Washington Heights/East Harlem ed., 3, 46, 14 November, 8.
Escobar, A. 2008. *Territories of Difference*. Durham, N.C.: Duke University Press.
Fennema, M. 1998. "Hispanidad and National Identity in Santo Domingo." *Journal of Political Ideologies* 3, 2: 193–212.
Fennema, M., and T. Loewenthal. 1987. *La Construcción de raza y nación en la República Dominicana*. Santo Domingo: Editora Universitaria-UASD.
Fiehrer, T. 1990. "Political Violence in the Periphery: The Haitian Massacre of 1937." *Race and Class*, 32, 2: 1–20.
Filkins, D. 2001. "In Some Immigrant Enclaves, Loan Shark Is the Local Bank." *New York Times*, 23 April, A1.
Firestone, D. 1996. "Zoning Plan for Warehouse-Style Stores Is Approved and Sent to Council in Close Vote." *New York Times*, 24 October, B4.
Flores, J. 2000. *From Bomba to Hip-Hop*. New York: Columbia University Press.
Foner, N. 2000. *From Ellis Island to JFK*. New Haven, Conn.: Yale University Press.
———. 2001. "Introduction: New Immigrants in a New New York." In Foner, ed., *New Immigrants in New York*, 1–31. Completely Revised and Updated Edition. New York: Columbia University Press.
Franks, J. 1995. "The *Gavilleros* of the East: Social Banditry as Political Practice in the Dominican Sugar Region, 1900–1924." *Journal of Historical Sociology* 8, 2: 158–81.
Galíndez, J. de. 1958. *La Era de Trujillo*. Buenos Aires: Editorial Americana.
Gandel, S., and J. S. Gold. 2003. "War Worries Bring Paralysis to NY Business." *Crain's New York Business* 19, 11, 17–23 March, 1, 36.
Geertz, C. 1962. "The Rotating Credit Association: A 'Middle-Rung' in Development." *Economic Development and Cultural Change* 10, 3: 241–63.

———. 1963. *Peddlers and Princes*. Chicago: University of Chicago Press.
———. 1973. "Person, Time, and Conduct in Bali." In Geertz, *The Interpretation of Cultures*, 360–411. New York: Basic Books.
Georges, E. 1984. "New Immigrants and the Political Process: Dominicans in New York." Occasional Paper 45. New York: New York University, Center for Latin American Studies.
———. 1990. *The Making of a Transnational Community*. New York: Columbia University Press.
Gilbertson, G. 1995. "Women's Labor and Enclave Employment: The Case of Dominican and Colombian Women in New York City." *International Migration Review* 29, 3: 657–70.
Gilbertson, G., and D. Gurak. 1992. "Household Transitions in the Migrations of Dominicans and Colombians to New York." *International Migration Review* 26, 1: 22–45.
———. 1993. "Broadening the Enclave Debate: The Labor Market Experiences of Dominican and Colombian Men in New York City." *Sociological Forum* 8, 2: 205–19.
Gilbertson, G., J. Fitzpatrick, and L. Yang. 1996. "Hispanic Intermarriage in New York City: New Evidence from 1991." *International Migration Review* 30, 2: 445–59.
Giménez, M. E. 1989. "'Latino/Hispanic'—Who Needs a Name? The Case Against a Standardized Terminology." *International Journal of Health Services* 19: 557–71.
Glick Schiller, N., L. Basch, and C. Blanc-Szanton, eds. 1992. *Towards a Transnational Perspective on Migration*. New York: New York Academy of Sciences.
Glick Schiller, N., and G. E. Fouron. 2001. *Georges Woke Up Laughing*. Durham, N.C.: Duke University Press.
Gonzalez, D. 1996a. "Small Markets Shopping for Same Deal." *New York Times*, 3 April, B1.
———. 1996b. "Lobbying for Markets (and Himself)." *New York Times*, 20 April, A23.
Gonzalez, E. 2004. *The Bronx*. New York: Columbia University Press.
Graeber, D. 2001. *Toward An Anthropological Theory of Value*. New York: Palgrave.
———. 2002. "The Anthropology of Globalization (with Notes on Neomedievalism, and the End of the Chinese Model of the Nation-State)." *American Anthropologist* 104, 4: 1222–27.
Graham, M. 1997. "Reimagining the Nation and Defining the District: Dominican Migration and Transnational Politics." In R. Pessar, ed., *Caribbean Circuits*, 91–125. New York: Center for Migration Studies.
Granovetter, M. 1995. "The Economic Sociology of Firms and Entrepreneurs." In A. Portes, ed., *The Economic Sociology of Immigration*, 128–65. New York: Russell Sage.
Grasmuck, S., and P. Pessar. 1991. *Between Two Islands: Dominican International Migration*. Berkeley: University of California Press.
Gregory, S. 1998. *Black Corona*. Princeton, N.J.: Princeton University Press.
———. 2007. *The Devil Behind the Mirror*. Berkeley: University of California Press.
Guarnizo, L. E. 1992. "One Country in Two: Dominican-Owned Firms in New York and

the Dominican Republic." Ph.D. dissertation, Johns Hopkins University, Department of Sociology.

———. 1997. "The Emergence of a Transnational Social Formation and the Mirage of Return Migration Among Dominican Transmigrants." *Identities: Global Studies in Culture and Power* 4, 2: 281–322.

Gudeman, S., and A. Rivera. 1990. *Conversations in Colombia.* Cambridge: Cambridge University Press.

Gupta, A., and J. Ferguson. 1997. "Discipline and Practice: 'The Field' as Site, Method, and Location in Anthropology." In Gupta and Ferguson, eds., *Anthropological Locations,* 1–46. Berkeley: University of California Press.

Gurak, D., and M. Kritz. 1982. "Dominican and Colombian Women in New York City: Migration Structure and Employment Patterns." *Migration Today* 10, 3-4: 14–21.

Gutiérrez, D. G., ed. 2006. *The Columbia History of Latinos in the United States Since 1960.* New York: Columbia University Press.

Hall, S. 1990. "Cultural Identity and Diaspora." In J. Rutherford, ed., *Identity,* 222–37. London: Lawrence and Wishart.

Hansen, T. B., and F. Stepputat, eds. 2005. *Sovereign Bodies.* Princeton, N.J.: Princeton University Press.

Hardt, M., and A. Negri. 2005. *Multitude.* London: Hamish Hamilton.

Hart, K. 2003. "British Social Anthropology's Nationalist Project." *Anthropology Today* 19, 6: 1–2.

Hartlyn, J. 1998. *The Struggle for Democratic Politics in the Dominican Republic.* Chapel Hill: University of North Carolina Press.

Harvey, D. 2005. *A Brief History of Neoliberalism.* Oxford: Oxford University Press.

Hays, C.L. 1994. "Congested. Expensive. Out of Date." *New York Times,* 29 May, 14, 1.

Hendricks, G. 1974. *The Dominican Diaspora.* New York: Teachers College Press.

Hernández, R. 2002. *The Mobility of Workers Under Advanced Capitalism: Dominican Migration to the United States.* New York: Columbia University Press.

Hernández, R., F. Rivera-Batiz, and R. Agodini. 1995. "Dominican New Yorkers: A Socioeconomic Profile, 1990." New York: CUNY Dominican Studies Institute.

Hispanic Federation. 2002. "Latino Political Participation in New York City: 2002." A Report of the Hispanic Federation (Released: March 12, 2002). New York: Hispanic Federation.

Hoetink, H. 1982. *The Dominican People, 1850–1900.* Baltimore: Johns Hopkins University Press.

———. 1986. "The Dominican Republic c. 1870–1930." In L. Bethell, ed., *The Cambridge History of Latin America,.* vol. 5. Cambridge: Cambridge University Press.

Hoffnung-Garskof, J. 2008. *A Tale of Two Cities: Santo Domingo and New York After 1950.* Princeton N.J.: Princeton University Press.

Holloway, L. 1994. "Neighborhood Report: College Point. Megastore Plan for Corporate Park Draws Fire." *New York Times,* 26 June, 13, 8.

———. 1996. "Big Stores Have Lower Prices, Mayor Says." *New York Times,* 25 November, B3.

Holston, J., and A. Appadurai. 1999. "Introduction: Cities and Citizenship." In Holston, ed., *Cities and Citizenship*, 1–18. Durham, N.C.: Duke University Press.

Howard, D. 2001. *Coloring the Nation*. Oxford: Signal Books.

Incháustegui Cabral, H. 1976. "Los Negros y las trigueñas en la poesía dominicana." *emeeme, Estudios Dominicanos* (Santo Domingo) 4, 24: 3–19.

Inda, J. X., and R. Rosaldo, eds. 2002. *The Anthropology of Globalization: A Reader*. Oxford: Blackwell.

Itzigsohn, J., and C. Dore-Cabral. 2001. "The Manifold Character of Panethnicity: Latino Identities and Practices Among Dominicans in New York City." In A. Laó-Montes and A. Dávila, eds, *Mambo Montage*, 319–35. New York: Columbia University Press.

Jones-Correa, M. 1998. *Between Two Nations*. Ithaca, N.Y.: Cornell University Press.

Jump, L. 1995. "Victory, Oh Victory, We Have the Victory!" *New York Beacon*, 2, 80, 23 August, 23.

Kearney, R. C. 1986. "Spoils in the Caribbean: The Struggle for Merit-Based Civil Service in the Dominican Republic." *Public Administration Review* (March/April): 144–51.

Kraly, E., and I. Miyares. 2001. "Immigration to New York: Policy, Population, and Patterns." In N. Foner, ed., *New Immigrants in New York*, 33–79. Completely Revised and Updated Edition. New York: Columbia University Press.

Krohn-Hansen, C. 1995. "Magic, Money and Alterity Among Dominicans." *Social Anthropology* 3, 2: 129–46.

———. 1996. "Masculinity and the Political Among Dominicans: 'The Dominican Tiger.'" In M. Melhuus and K. A. Stølen, eds., *Machos, Mistresses, Madonnas*, 108–33. London: Verso.

———. 1997. "The Construction of Dominican State Power and Symbolisms of Violence." *Ethnos* 62, 3–4: 49–78.

———. 2001. "A Tomb for Columbus in Santo Domingo: Political Cosmology, Population and Racial Frontiers." *Social Anthropology* 9, 2: 165–92.

———. 2005. "Negotiated Dictatorship: The Building of the Trujillo State in the Southwestern Dominican Republic." In Krohn-Hansen and K. G. Nustad, eds., *State Formation*, 96–122. London: Pluto Press.

———. 2009. *Political Authoritarianism in the Dominican Republic*. New York: Palgrave Macmillan.

Kryzanek, M. J., and H. J. Wiarda. 1988. *The Politics of External Influence in the Dominican Republic*. New York: Praeger.

Kugel, S. 1999. "Neighborhood Report: Washington Heights—Buzz; for Dominicans, Minimum Wage, Maximum Uncertainty." *New York Times*, 5 September, 147.

Lamphere, L., A. Stepick, and G. Grenier, eds. 1994. *Newcomers in the Workplace*. Philadelphia: Temple University Press.

Laó-Montes, A. 2001. "Introduction." In Laó-Montes and A. Dávila, eds., *Mambo Montage*, 1–53. New York: Columbia University Press.

Latour, B. 1991. "Technology Is Society Made Durable." In J. Law, ed., *A Sociology of Monsters*, 103–31. London: Routledge.

Law, J. 1992. "Notes on the Theory of the Actor-Network: Ordering, Strategy, and Heterogeneity." *Systems Practice* 5, 4: 379–93.
Lazar, S. 2008. *El Alto, Rebel City*. Durham, N.C: Duke University Press.
Levitt, P. 2001. *The Transnational Villagers*. Berkeley: University of California Press.
Lewis, J. 1976. "Washington Heights and Changing Times." *New York Daily News*, 25 January.
Liff, B., and M. O. Allen. 1996. "Rudy in Megastore Food Fight." *New York Daily News*, 27 November, 6.
Limonic, L. 2008. "The Latino Population of New York City, 2007." Latino Data Project Report 20, December 2008. New York: City University of New York, Graduate Center, Center for Latin American, Caribbean and Latino Studies.
Linares, G. 1989. "Dominicans in New York: The Struggle for Community Control in District 6." *Centro Bulletin* 2, 5: 77–84.
Llanes, J. L. 2003. "The New York City Taxi and Limousine Commission Is a Cash Cow for the Mayor's Office." *Voices That Must Be Heard*, 19 June (originally published in Spanish in *Hoy*, 12 June 2003; trans. Nicole Lisa). http://www.indypressny.org/nycma/voices/70/news/news_3/, accessed 8 October 2010.
Lomnitz, C. 2005. *Death and the Idea of Mexico*. New York: Zone Books.
Lomnitz, L. 1977. *Networks and Marginality*. New York: Academic Press.
Lowenstein, S. M. 1989. *Frankfurt on the Hudson. The German-Jewish Community of Washington Heights, 1933–1983: Its Structure and Culture*. Detroit: Wayne State University Press.
MacGaffey, J., and R. Bazenguissa-Ganga. 2000. *Congo-Paris*. Oxford: James Currey; Bloomington: Indiana University Press with International African Institute.
Mahler, S. 1989. "La dinámica de la legalización en Nueva York: Un enfoque hacia los dominicanos." In E. Georges et al., *Dominicanos ausentes: Cifras, políticas, condiciones sociales.*, 9–38. Santo Domingo: Fondo para el Avance de las Ciencias Sociales/Fundación Friedrich Ebert.
Malinowski, B. 1935. *Coral Gardens and Their Magic: A Study of the Methods of Tilling the Soil and of Agricultural Rites in the Trobriand Islands*. 2 vols. New York: American Book.
Manhattan Times. 2002. Washington Heights/East Harlem ed. 3, 30, 25–31 July.
Mankekar, 2002. "'India Shopping': Indian Grocery Stores and Transnational Configurations of Belonging." *Ethnos* 67, 1: 75–98.
Mar, D. 1991. "Another Look at the Enclave Economy Thesis: Chinese Immigrants in the Ethnic Labor Market." *Amerasia Journal* 17, 3: 5–21.
Martin, J. B. 1966. *Overtaken by Events*. New York: Doubleday.
Martinez Alequin, R. 1991. "Who's Running the Bodega?" *New York Newsday*, 29 August.
Martinez, J. 2005. "Violent City Deaths Hit Historic Lows." *New York Daily News*, 2 January.
Martínez, S. 1995. *Peripheral Migrants*. Knoxville: University of Tennessee Press.

——. 1997. "The Masking of History: Popular Images of the Nation on a Dominican Sugar Plantation." *New West Indian Guide* 71, 3–4: 227–48.

——. 1999. "From Hidden Hand to Heavy Hand: Sugar, the State, and Migrant Labor in Haiti and the Dominican Republic." *Latin American Research Review* 34, 1: 57–84.

Massey, D. S., and N. A. Denton. 1993. *American Apartheid*. Cambridge, Mass.: Harvard University Press.

Mateo, A. L. 1993. *Mito y cultura en la era de Trujillo*. Santo Domingo: De Colores.

Maurer, B. 1997. *Recharting the Caribbean*. Ann Arbor: University of Michigan Press.

Mauss, M. 1923–24. "Essai sur le don. Forme et raison de l'échange dans les sociétés archaïques." *Année Sociologique* 2nd ser. 1: 30–186.

Mintz, S. W. 1985. *Sweetness and Power*. Harmondsworth: Penguin.

——. [1974] 1989. *Caribbean Transformations*. Morningside ed. New York: Columbia University Press.

——. 1998. "The Localization of Anthropological Practice: From Area Studies to Transnationalism." *Critique of Anthropology* 18, 2: 117–33.

Mirabal, N. R. 2001. "'No Country But the One We Must Fight For': The Emergence of an Antillean Nation and Community in New York City, 1860–1901." In A. Laó-Montes and A. Dávila, eds., *Mambo Montage*, 57–72. New York: Columbia University Press.

Mitchell, A. 1992. "Where Markets Are Never Super; Some Urban Neighborhoods Fight Absence of Major Chains." *New York Times*, 6 June, 1, 25.

Moore, J., and H. Pachón. 1985. *Hispanics in the United States*. Englewood Cliffs, N.J.: Prentice-Hall.

Morgen, S., and J. Maskovsky. 2003. "The Anthropology of Welfare 'Reform': New Perspectives on U.S. Urban Poverty in the Post-Welfare Era." *Annual Review of Anthropology* 32: 315–38.

Moya Pons, F. 1986a. "Etnicidad, Identidad Nacional y Migración." In Moya Pons, *El Pasado Dominicano*, 235–51. Santo Domingo: Fundación J. A. Caro Alvarez.

——. 1986b. "Los Historiadores y la percepción de la nacionalidad." In Moya Pons, *El Pasado Dominicano*, 253–64. Santo Domingo: Fundación J. A. Caro Alvarez.

——. 1990. "The Dominican Republic Since 1930." In L. Bethell, ed., *The Cambridge History of Latin America*, vol. 7. Cambridge: Cambridge University Press.

——. 1998. *The Dominican Republic: A National History*. Princeton, N.J.: Marcus Wiener.

Murray, G. F. 1996. *El Colmado*. Santo Domingo: Fondo para el Financiamiento de la Microempresa, Inc. (FondoMicro).

Navarro, M. 2002a. "Speaking the Language, and the Issues, Pataki Makes Inroads with Latino Voters." *New York Times*, 16 October, B6.

——. 2002b. "Pataki's Success Among Latinos Worries Some Democrats." *New York Times*, 9 November, B1.

New York City Taxi Magazine. 2004. 11, October–November.

New York State Federation of Taxi Drivers. 2002. *Reglamentos de TLC para la Industria del Taxi*. New York: New York State Federation of Taxi Drivers.

Noel, P. 2000. "Africans Are Dying, Too: The Forgotten Victims of the Livery Cabbie Murders." *Village Voice*, 18 April.

Nossiter, A. 1995. "Warrior for the Bodega Owners." *New York Times*, 18 June, 13, 4.

Oboler, S. 1992. "The Politics of Labelling: Latino/a Cultural Identities of Self and Others." *Latin American Perspectives* 19, 4: 18–36.

———, ed. 2006. *Latinos and Citizenship*. New York: Palgrave Macmillan.

Office of the Governor for the State of New York, David A. Paterson. 2008. "Governor Paterson Signs Bill to Deliver Workers' Benefits to New York Livery Cab Drivers, Protect Crucial City Industry." Press release, 25 July.

Office of the Governor for the State of New York, George E. Pataki. 2001a. "Governor Presides at Swearing in of Taxi Federation President." Press release, 16 April.

———. 2001b. "Governor Proposes Bill to Help Families of Slain Livery Drivers." Press release, 9 May.

Olwig, K. F. 1993. *Global Culture, Island Identity: Continuity and Change in the Afro-Caribbean community of Nevis*. Philadelphia: Harwood Academic.

———. 2007. *Caribbean Journeys*. Durham, N.C.: Duke University Press.

Omi, M., and H. Winant. 1994. *Racial Formation in the United States from the 1960s to the 1990s*. 2nd ed. New York: Routledge.

Ong, A. 1998. *Flexible Citizenship*. Durham, N.C.: Duke University Press.

———. 2006. *Neoliberalism as Exception*. Durham. N.C.: Duke University Press.

Ortner, S. 1995. "Resistance and the Problem of Ethnographic Refusal." *Comparative Studies in Society and History* 37, 1: 173–93.

———. 1996. "Making Gender: Toward a Feminist, Minority, Postcolonial, Subaltern, etc., Theory of Practice." In Ortner, *Making Gender*. Boston: Beacon Press.

———, ed. 1999. *The Fate of "Culture"*. Berkeley: University of California Press.

———. 2003. *New Jersey Dreaming*. Durham, N.C.: Duke University Press.

Osofsky, G. [1966] 1996. *Harlem: The Making of a Ghetto*. Chicago: Ivan R. Dee.

Padilla, F. M. 1985. *Latino Ethnic Consciousness*. South Bend, Ind.: University of Notre Dame Press.

Park, K. 1997. *The Korean American Dream*. Ithaca, N.Y.: Cornell University Press.

Pear, R. 2010. "In a Tough Economy, Old Limits on Welfare." *New York Times*, 10 April.

Pessar, P. 1987. "The Dominicans: Women in the Household and the Garment Industry." In N. Foner, ed., *New Immigrants in New York*, 103–29. New York: Columbia University Press.

———. 1994. "Sweatshop Workers and Domestic Ideologies: Dominican Women in New York's Apparel Industry." *International Journal of Urban and Regional Research* 18, 1: 127–42.

———. 1995. *A Visa for a Dream*. Boston: Allyn and Bacon.

———, ed. 1997. *Caribbean Circuits*. New York: Center for Migration Studies.

Portes, A. 1995. "Economic Sociology and the Sociology of Immigration: A Conceptual Overview." In Portes, ed., *The Economic Sociology of Immigration*, 1–41. New York: Russell Sage.

Portes, A., and L. E. Guarnizo. 1991. *Capitalistas del Trópico*. 2nd ed. Santo Domingo: Programa FLACSO—República Dominicana; Baltimore: Johns Hopkins University.

Portes, A., and R. G. Rumbaut. 1996. *Immigrant America: A Portrait*. 2nd ed. Berkeley: University of California Press.

Price, R. 1983. *First-Time*. Baltimore: Johns Hopkins University Press.

———, ed. [1979] 1996. *Maroon Societies*. 3rd ed. Baltimore: Johns Hopkins University Press.

Pristin, T. 1999a. "Big vs. Local in Harlem Supermarket Proposals." *New York Times*, 15 June, B12.

———. 1999b. "Team Chosen to Build Harlem Market." *New York Times*, 19 June, B3.

———. 2001. "2 Years Later, Harlem Still Waits for a Supermarket It Needs." *New York Times*, 20 May, A43.

Rashbaum, W. K. 2000. "After Deaths, City Plans Millions for Livery-Cab Safety." *New York Times*, 15 April, B3.

Richburg Hayes, L. 2000. "Do the Poor Pay More? An Empirical Investigation of Price Dispersion in Food Retailing." Working Paper 446, Princeton University, Industrial Relations Section, 1 September. http://papers.ssrn.com/sol3/papers.cfm?abstract_id=242535.

Ricourt, M. 2002. *Dominicans in New York City*. New York: Routledge.

Ricourt, M., and R. Danta. 2003. *Hispanas de Queens*. Ithaca, N.Y.: Cornell University Press.

Rodríguez, C. E. 1996. "Puerto Ricans: Between Black and White." In Rodríguez and V. E. Sánchez Korrol, eds., *Historical Perspectives on Puerto Rican Survival in the United States*, 25–35. Princeton, N.J.: Marcus Wiener.

Rodríguez, J., and J. Rodríguez. 2004. "High Class, crecimiento, expansión y éxito." *El Taxista* (Manhattan-El Bronx-Queens-Brooklyn), 5, 114 (July), 4, 5.

Rodriguez, L. 2000. "Faith, Hope and Caridad: A Name That Rings Bells for Dominican Diners Has Proliferated to the Point of Confusion." *New York Times*, 17 September, 4.

Roorda, E. 1998. *The Dictator Next Door: The Good Neighbor Policy and the Trujillo Regime in the Dominican Republic, 1930–1945*. Durham, N.C.: Duke University Press.

Rosaldo, R. 1994. "Cultural Citizenship and Educational Democracy." *Cultural Anthropology* 9, 3: 402–11.

Rouse, R. [1991] 2002. "Mexican Migration and the Social Space of Postmodernism." In J. X. Inda and R. Rosaldo, eds., *The Anthropology of Globalization: A Reader*, 157–71. Oxford: Blackwell.

Sagás, E. 2000. *Race and Politics in the Dominican Republic*. Gainesville: University Press of Florida.

Sainz, R. A. 1990. "Dominican Ethnic Associations: Classification and Service Delivery Roles in Washington Heights." Ph.D. dissertation, Columbia University, School of Social Work.

Sánchez Korrol, V. E. 1994. *From Colonia to Community*. Berkeley: University of California Press.

Sanders, J., and V. Nee. 1987. "Limits of Ethnic Solidarity in the Ethnic Enclave Economy." *American Sociological Review* 54: 809–20.

Sanjek, R. 1998. *The Future of Us All*. Ithaca, N.Y.: Cornell University Press.

———. 2003. "Rethinking Migration, Ancient to Future." *Global Networks: A Journal of Transnational Affairs* 3, 3: 315–36.

San Miguel, L. 1997a. *Los Campesinos del Cibao*. San Juan: Editorial de la Universidad de Puerto Rico.

———. 1997b. *La Isla imaginada*. San Juan: Isla Negra/La Trinitaria.

Sassen, S. [1991] 2001. *The Global City: New York, London, Tokyo*. 2nd ed. Princeton, N.J.: Princeton University Press.

Sassen-Koob, S. 1982. "Recomposition and Peripheralization at the Core." *Contemporary Marxism* 5: 88–100.

———. 1987. "Formal and Informal Associations: Dominicans and Colombians in New York." In C. R. Sutton and E. M. Chaney, eds., *Caribbean Life in New York City*, 261–77. New York: Center for Migration Studies.

Schaller Consulting. 2004. *The New York City Taxicab Fact Book*. New York: Schaller Consulting, June. www.schallerconsult.com/taxi, accessed 25 January 2005.

Scott, J. C. 1976. *The Moral Economy of the Peasant*. New Haven, Conn.: Yale University Press.

———. 1985. *Weapons of the Weak*. New Haven, Conn.: Yale University Press.

———.1990. *Domination and the Arts of Resistance*. New Haven, Conn.: Yale University Press.

Serant, C. 1995a. "Bizman Is Set for Food Fight: Fixes Up W'Burg Market." *New York Daily News*, 5 June, Suburban Section, 3.

———. 1995b. "Small Biz Pushes for City Aid: Say Big Stores Favored." *New York Daily News*, 24 July, Suburban Section, 3.

Sharpe, K. E. 1977. *Peasant Politics*. Baltimore: Johns Hopkins University Press.

Shaw, R. 2010. "As Progressives Predicted, Clinton Welfare Reform Law Fails Families." *BeyondChron: San Francisco's Alternative Online Daily*, 19 April. http://www.beyondchron.org/news/index.php?itemid=8029, accessed 14 January 2012.

Silverman, E. 1991. "The New Nueva York: Taking Care of Business." *New York Newsday*, 21 October.

Simmons, K. E. 2009. *Reconstructing Racial Identity and the African Past in the Dominican Republic*. Gainesville: University Press of Florida.

Smith, R. C. 2005. "Racialization and Mexicans in New York City." In V. Zúñiga and R. Hernández-León, eds., *New Destinations: Mexican Immigration in the United States*, 220–43. New York: Russell Sage Foundation.

———. 2006. *Mexican New York*. Berkeley: University of California Press.

Sommer, D. 1991. *Foundational Fictions*. Berkeley: University of California Press.

Sontag, D., and C. W. Dugger. 1998. "The New Immigrant Tide: A Shuttle Between Worlds." *New York Times*, 19 July, A1, A27–28.

Soto, J. 1996. "El Consejo rechaza plan para construir supertiendas: Duro revés para Giuliani." *El Diario/La Prensa*, 12 December, 3.

Stolcke, V. 1995. "Talking Culture: New Boundaries, New Rhetorics of Exclusion in Europe." *Current Anthropology* 36, 1:1–24.

Stoller, P. 2002. *Money Has No Smell*. Chicago: University of Chicago Press.

Suárez-Orozco, M. M. 2000. "Everything You Ever Wanted to Know About Assimilation But Were Afraid to Ask." *Daedalus* 129, 4: 1–30.

Suárez-Orozco, M. M, and M. M. Páez, eds. 2002. *Latinos: Remaking America*. Berkeley: University of California Press.

Tabb, W. 1982. *The Long Default: New York City and the Urban Fiscal Crisis*. New York: Monthly Review Press.

El Taxista (Manhattan-El Bronx-Queens-Brooklyn). 2002. 4, 87 (August).

———. 2003. 5, 101 (October).

Thompson, E. 1971. "The Moral Economy of the English Crowd in the Eighteenth Century." *Past and Present* 50: 76–136.

———. 1991. "The Moral Economy Reviewed." in Thompson, *Customs in Common*, 259–351. London: Merlin Press.

Tienda, M., and V. Ortíz. 1986. "Hispanicity and the 1980 Census." *Social Science Quarterly* 67, 1: 3–20.

Torres-Saillant, S. 1998. "The Tribulations of Blackness: Stages in Dominican Racial Identity." *Latin American Perspectives: Race and National Identity in the Americas* 25, 3: 126–46.

———. 1999. *El Retorno de las Yolas*. Santo Domingo: Librería La Trinitaria y Editora Manatí.

———. 2002. "Epilogue: Problematic Paradigms: Racial Diversity and Corporate Identity in the Latino Community." In M. M. Suárez-Orozco and M. M. Páez, eds., *Latinos: Remaking America*, 435–55. Berkeley: University of California Press.

Torres-Saillant, S., and R. Hernández. 1998. *The Dominican Americans*. Westport, Conn.: Greenwood.

Trouillot, M.-R. 1995. *Silencing the Past*. Boston: Beacon Press.

———. 2001. "The Anthropology of the State in the Age of Globalization." *Current Anthropology* 42, 1: 125–38.

———. 2003. *Global Transformations*. New York: Palgrave Macmillan.

Turits, R. L. 2003. *Foundations of Despotism: Peasants, the Trujillo Regime, and Modernity in Dominican History*. Stanford, Calif.: Stanford University Press.

El Universal (Nueva York-Santo Domingo). 2002. 8, 91 (August).

Vega, B. 1986. *Control y Represión en la Dictadura Trujillista*. Santo Domingo: Fundación Cultural Dominicana.

Vega, M. 1995a. "Lio de bodegueros: La 'bodega grande' enfrenta a pequeños supermercados en El Barrio." *El Diario/La Prensa*, 13 April, 3.

———. 1995b. "Aprueban el 'Pathmark' para El Barrio: En una candente sesión y por un solo voto." *El Diario/La Prensa*, 28 April, 2.

Verdery, K. 1999. *The Political Lives of Dead Bodies*. New York: Columbia University Press.
Wade, P. 1997. *Race and Ethnicity in Latin America*. London: Pluto Press.
Waldinger, R. 1986. *Through the Eye of the Needle*. New York: New York University Press.
Walker, M. T. 1970. "Power Structure and Patronage in a Community of the Dominican Republic." *Journal of Inter-American Affairs* 12, 4: 485–504.
———. 1972. *Politics and the Power Structure*. New York: Teachers College Press, Columbia University.
Weiner, A. B. 1988. *The Trobrianders of Papua New Guinea*. New York: Holt, Rinehart.
Williams, M. 1999. "Flak in the Great Hair War: African-Americans vs. Dominicans, Rollers at the Ready." *New York Times*, 13 October, B1, B8.
Williams, R. 1977. *Marxism and Literature*. Oxford: Oxford University Press.
Wilson, P. J. 1969. "Reputation and Respectability: A Suggestion for Caribbean Ethnology." *Man* 4, 1: 70–84.
Yanagisako, S. 2002. *Producing Culture and Capital*. Princeton, N.J.: Princeton University Press.

INDEX

Abyssinian Development Corporation, 214
African Americans: Dominican Bronx, 45–46; Dominican cooperation and alliances with, 199, 280n20; Dominican-owned beauty salons serving, 89; and Dominican system of racial classification, 180; Dominican Upper Manhattan, 40–41, 43; history of migration from the South, 40–41; and U.S. system of racial classification, 181, 183–84
Aid to Families with Dependent Children (AFDC), 277n10
Alianza Dominicana, 164
Alvarez, Caridad, 83
Alvarez, Consuelo, 84
American immigrant success stories, 224–26
Amsterdam Car Service, 77–78
anthropological fieldwork and research, 5–22; and gender issues in Dominican immigrant population, 7–10; and international migration research, 13–22; living with first-generation immigrant family, 5–6, 8–10; and so-called transnational migrant circuit, 20–22; studying belonging (negotiation and building of identities), 20–22; studying economic practices and income-producing strategies, 13–16; studying everyday life, 16–18; studying political life, 18–20, 267; and trope of ethnic enclave, 10–13. *See also* international migration studies
anti-immigration legislation, 283n1
Arrighini, Nicola, 192
La Asociación de Bases de Nueva York (Livery Owners Coalition of New York), 80, 245, 282n8
Associated Wholesalers (and Associated stores), 59–61, 64, 65–66, 97
Audubon Car Service, 140

Audubon Partnership for Economic Development, 96, 244, 247, 251
Autonomous University of Santo Domingo (UASD), 33

Balaguer, Joaquín: *El Cristo de la Libertad: Vida de Juan Pablo Duarte*, 191; regime, 34–35, 37, 189, 191, 192, 272nn7–8
Baruch College, 63, 84, 109, 148
Bazenguissa-Ganga, Rémy, *Congo-Paris* (2000), 15, 270n6
beauty salons, Dominican-owned, 87–89, 114, 120–21, 273n1; and sustaining female networks, 129–30; working conditions, 114, 120–21
black-car services, 69, 74n7, 137, 158–60, 243
Blanco, Salvador Jorge, 35
Bloomberg, Michael: and El Día del Taxista, 260–61; and Latino vote, 246; and National Supermarkets Association, 194, 224
bodegas, Dominican-owned, 2, 47, 52–57, 63–69, 86, 126–29, 130–31, 273n1; beer sales and in-store beer consumption, 129; and business partnerships (*sociedades*), 50–51, 63, 67; and city economic conditions, 54–56, 68–69; crime and violence, 55; defining, 52; and Dominican *colmado*, 126–27; family labor, 56, 67; informal and illegal activities, 129; as place to share news and gossip, 128, 129; racial discrimination from suppliers, 55–56; raising capital, 51–52, 63–64, 67; regular customers, 127–28; rents and landlords' exploitation, 56; role in community, 53, 56–57, 126–29, 130–31; self-exploitation and owners' long working hours, 54, 56, 57, 113, 114–16; selling Dominican commodities, 53, 128, 130–31, 187; working conditions, 118. *See also* supermarkets, Dominican-owned

bookstores, Dominican-owned, 109–10, 111–12
Bosch, Juan, 33, 189
Bourdieu, Pierre, 131
Bronx, Dominican, 38–39, 44–46; black and Latino community, 44, 45–46; revitalization and renewal, 45
Bush, George W., 193–94, 242

Camacho, Nelson, 72–77, 79, 149–51, 165
Candelario, Ginetta, 88
capital, processes for obtaining, 95–110; bank loans, 64, 84, 95–98, 107, 141–42; bodega-owners, 51–52, 63–64, 67; businesses undermined by "uncontrolled solidarity," 103, 276n3; business partnerships and rotating credit associations (*sanes* or *sociedades*), 50–51, 63, 67, 108–10, 111–13, 151, 273n2, 274n3; discourse on transition from being "nonbankable" to "bankable," 97–98; drawing on friendships, 61, 98–103, 106–8, 141–42; drawing on kinship and family, 51–52, 61, 63–64, 67, 98–104; and interest rates, 96–97; non-profit groups that make small business loans, 96; *los prestamistas* (private moneylenders/loan sharks), 95–97, 106, 276n1; social mobility/class and access to credit, 97; supermarket owners, 61, 64, 97–98, 101–3, 107
Caridad restaurants, Chelo Ramírez's, 82–86, 87, 99, 104, 112
Caro, Robert, 41
Carrión, Adolfo, Jr., 222, 224
car services. *See* livery-cab operations, Dominican-controlled
Centro Cívico Cultural Dominicano, 191–92
Chase Manhattan Bank (now JP Morgan Chase), 64, 97, 107
Chock, Phyllis Pease, 225
City College of New York, 124, 194–95
Clinton, Bill, 234, 277n10
Club Cívico Cultural Juan Pablo Duarte, 192
clubs. *See* voluntary associations (*clubes*)
colmados, 126–27
Comité Pro-Defensa de los Taxistas sin Medallón (Committee for the Defense of the Nonmedallion Cab Drivers), 73–74, 75, 76, 282n8
Community Association for Progressive Dominicans, 195, 196, 198, 202

Community Association of East Harlem Triangle, Inc., 214
Community Food Resources Center, Inc., 215
Compare supermarkets, 60, 65–66
compartir, 166–67, 169–70
crime and violence: against bodega-owners, 55; against livery-car drivers, 79, 166, 237–40, 274n9, 282n6
C-Town supermarkets, 59–60, 113–14, 122, 132–33, 229
Cuban immigrants, 23–25, 42–43, 227, 270n10; and restaurant business, 83, 84
Cuomo, Mario, 74

Danta, Ruby, 178
Daus, Matthew W., 243, 244–45, 247
Dávila, Arlene, *Latinos, Inc.: The Marketing and Making of a People* (2001), 178–79, 182, 184
Delgado, Walther: and Audubon Partnership, 244, 247, 251, 253; and New York City For-Hire Base Group, 244, 247, 251
Delio Marte, José, 1–3, 49–57, 72–73, 102–3, 107; and bodega business, 49–57, 127; financing celebrations of Duarte's birthday, 192–93, 280n13
Democratic Party, 19, 165, 189, 200, 202, 246–47
deportations, 264, 283n1
El Día del Taxista (Livery Cab Drivers Day), 257, 259–61, 262
El Diario/La Prensa (newspaper), 5, 115, 128, 179, 238
Díaz, Hugo, 50, 204
Díaz, Mariano, 207, 217
Díaz, Mary, 226
Díaz, Ruben, 74, 261
Dinkins, David, 199, 202, 203
divorce and separation rates, 168, 169
Dominican community in New York City: borough statistical data, 38; Bronx, 38–39, 44–46; and city economic restructuring, 4, 94–95, 264; distribution in late 1960s-early 1970s, 39–40; and "Dominicanization," 5, 37, 266–68; education levels, 44, 273n16; female-dominated reciprocity networks, 8–10, 129–30; female-headed households, 7–8, 123–24, 142–43, 145–46, 277n10; housing arrangements and variations, 40; and Latinization of city, 23–26, 267–68;

naturalized citizens, 44; and neoliberalism, 23, 26–27, 229; from nineteenth century to 1950s, 271n5; and non-Hispanic white populations, 43; political culture and activism, 18–20, 188–200, 201–29, 230–63, 267; population growth/statistics, 3; since 1970s, 3–5, 23–27; Upper Manhattan, 38–39, 40–44. *See also* Dominican immigrants; Upper Manhattan, Dominican (Washington Heights-Inwood area)

Dominican Day and Parade, 109, 190

Dominican immigrants, 3–4, 24–26, 31, 32–37, 189, 271n6; belonging and identity, 20–22; dissimilarities among first-generation immigrants, 15–16; earliest politically-driven mass emigration, 33, 189; economic practices and income-producing strategies, 13–16; everyday life, 16–18; naturalized citizens, 44; participation in political life, 18–20, 267; post-2000 slowdown in migration, 46; and post-Trujillo economic and political shifts, 34–36; pre-1962 migration, 271n5; regularized status/legal residents, 37; and U.S. economic and military imperialism in Caribbean, 33–34, 37, 271n6; and U.S. Immigration Reform Act, 269n4, 271n6, 272n10; visas, 33, 36–37, 271n6

Dominican Independence Day, 192, 193, 221

dominicano/a, 3, 173–75, 185–88, 200, 228

Dominican racial and ethnic identity, 20–22, 26, 173–200; defining identity/production of "identities," 22, 200; everyday life, 16–18, 175–79; expressions of memory of Duarte, 190–98; "Hispanic" and "Latino," 174, 181–84, 228, 279n4; Hispanic panethnicity, 22, 174, 177–79, 181–84, 185–88, 228, 255–61; identification *dominicano/a*, 3, 173–75, 185–88, 200, 228; identification *hispano/a*, 174–75, 182–83, 184, 185, 187, 200; intermarriage patterns among Hispanic groups, 178, 279n2; and Latinization of New York, 23–26, 267–68; and livery-cab industry, 255–61; local shopping and Dominican commodities, 53, 128, 130–31, 187; and marketing practices, 185–88; and racial classification practices, 174, 179–84, 197, 227–28; and Spanish language, 147, 176–77, 178–79, 256–59; supermarket owners' social and cultural activities, 219–26

Dominican Republic, 31–46; Balaguer regime, 34–35, 37, 189, 191, 192, 272nn7–8; Bosch and PRD, 33–34; Caribbean island of Hispaniola ("Quisqueya"), 31; civil war (1965), 33–34; Duarte and founding as independent nation, 190–91; economic boom of late 1970s/early 1980s, 35; election of Fernández and PLD, 272n9; election of Mejía and PRD, 272n9; falling wages and debt problems, 35–36; La Descubierta, 5, 100–101, 103–4, 191; massacres in Dominican-Haitian borderlands (1937), 32, 271n4; Partido Reformista (PR), 34; Partido Revolucionario Dominicano (PRD), 33–34, 35, 73, 165, 272n9; political turbulence (1960s through 2000s), 32–37; post-Trujillo economic and political shifts, 34–36; post-Trujillo mass immigration, 3–4, 24–26, 31, 32–37, 189, 271n6; racial classifications and nationalist discourse, 179–80, 184, 190–91, 197; Trujillo administration/dictatorship, 3, 32, 179–80; Trujillo's socioeconomic restructuring and agrarian production policies, 32; U.S. economic and military imperialism, 33–34, 37, 271n6; U.S. military intervention (1965), 33–34; U.S. occupation (1916-1924), 32

Dore-Cabral, Carlos, 180

"Do the Poor Pay More? An Empirical Investigation of Price Dispersion in Food Retailing" (Richburg Hayes), 211–12

Duany, Jorge, 12

Duarte, Juan Pablo, cult of (*el padre de la patria*), 190–98; annual birthday celebrations, 192–93; and anti-Haitian nationalist discourse, 190–91, 197; and El Carnaval del Boulevard, 196–97; and Instituto Duartiano of New York, 192–93, 197; renamed schools and city streets, 194, 195–96; statue on Duarte Square, 192; and voluntary associations, 190–98

East Harlem Abyssinian Triangle Corporation, 214–15

economy. *See* small-business economy, Dominican

English language: first-generation immigrants, 94; and livery-cab drivers, 80–81, 140, 235–36, 241

Espaillat, Adriano: and El Día del Taxista, 259; and National Supermarkets Association, 219, 222, 224, 281n12; and New York City For-Hire Base Group, 243, 245, 253; and Workers' Compensation for livery-cab drivers, 253, 282–83n13
Espinal, Pablo, 207, 216, 217, 229
ethnic enclave, trope of, 10–13
Eusebio, Nelson, 207
Excellent Car Service, 143–44
Executive Transportation Group, 159

family. *See* kinship/family (*la familia*)
Federation of Dominican and Hispanic Merchants and Businessmen, 2–3
Federation of Social Clubs, 190
Fernández, José, 222
Fernández, Leonel, 272n9
Fernández, Paul, 207
Ferrer, Fernando, 74, 165
First Class (Dominican-owned livery base), 139
Foner, Nancy, 4
Food Stamp Program, 205–6, 280n3
friendship networks, 106–8, 125; and *confianza* or trust, 106–8; and independent supermarket owners, 61, 98–103; and livery-cab operations, 141–42, 164, 166–67, 169–70; masculinity and *compartir*, 166–67, 169–70; processes for raising capital, 61, 98–103, 106–8, 141–42; and *serio* ("serious"), 106, 276n5; sports activities, 164

Galiber, Joseph, 75
garment industry, 50
Geertz, Clifford, 17, 273n2
gender roles, 7–10; and female-dominated reciprocity networks, 8–10, 129–30; and gender hierarchies, 276n6; *hombre independiente*, 166; *hombre valiente*, 166; ideas about masculinity, 100, 165–70; and livery-cab industry, 165–70; men and *compartir*, 166–67, 169–70; men as *serio* (serious), 167; *mujeriegos* (womanizers), 167–68; and paradoxical relations between men and women, 100, 168–69; single female-headed households, 7–8, 100–101, 123–24, 142–43, 145–46, 277n10
Georges, Eugenia, 188–89, 201–2
Gilbertson, Greta, 122
Giuliani, Rudolph: megastore development plans, 203, 212–13; and New York State Federation of Taxi Drivers, 237–40, 247
Gonzalez, Evelyn, 44
Graeber, David, 21, 131, 270n8
Granovetter, Mark, 95–96, 103, 105
Gregory, Steven, 22, 264–65; *Black Corona*, 264–65
grocery wholesalers, 59–61, 64, 97, 98
Guarnizo, Luis, 4, 87
Guzmán, Antonio, 35, 272nn7–8

Haiti: Dominican nationalist anti Haitian discourse, 180, 190–91, 197; immigration to Dominican Republic in search of work, 180; immigration to New York City, 270n1; Trujillo-regime massacres in Dominican-Haitian borderlands, 32, 271n4
Hall, Stuart, 200
Hardt, Michael, 18, 267
Harvey, David, 26–27, 229; *A Brief History of Neoliberalism* (2005), 26–27
Hendricks, Glenn, 39–40
Heredia, Pedro: and Dominican belonging/Hispanic panethnic identity, 256; and New York City For-Hire Base Group, 158, 243–55, 282–83n13; and Workers' Compensation for livery-cab drivers, 245, 251–53, 282–83n13
La Hermandad Quisqueyana Community Center, 73, 149–51, 199
Hernández, R., 201
Hernández, Ramona, 7–8, 264; *The Mobility of Workers Under Advanced Capitalism* (2002), 7–8
Highbridge (Dominican-controlled livery-car base), 137, 160, 278n3
High Class Car Service, 157–58, 161, 252
Hispanic panethnicity, 22, 174, 177–79, 181–84, 185; and advertising of national companies, 187; and everyday tenement life, 177–79; identification *hispano/a*, 174–75, 182–83, 184, 185, 187, 200, 228; intermarriage and partnership patterns among Hispanic groups, 178, 279n2; and livery industry, 255–61; and small businesses, 185–88; and Spanish-language television, newspapers, magazines, 178–79, 256–59
Hispanics Across America (HAA), 242
Hoffnung-Garskof, J., *A Tale of Two Cities* (2008), 271n6

Hostos Community College (Bronx), 109
Hoy (newspaper), 179

identity, Dominican. *See* Dominican racial and ethnic identity
"immigrant ghetto"/"immigrant inner city," 10. *See also* ethnic enclave, trope of
immigration. *See* Dominican immigrants; international migration studies
indios, 180
Inoa, Orlando, 221
Instituto Duartiano of New York, 192–93, 197
international migration studies, 1–28; anthropological fieldwork and research, 5–13; belonging (negotiation and building of identities), 20–22; combining interviews with other forms of production of data, 17–18; culture and politics, 19–20; economic practices and income-producing strategies, 13–16; everyday life, 16–18; and four sets of processes in immigrants' lives, 13–22; and participation in political life, 18–20, 267; so-called transnational migrant circuit, 20–22; social actors and cultural worlds, 17; and trope of ethnic enclave, 10–13
International Monetary Fund (IMF), 35
Itzigsohn, J., 180

Jackson, Jesse, 199
Jewish New Yorkers: Highbridge livery-base customers, 278n3; independent supermarket-owners, 60–61; Washington Heights community, 42
Johnson, Lyndon, 33
Jones-Correa, M., 279n8

Kennedy Car Service, 161
Kerrison, Ray, 213
Kim, Sung Soo, 208, 212–13, 222, 281n4
kinship/family (*la familia*), 37, 98–104, 125; *cadena*, 37; and "chains" in migration process, 37, 102–3; female-headed households, 7–8, 100–101, 123–24, 142–43, 145–46, 277n10; labor and exploitation of family members (as unpaid "help"), 56, 67, 116–17, 120; large families, 99–103; looseness and flexibility in, 102; mobilizing to raise capital, 51–52, 61, 63–64, 67, 98–104; personal kindreds, 98–104; reasons Dominican businesses do not seems to be eroded by excessive claims of relatives, 103–5; and ties between immigrants and Dominican Republic, 101; and trust/"enforceable trust," 101–2
Kiss (Dominican-owned livery base), 137–38
Koch, Ed, 45, 68, 75, 202
Korean American Small Business Service Center, 208
Korean Produce Association, 208
Krasdale Foods, 59–61, 97

labor and Dominican-owned small businesses, 94, 111–24; average wages for female employees, 122; beauty salons, 120–21; bodegas, 54, 56, 57, 113, 114–16, 118; co-owners (*socios*) and respective work contributions, 111–13; exploitation of family members (as unpaid "help"), 56, 67, 116–17, 120; flexibility for workers, 123–24; independent supermarkets, 117–18; long working hours (self-exploitation), 54, 56, 57, 113–22; personal networks and recruiting new employees, 121, 136–37; restaurant waitresses, 118–20, 123–24; and segmented labor market, 93–94; single mothers with small children, 123–24, 277n10; and small-business economy in New York, 121–22, 131–33; and unions/unionization, 122; wages, 94, 117–22; working conditions for employees, 117–22; working *por comisión*, 120–21
Lara Flores, Bienvenido, 193, 280n14
Latinos. *See* Hispanic panethnicity
Latour, Bruno, 270n6
Law, John, 270n6
Lazar, Sian, 18
Legal-Aid Society (Manhattan), 251
Levitt, Peggy, *The Transnational Villagers* (2001), 184
Lewis, John, 47
Lhota, Joe, 240
Linares, Evelyn, 195, 199
Linares, Guillermo, 165, 194–98; and Community Association for Progressive Dominicans, 195, 196, 198, 202; and Democratic Party, 202; and Duarte celebrations, 191, 194–98; and New York City Council, 163, 189, 191, 196, 216–18; political conflict with National Supermarkets Association, 216–19
Lipsky, Richard, 216

Liu, John C., 248
livery-cab bases, 70, 72–81, 134–65; annual elections for board and leadership, 78, 134, 150–53; base president, 134, 139, 150–53; base station, 70, 134; and car-repair shops, 157–58, 161; and *choferes particulares*, 134, 139; cooperatives/groups of owners (*los socios*), 70, 76–78, 109, 134, 135, 136–39, 278n2; Discipline Department, 150, 153–56, 183; dispatchers and secretaries, 146–48; economic diversification, 156–61; establishing, 135–39; founding drivers (*fundadores*), 139; as "*la compañía*" (the company), 161–65; leadership and discipline, 148–56, 162; non-affiliated drivers, 278n1; paperwork and obtaining licenses, 136; political activism and collective struggle for rights, 73–76, 79–81; political activism and neighborhood projects, 162, 164–65; Puerto Rican-owned, 73–74, 76, 137, 278n3; real estate purchases, 156–58, 161; recruitment of drivers, 136–37; rivalries and competition between, 138–39; rules and norms, 143, 153–56; sports teams and social rituals, 161–64; vehicle-standards, 138–39; as voluntary associations, 148–51, 170
livery-cab drivers, 78–79, 140–46, 237–38; choosing the work, 72, 146, 278n4; combining work and school/college, 72, 140; day shifts/night shifts, 144; expected income, 144–45; founding drivers (*fundadores*), 139; independence, 143–44; insurance and premiums, 81, 141, 145; killings/violence against, 79, 166, 237–40, 274n9, 282n6; knowledge of English/Spanish, 80–81, 140, 147, 235–36, 241; long hours, 144–46; non-affiliated drivers, 278n1; obtaining a vehicle, 78–79, 138–39, 140–43; personal networks and recruitment, 136–37; regular travel to Dominican Republic, 143–44, 146; self-discipline and hard work, 168; women as, 140, 142–43, 145–46, 278n4; working for a base, 78–79, 143–44
livery-cab operations, Dominican-controlled, 69–81, 134–70, 230–63; and black-car services, 69, 74n7, 137, 158–60, 243; city authorities and regulatory power, 74–75; friendship networks, 141–42, 164, 166–67, 169–70; gender and masculinity, 165–70; history of emergence of, 70–76; and New York City Taxi and Limousine Commission, 69, 70–72, 74–75, 80–81, 136, 143, 145, 232–33, 241, 244–45, 248–50, 253–54, 258, 274n7; oral histories, 47, 69–81; street hails/street pick ups forbidden, 69, 75, 81; and unlicensed "gypsy" cabs, 70, 74; women drivers, 140, 142–43, 145–46, 278n4; yellow taxis ("medallion taxis"), 63, 69, 71–72, 274n7

livery industry, political culture and activism in, 73–76, 79–81, 203, 230–63; and La Asociación de Bases de Nueva York, 80, 245, 282n8; celebrations of El Día del Taxista, 257, 259–61, 262; and El Comité pro Defensa de los Taxistas sin Medallón, 73–74, 75, 76; and Complaint Review Board, 248–49, 258; demands for a driver's handbook, 248; demands for open-door hearings, 249–50; and Democratic politics, 246–47; discourse of injustice, 80–81, 250–51, 255; industry publications, 256–59; and killings/violence against livery drivers, 79, 166, 237–40, 274n9, 282n6; Mateo's leadership, 69, 80, 203, 231–43, 245–47, 253–54, 262–63; neighborhood improvement projects, 164–65; New York City For-Hire Base Group, 158, 230, 243–55, 262; New York State Federation of Taxi Drivers, 69, 80, 203, 230, 231–43, 254–55, 256, 262; and panethnic Latino identity/Dominican belonging, 255–61; protests against abusive fines, 253–54; and Republican politics, 242, 246–47; and Spanish-language edition of rules and regulations, 241; and Workers' Compensation coverage, 245, 251–53, 282n13
Livery Operators Workers' Compensation Insurance Task Force, 245
Lowenstein, Steven, 41–42, 43

MacGaffey, Janet, *Congo-Paris* (2000), 15, 270n6
Maldonado, José, 213
Malinowski, Bronisław, 16
Manhattan Borough Board, 214–15, 216, 219
Marble Hill neighborhood, 81–87, 274n10
Martínez, Miguel: and El Día del Taxista, 259, 261; and National Supermarkets

Association annual banquet, 222; and New York City Council, 189, 193, 200, 258, 279n10, 280n14; and New York City For-Hire Base Group, 243, 247–49, 253, 254
Martinez, Ray, 245
masculinity, 100, 165–70. *See also* gender roles
Mateo, Fernando: and El Día del Taxista, 261; and Hispanics Across America (HAA), 242; and killings of livery-cab drivers, 238–40; life and career, 231, 233–36; and New York State Federation of Taxi Drivers, 69, 80, 203, 231–43, 245–47, 253–54, 262–63, 282n1; and Republican politics, 242, 246–47
Mateo Express, 234
megastores: Dinkins administration plan, 203; fight over Pathmark supermarket in East Harlem, 203–4, 214–19, 229; Giuliani administration plan, 203, 212–13; loans and tax abatement packages from city, 215, 281n10; and National Supermarkets Association, 203–4, 212–19, 228–29. *See also* National Supermarkets Association
Mejía, Hipólito, 272n9
Méndez, Olga, 215, 246
Messinger, Ruth, 215, 216
mestizaje, 180, 228
Metropolitan Life Insurance Company (MetLife), 109
Miller Brewing Company, 223
Mirabal, Nancy Raquel, 23–24
Morrisania (Southern Bronx), 45
Moya Pons, Frank, 181
Murray, Gerald, *El Colmado* (1996), 126–27
Murtaugh, John Brian, 2, 189

National Supermarkets Association, 57, 58–62, 201–29; annual banquet, 221–26; capitalism and fair economic competition, 215, 228–29; college scholarship program, 220–21; and corporate chain supermarkets, 203–4, 210–19, 228–29; and Dominican/American identity and belonging, 219–26; emergence of, 203, 204–9; and Espaillat (state politician), 219, 222, 224, 281n12; members and stores, 58–59, 204–5, 207; opposition to megastore development plans, 203–4, 212–19, 228–29; and Peña, 62, 204–7, 219, 227; political neutrality/political role, 208–9; presidents of, 206–7; Queens headquarters, 193–94; recruitment through personal networks, 205; and Salcedo, 57, 58–59, 98, 194, 205–9, 210, 213, 217, 221–26, 229; social and cultural activities, 219–26. *See also* supermarkets, Dominican-owned
Negri, Antonio, 18, 267
neoliberalism, 23, 26–27, 229
New York City: borough statistical data, 38; Dominican Bronx, 38–39, 44–46; Dominican Upper Manhattan, 38–39, 40–44; economic restructuring since 1960s, 4, 26–27, 54–56, 94–95, 264; fiscal crisis of mid-1970s and 1980s, 26–27, 105–6; Latinization of, 23–26, 55–56, 266–68; three economies, 14
New York City Council, 4; Linares's seat, 163, 189, 191, 196, 216–18; Martínez's seat, 189, 193, 200, 258, 279n10, 280n14; and megastore plan, 213; and National Supermarkets Association, 208, 213; and New York City For-Hire Base Group, 245, 249; and New York City Taxi and Limousine Commission, 71, 247, 249; and renamed schools, 194, 196
New York City Department of Consumer Affairs, 213; "The Poor Pay More . . . for Less" (1991 report), 210–11
New York City For-Hire Base Group, 158, 230, 243–55, 262; and Audubon Partnership for Economic Development, 244, 247, 251; and Complaint Review Board, 248–49, 258; and Democratic politics, 246–47; discourse of injustice, 250–51; and Dominican-community politicians, 253; as grassroots, loose network, 246; and Heredia, 158, 243–55, 282–83n13; and New York City Taxi and Limousine Commission, 244–45, 248–50; nonsupport for Mateo's leadership, 245–47; and panethnic Latino identity/Dominican belonging, 256; protest against abusive fines, 253–54; reasons for establishment, 245–47; state funding/financing, 253; three projects, 248–50; and Workers' Compensation coverage, 245, 251–53, 282n13
New York City Police Department Taxi Unit, 71

New York City Taxi and Limousine Commission, 69, 70–72, 74–75, 80–81, 136, 143, 232–33, 241, 248–50, 253–54, 258, 274n7; annual fees, 145; base presidents and meetings with, 153; Complaint Review Board, 248–49, 258; driver's handbook for livery-cab drivers, 248; English language rules and regulations, 241; and Federation of Taxi Drivers, 232–33, 241, 253–54; July 2003 protest against abusive fines by, 253–54; and New York City For-Hire Base Group, 244–45, 248–50; open door hearings, 249–50

New York City Taxi Magazine, 257, 258–59

New York Crime Victim Board, 240

New York Daily News, 47, 238

New York State Assembly, 4; Espaillat's seat, 2, 189, 191, 200, 218, 219, 269n2

New York State Federation of Hispanic Chambers of Commerce, 3, 50, 204, 222

New York State Federation of Taxi Drivers, 80, 203, 230, 231–43, 254–55, 256, 262; base representatives (*delegados*), 237; Bronx neighborhood office, 237; founding, 80, 203, 232–33; and Giuliani administration, 237–40, 247; legal services for members, 236–37; Mateo's leadership, 69, 80, 203, 231–43, 245–47, 253–54, 262–63; and New York City Taxi and Limousine Commission, 232–33, 241, 253–54; obtaining protection and safety for drivers, 237–40, 282n6; organization structure and political activities, 236–43; and panethnic Latino identity/Dominican belonging, 256; and Pataki administration, 240–41, 242, 282n6; protest against abusive fines, 253–54; publishing *Reglamentos de TLC para la Industria del Taxi*, 241; weekly fees, 236; and Workers' Compensation coverage, 240

New York Times, 89, 123, 213, 229, 238, 276n1

Nixon, Richard, 27

Noticias del Mundo (newspaper), 179, 238, 260

Null, Steve, 281n4

Oboler, Suzanne, 174

Ortner, Sherry, 131

Pagan, Antonio, 215

Park, Kyeyoung, 93–94, 270n7

Partido de la Liberación Dominicano (PLD), 80, 272n9

Partido Reformista (PR), 34

Partido Revolucionario Dominicano (PRD), 33–34, 35, 73, 165, 272n9

Pataki, George: and El Día del Taxista, 260; and Latino vote, 246; and National Supermarkets Association's annual banquet, 224; and New York State Federation of Taxi Drivers, 240–41, 242, 282n6; and Workers' Compensation for livery-cab drivers, 240–41, 251–52

Paterson, David, 282n13

Pathmark supermarket in East Harlem, 203–4, 214–19, 229

Peña, Eligio: as bodega owner, 62–66, 104, 107–8; and National Supermarkets Association, 62, 204–7, 219, 227

Peralta, Armando, 233, 235, 237

Peralta, José, 222

Pérez, Freddy, 74, 75, 76

Perez, Luis Francisco, 238

Personal Responsibility and Work Opportunity Reconciliation Act (1996), 277n10, 283n1

Pessar, Patricia, 277n10

Placeres, Alfredo: and National Supermarkets Association's annual banquet, 222, 224; and New York State Federation of Hispanic Chambers of Commerce, 3, 50, 204, 222; and Small Business Congress of New York City, 281n4

political culture and activism of Dominican New Yorkers, 18–20, 188–200, 201–29, 230–63, 267; and broad anthropological understanding of politics, 19–20, 267; collective bargaining, 202; cooperation and alliances with other minority groups, 199, 280n20; and Duarte cult, 190–98; electoral representation, 2, 4, 189, 191, 200, 279n10; livery-car industry, 73–76, 79–81, 203, 230–63; small-business associations and interest organizations, 18, 202–3, 270n7; voluntary associations (*clubes*), 18–19, 148–56, 162, 170, 188–200, 201–2. *See also* National Supermarkets Association; New York City For-Hire Base Group; New York State Federation of Taxi Drivers

"The Poor Pay More . . . for Less" (1991

report of New York City Department of Consumer Affairs), 210–11
Portes, Alejandro, 4, 101–2
Powell, Adam Clayton, IV, 215, 217
practice theory, 131
los prestamistas (private moneylenders/loan sharks), 95–97, 106, 276n1
profesionales, 275n11
Puerto Rican immigrant community, 23–26, 38, 273n15; Dominican cooperation and alliances with, 199, 280n20; grocery store owners, 55; immigration patterns, 23–24, 42–43; intermarriage and partnership patterns between Dominicans and, 178, 279n2; and livery industry, 73–74, 76, 137, 278n3; and *sociedades*, 51

"Quisqueya," 31
Quisqueya Tours (travel agency), 186, 275n11

racial classifications, 174, 179–84, 197; based on skin color, 179–81, 228; and Dominican nationalist discourse, 179–80, 184, 190–91, 197; *indios*, 180; *mestizaje*, 180, 228; and racial discrimination, 55–56. See also Dominican racial and ethnic identity
radio taxis, 274n7
Ramírez, Chelo, 99; and Caridad restaurants, 82–86, 87, 99, 104, 112
Rangel, Charles, 202, 215, 282–83n13
Reglamentos de TLC para la Industria del Taxi (2002), 241
rents, commercial, 56, 68–69, 132–33
Republican politics, 242, 246–47
restaurants, Dominican-owned, 81–87; Caridad restaurants, 82–86, 87, 99, 104, 112; contributions to social networks, 125–26; and Cuban-owned restaurants, 83, 84; employees, 84–85; Inwood, 1–3; Marble Hill neighborhood, 81–87; raising capital, 84; and *socios*, 85–87, 99, 112; typical names, 82; working conditions for waitresses, 118–20, 123–24
Richburg Hayes, Cashawn, 211–12
Ricourt, Milagros, 178
Rivera, José, 74, 75, 165
Rodríguez, Alfredo, 215–16, 217
Rodríguez, José, 257, 258
Rodriguez, William, 207

Rodríguez, Ydanis, 279n10
Rosaldo, Renato, 12, 228
Rouse, Roger, 20

Safir, Howard, 239
Sainz, R. A., 192
Salcedo, Luis A., 57–62, 98, 99, 107; and National Supermarkets Association, 57, 58–59, 98, 194, 205–9, 210, 213, 217, 221–26, 229; on unionization, 122
sanes (rotating credit associations), 50–51, 151, 274n3. See also *sociedades*
Sanjek, Roger, 24, 68, 94–95, 132, 270n7; *The Future of Us All*, 94–95
Sara Lee Corporation, 55
Sassen-Koob, Saskia, 51
Schneiderman, Eric, 217–18
Schumer, Charles, 260–61
Seaman (Dominican-owned livery base), 156–57, 161
serio (serious), 106, 167, 276n5
service-sector jobs, 4, 94, 264
Small Business Congress of New York City, 208, 212, 213, 281n4
small-business economy, Dominican: and Dominican identity/Hispanic panethnicity, 185–88; economic-cultural networks (three components of), 15; effects of wider political economy, 121–22, 131–32; immigrants' economic practices and income-producing strategies, 13–16; minorities' entrepreneurial activity in a weakened economy, 105–6; and New York City's three economies, 14; reasons for preferring employment in, 122–24; small-business associations and political activity, 18, 270n7; and social networks, 124–30. See also labor and Dominican-owned small businesses
social networks and neighborhood businesses, 124–30; beauty salons and female networks, 129–30; bodegas, 126–29, 130–31; livery bases' sports teams and social rituals, 161–64; and a practice-theory position, 131; recruiting new employees, 121, 136–37; restaurants, 125–26. See also friendship networks; kinship/family (*la familia*); voluntary associations (*clubes*)
sociedades, 50–51, 63, 67, 108–10, 111–13, 151, 273n2, 274n3

socios: and cooperative livery bases, 70, 76–78, 109, 134, 135, 136–39, 278n2; and recreational or social clubs, 18–19, 149–53, 188; rotating credit associations and business partnerships (*sociedades*), 50–51, 63, 67, 108–10, 111–13, 151, 273n2, 274n3

Spanish-Cuban-American-Filipino War (1898), 24

Spanish language: everyday life, 147, 176–77; and Hispanic panethnicity, 178–79; and livery-cab drivers, 80–81, 140, 147, 235–36, 241, 256–59; television, newspapers, magazines, 178–79, 256–59

Special Supplemental Nutrition Program for Women, Infants, and Children (WIC), 205–6, 280n3

sports teams and livery bases, 161–64

supermarkets, Dominican-owned, 58–62, 64–66, 97–98, 106–7, 201–29; and bank loans, 64, 97, 107; and grocery wholesalers, 59–61, 64, 97, 98; independent Compare supermarkets, 60, 65–66; and Jewish-owned supermarkets, 60–61; kinship and friend networks, 61, 98–103; and Korean greengrocers, 208; licenses to accept food stamps and WIC coupons, 205–6; owners' career patterns, 65; owners' working hours (self-exploitation), 113–14; political activism, 57, 58–62, 201–29; raising capital, 61, 64, 97–98, 101–3, 107; role in community, 61–62; social class and access to credit, 97; women owners, 113–14, 276n6; working conditions, 117–18. *See also* National Supermarkets Association

Taveras, Carmen, 226
El Taxista, 66, 163, 257–58, 259
Telemundo, 178–79
Temporary Assistance for Needy Families, 277n10
tenement life, 16–18, 175–79
Torres-Saillant, Silvio, 201, 266
"Toys for Guns" program, 234
transnational migrant circuit, 20–22
travel agencies, Dominican-owned, 275n11
Trujillo, Rafael Leónidas: administration/dictatorship, 3, 32, 179–80; assassination, 3, 32; racial classification practices/racist discourses, 179, 180

Turits, R. L., *Foundations of Despotism* (2003), 32

United States: economic and military imperialism in Caribbean, 33–34, 37, 271n6; Immigration Reform Act (1965), 269n4, 271n6, 272n10; military intervention in Dominican Republic (1965), 33–34; occupation of Dominican Republic (1916–1924), 32; system of racial classification, 180–84, 228; visa system, 33, 36–37, 271n6

Univisión, 178–79, 225

Upper Manhattan, Dominican (Washington Heights-Inwood area), 38–39, 40–44; and African American migration from South, 40–41; education levels, 44, 273n16; foreign-born/U.S.-born Dominicans, 44, 46; German Jewish population, 42; housing shortages and "slum" clearance projects (late 1940s and 1950s), 41; internal socioeconomic differentiation, 43; Latino and non-Hispanic white populations, 43, 273n15; median household incomes, 43–44; neighborhood boundaries (streets), 43; pre-World War II, 41–42; social history and demographics, 40–44, 46; urbanization, 41–42; white exodus (1960s and 1970s), 42–43

Upper Manhattan Empowerment Zone, 244
U.S. Immigration Reform Act (1965), 269n4, 271n6, 272n10

Vargas, Jaime, 76, 79–80
Vargas, José, 244–45
Vega, Amelia, 226
Viloria, José: and El Día del Taxista, 260; and *New York City Taxi Magazine*, 258–59; and New York State Federation of Taxi Drivers, 163, 231–33, 235, 236, 237–39, 241, 282n1
visas, U.S., 33, 36–37, 271n6; falsified/forged documentation, 37, 272n11; immigrant visas, 33, 36–37, 271n6; nonimmigrant (tourist and student visas), 36–37
voluntary associations (*clubes*), 18–19, 148–56, 162, 170, 188–200, 201–2; annual Dominican Day, 109, 190; *clubes regionalistas* (place-based associations), 188; community development and advocacy, 188; early and mid-1960s, 188; efforts to integrate and unify (late 1970s), 189–90;

elected boards, 149, 150; and expressions of Duarte cult, 190–98; Federation of Social Clubs, 190; and livery-cab bases, 148–51, 170; mid- to late-1970s, 189; non-Dominican members, 199; recreational or social clubs, 18–19, 149–53, 188; *socios* (club members), 149–53; types and organizational features, 149; and women, 279n8

wage, minimum, 94, 122
Wal-Mart, 122
Washington Heights and Inwood Development Corporation, 96
welfare reform, 277n10
White Rose Foods, 59–61, 64
women, Dominican: average wages in Hispanic-owned businesses, 122; beauty salon-owners, 87–89, 114, 120–21; female-dominated reciprocity networks, 8–10, 129–30; female-headed households, 7–8, 100–101, 123–24, 142–43, 145–46, 277n10; and ideas about masculinity in livery-cab industry, 165–69; livery-base secretaries, 148; livery-cab drivers, 140, 142–43, 145–46, 278n4; paradoxical relations between men and, 100, 168–69; and voluntary associations, 279n8; waitresses, 118–20, 123–24. *See also* gender roles
Wonder Bread products, 55
Workers' Compensation coverage for livery-cab drivers, 240, 245, 251–53, 282n13

Yanagisako, Sylvia, *Producing Culture and Capital* (2002), 15
yellow taxis ("medallion taxis"), 63, 69, 71–72, 274n7

ACKNOWLEDGMENTS

The research on which this book about Dominican immigrants in New York is based was shaped and started in the period 2001–2004. During these years, I took part in an expanded research program at the Department of Anthropology, University of Oslo, on the anthropology of globalization. The program, called Transnational Flows of Substances and Concepts, was directed by Marianne E. Lien and supported financially by the Norwegian Research Council. The other participants were Thomas Hylland Eriksen, Erik Henningsen, Signe Howell, Sarah Lund, and Marit Melhuus. Others who definitely helped to give academic shape and substance—and inspiration—to the program were Odd Are Berkaak, Kathinka Frøystad, Keith Hart, Penny Harvey, Eric Hirsch, Knut G. Nustad, and James C. Scott. I thank all these people for lively exchanges and for backing, critique, and help; and the Norwegian Research Council for its economic support.

During my six-month fieldwork in New York City in the second half of 2002, I was affiliated with the Department of Anthropology at Queens College, City University of New York. I thank this institution for its generosity and hospitality. The year before, in 2001, I had for the first time, but briefly, met Roger Sanjek. We had discussed my new research plans—the project and the fieldwork I wanted to start among Dominicans in the city—over breakfast in Manhattan. Since this first conversation about my thoughts and plans, Roger has all along been an enormous support. He helped me shape my project; he got me the formal affiliation with the Department of Anthropology at Queens College (his own workplace); he reacted to empirical findings, ideas, and tentative arguments I presented in conversations; and not least, he read, and commented on in a detailed manner, the whole book manuscript in crucial phases.

Two others who met me with patience and aided me (more than they presumably think or remember) at an early stage of my research in New York were respectively Arlene Dávila and Ric Curtis. The latter also put me in contact with Rose M. Lindenmayer. During 2002–2004 Rose transcribed a long list of taped conversations and interviews for me (the majority in Spanish, a small number in English), and did a brilliant job.

I would like to thank all whom I met and got to know in the field, or in Dominican New York. Not only did they give readily of their time, hospitality, and knowledge, but also overall they shaped my investigation by providing contexts, insights, and views decisive for making this book. Special thanks are given to the following persons: Nelson Camacho, Hugo Díaz, Pedro Heredia, María Khury-Anton, Luis A. Salcedo, Silvio Tolentino, and José Viloria. My major debt in Dominican New York is to Magdalena Flores and her children and grandchildren. I am profoundly grateful.

The Department of Anthropology at the University of Oslo supported my research economically through financing my trips to New York in 2004–2008. At the department, I have on several occasions presented work in progress— that is, a part of my research on Dominican New York. I thank my colleagues at the department for their comments and encouragements.

I began writing the manuscript that became this book in 2005, when I spent five months as a visiting researcher at the Department of Anthropology at the University of Michigan in Ann Arbor. The same year I presented a paper at the Department of Anthropology at the University of Edinburgh where I used the opportunity to try out a set of arguments based on my investigations among Dominican New Yorkers. I sincerely thank these two institutions for the opportunities that they offered me—and for the scientific benefit and the generosity I experienced in both places.

In June 2008, I organized, together with Knut G. Nustad, a small international workshop in Oslo on the anthropological and ethnographic study of contemporary forms of urban politics. At the workshop I presented the paper "Immigrants, Small Business and Politics: Dominican Supermarket Owners' Political Activism in New York City." I thank the other participants for their reactions and questions. Special thanks go to Knut Nustad for highly stimulating and productive cooperation and many enriching conversations about critical anthropology and ethnography, about examinations of forms of power, about the study of the state, and about a large number of other issues. Thanks go as well to Kent Enstrøm for his preparation of maps of Upper Manhattan and the Bronx, and to Jonathan Derrick for important help with editing and language.

I owe a great deal to Peter Agree at Penn Press for encouraging and helping me through the end of this intellectual project. My sincere thanks as well to the Press's anonymous readers, who provided challenging, useful comments as I finished the book.

But my deepest debt is, without a doubt, to Rigmor and Arne, without whose trust, understanding, and companionship this study would hardly have been possible.

Earlier versions of a few paragraphs of the Introduction appeared in "The Understanding of Migration and the Discourse of Nationalism: Dominicans in New York City," in *Holding Worlds Together: Ethnographies of Knowing and Belonging*, ed. Marianne Elisabeth Lien and Marit Melhuus (Oxford: Berghahn, 2007), 77–102.